T0313742

MARKETS, MINDS,
AND MONEY

Markets, Minds, and Money

WHY AMERICA LEADS THE WORLD IN UNIVERSITY RESEARCH

MIGUEL URQUIOLA

 Harvard University Press

Cambridge, Massachusetts · London, England · 2020

First printing

Library of Congress Cataloging-in-Publication Data

Names: Urquiola S., Miguel (Urquiola Soux), author.
Title: Markets, minds, and money : why America leads the world in
    university research / Miguel Urquiola.
Identifiers: LCCN 2019046786 | ISBN 9780674244238 (cloth)
Subjects: LCSH: Education, Higher—Research—United States—History. |
    Education, Higher—Economic aspects—United States—History. |
    Universities and colleges—Graduate work—History. | Free
    enterprise—United States—History. | Education, Higher—Aims and
    objectives—History.
Classification: LCC LB2326.3 .U74 2020 | DDC 378.007—dc23
LC record available at https://lccn.loc.gov/2019046786

Contents

Preface

THIS BOOK HAD ITS origin at a dinner hosted by the president and the provost of Columbia University. The invitation specified a topic for discussion: the impact that technologies like online education might have on research universities. The guests were academics and entrepreneurs.

Most of the participants did not think new technologies posed an existential threat to research universities. But a nontrivial minority suggested that the end was nigh. How could institutions charging astronomical tuition face outfits delivering online instruction for free? Nimble disruptors were on the horizon; for dinosaurs like those in the Ivy League, deep pockets would only buy time.

In short, the dinner concerned the effects of competition on schools, a topic I have researched for years. For me it raised questions like: How did American research universities rise to preeminence in the first place? How were they able to outshine their historically stronger European counterparts? Could their position be easily reversed?

After dinner one guest expressed an interest in my research—he thought it relevant to such questions. He was right, but I wondered if he would find it of much use. Like most economists' work, mine consists of short, technical articles. There are benefits to that format: it forces one to carefully establish theoretical and empirical relationships; it leaves little room for speculation. There are also costs: it hinders tackling "big" questions; it leaves little room for speculation.

I decided to write a book on the questions raised above. The result, which is in your hands, draws on economists' study of education markets and covers much educational history. That said, it is not historical research; for instance, the book makes very limited use of primary sources. Rather, my goal is to use economics to make sense of a large historical record, hopefully illuminating interesting questions.

MARKETS, MINDS,
AND MONEY

The institutions of . . . education . . . are always a faithful mirror
in which are sharply reflected the national history
and character.

—Charles Eliot, President of Harvard, 1869

We must consider that we shall be as a City upon a Hill . . .

—John Winthrop, First Governor
of the Massachusetts Bay Colony, 1630

Let every one provide for his own house . . .

—Theodore Frelinghuysen, Minister
of the Dutch Reformed Church, 1755

PART I

American Research Performance

CHAPTER 1

A Puzzle

T HE UNITED STATES, one often hears, is falling behind. Influential academics argue that while it once led on key measures of social success, it is now sliding "from the front to the back of the pack." Concerning education, several add that while the United States was once ahead, today its schools are "endangering prosperity," its test results are "mediocre," and its educational institutions "decadent."[1]

Figure 1.1 illustrates developments that prompt such statements by plotting data for four countries: France, Germany, the U.K., and the United States. The left panel shows that around 1870, Americans on average had about twice as many years of schooling as Germans, and four times as many as the citizens of France and the U.K. These gaps have since all but disappeared.

Even if one valued American performance above all, however, this is not necessarily alarming. It could simply reflect that it might be easier to raise school enrollments in countries where they are initially low. The right panel shows that greater reason for concern arises when one considers what children learn at school. It plots, for the same countries, average scores in international math tests. Such exams have appeared only recently—the figure begins in 2003 rather than 1870. Here the United States trails France, Germany, the U.K., and, incidentally, almost every other wealthy country. While interpreting international test results requires care, such figures illustrate why observers of American education often despair.[2]

This book studies a different product of educational systems: university research. By research we mean the specialized work that leads to papers in prestigious journals and, in a few cases, to major awards like Nobel prizes.

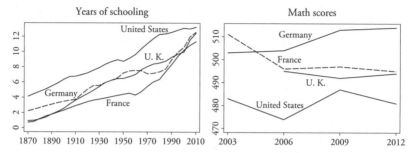

FIGURE 1.1 The left panel uses data from Barro and Lee (2013) to plot average years of schooling among individuals aged 15 to 64. The right panel plots average math scores from the Programme for International Student Assessment (PISA, gpseducation.oecd.org).

It is difficult to measure long-term performance in this area. Figure 1.2 provides an approximation by describing the frequency with which universities in different countries appear in Nobel prize winners' biographies. We will describe this measure in detail soon—for now simply note that it captures which universities hosted prize winners either as students or professors.

The picture that emerges is strikingly different from those above. By this measure, the United States was dead last around 1870, and Germany led the world. American universities subsequently took a commanding lead, however, and have not relinquished it. In short, here one sees the United States moving from the back to the front of the pack!

The broad patterns in Figure 1.2 are consistent with contemporary perceptions and actions. For example, in the 1800s young American academics typically traveled to Europe for doctoral training, and Cole (2009, 18) states that many of them were "simply envious" of the research conditions they found there. Nicholas Butler, a president of Columbia University, wrote that an 1885 visit to Germany as a young man "left an ineffaceable impression of what scholarship meant, of what a university was, and of what a long road higher education in America had to travel before it could hope to reach a place of equal elevation."[3]

In contrast, today the consensus is that American universities produce better research than those of any other country. For example, a recent iteration of the Shanghai ranking has nineteen American universities among the top twenty-five.[4]

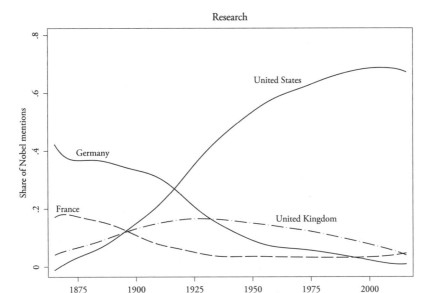

FIGURE 1.2 The figure describes the frequency with which Nobel winners' biographies mention universities in different countries. It plots fitted values of locally weighted regressions of each country's share of total mentions on the year. This chapter and Appendix Section I provide further detail on the data and its presentation.

These developments matter because university research contributes to economic growth and human welfare. For example, it directly led to medical tools like x-rays and magnetic resolution, and it helped scale up the use of antibiotics; it underlies promising techniques like gene-editing. It is also behind technologies used by numerous companies; for example, audio recording by RCA, jet travel by Boeing, algorithms by Google, and positioning systems by Uber.[5] Indeed, American universities' lead in research may help compensate for the country's underperformance in other educational dimensions. It may help account for why the United States continues to have one of the most dynamic economies, and it may be crucial to ensuring that remains the case.[6]

Taken together, the figures above raise two sets of questions that motivate this book:

- In terms of research output, why was the American university system at the bottom of the pack well into the 1800s? How was it later able to reach the top? Why does it continue to outperform European systems it previously trailed?

- Why does the American educational system excel at producing research, even as it disappoints in other dimensions?

Our answer to these questions centers on the fact that among rich countries, the United States is unique in taking a *free market* approach to education. This book will argue that this approach accounts for why American universities were weak at research initially, for why they improved, and for why they have retained their lead. For good measure, this approach helps explain why American educational institutions are better at producing research than outputs like test scores.

Before expanding on this idea, this chapter elaborates on the data behind Figure 1.2, presenting some more facts for explanation.

A New Measure of Research Performance

In recent years it has become easier to measure universities' research output. For example, today bibliographic databases exhaustively describe professors' publications. For our purposes, however, these have a disadvantage: most cover at best a few decades, while our goal is to understand research performance over a longer period.[7]

We therefore use Nobel prize winners' biographies to assess universities' involvement in research. This produces a coarse and imperfect measure but allows us to observe research activity as far back as the 1850s. In addition, in recent periods the results generally match well with more elaborate rankings, and in earlier periods with consensus perceptions of schools' performance.

The idea behind this measure is perhaps best illustrated by an example. Consider Wilhelm Röntgen, who received the first Nobel Prize in Physics in 1901. While the prize goes to an individual, the institutions that host him or her receive some reflected glory. Which universities should receive credit for Röntgen's feat? Some clearly seems due to the University of Munich, at which Röntgen was a professor at the time of the award. Röntgen's presence there suggests that Munich offered an attractive atmosphere for researchers.

In addition, Röntgen remained at Munich for more than twenty years, and thus had the chance to teach many students and influence multiple colleagues, potentially enhancing the university's research. Rigorous studies suggest that leading scholars can have such an impact.[8]

On the other hand, Röntgen only moved to Munich in 1900, a year before his award. So perhaps credit should also go to the universities he worked at earlier: Warzburg, Strasbourg, Hohenheim, and Giessen. These schools might have benefited from Röntgen's presence even more than Munich if they had him when he was most productive; for instance, Röntgen's discovery of x-rays happened at Giessen. Consistent with this hypothesis, if one asks professors whether they would rather have as a colleague a Nobel prize winner or the younger, pre-Nobel version of the same person, they usually choose the latter.

There is also a case for assigning credit to institutions Röntgen was at even earlier, such as the University of Zurich, where he got his PhD. As academics know, individuals like Röntgen do not simply arrive at a place like Giessen and all of a sudden do amazing research. They bring with them an enormous amount of training, and it usually takes active researchers to train future researchers; for example, Röntgen's biography states that his advisors greatly influenced his development.[9] Thus his prize suggests that Zurich had good researchers itself. An analogous case might be made for winners' undergraduate institutions since they teach crucial foundational skills; in Röntgen's case, this was ETH Zurich.[10]

Our measure therefore assigns credit for Röntgen's work to all the mentioned universities. More generally, we take all 1901–2016 winners of the Chemistry, Economics, Medicine, and Physics prizes, and use biographical information to identify the universities at which they were students or professors. We then assign these schools to the countries they are located in at present. For example, in Röntgen's case all the institutions he studied at are in Switzerland, and all he worked at are in Germany, except for the University of Strasbourg, which is now in France. Thus, we do not consider winners' nationalities—the issue is not where they were born, but in which universities they studied or worked. We consider a total of 639 prize winners whose biographies cite universities (strictly speaking, degree-granting institutions) 3,120 times. We assign each of these schools a "mention." Each mention is associated with a specific year: the year of graduation for universities the winners were students at; the year of the award for universities that hosted them at that point; and the year of arrival for all other schools they worked at. The precise year used does not affect the key findings (further details are in Appendix Section 1).

As advertised, this approach has the advantage of reaching relatively far back: the first mention is for 1855. It also has disadvantages. First, the Nobel field coverage is partial; for instance, it excludes the humanities. Second, the Nobel prize is a coarse indicator of research activity in that it goes only to top achievers; a university could produce good research and yet have employed no Nobel winners.[11] This concern is mitigated because we also consider winners' affiliations as students, and 446 schools receive mentions, in total. Third, the Nobel prize is a "trailing indicator," typically awarded for work done earlier in individuals' careers. Because universities cannot be mentioned in winners' biographies until they win, our measure penalizes "up and coming" schools. For instance, in recent decades, countries like China and South Korea have invested in their universities. To the extent that these are now training outstanding students, they will take years to show up in Nobel biographies. That said, our results for recent decades match up well with rankings that use bibliographical data likely to reflect progress more rapidly. In addition, this book's focus is not on recent developments, but on the rise to dominance of American research universities.

Table 1.1 uses the resulting data to list the number of times winners' biographies mention universities in different countries.[12] The first column shows that U.S. schools account for half of the total 3,120 mentions. Only three other countries contain universities with more than one hundred: the U.K., Germany, and France. This begins to clarify why we will often focus on these four countries.

The remaining columns describe countries' mentions by roughly forty-year periods. These reveal a few relatively steady performers; for example, Switzerland and the U.K. hold relatively constant ranks. A salient case of improvement is the United States, which placed fourth in 1855–1890, but by

Table 1.1   Country-level university mentions

Rank	Country	Total mentions	1855–1900	1901–1940	1941–1980	1981–2016
1	United States	1,548	13	298	862	375
2	United Kingdom	424	22	151	205	46
3	Germany	388	87	187	98	16
4	France	151	33	51	50	17
5	Japan	77		7	39	31
6	Switzerland	71	9	29	27	6
7	Canada	53		10	35	8
8	Sweden	50	7	20	19	4
9	Netherlands	38	10	13	10	5
10	Denmark	36	6	18	10	2
11	Austria	35	9	24	2	
12	Russia	30	5	12	9	4
13	Australia	25		7	15	3
14	Israel	24			17	7
15	Italy	23	1	13	7	2
16	Norway	17		4	7	6
17	Belgium	16	2	6	7	1
18	China	14			6	8
19	India	12		5	6	1
20	Finland	10		5	3	2
21	Hungary	10		4	6	
22	Poland	10	2	8		
23	South Africa	8			8	
24	Argentina	7		2	5	
25	Spain	7	4	3		
26	Ireland	5		2	2	1
27	New Zealand	5	2		3	
28	Czech Republic	4		4		
Total		3,120	221	884	1,468	547

The table lists the number of times Nobel winners' biographies mention universities in different countries. It lists only countries with universities accounting for four or more mentions. The countries with institutions accounting for three are Estonia, Pakistan, Portugal, and the Ukraine. Egypt accounts for two, and eight other countries account for one. The totals in the table cover all countries. Appendix Section 3 presents analogous results including non-degree-granting institutions. For details on the data, see the text and Appendix Section 1.

1941–1980 collected more mentions than all other countries combined. A salient case of decline is Germany, which went from holding the first rank in the first period to placing fifth by the last.

Table 1.1 makes no adjustments for income or population because that does not change the two facts this book seeks to explain: American universities' initial weakness and later leadership. To illustrate, by 1875 the United States already had population and per capita income levels above those of France and Germany, yet it distinctly underperformed these countries at research. Today the U.S. population is significantly smaller than that of the European Union, yet its universities receive twice as many mentions as those of all European countries combined (Appendix Section 4 presents variants of Table 1.1 that control for income and population—the two key facts mentioned remain).

Table 1.1 also highlights that American improvement was gradual, a point that is often underappreciated. Observers often credit the rise in American universities' research performance to events surrounding World War II. For example, Cole (2009, 75) states, "If just one moment in history could be set to mark a decisive turning point for the rise of the American Research University, it would be January 1933. Hitler came to power that month . . . ." Similarly, Graham and Diamond (1997, 200) highlight the role of war-related federal funding: "For more than two centuries, higher education in America remained fragmented, financially undernourished, intellectually provincial, and culturally parochial. Then came World War II, the Manhattan Project, the Cold War, and the revolution in federal science policy." And recently, Gruber and Johnson (2019, 19) state that "Throughout the pre-World War II period . . . American universities remained small and more focused on teaching than on research."

There is no question that events surrounding World War II improved American universities' research. The Nazis' rise to power saw a large migration of academics to the United States, and we will stress the impact of federal research funding later.[13] Table 1.1 makes clear, however, that American improvement began much earlier. Table 1.2 elaborates on this by presenting country-level results by decades rather than forty-year periods. For brevity, it only lists the top ten countries (by cumulative mentions) and ends in 1930. It shows that while American universities received no

Table 1.2 Country-level university mentions

Cumulative rank	Country	Total number of mentions in:						
		1855–1870	1871–1880	1881–1890	1891–1900	1901–1910	1911–1920	1921–1930
1	United States		2	4	7	24	45	75
2	United Kingdom	1	4	6	11	17	32	38
3	Germany	11	15	18	43	45	36	70
4	France	2	15	7	9	20	7	10
5	Japan							2
6	Switzerland	2	1	3	3	3	11	11
7	Canada					3	2	3
8	Sweden			4	3	4	3	9
9	Netherlands		5	4	1	3	2	3
10	Denmark			3	3	4	4	9

The table lists the number of times that Nobel winners' biographies mention universities in different countries. It lists only the ten countries with the most cumulative mentions in Table 1.1. For details on the data, see the text and Appendix Section 1.

mentions in the first decade covered, they began to do so in the 1870s. By 1901–1910, the United States had overtaken France and the U.K.; by 1911–1920 it was also ahead of Germany.

In other words, Table 1.2 is more consistent with Geiger's (1993, 4) statement that: "[American] science had advanced from an apprenticeship status prior to World War I to full parity with Europe's best . . . by the early 1930s."[14]

Our results are also consistent with how aspiring academics "voted with their feet." Veysey (1965, 131) notes that American enrollments in European graduate programs peaked around 1895; by 1900 there was a sense that American graduate education was moving ahead. He quotes a student: "There is but one verdict given by the men who come back from Germany these days, and that is that one could get more from his Professors in any of our large universities than he could get from his Professors in a German University."

The fact that U.S. universities were on the upswing well before 1930 emerges even more clearly if one looks only at Nobel winners' affiliations as doctoral and undergraduate students. By the early 1900s, American universities were already the most active at training individuals who would go on to win prizes. For example, in 1901 future Nobel winner Theodore Richard—trained at Haverford and Harvard—became the first American to be offered a professorship at a German university.[15] The bottom line is that while the exact year in which the United States overtook Europe naturally depends on the measure used, its ascent was well underway by the early 1900s (for further details see Appendix Section 5).

These observations are not meant to discount the impact of World War II—indeed, it would seem hard to explain the German decline without it. This book's focus, however, is on providing an explanation for the American rise, and the point is that one cannot be offered relying solely or even primarily on events in Europe. In particular, an account of American schools' research performance must address why improvement was underway before 1900, and it likely must feature developments in the United States itself.[16]

Table 1.3 moves on to results at the institution level, listing only universities mentioned seven or more times (those with two to six mentions are in Appendix Section 6). Somewhat improbably, Cambridge and Harvard tie exactly for first place, with 170 mentions each. Rounding out the top ten

Table 1.3 Cumulative Nobel mentions by university

Institution	Mentions	Institution	Mentions	Institution	Mentions	Institution	Mentions
Harvard University	170	University of Wisconsin	30	Univ. of Calif., San Diego	17	Free University of Brussels	9
University of Cambridge	170	University of Copenhagen	29	University of Edinburgh	17	Univ. of Calif., Santa Barbara	9
Columbia University	106	University of Strasbourg	26	University of Washington	16	University of Birmingham	9
University of Chicago	102	Carnegie Mellon University	24	University of Würzburg	16	University of Colorado	9
Univ. of Calif., Berkeley	95	Technical Univ. of Munich	24	Karolinska Institute	15	University of Tübingen	9
Massachusetts Inst. of Tech.	81	New York University	22	Kyoto University	15	Hebrew Univ. of Jerusalem	8
Stanford University	74	University of Minnesota	22	Nagoya University	15	Purdue University	8
Princeton University	59	École Normale Supérieure	21	University of Frankfurt	15	Technion	8
University of Oxford	59	Univ. of Calif., Los Angeles	21	University of Freiburg	15	University of Bonn	8
University of Paris	54	University College London	21	University of London	15	University of Liverpool	8
California Inst. of Tech.	53	Heidelberg University	20	University of Marburg	15	University of Rome	8
Humboldt Univ. of Berlin	52	University of Michigan	20	Case Western Reserve	15	University of Wroclaw	8
Yale University	51	University of Texas	20	University of Graz	14	Pasteur Institute	7
University of Göttingen	44	Washington Univ. in St. Louis	20	University of Vienna	14	University of Basel	7
University of Munich	44	City University of New York	18	University of Tokyo	14	University of Buenos Aires	7
Cornell University	42	Imperial College London	18	Leipzig University	12	University of Geneva	7
Johns Hopkins University	41	Leiden University	18	Northwestern University	11	University of Hamburg	7
ETH Zurich	36	McGill University	18	University of Toronto	11	University of Helsinki	7
University of Illinois	33	University of Zurich	18	Technical Univ. of Berlin	10	University of Virginia	7
University of Manchester	33	Uppsala University	18	University of Kiel	10	Weizmann Inst. of Science	7
University of Pennsylvania	33	Utrecht University	18	University of Oslo	10		
Rockefeller University	30	London School of Economics	17	Duke University	9		

The table lists the total number of times Nobel winners' biographies mention specific universities. It includes only institutions with at least seven mentions; Appendix Section 6 lists those with fewer. For details on the data, see the text and Appendix Section 1.

are Columbia, Chicago, Berkeley, MIT, Stanford, Princeton, Oxford, and Paris.[17] All the schools in the top twenty—except ETH Zurich—are in France, Germany, the U.K., or the United States.

Table 1.3 also shows that in the world in general, and in the United States in particular, relatively few universities account for a large share of Nobel mentions. For instance, Chicago, Berkeley, and MIT each account for more than all Japanese universities combined. While the United States has about 4,700 post-secondary degree-granting institutions, only thirty two of them appear in Table 1.3.[18] Other measures of research output would suggest less concentration, but the fact is that an explanation of American research performance must also account for why—particularly in terms of the highest quality output—it is driven by about 1 percent of schools.

Table 1.4 explores the evolution of university mentions by listing the twenty-five schools that ranked highest within roughly forty-year periods.[19] In 1855–1900, European institutions dominated, with the most mentions going to Berlin, followed by Cambridge and Munich. No American university made it into the top twenty-five. By 1901–1940, Cambridge was in first place, and Harvard and Columbia had joined the top five. By 1941–1980, Harvard was in the lead, and six of the top seven were American. By 1981–2016, only American universities remain in the top seven. The results for this last period display significant overlap with recent rankings; for instance, seven of the top ten schools in our listing are also in the top ten in the Shanghai ranking.

To summarize, a story that explains the evolution of American research performance must provide reasons for: the weakness of American schools into the 1800s; the onset of improvement decades before World War II; the outsized role of a few specific schools in leading that improvement; and the concentration of research output—particularly that of high quality— in a small fraction of institutions. We now present a brief overview of the story this book will offer. Before proceeding, we note, for interested readers, that Appendix Section 7 contains some "inside baseball." It presents rankings specific to chemistry, economics, medicine, and physics. There is interesting variation across these fields, but it does not change the key conclusions above.

Table 1.4 University-level mentions in given time periods

Total number of mentions in:

1855–1900		1901–1940		1941–1980		1981–2016	
Humboldt Univ. of Berlin	19	University of Cambridge	63	Harvard University	101	Harvard University	32
University of Cambridge	11	Harvard University	35	University of Cambridge	83	Stanford University	28
University of Munich	10	Humboldt Univ. of Berlin	31	Columbia University	64	Massachusetts Inst. of Tech.	27
University of Strasbourg	10	Columbia University	29	University of Chicago	64	Univ. of Calif., Berkeley	20
University of Paris	9	University of Göttingen	27	Univ. of Calif., Berkeley	62	University of Chicago	18
Leiden University	8	University of Munich	25	Massachusetts Inst. of Tech.	48	Yale University	17
University of Wurzburg	7	University of Paris	21	Stanford University	46	Princeton University	16
Heidelberg University	6	University of Chicago	20	University of Oxford	33	University of Cambridge	13
University of Copenhagen	6	University of Manchester	18	Princeton University	32	Columbia University	12
University of Göttingen	6	University of Oxford	17	California Inst. of Tech.	29	University of Texas	12
ETH Zurich	5	ETH Zurich	16	Yale University	26	Johns Hopkins University	10
University of Bonn	5	California Inst. of Tech.	15	Cornell University	23	California Inst. of Tech.	9
University of Vienna	5	University of Copenhagen	15	University of Illinois	20	Rockefeller University	9
École Normale Supérieure	4	University of Wisconsin	15	University of Paris	20	Cornell University	8
University of Manchester	4	Johns Hopkins University	14	Carnegie Mellon University	19	Nagoya University	8
Leipzig University	3	Univ. of Calif., Berkeley	12	University of Pennsylvania	19	Northwestern University	8
University of Giessen	3	University of Marburg	12	Johns Hopkins University	15	University of Pennsylvania	8
University of Graz	3	Uppsala University	12	New York University	15	Univ. of Calif., San Diego	7
University of Lyons	3	Cornell University	11	Rockefeller University	15	Univ. of Calif., Santa Barbara	7
University of Stockholm	3	Princeton University	11	Technical Univ. of Munich	15	University of Oxford	7
University of Tartu	3	University of Graz	10	Univ. of Calif., Los Angeles	15	Duke University	6
University of Zurich	3	University of Illinois	10	Washington Univ. in St. Louis	15	University of Colorado	6
Uppsala University	3	University of Zurich	10	McGill University	14	University of Washington	6
Utrecht University	3	University College London	9	University of Wisconsin	14	Univ. of Calif., Los Angeles	5
Aachen University	2	University of Vienna	9	University of Michigan	13	Arizona State University	4

The table lists the number of times Nobel winners' biographies mention specific universities in given time periods. It only lists the top 25 schools within each period. For details on the data, see the text and Appendix Section 1.

The Argument

Why do some university systems perform well at research? Consider first a superficial answer to this question: to excel at research, a university system must have some schools with ample minds and money. By "minds" we will mean people with research talent (there are certainly other types of talent, and we will discuss some of them); by money we will mean financial resources. It is worth elaborating on these two elements briefly before attempting a deeper answer.

Leading American universities are able to identify and recruit talented individuals. Each of their academic units (e.g., a chemistry department) deploys search committees on an almost constant basis. These often look for younger faculty in formal searches that can attract hundreds of promising candidates from around the world. Committees read applicants' papers and letters of recommendation and conduct interviews. They invite finalists for day-long visits during which they present their work. Committee members look for senior scholars relying on arguably even richer information. For example, they will almost always have peer-reviewed potential candidates' work and have seen them present it.

One reason these schools can attract the best minds is that they offer them money. Not only do they pay professors well, they give them funding—often in the millions of dollars—for items like laboratories staffed by bright students. They also offer time; professors at top universities often teach relatively little.

It is not hard to see that a system that features at least some schools with ample minds and money will tend to produce good research. The deeper question is: Why did the United States initially lag behind Europe in generating such schools, and why did this change? This book's answer centers on the fact that the United States takes a free market approach to education. To be precise, we will say a university system operates as a free market when it has three traits:

- *Self-rule.* A university system features self-rule when its schools are free to set their own direction. Self-rule can exist even

when states fund universities, as long as they allow them wide
latitude of action.

- *Free entry.* A system displays free entry when it is relatively easy to
open a new school.
- *Free scope.* A university system features free scope when institutions are allowed to supply a wide variety of services.[20]

The American university system displays these traits much more than those
of most wealthy countries. First, its private institutions are largely independent, and most of its public schools enjoy substantial autonomy as well.
Second, states, foundations, and for-profit companies can easily create new
universities. Third, universities face few constraints on their activities—for
example, many offer a large variety of degrees at the same time as they operate hospitals and revenue-generating athletic teams.[21]

Attributing American universities' initial weakness *and* later strength to
these traits implies that in education there is no automatic link between a
free market approach and good performance. To many readers, this might
seem an unusual claim; how can a market approach help at certain times and
hinder at others?

This is possible because education is an unusual good. As Becker (1964)
pointed out in Nobel prize-winning work, when people purchase schooling,
they do not buy a consumer good like a phone—they make an investment
to prepare for subsequent markets. For example, individuals go to school
to prepare for a career, or to render themselves more attractive to potential
partners. In other words, they see education creating an asset that Becker
called human capital.

Importantly, schools provide two services to such customers: *teaching* and
sorting. By teaching we refer to aspects that concern teachers and what they
do: who they are, what skills they seek to transmit (i.e., the curriculum), and
what methods they use to do so. By sorting we refer to who students meet
at school. When a school produces sorting, it implicitly "sells" peer groups.
In many cases, this involves delivering some type of homogeneity. For example, a given school may cater to students who are smart, or wealthy, or
artistic, or headed to particular careers. By so doing it appeals to students

who wish to be exposed to or associated with such people. Sorting can apply to faculty members too. A given university may attract the best professors in a given area of chemistry, and it may thus appeal to academics who wish to be exposed to or associated with them. Sorting people into such bins is a fundamental service schools provide.

This book will argue that the free market provision of these two services— teaching and sorting—hindered American universities' research performance until about the Civil War and has enhanced it since. More precisely, the market provision of these services initially prevented all schools from getting much in the way of minds and money; later it helped a few dozen secure enormous amounts of each.

To see this, note that in a free market firms must provide customers what they want, and well into the 1800s, American households demanded denominational sorting. For example, Baptists wished to attend college with Baptists, Presbyterians with Presbyterians, and so on. Further, most strongly preferred colleges located close to home. Together, these factors produced massive entry: while at independence the United States had nine colleges, about another 900 opened before the Civil War. Mass entry allowed colleges to satisfy the demand for sorting: they catered to students from denominationally homogeneous regional elites. At the same time, mass entry stunted the colleges' teaching: small and underfunded, they could only offer a narrow, rigid curriculum taught by unspecialized and poorly paid professors. In short, the colleges had little need for research talent and few resources to pay for it. There was almost no way they could compete at research with European universities, and they did not.

Since the colleges' teaching and sorting had gotten them into the doldrums, teaching and sorting reform would be necessary to get them out. The need for teaching reform became apparent as colleges observed a gap grow between the skills they taught and those their customers demanded. For example, with industrialization interest grew around areas college curricula essentially ignored (e.g., engineering, business). Yet teaching reform proved hard to implement. Following many failed attempts, after the Civil War two entrants, Cornell and Johns Hopkins, succeeded—they showed that survival could lie in offering specialized and advanced instruction in a range of areas, rather than in providing denominational sorting. Self-rule allowed incumbents like Harvard and Columbia to respond forcefully, and soon Chicago, MIT, Stanford, and a couple of dozen others had joined the fray. All these schools soon realized that the new teaching favored a new type of teacher: a specialist at the frontier of a field—that is, someone who could do research. The academic system responded by providing additional measures of research quantity and quality. This allowed schools to identify talent and set in motion a sorting process that began to concentrate the best minds in the schools that had led in teaching reform.

These schools were also pleased to see their enrollments grow rapidly, but this began to threaten the match between the sorting they provided and that which key students demanded. Specifically, enrollment growth often originated with less wealthy students and with Jewish students, and—in a period of rising antisemitism—alienated the elites the colleges had traditionally served. By the 1920s, some schools were engaging in sorting reform: Columbia and Harvard implemented selective admissions, and several followed soon after. Selectivity set in motion another sorting process, one that concentrated high-ability students at such schools.

In the end, the schools that first engaged in teaching and sorting reform offered students a compelling package: the best peers and teachers who, by virtue of their research talent, were certified to deliver specialized and advanced instruction. This tended to produce satisfied customers who later donated to their alma mater. For the schools that put this package together by dint of hard work, vision, privilege, or luck, it created a virtuous circle: reforms procured minds and money, which allowed them to procure more of each. The flip side was a vicious circle for schools that saw good students or researchers slip away. After World War II, federal research funding reinforced these dynamics. The result is a system that finds top talent and matches it with enormous resources at a few dozen research universities. In addition, for reasons we will discuss, these schools can direct a disproportionate share of their energy to research.

In short, as stipulated, this argument can explain the initial weakness of American universities' research, and the fact that improvement began decades before World War II. Further, it assigns agency to American schools—particularly to a handful whose leaders will turn out to be key characters in the story—rather than to a European *deus ex machina*.

Finally, for reasons we will discuss, the market approach does not enhance American performance in other educational dimensions. In K through 12, for instance, sorting dynamics complicate the identification of (teaching) talent, and at times direct resources to *less* productive schools. Further, while American production of top-quality research can largely depend on what happens at a few dozen universities, outcomes like international test scores necessarily depend on the state of thousands of K–12 schools.

Even if this story successfully accounts for salient aspects of American educational performance, it leaves open a key question: Why does the United States have a market-oriented university system, while European countries mostly do not? For example, almost all French universities are publicly funded and tightly controlled from Paris; while Germany has a federal structure, each state exerts similar control within its borders.[22]

Part II of the book shows that, ironically, Europe *invented* the expansive, unfettered university market—one existed there for centuries. That setup ended, however, with the Protestant Reformation, as states became willing and able to control still religiously oriented universities. Also ironically, the American colonies that first created colleges—Massachusetts, Connecticut, Virginia—in many ways adopted European-style control of their schools. In other words, if the United States had consisted only of such colonies, its university sector might not display much in the way of self-rule or free entry. However, once college founding moved into the Middle Atlantic—New Jersey, New York, Pennsylvania—the system took on the market orientation it still displays today. In addition, institutional development ultimately made American universities more nimble than their European counterparts.

The book proceeds as follows. Chapter 2 describes the teaching services of American colleges before the Civil War. Chapter 3 discusses how teaching reform began to concentrate talent, and Chapter 4 how sorting reform did the same for resources. Chapter 5 surveys aspects that ensure these inputs are used productively. Chapters 6 and 7 explain why the free market approach prevails (or not) in the United States and Europe. Chapter 8 considers the future of American university research performance.

CHAPTER 2

The Antebellum College

WELL INTO THE 1800S, the American educational system produced little research. This chapter argues that this was because market forces left its component colleges short of minds (research talent) and money. It begins by observing that these schools' *teaching* covered few fields and rarely featured advanced instruction; thus, it did not demand specialized professors who might engage in research. The chapter then explains that these shortcomings arose because in other dimensions, colleges were performing well: they were supplying the *sorting* their customers desired, along with rapid educational expansion. In other words, market conditions induced a tradeoff in which teaching and research suffered.

A note on terminology before proceeding: we will call the colleges that operated before the Civil War *antebellum* colleges. In other words, by the antebellum period we understand the entire history of American colleges up to the Civil War: 1636 to 1861. While this is a longer period than the term usually applies to, it provides a useful demarcation point—the 1860s are a watershed in the research orientation of American universities.[1] We also note that treating the antebellum period as a single unit requires significant generalization. Conditions changed over more than two hundred years. In many cases we gloss over such developments; the argument is that conditions relevant for research performance did not vary drastically until about 1860.

Teaching

One can get a sense of the antebellum colleges' teaching by considering three questions: Who were the teachers? What did they teach? How did they teach?

Who were the teachers?

The antebellum college had three types of teachers: presidents, professors, and tutors. To people familiar with modern American universities, it might seem strange to include presidents on this list. Today university presidents are usually distant figures: many rarely set foot in a classroom and have never met most senior professors. By contrast, the antebellum president often taught a "capstone" course to the entire senior class and knew many students by name. An 1812 entry in the diary of Princeton President Ashbel Green is illustrative: "This morning the faculty admonished four students and dismissed two . . . I took the examination of the senior class on belles lettres and wrote the parents of the two dismissed students. The faculty met in the evening and a pistol was fired at the door of one of the tutors. I ought to be very thankful to God for his support this day."[2]

Following the president in rank were professors, who for a long time only made an appearance at the wealthiest schools; for example, Harvard did not appoint one for almost a century after its creation. Professors' scarcity reflected that being older and relatively distinguished, they were more expensive than tutors, who occupied the third rank. Tutors were typically graduates who stayed on to teach for a few years; in age and experience, they resembled our modern graduate students. Initially, the vast majority of all three types were men.

One way to characterize them is to consider their alternative employment. What would they have done had they not been teaching? Particularly earlier in this period, many would have been clergymen. For example, 100 percent of teachers at Lafayette College in 1841 had a ministerial background or primarily theological training. Corresponding estimates are 60 percent at Dartmouth in 1862, and 70 percent at Princeton in 1868.[3] In many cases, these individuals preferred ministerial positions to college appointments. For example, Increase Mather, who became the president of Harvard in 1692, wondered why anyone would trade preaching to one thousand people for teaching forty students.[4] Other men took professorships only after loss of voice or hearing rendered the pulpit impractical.[5] Tutors' youth reflected that they too were on the lookout for alternatives, often as junior ministers (or, particularly later in the antebellum period, as apprentices to lawyers).

All this was natural at a time when colleges' key missions included training ministers, and when most were closely identified with a denomination (e.g., Baptist, Lutheran, Methodist). As a result, religious criteria often went into the selection of teachers. For example, the desire for a clear sense of denominational sympathies often led colleges to prefer their own graduates, or to resist sending them away for further training. In 1879 Princeton President James McCosh wrote to an alumnus studying in Germany: "You are aware that the Trustees . . . are resolute in keeping the college a religious one. You have passed through varied scenes since you left us . . . If a man has the root in him he will only be strengthened in the faith by such an experience. It will be profitable to me to find how you have stood all this."[6]

Wealth-related criteria could matter too. Rudolph (1962, 195) writes that: "From 1835 to 1852 chemistry at Williams was taught by a man of independent wealth who spent his token salary on laboratory equipment. The appointment of Henry D. Rogers as the first professor of geology . . . at the University of Pennsylvania . . . was a response to his offer to serve without salary. Amasa Walker joined the Oberlin faculty as a professor of political economy on the same terms . . . ."

This reflects that although they conferred prestige, professorships often paid relatively little. Historians state that even into the 1860s, professors' salaries at Harvard and Yale were "below the cost of living," and those of tutors not much above the pay of artisans.[7] Colleges were known to go into arrears, arbitrarily cut faculty salaries, and make fundraising a condition for payment.[8] Of course, low teacher pay could be convenient for cash-strapped schools, and thus it is not shocking that in 1869 Harvard President Charles Eliot stated: "The poverty of scholars is of inestimable worth in this money-getting nation. It maintains the true standards of virtue and honor. The poor friars, not the bishops, saved the Church. The poor scholars . . . defend the modern community against its own material prosperity. Luxury and learning are ill bed-fellows."[9]

Given the salience of religion and wealth in faculty hiring, expertise could take a back seat. For example, in 1802 Yale President Timothy Dwight recruited Benjamin Silliman to teach chemistry and natural history. That Silliman would go on to an illustrious teaching career would not have been obvious at the time; as Kelley (1974, 129) notes,

> Silliman had never studied chemistry and knew almost nothing about it. . . . Dwight chose Silliman because he knew it would be difficult to find anyone in America with knowledge of chemistry and natural history, and he was afraid to select a foreigner. . . . Dwight's reasons for choosing Silliman did not stop there. Even more than foreigners he seems to have feared intellectuals. Dwight had described people focused on intellectual endeavors thus: "In his study he dwells: in his books he passes his life. . . . He has not discovered that science is a means, and not an end."

Finally, the antebellum colleges did not have many teachers. Geiger (1986) states that earlier in this period the typical college had fewer than five. In 1814, Dartmouth was described as one of the country's thriving colleges when it had three professors and two tutors; Harvard had fewer than five tutors for its first hundred years.[10] In addition, faculty numbers were volatile not only because many professors left, but also because others were easily fired, given that they had few job protections.

That said, the tendency over the antebellum period was one of growth. For example, by the 1850s Harvard and Yale had about twenty faculty members; Dartmouth, Hampden Sydney, NYU, and Union, between ten and fifteen.[11] Of course, even these numbers are tiny by modern standards. In 2017, Carnegie Mellon and the University of Texas at Austin reported having about 1,400 and 3,700 full-time faculty, respectively—numbers that would have astounded the antebellum professors.[12]

This characterization of the antebellum colleges' faculty provides a first sense of why their teaching displayed limitations. The professors were not numerous and often hired for reasons unrelated to their expertise. Their positions had few attributes that would have induced or even allowed them to attain cutting-edge knowledge.

What Did They Teach?

The seed of the antebellum curriculum arrived at Harvard with Puritans whose leaders mostly studied at Cambridge and at Calvinist universities in Holland and Switzerland. The course of study they brought descended—via the medieval university—from the Roman "liberal arts"; i.e., the teachings considered appropriate for a free man. The subjects it covered included grammar, logic, rhetoric, mathematics, music, the physical sciences ("natural philosophy"), and ethics and politics ("moral philosophy").[13] Thanks to humanism there was also an emphasis on ancient texts in Greek and occasionally Hebrew. In the sciences, the approach was deductive: one started with truth as revealed in authoritative texts, and then applied logic to derive explanations for physical phenomena.

Initially, the only prerequisite for this curriculum was some competence in Latin and Greek. In 1642 Harvard President Henry Dunster stated that "When any scholar is able to read Tully or such like classical Latin Author ex tempore, and make and speake true Latin in verse and prose . . . , and declaim perfectly the paradigms of nounes and verbes in ye Greeke tongue, then may hee bee admitted into ye College . . . ."[14] In the next century, colleges added requirements in math, geography, and English. A glimpse of the admission exam circa 1824 comes from Frederick Barnard, President of Columbia, who described the exam he underwent as a young man at Yale: "The examination was entirely oral. . . . One officer conducted the examination in all the subjects . . . my examiner was Professor Silliman, who, though professor of Chemistry, took us up on Virgil, Cicero, the Greek Testament, . . . Geography, and Arithmetic, all apparently with equal facility."[15]

The curriculum was highly structured and did not feature electives. Barnard elaborated that in his first three years at Yale he had no choice of courses and "studied mainly Greek, Latin, and mathematics (algebra, geometry, and spherical trigonometry) . . . [and] a smattering of geography, history, science, astronomy, and English grammar and rhetoric."[16] In the senior year the focus was on a "capstone" moral philosophy course, often taught by the president. It summarized and related all subjects covered, a task that was feasible given the belief that all knowledge was ultimately about God, and hence all fields could be unified.

To summarize, a school's curriculum provides a sense of what it is trying to do. That of the antebellum college makes clear that research was not one of its central goals. The course did not accommodate the depth of material synonymous with elective and graduate courses, and its approach to knowledge was often at odds with inductive theorizing. In addition, it did not cover practically oriented areas like business or engineering.

How Did They Teach?

As all teachers know, it is easier to motivate students when they have chosen to take a class. Since antebellum colleges offered essentially no electives, it is not surprising that they produced numerous reports of student boredom and disinterest. Furthermore, the teaching methods may have aggravated matters. Patton and Field (1927, 41) cite a student who said of his 1850s Harvard education:

> the poor old college prepared us to play our parts in this world by compelling us . . . to devote the best part of our school lives to acquiring a confessedly superficial knowledge of two dead languages . . . Nor in my time did the mischief end here. On the contrary, it began here. As a slipshod method of training was accepted in those studies to which the greatest prominence was given, the same method was accepted in other studies. . . . Even now, I do not know how I could have got solid . . . teaching in the classroom even if I had known enough to want it.

Considering the approaches the colonists imported from Europe clarifies this student's statement. When universities emerged there, the basic instructional exercise was the lecture (*lectio*—literally translated, the "reading"), in which the teacher read out loud a classic text, perhaps inserting some commentary. Considerations of principle and practicality surrounded this exercise. Since the classic books contained given truth, reading them carefully was justified. In addition, universities appeared before the printing press had reduced the price of books, and thus careful note-taking allowed economies. Another key exercise was the recitation (*recitatio*), essentially a repetition of the material, presided over by a *baccalorius* (the term from which our bachelor's degree originates), the equivalent of a graduate student. This repetition ensured everyone had understood the reading, or at least that their notes were somewhat accurate.[17]

These two exercises were modified but not abandoned during the Reformation, and their essence weathered the transatlantic voyage reasonably well. A key change was that in some sense the American colleges merged the two practices: the reading was mainly done by students under teacher supervision, and seems to have involved a measure of memorization. For example, James (1930, 37) indicates that in the mid-1800s at Harvard, "almost all the instruction was given schoolmaster fashion and by means of textbooks out of which the boys recited to the teacher."

Further detail comes thanks to Yale President Jeremiah Day, who in 1817 asked his faculty to report on their teaching methods. Most reported calling on students to read or repeat passages. For example, a professor of mathematics stated: "The manner in which the text books are recited is the following: lessons are given out varying from three to . . . eight pages, according to the difficulty of the subject. The propositions, rules, and general principles are required to be committed to memory. The proofs and illustrations are expected to be given in substance, by the student. . . ."[18]

From the teachers' perspective, recitations were a mixed bag. On the one hand, many found the practice boring. In 1851 Noah Porter, a future president of Yale, made an "earnest plea" to be permitted to do some real teaching rather than just hear recitations.[19] On the other hand, professors must have appreciated that recitation could save effort: checking that students can read or memorize material is much easier than explaining it. This mattered because particularly at less wealthy schools, it was common for a single professor to teach classes spanning a wide segment of the curriculum. One faculty member at Williams taught rhetoric, English literature, aesthetics, and political economy. Dartmouth tasked another with teaching "English, Latin, Greek, Chaldee and such other languages as he shall have time for."[20]

Even more extreme, early in the antebellum period tutors were assigned a class (e.g., the class of 1776) and made responsible for delivering its entire instruction, in all subjects, into the junior year.[21] Given such a task, I suspect, modern professors would begin to sing the praises of recitations!

The bottom line is that once one gets a sense of the antebellum colleges' teaching, it is not a shock that they produced little research. The curriculum did not require specialized professors; to the extent the colleges had any—and they occasionally did, as we will see shortly—it rarely reflected necessity. The instructional methods did not make professors' lives interesting, nor did they require that they connect their teaching to their scholarship. In particular, in the classroom, researchers are most at home explaining material close to their own work. Such an exercise was rarely called for, rewarded, or even allowed in the antebellum college. This disconnect, combined with low pay and job insecurity, did not help make college teaching an attractive career. It is not shocking that around the Civil War, Charles Eliot stated: "It is very hard to find competent professors for the University. Very few Americans of eminent ability are attracted to this profession. The pay has been too low, and there has been no gradual rise out of drudgery. . . ."[22]

Meanwhile in Europe

We have cited the nature of the antebellum colleges' teaching in explaining why they did less research than European universities. This argument might seem strange because we have also stated that to a large extent, the colleges' imported their teaching practices from Europe. Were not the same practices impeding research there?

The thing to realize is that even as many of these practices persisted in the United States, they were generally eliminated in Europe—particularly in Germany—amid gradual educational reforms brought on by the Enlightenment.[23] For instance, over the 1700s the teaching of the liberal arts was mostly removed from European universities and transferred into improved secondary schools like the German *gymnasia* and the French *lycées,* which catered mainly to the children of the elite.[24] Universities, in turn, abandoned the practice of having the same professor teach a wide variety of courses. Rather, they began requiring that professors specialize and teach advanced subjects in departments or institutes, including some that served to incorporate emerging scientific work into universities.[25] These changes gradually introduced the arrangement most common in Europe today: students complete their "general" instruction in secondary school and enter university by applying to specific fields—the equivalent of American majors.[26] These reforms were facilitated by increased public educational spending, which allowed universities to build their infrastructure and attract talented professors, from whom they began to expect academic publications.[27] By the 1850s, Europe had several strong universities; for example, Göttingen had a well-appointed library and about one hundred faculty members, many lecturing on specialized topics and carrying out scholarship. It is not surprising that by our measure of research output, around these years it outperformed all its American counterparts (Table 1.4). One could make analogous statements about universities including Berlin, Edinburgh, Glasgow, Halle, Heidelberg, Leipzig, and Leyden.

In short, thanks to reforms induced by the Enlightenment, by the 1800s European universities were delivering teaching at a relatively specialized and advanced level and, associated with that, were outperforming American colleges in research.

This is not to say that the Enlightenment spirit did not reach American colleges. It would be strange if it had not, given the contact between Europe and the United States, the tendency of American elites to emulate their continental counterparts, and the fact that both places experienced processes like industrialization. In fact, Enlightenment impulses certainly registered in the antebellum colleges, but their impact was ultimately stunted.

To elaborate, the colleges displayed a clear interest in science even before independence. As early as 1659, Harvard tutors were teaching Copernican astronomy, and in 1672 the college acquired a telescope. By 1728, it had created the Hollis Professorship of Mathematics and Natural Philosophy. By the 1790s, several others had analogous positions—for example, Columbia had a professor of botany, and Princeton one of chemistry.[28] All invested in "philosophical apparatus," as scientific instruments were then known. For instance, Oberdorfer (1995, 45) states that when Princeton President John Witherspoon learned that David Rittenhouse, "a renowned Philadelphia scientist, had created a mechanical replica of the movement of the planets called an orrery, [he] rode to Rittenhouse's home and purchased the delicate mechanism for 220£. This was an extraordinary expenditure at a time when . . . the annual budget of the college was less than 2000£."

Professors too showed an interest in science and research. Edward Hitcock, who taught chemistry and natural history at Amherst, completed the first geological survey of Massachusetts; Asa Gray, his counterpart at Harvard, was one of three recipients of an advance copy of the Origin of the Species.[29] Such teachers generated interest among students too. By the early 1800s, Benjamin Silliman was having enough success teaching science at Yale for a member of Yale's board to ask him: "Why, Domine, ... is there not danger that with these physical attractions you will overtop the Latin and the Greek?"[30]

His concern reflected that these years also saw a willingness to diverge from a single-minded focus on classical languages. In 1769, Harvard began allowing students to take French—with parental permission—and by 1850 most colleges taught some English, French, and German literature.[31]

The Enlightenment spirit was also evident in the stated aims with which new colleges entered the market. While decidedly religious goals animated the creation of Harvard and Yale, by the 1750s founders were citing other motives. In 1754, Columbia claimed its curriculum would feature surveying, navigation, geography, history, natural philosophy, and "the Knowledge . . . of every Thing useful for the Comfort, the Convenience, and Elegance of Life. . . ."[32] Meanwhile, Pennsylvania advertised a curriculum with a third of instructional time going to science and practical topics. There were even forays into graduate instruction. For example, Columbia granted an MD in 1767, and by 1834 Harvard had students studying theology, medicine, and law.[33]

And yet all these advances failed to produce a transformation of teaching like that which happened in Europe. Many of the changes, in the end, were superficial. For example, despite enjoying a higher profile, science often continued to be taught with a deductive orientation and little experimentation. For all the expense, no antebellum college acquired a faculty nearly large or sophisticated enough to compete with a good European university.

In fact, to the extent that teaching began to cover applied science in the United States, this tended to happen outside colleges. A notable venue was the Rensselaer Polytechnic Institute (RPI), which emerged in 1824 when Steven Van Rensselaer donated funds to promote the application of science "to the common purposes in life."[34] RPI offered courses in engineering, surveying, and applied science, and featured some of the first laboratories in the United States. Until the Civil War, it accounted for the majority of the country's formally trained engineers, and its graduates were central to the growth of railroads. At this time RPI's main competitors were not colleges, but rather federal institutions focused on European-style military science: the United States Military Academy at West Point, and the Citadel in South Carolina.[35]

Despite their success, however, schools like RPI also offered relatively narrow teaching services and little in the way of advanced instruction. Rudolph (1977) states that around 1830, a motivated college graduate could have earned an RPI degree in twenty-four weeks. And schools like RPI were not research-oriented either; Curti and Nash (1965, 109) observe that even their ardent supporters "conceived of these not in the spirit of a university dedicated to the increase of knowledge, but rather as providing a narrow training for scientific farming, engineering, and mining."

To make matters worse, the existence of institutions like RPI facilitated colleges' claim that science properly belonged elsewhere. When Williams College first hired Ira Remsen to teach chemistry, he asked for a small room in which he might set up a laboratory at his own expense. The response was: "You will please keep in mind that this is a college and not a technical school."[36]

Why Did College Teaching Not Change?

Why did the Enlightenment have a muted effect on antebellum college teaching? The free market blunted its impact: the demands consumers placed on the college sector led it to respond in ways that largely foreclosed teaching reform. This section discusses two sets of such demands: (i) that for sorting and proximity, and (ii) that for educational expansion.

Demand for Sorting and Proximity

In addition to teaching, schools provide sorting. When a school produces sorting, it at least implicitly curates and "sells" peer groups, usually delivering some type of homogeneity. For example, in many countries "elite" high schools admit only students who perform well on specific tests, and some private schools cater to wealthy students. In the United States, some charter schools attract motivated children.[37] In all these cases, these schools appeal to students who wish to be exposed to or associated with the peers they provide. In other words, sorting arises when schools' customers care about the identity of other customers.

Education is not the only industry in which such concerns arise. For example, when people choose restaurants, they consider the quality of the food; but they also often pay attention to who else is buying it. Do the customers at neighboring tables have small children, or do they seem to welcome those who do? Do they appear elegant or "hip"? Are they so-called "foodies"? By delivering specific types of diners, restaurants also perform sorting.

In the case of schools, however, sorting can involve higher stakes because the peers that students have at school can affect their long-term outcomes. We briefly note three reasons for this here (we will return to these below). First, there is evidence that students at schools with able peers land better jobs; this may reflect that employers recruit at such schools, or that friends made at school help graduates land positions.[38] Second, school-based social circles can impact outcomes like marriage.[39] Third, students may learn more when they have peers who are smart or close to themselves in ability; in this sense the quality of a school's sorting can affect the quality of its teaching.[40]

The antebellum colleges certainly produced sorting, but often along dimensions other than those we focus on today. Current discussions around sorting often focus on characteristics like social class or race; for example, ongoing litigation surrounds the role race plays in Harvard's admissions, and many observers worry that low-income children are underrepresented at elite schools.[41]

By contrast, in the antebellum period the concern for sorting often involved denominational affiliation: many households desired schools catering to people whose beliefs were similar to their own, for example, on the proper protocol for baptism. Such concerns might seem obscure to most modern parents on campus tours, who view chapels as pretty but otherwise incidental objects. But their 1776 counterparts would have had no trouble pointing out that Dartmouth, Harvard, and Yale were largely controlled by Congregationalists; Princeton by Presbyterians; Columbia and William and Mary by Anglicans; Brown by Baptists; and Rutgers by the Dutch Reformed.[42] Of course, denominational preferences may not have purely reflected religion, since as discussed below, denominations differed in their socioeconomic composition. Thus, for example, a desire to attend school with Presbyterians rather than Baptists might have—beyond attitudes toward baptism—reflected a desire to enroll with people of certain social backgrounds.

In addition to denominational homogeneity, antebellum parents often preferred proximity: they wished for their children to attend college relatively close to home. This preference persists today, but it was perhaps more intense when travel was slower and communication more difficult.[43] One reason this mattered is that in this period small local donations were often crucial to college survival. For example, Curti and Nash (1965, 52) report that when Western Reserve College was founded in 1826, local farmers "pledged support in kind or in labor. . . . One man took responsibility for bringing stone for buildings from a quarry ten miles away; the job required the work of an entire winter. A farmer's wife promised fifty dollars annually from the butter and egg money and bore this sacrifice for ten years." Furthermore, reports suggest that such donations were easier to obtain locally. Philander Chase, who helped found Kenyon and other Midwestern colleges, summarized the situation thus: "Place the [college] near the town or village I inhabit and I will give, liberally give, but otherwise not a cent from my pocket shall you have."[44]

The desire for a nearby college was strong enough for some colleges to place their location for sale. For example, in 1819 the trustees of Williams accepted bids from multiple towns, although in the end, the legislature ruled that the college should remain in Williamstown. Similar concerns helped the creation of colleges in Brunswick, Maine (Bowdoin) and Columbia, South Carolina (South Carolina College).[45]

After independence, such concerns produced college entry on a scale that would have shocked European observers, who by that point were used to states funding universities and strictly controlling their number. The pace of entry was such that for much of the 1800s no centralized college registry

Table 2.1　Colleges created before the Civil War, by state

| State | Colleges in sixteen states | | | |
	Open (1)	Closed (2)	Total (3)	Mortality rate (4)
Pennsylvania	16	15	31	0.48
New York	15	21	36	0.58
Ohio	17	26	43	0.60
Virginia	10	22	32	0.69
North Carolina	7	19	26	0.73
Maryland	5	18	23	0.78
Alabama	4	19	23	0.83
Tennessee	7	39	46	0.85
Georgia	7	44	51	0.86
Louisiana	3	23	26	0.88
Missouri	8	77	85	0.91
Mississippi	2	27	29	0.93
Texas	2	38	40	0.95
Kansas	1	19	20	0.95
Florida	0	2	2	1.00
Arkansas	0	3	3	1.00
Total	104	412	516	0.80

This table draws on data in Tewksbury (1932). It describes the number of colleges opened and closed in sixteen states, where these are ordered by the number of institutions still open in 1861.

exists, and it is hard to know how many schools there were. The main reference has been work by Tewksbury (1932).[46]

While nine colleges were in place by 1776, Tewksbury estimates there were 182 in 1861; Hofstadter (1955) and Burke (1982) suggest somewhat higher numbers: 250 and 241, respectively. These figures do not capture the full extent of entry because many colleges closed before the war. Counting these is even harder, and Tewksbury reports data for only sixteen states. Table 2.1 presents data for these, with column (1) showing that at the eve of the war, they contained 104 colleges. Column (2) shows that an additional 412 had closed, making for a total of 516 ever in existence. Column (4) contains the mortality rate—the ratio of schools closed to the total ever open; overall, this statistic stands at 0.80. If the same mortality rate applied in all states, then one would conclude, admittedly roughly, that about 900 colleges entered the market before the Civil War. One can see why observers like Hofstadter (1955, 114) say that in this period college creation got "completely out of hand."[47] By comparison, around these years France, Germany, and the U.K. had twenty-two, twenty-two, and eleven universities, respectively.

Contemporary observers agreed that demands for denominational sorting and proximity—in many cases acting in concert—helped propel this entry. Frederick Barnard, who would later preside Columbia, stated in 1856: "Nearly all our colleges are . . . the creations of the different religious denominations which divide our people. They are regarded as important instrumentalities, through which the peculiarities of doctrine . . . are to be maintained, propagated, or defended. It is this which has led to the great multiplication of collegiate institutions in our country . . . ."[48] Phillip Lindsley, President of Princeton and later of the University of Nashville stated that "A principal cause of the . . . multiplication . . . of western colleges is, no doubt, the diversity of religious denominations among us. Almost every sect will have its colleges, and generally one at least in each state."[49]

To elaborate, two groups, Congregationalists and Presbyterians, were initially the most active in college creation. This is not surprising given that as Calvinists, both stressed a trained clergy and a literate flock. Further, each of these groups had a predominant institutional origin: Congregationalists often hailed from Yale and Presbyterians from Princeton. For example, Rudolph (1977) considers the presidents of seventy-five colleges in 1840 and indicates that thirty-six and twenty-two were Yale and Princeton graduates, respectively. As a result, observers sometimes called these two schools "mothers of colleges."[50] Yale, in particular, extended its influence across the country, and at several points in the antebellum period was the largest and most "national" school—that is, one of the very few capable of attracting students from far away. The fact that Yale rather than the older Harvard occupied this position itself reveals the salience of religious sorting. Yale was founded by Connecticut Congregationalists who, in addition to desiring a college physically closer than Cambridge, Massachusetts, also wanted one that was more orthodox than the also Congregationalist Harvard.[51]

As the 1800s progressed, Baptists, Catholics, Episcopalians, Lutherans, Methodists, Quakers, and others enthusiastically joined the fray. Table 2.2 draws on Tewksbury's data to show that by 1861, four denominations

Table 2.2   Colleges created before the Civil War by affiliation

Denominational or state affiliation	Colleges
Presbyterian	49
Methodist	34
Baptist	25
Congregational	21
Catholic	14
Episcopal	11
Lutheran	6
Disciples	5
German Reformed	4
Universalist	4
Friends	2
Unitarian	2
Christian	1
Dutch Reformed	1
United Brethren	1
Semi-State	3
Municipal	3
State	21
Total	207

This table draws on data from Tewksbury (1932) to list the religious
and state affiliations of colleges in existence before the Civil War.
The total (207) exceeds the number cited earlier (182) because some
colleges were affiliated with more than one denomination or in some
cases with a denomination in addition to a state. As in Table 2.1, the
numbers do not include schools closed before the Civil War.

accounted for more than twenty colleges each, and six for more than ten.
In addition, twenty-one state colleges had appeared, in a few cases to provide denomination-free schooling. For example, the University of Virginia
was created in part because William and Mary—which the state had historically helped support—would not give up its Episcopalian affiliation when
Thomas Jefferson and others pushed for the creation of a nondenomina-
tional institution.[52]

The bottom line is that in terms of college creation, the United States
lived up to its image as the Wild West. In the words of Jencks and Riesman
(1968, 156): "instead of a national system of higher education, America got a
Balkanized pattern that made even the decentralized and polycentric
German approach look orderly and monolithic . . . ."

A key consequence of this massive entry was that the antebellum colleges faced significant resource constraints. First, most had few students; Geiger (1986) reports that before the Civil War, the typical college had less than one hundred. There was of course variation around this; the largest Eastern schools approached four hundred students, while Rudolph (1962) reports cases like that of Lafayette, which in 1848, about twenty years after its creation, had more trustees than students.[53]

Low enrollments mechanically implied low tuition revenues, particularly given anecdotal evidence that many colleges had trouble raising their prices or collecting tuition. For example, at certain points in the 1800s, no student paid tuition at Cumberland College; in the 1820s, Dartmouth's President John Wheelock reported "no difficulty in securing sufficient numbers of students, so long as he charged nothing for the services of the college."[54]

The result was that, in the words of Boyer (2015, 11), most schools hovered between "genial penury and unmitigated fiscal disaster." This helps explain the mortality rate observed in Table 2.1—where there is free entry there can be free exit. Indeed, some schools even went in and out of existence; for example, financial difficulties forced Rutgers to close twice before 1825.[55]

In several states, mortality was not higher only thanks to public aid that benefitted schools including some of which we now think of as private and wealthy. For example, Williams received fifty thousand dollars from Massachusetts between 1793 and 1823, an amount equivalent to all it was able to raise, including via state-authorized lotteries. Without a subsequent additional hundred thousand dollars from the State, President Mark Hopkins said, "I do not see how the College could have gone on."[56] Rudolph (1962) cites similar potentially lifesaving public grants at Dickinson, NYU, Pennsylvania, and Union.

The antebellum colleges' financial condition contributed to limiting their teaching services. For resource-poor institutions, few students mechanically imply few professors, and with a small faculty it is difficult to offer specialized or advanced instruction. It is worth elaborating on this point. University administrators readily point out that providing advanced education is expensive and risky. One must add new classes and recruit new

Table 2.3   Top ten institutions in terms of endowment per student, 2016

Rank	Institution	Endowment per student (millions of dollars) (1)	Total endowment (billions of dollars) (2)	Enrollment (3)
1	Princeton University	2.7	22.2	8,181
2	Yale University	2.0	25.4	12,312
3	Harvard University	1.6	34.5	21,000
4	Stanford University	1.4	22.4	15,877
5	Pomona College	1.2	2.0	1,663
6	MIT	1.2	13.1	11,319
7	Swarthmore College	1.1	1.7	1,581
8	Amherst College	1.1	2.0	1,849
9	Olin College of Engineering	1.0	0.4	350
10	Williams College	1.0	2.3	2,245

The table lists the institutions with the highest endowments per student. The data are drawn from http://www.reachhighscholars.org/college endowments.html, which in turn uses data from NACUBO (National Association of College and University Business Officers).

faculty; average class sizes fall, raising costs per student. For an illustration of how financially minded stakeholders resist going down this path, let us move ahead in time and consider the present-day Princeton, by some measures the wealthiest university in the world. Specifically, Table 2.3 shows that while Princeton does not have the highest endowment among American universities, it does have the greatest resources per student (column 1). In 2016, these amounted to 2.7 million dollars—a sum beyond the antebellum colleges' wildest dreams.

And yet even at the modern Princeton, offering advanced instruction is viewed as financially questionable. To wit, President William Bowen (2010, 76) wrote in his recent memoir:

A recurring debate at Princeton . . . centers on [the] weight to be given to PhD programs . . . versus the undergraduate college. . . . [I]t was necessary to communicate over and over to the trustees . . . that there is a powerful complementarity between teaching at the two levels. Business executives, in particular, are used to thinking of "product lines" and the need to avoid spending resources on the relatively "unproductive" ones. . . . It was natural for such trustees to ask me why we kept spending so much money . . . on what seemed like esoteric PhD programs of relatively small scale when resource constraints overall were tight.

Such concerns would have been much more salient in the antebellum period.

The bottom line is that massive entry blunted any push for teaching reform. Indeed, some historians argue that rapid entry did not produce as much stagnation as decline; for example, Hofstadter (1955, 209) refers to the decades after independence as the "great retrogression." He states that "one of the primary factors in the backsliding of the collegiate system was that the sponsors of collegiate education, instead of developing further the substantial and altogether adequate number of institutions that existed in 1800, established new institutions far beyond the number demanded by the geography of the country."

Demand for Educational Expansion

While the demand for sorting held back teaching reform, so did a demand for rapid educational expansion. To see why, a good starting point is Goldin and Katz's (2008) observation that the United States expanded access to formal education much faster than most European countries. Specifically, after independence many Americans who had not themselves acquired much schooling desired that their children do so, and the educational and political systems accommodated this demand. For example, local jurisdictions aggressively opened elementary and later secondary schools.[57]

This demand was essentially the same that produced grassroots benefactions for new colleges and helped propel denominations' college building. To illustrate, recall that the initial college founders *par excellence* were Calvinists: Congregationalists and Presbyterians, but also Dutch Reformed and German Reformed. Later, all these groups were eclipsed by the Baptists and Methodists, who had historically placed less emphasis on clerical training and attracted a membership that was on average of lower socioeconomic status. Rudolph (1962, 57) states, however, that both of these denominations turned aggressively to college building once they realized that "opportunity in the United States being what it was, no church could establish itself as the permanent refuge for the permanently meek and disinherited. American life did not work that way . . . ." Thanks to such developments, by the Civil War Americans had significantly more years of schooling than their British, French, and German counterparts (Figure 1.1).

One reason why the United States was able to take the lead in this dimension is that Europe approached educational expansion more slowly and systematically. For example, many European school systems adopted formal tracking: exams and teacher assessments performed at relatively young ages directed children into different types of schools. Those perceived as most prepared—typically the children of the elite—were directed to academic schools, with the remainder sent to more vocational establishments.[58] This practice implied that the size of different parts of the school sector could be restricted, since no segment was expected to accommodate all. In addition, the academic high schools could teach the liberal arts at a relatively high level, given that they only needed to serve an educational elite. Finally, in time formalized exams that certified completion of secondary school became gateways to university, creating a clear demarcation between the tasks assigned to each part of the system.

European countries were able to craft such orderly systems in part because they developed an institutional machinery that included centralized states willing and able to regulate education. An oft-repeated story states that the French Minister of Education knows, at any given time of any day, exactly what is being taught at any school in France. While this surely involves exaggeration, it captures the centralized spirit of education in Europe.

By comparison, American educational expansion was so decentralized that, as we have seen, the authorities often did not know how many colleges existed. In addition, schools ensured that most children had access to and moved through the educational system, and this at times entailed lowering the teaching level. Goldin and Katz (2008, 133) state that: "around 1900 . . . U.S. schooling was not an elite system in which only a small number of bright young boys could attain an upper secondary school education and thus continue their studies in . . . university. [American] schools were, by and large, open to all and were forgiving to those who did not shine in the lower grades." They elaborate on two key terms: "By 'open' we mean that almost all children could attend school. By 'forgiving' we mean that one could advance to higher grades and institutions even if one failed to perform adequately in a lower grade" (154). In other words, the goal was that schools receive and hopefully graduate everyone. Incidentally, in many ways this spirit remains alive and well. The Bush administration titled its key education legislation "No Child Left Behind"; not to be outdone, the Obama administration labeled its successor "Every Student Succeeds."

For their part, colleges desperate for enrollments were inclined to accept students with any amount of preparation. In this sense, their teaching—for example, the lack of advanced instruction—was simply a consequence of the demand they encountered; there was only so much preparation they could expect from their students. It is thus not surprising that when some called for colleges to adapt German-style university curricula, Harvard's Charles Eliot replied that this would suit his freshmen "about as well as a barnyard would suit a whale."[59]

Now one might think that some colleges could have catered only to the elite and supplied a different type of teaching. But as we will see later (Chapter 4), college selectivity would not appear in the United States until well into the 1900s. Before the Civil War, the vast majority of schools not only struggled financially but—with very few exceptions like Princeton and Yale—drew students from local markets. Many of these markets were too small to allow a school to choose students. In addition, this was still a time in which observers took the size of a college as a "first pass" indicator of its quality, and it would have been strange to turn students away. The bottom line is that even the colleges with the best reputations tended to accept all applicants who fulfilled modest prerequisites.

For another illustration of how rapid expansion contributed to low teaching standards, note that in many areas the college system was built simultaneously with the school system, if not earlier. For example, Thelin (2004, 40) observes that in the East, the original colonial college system consisting of nine schools was constructed "without a strong, coherent base of elementary and secondary education even among . . . elite families, let alone [the] general population." Or as Rudolph (1962, 48) puts it, one early law of

American education was that "Where there are no elementary or secondary schools, there you will find a college."

One sees further indication of this in language surrounding the creation of the first three colleges—in each case the word "school" appears either before or instead of the word "college": in 1636, the Massachusetts' colonial government allocated "400£ towards a schoale or colledge"; in the 1690s, the Virginia Assembly instructed the future president of William and Mary to "make it your business to peruse the best charters in England whereby free schools and colleges have been founded"; in 1701, the Connecticut General Court discussed "suitably endowing & ordering a Collegiate School within his Majties Colony of Connecticot . . . ."[60]

Part II will discuss that the colonists had legal and political reasons to mention schools in these passages. Another possibility, however, is that they used ambiguous language because they realized that given the colonies' educational condition, they needed schools as much as they needed colleges. Consistent with this, William and Mary's charter allowed for the creation of four schools: "a common school for Indian children," a grammar school centered on Greek and Latin, a divinity school, and a college. The schools operated for decades before the college itself got running.

Additionally, the simultaneous construction of schools and colleges meant that for a long time, the boundary between these was unclear. For example, arriving in New York in 1773, Alexander Hamilton considered enrolling at Princeton but opted for Columbia because the latter was willing to grant him advanced placement. One reason for his hurry was his age: he was eighteen at a time when most students entered college aged thirteen or fourteen.[61] Almost a century later, in 1849, Charles Eliot entered Harvard at age fifteen.[62]

Given that antebellum colleges often enrolled students we now consider of high school age, it is not surprising that many in fact provided teaching that was at that level. For example, Hofstadter (1955) observes that the designation "college" was used liberally, and for some institutions "high school" would have been more appropriate. Jencks and Riesman (1968, 29) elaborate:

> public high schools remained relatively rare until the very end of the century, and students who wanted to continue beyond elementary

school usually had to enroll away from home. Some enrolled in private academies, but others went directly into "preparatory departments" of places that called themselves colleges. In some cases these were in fact exclusively preparatory institutions. In other cases they offered only introductory college-level work. In still other cases they offered a regular college course, but enrolled the majority of their students in precollege programs. Given this mixing of different levels of instruction and different age groups within institutions, the distinction between secondary and college level instruction was extremely hard to draw.[63]

Offering preparatory work also helped schools attract enrollments. For example, in 1865 Wisconsin had 331 students, but only 41 of them were in "regular" college classes; the rest enrolled in a preparatory program. During its initial years, Georgetown only enrolled students aged between eight and fourteen.[64] Graham (2005) adds that such patterns were at times viewed favorably by local authorities, as they eased pressures on cash-strapped local "common" schools. In addition, this pattern helps explain the presence of young students who had difficulty paying full tuition.

The entire picture is consistent with Burke's (1982, 35) statement that "The development of the antebellum colleges cannot be understood unless it is viewed as an integral part of the struggles and successes of the general expansion . . . of American education." It also helps explain how nine hundred colleges opened before the Civil War, and why so many of them closed. Likely only a portion of these schools actually operated at the college level, and those that provided secondary-level teaching would have found it hard to survive as lower-priced public high schools appeared.[65] Consistent with this, Burke (1982) presents a count of colleges alternative to Tewksbury's (1932) and finds a much lower mortality rate. The difference mainly arises because Burke does not count as colleges those establishments that appear to have offered only secondary-level instruction.

For our purposes, it is not important to determine what institutions should or should not have been called colleges. First, just as some colleges engaged in secondary-level teaching, the opposite was possible too. For example, before assuming the Yale presidency in 1795, Timothy Dwight established an academy that carried students "all the way through college work" in a way many considered gave Yale a run for its money.[66] Second, the very existence of the labeling ambiguity illustrates the massive and often chaotic entry that helped arrest the development of colleges' teaching services.

A final implication is that in terms of the material covered, four years in an American college would likely not have been equivalent to four years in a European university. The above discussion suggests that in the extreme, American college students studied the humanist curriculum that their European counterparts covered in secondary school. While one can push such reasoning too far, the idea was entertained by contemporary observers well acquainted with both systems. Yale president Jeremiah Day (in office 1817–1846) stated that the German institution most equivalent to the college was the *gymnasium*.[67] Geiger (1986, 4) notes that Henry Tappan, president of the University of Michigan in the 1850s, "recognized that the offerings of the American college corresponded in large part with the classical regimen of the gymnasium or lycée. It seemed clear to [him] that advanced study, such as that cultivated by the German universities, ought to follow the completion of the American bachelor's degree." Although not crucial for our argument, this raises the possibility that the left panel of Figure 1.1 overstates the historical American educational advantage; this may not have been as large measured by skills rather than by years of schooling.[68] Indeed this consideration to some extent still applies today: Hoxby (2014, 1) discusses current instruction at the lower end of nonselective American colleges, stating that "a non-trivial share of [their] courses cover the same material that appears in secondary school curricula. Most [of these] courses are designed for students who are no more than minimally college-ready . . . ."

Demand for Discipline

This chapter has argued that the condition of antebellum college teaching stemmed from market conditions. Survival required that schools cater to often underprepared customers who demanded denominationally oriented schooling close to home. This produced underfunded, understaffed colleges that had no choice but to offer a rigid curriculum taught mainly by unspecialized professors using rote exercises.

In closing we note, however, that many antebellum college presidents and professors did not blame the state of affairs on external forces. Rather, they made an affirmative case for the antebellum teaching. They held it was appropriate, regardless of whether resource constraints made it difficult to pursue any other. Considered ex post, this can seem like a rationalization; still, it is worth considering because it was an influential view, and because it will be relevant to later discussions of teaching reform.

The salient exposition of this positive case is the so-called Yale Report of 1828. This document was authored by a committee, although historians suggest that Yale President Jeremiah Day and Professor James Kingsley had lead roles in its authorship.[69] The report defended the antebellum curriculum—which as we review below already had critics—using arguments related to modern notions of neuroplasticity, holding that learning can modify the brain. In the report's terminology, a college education expanded the faculties of the mind: attributes like persistence, attention, memory, discipline, and abstraction. This view was influential, as evidenced by Princeton President James McCosh's 1868 statement: "I do hold it to be the highest end of a university to educate; that is, draw out and improve the faculties God has given."[70]

Storr (1953) explains the Report's position with an analogy. It held that college trained the student's mind for something like a decathlon; its appropriate role was that of a coach who ensures the athlete prepares for all events. It would be a mistake, in this view, to allow him to focus on only one event because he preferred it; that would leave him unprepared. In this spirit, the fixed classical four-year curriculum ensured the student's exposure to all necessary forms of practice; hence the resistance to electives and specialization. Further, in each area recitations featuring a measure of memorization were essential. For instance, the Report pushed back against calls for modern lectures, stating that these "do not always bring upon the student a pressing and definite responsibility. He may repose upon his seat, and yield a passive hearing . . . without ever calling into exercise the active powers of his own mind."[71] Indeed, the fact that Greek and Latin were difficult and in some sense irrelevant to modern life made them ideal for intellectual exercise.

In this view, the college's role was to expand the mind's capacity—not to fill it; that would happen later in the graduate's life. For example, if one practiced the conjugation of Latin verbs, one's mind would be ready to deal with legal issues, or with the challenges of running a business. But it was not the college's role to teach the details of such endeavors; hence the resistance to practical subjects. To summarize, it is useful to cite the report itself:

> The two great points to be gained . . . are the discipline and the furniture of the mind; expanding its powers, and storing it with knowledge. The former of these is, perhaps, the more important of the two. A commanding object, therefore, . . . should be, to call into daily and vigorous exercise the faculties of the student. Those branches of study should be prescribed, and those modes of instruction adopted, which are best calculated to teach the art of fixing the attention, directing the train of thought, analyzing a subject proposed for investigation. . . . We doubt whether the powers of mind can be developed . . . by studying languages alone, or mathematics alone, or natural or political science alone. . . . As our course of instruction is not intended to complete an education . . . neither does it include all the minute details of mercantile, mechanical, or agricultural concerns. These can never be effectually learned except in the very circumstances in which they are to be practiced.[72]

In other words, the colleges' teaching was fit for the elite. To stoop to anything else would be a disservice to society.

Whether a rationalization or not, the report's recommendations dovetailed neatly with the resource constraints facing the colleges. In Rudolph's (1962, 135) words:

> The privileged orders were pleased that Yale chose to withstand the demands for a more popular and practical education, . . . And these—the religious, the very pious, the privileged—were the people who ran the colleges, people who also knew that the American college was running on a shoestring and that the old course of study, while the best, was also the cheapest.

More generally, the report's emphasis on control of academic activity dovetailed with the notion that schools should control student conduct—that is, with the idea that a college should act *in loco parentis*—a current of paternalism that runs in American higher education. Even after the Civil War, many colleges had pages-worth of regulations on student behavior. For example, in 1885 Princeton ruled that "should any students continue to have their washing done in town . . . , it must be done under the supervision of the College Office."[73] President McCosh took measures to limit gambling, drinking, and visits to Trenton, which he called "the graveyard of purity."[74] At Swarthmore in the 1870s, President Edward McGill issued numerous rules, including that "Students of the two sexes, except brothers and sisters, shall not walk together on the grounds of the College . . . , nor to or from the railroad station or the skating grounds. They shall not coast upon the same sled."[75] This impulse also remains alive and well. Witness the heavily scheduled orientations that modern American universities hold for first-year students, including workshops detailing the subtleties of acceptable and unacceptable physical contact between students.

In closing this chapter, note that historians have debated whether the antebellum colleges get a fair shake. Axtell (1971) argues that their state was not as depressing as Hofstadter (1955) and others have made it out to be. On the one hand, this chapter has taken a view close to Hofstadter's by arguing that massive entry produced colleges short on resources, with consequences evident in their research performance. On the other hand, it has also argued that the colleges produced value for their customers by supplying denominationally homogeneous peer groups and relatively basic instruction, close to home. In other words, while massive entry may have stunted their *teaching*, it allowed the colleges to supply the *sorting* people demanded. That is to say, market conditions induced a tradeoff in which research may have suffered, but focusing on only one dimension of schools' performance is unfair.[76] This assessment is in the spirit of Burke's (1982, 51) statement that "By assuming that every educational institution with the term 'college' in its title was designed to compete with what the historians viewed as the legitimate higher educational institutions, they misinterpreted the reasons why the institutions were founded." In other words, our case is at odds with the characterization of the antebellum colleges as failures that Blackburn and Conrad (1986) attribute to the "traditionalist" view.

Whether one sets out to defend or indict the antebellum college, the bottom line is that, lacking minds and money, it produced little research. How could this system possibly catch up to Europe by the early 1900s, overtaking it soon after? That is the topic of the next three chapters. They cover, respectively: teaching reform, sorting reform, and factors that enhance research productivity.

CHAPTER 3

Teaching Reform

W HILE FREE ENTRY allowed the antebellum colleges to satisfy their customers' demand for sorting, it also allowed a gap to develop between the teaching they offered and that many potential customers demanded. This gap grew as industrialization intensified the need for specialized and scientific training. For example, Goldin and Katz (1998) note that in the 1800s, industries like steel, rubber, and drugs began to require workers with training in chemistry, biology, and physics; similarly, social problems related to industrial and urban development increased demand for social scientists. Analogous needs developed in agriculture and business.[1]

By the late 1800s many observers could argue that the colleges were not meeting entire facets of educational demand. In 1889, for instance, Andrew Carnegie stated that : "While the college student has been . . . trying to master languages which are dead, . . . the future captain of industry is hotly engaged in the school of experience . . . College education as it exists is fatal to success in that domain."[2] For their part, academics noted the colleges' failure to supply advanced training, and pointed to the growth of noncollegiate institutions like RPI. Charles Adams, professor at Michigan and later president of Cornell, summarized their mood: "the sad fact stares us in the face that the training which has long been considered essential to finished scholarship has been losing ground . . . in the favor of the people."[3]

What do we see if we fast forward to the present? First, even further entry. The United States now has about 4,700 postsecondary institutions, more than twenty times as many as in 1860. The logic in the previous chapter might lead one to think this would have further hindered the production of research. And yet, about 100 of these 4,700 schools—often called "Research I" universities—allow the country to lead the world in university research.[4] Interestingly, at these institutions, undergraduate colleges—direct descendants of their antebellum counterparts—often occupy pride of place.

In short, to an extent the inhabitants of the antebellum colleges could not have imagined, some of their schools transformed into universities that command enormous amounts of minds and money. The next three chapters describe how this transformation happened.

This chapter describes how the process started as a few schools undertook teaching reform. These aimed to show that survival could lie in offering advanced, specialized instruction in a broad range of areas, rather than in providing denominational sorting. This reform amounted to a radical transformation of the prevalent "business model," and was not easy to implement. Efforts toward it started much before the Civil War, and their failures provided lessons that helped shape later attempts. Finally, the schools that succeeded realized that delivering the new advanced/specialized teaching required a new kind of teacher: one at the frontier of a field, and this began to be ascertained by professors' ability to do research. As the academic system provided increasingly sophisticated measures of this ability, a sorting dynamic began that allowed these schools to corner more than their fair share of research talent.

Pre–Civil War Failures

Teaching reform did not happen instantaneously. The antebellum period saw efforts that almost always failed, sometimes spectacularly. These merit discussion, however, not only because they are interesting in their own right, but because they illuminate the ingredients later reformers would need to achieve success. The first section of this chapter, therefore, reviews a sample of these early attempts.[5] The lessons that emerge recur in the second section, which covers successful postwar reforms.

The trees we will describe are specific efforts at specific schools. To not lose sight of the forest, we preview three types of reforms and resulting lessons:

- First, teaching reforms that in retrospect should have been noncontroversial. Not only were their key features later widely implemented, but they did not even cost much. They nonetheless encountered fatal opposition, illustrating that reformers would have to contend with conservative resistance.
- Second, teaching reforms with features that also eventually became commonplace, but that were costly and hence ran into resource constraints. These illustrated that successful reform would require deep pockets.
- Third, reforms that were flawed in that they did not adequately consider how changes to schools' teaching would affect their sorting. Success would also require attention to this crucial university product.

A final note before proceeding is that this chapter focuses on reforms spearheaded by individuals, and sometimes provides brief biographical background on them. This approach reflects that partly due to self-rule, free entry, and the substantial power vested in boards and presidents, individuals can have a large impact on American schools.[6] Of course, some of the time universities see presidents, deans, and professors who have little in the way of a vision to change their schools. The individuals covered here are the polar opposite—they sought major changes, whether they succeeded or failed.

George Ticknor (Harvard)

George Ticknor, a Dartmouth graduate, was among the first Americans to pursue advanced studies in Germany, where he spent time at Göttingen beginning in 1815. After returning to the United States, Ticknor taught French, Spanish, and literature at Harvard, where he began to stress the need for reform. In 1821 he wrote that Harvard was neither a "University, which we call ourselves nor a respectable high school which we ought to be . . . ."[7] He began to float numerous ideas for teaching reform. First, he wished to introduce tracking, that is, to separate students by ability. He criticized "the attempt to force together sixty or eighty young men . . . of very unequal ages, talents, attainments, [and] habits . . . to advance *pari passu* during four . . . valuable years of life, giving to the most industrious and intelligent no more and no other lessons, than to the most dull and idle . . . ."[8] It would be better, he argued, to separate students into different ability groups, tailoring lessons to each.[9] Second, he called for the addition of courses that would be offered on an elective basis, allowing students to deviate from the prescribed curriculum to opt for specialized instruction. He asked: "And why should not the student . . . determine in a greater or less degree, what studies he shall pursue . . . ? College could be thus more intimately connected with the remainder of life, and rendered more directly useful to it."[10] Third, Ticknor wished to give professors more time for research, and freedom to gradually substitute recitations for lectures with an emphasis on "commentary, explanation, and illustrative material."[11] Fourth, he wanted to organize the college into departments that would eventually branch into graduate teaching. Fifth, he wished Harvard would broaden its scope, entering areas covered by schools like RPI; that is, that it would "marshall . . . resources to render unnecessary the establishment of . . . agricultural schools, law schools, and other establishments for special purposes . . . ."[12]

Harvard's President John Kirkland displayed some sympathy toward Ticknor's ideas, but warned him also that Harvard was "poorer than you think."[13] In 1826, a committee supported Kirkland, stating:

> We are not insensible how great a benefit it would be to the public, and how great an honor to the College, if we had Professors, who might confine their instruction in each department, to such as had mastered its rudiments, and who might immediately make known here, the discoveries of other learned men in all countries, and extend the boundaries of science by their own. But . . . the income of the college is so reduced that this object cannot be attained.[14]

Perhaps in response to such objections, Ticknor ultimately focused his energy on tracking, the least expensive of his proposals; this was the only one that made it beyond paper. With Kirkland's support, he demonstrated it himself, separating the freshmen taking French into four sections of varying difficulty.

But the idea failed to take hold elsewhere in the college. Rudolph (1977, 77) notes that skeptical professors found a model in a colleague who made "a great display of dividing the class into groups and then assigning identical lessons to all of them." He adds that even Kirkland voiced doubts, noting that reformers wished to legislate "that professors shall be amiable, tutors popular, and students loving." In 1835, Ticknor resigned.

In short, the one reform Ticknor managed to implement fell victim to resistance from conservative stakeholders. Perhaps Harvard's very age made it a tough setting for experimentation. In closing, we note that Ticknor was prescient not just about reforms Harvard would eventually adopt, but also about the role free entry would play in making them viable. In 1821 he wrote: "Every day persuades me anew . . . that at Cambridge we shall never become what we might be very easily unless we are led or driven to it by a rival."[15]

Samuel Ruggles (Columbia)

In 1853 James Renwick, Columbia's professor of natural philosophy, announced his retirement. The Board of Trustees immediately began to search for a replacement, all the more given Renwick's observation that he alone taught the physical sciences at Columbia, whereas Harvard, Princeton, and Yale had separate professors for physics, chemistry, and geology.

At the time, the board consisted of twenty-four men, six of them were clergy, all were members of Episcopalian and Dutch Reformed groups that historically made up New York's elite. The board had a reputation for conservatism, not least because some of its seats were effectively hereditary.[16] The salient board member, for our purposes, was Samuel Ruggles—a real estate investor and politician who became an advocate for the transformation of Columbia into a university.[17] Ruggles was among the first to realize that this would require the school to reform its teaching and hence its personnel policy.

Among the candidates considered was Wolcott Gibbs, a chemist with sterling credentials. Some trustees, however, soon noticed a blemish: Gibbs had been raised Unitarian. Ruggles tried to preempt the opposition, proposing a motion that:

Whereas the original charter incorporating King's . . . College . . . provides that [its] laws . . . shall not "extend to exclude any person of any religious denomination whatever, from equal Liberty and advantage of Education" . . . RESOLVED that in filling [this] Professorship, the Trustees are legally and morally bound to select such Professor, with reference solely to his fitness for the place, without regard to his religious opinions.[18]

Everyone realized that the issue went beyond Gibbs's denomination—if expertise became the key criterion for academic appointments, the trustees would lose control of faculty hiring. Seeing the larger stakes, Ruggles's son-in-law, one of his allies on the board, stated that he would willingly sacrifice Gibbs "for the sake of eliminating some half dozen obstructive colleagues."[19]

As the controversy spilled into the press, Ruggles published a pamphlet titled "The Duty of Columbia College to the Community." It raised a contrast between Columbia and Göttingen, pointing out that both were founded by George II, and hence were about the same age. Yet Columbia had six professors and 150 students, whereas Göttingen had 89 and 1,545, respectively. Ruggles (1854, 17) also echoed themes raised by Ticknor:

A deep, premonitory feeling now pervades the public mind, that a great . . . University is needed, not a College, in our narrow sense of the term, a mere gymnasium or grammar-school, where some half dozen professors repeat . . . the same rudiments, but a broad, comprehensive seat of learning . . . where every student may pursue any path he may select, to its extremest attainable limit, and above all, where research . . . by the ablest men the world can furnish, shall add daily to the great sum of human knowledge.

He implied, for good measure, that his colleagues were in breach of fiduciary duty: "For I expressly maintain, that we hold a distinct relation to the community and owe it a definite duty . . . Our Board . . . is not a fraternity, nor a religious order, set apart from and independent of the community . . . ."

(13). Ruggles had overplayed his hand, and the majority dropped Gibbs from consideration. (Gibbs went on to teach at City College and Harvard.)

To summarize, Ruggles's effort shared multiple attributes with Ticknor's: it attempted to improve teaching, emphasizing expertise; it was prescient, as today professors, *de facto*, select who is to fill faculty vacancies; it was low cost, since at root it could be only about replacing instructors; its failure originated in conservative resistance.

We now consider a type of reform that, while eventually also widely adopted, was not cheap.

Graduate Instruction

At some schools, proposals for teaching reform centered on adding graduate instruction, an ambitious step for schools in fiscally precarious positions, particularly at a time when virtually no job in the country required a master's degree.

One initiative happened at NYU as it prepared to open under the leadership of men including Albert Gallatin, a Swiss immigrant who became the longest-serving secretary of the treasury. This group felt that a city was the proper place for a university, and when NYU opened in 1832, it offered an MA in addition to a BA degree. But demand was low and amid money troubles, the school dropped the MA.

Another effort took place at Albany and was led remotely by men including Samuel Ruggles and Louis Agassiz, the latter another Swiss immigrant and PhD-trained professor of geology at Harvard. These men's participation likely reflected their assessment of the prospects for graduate instruction at their home institutions. The group stated: "There is a great and growing demand in our country for something higher than college instruction; and one great University, if fairly set in motion, would thrive. . . . There are men enough to make one very brilliant institution . . . ."[20] The demand they perceived, however, was insufficient to call forth the private donations or public subsidies needed, and they abandoned the project. Another initiative at Pennsylvania, also endorsed by Agassiz, immediately met with questions regarding demand and financial feasibility. One skeptical professor stated: "I do not think that there exists at present, in our country, any extensive demand for . . . opportunities of further acquirement of knowledge . . ."[21] Another dismissed Agassiz's endorsement on the grounds that he was a foreigner.

These episodes suggest that a school could only sustain graduate instruction if it received consistent outside support, or if it could cover losses using profits from other activities. In part because of this, the only antebellum school that had lasting success with graduate instruction was, perhaps ironically, Yale. Around 1850, the school had one of the best reputations and largest stocks of alumni; thus it was arguably well placed to generate demand for graduate teaching, and to absorb the associated financial losses.

The key developments happened under President Theodore Woolsey, who perhaps aware of resistance to reform, characterized himself as a "progressive conservative."[22] His inaugural address stated that while Yale was not a high school, neither was it a university, and called for measured steps toward becoming the latter. Soon after, he established a department of philosophy which would eventually develop into Yale's graduate school. The experiment was a success and, in 1861, Yale awarded the first PhD degree in the United States.

On the other hand, this did not radically alter the institution's focus, which as we shall see remained centered on its college for many years. Perhaps this is why in 1869 Charles Eliot declared Yale's foray into graduate teaching a success "on a really high level, if also on a modest scale."[23]

All the above reforms ran into trouble despite their good attributes. We now turn to a set of proposals that had design drawbacks related to sorting.

Francis Wayland (Brown), Parallel Programs, and Scientific Schools

Francis Wayland was the president of Brown during the 1840s, when it repeatedly faced declining enrollments.[24] Wayland (1850, 34) claimed that stagnant demand was a generalized problem in the college market, and in what became famous words remarked: "We have produced an article for which the demand is diminishing. We sell it at less than cost, and the deficiency is made up by charity. We give it away, and still the demand diminishes. Is it not time to inquire whether we cannot furnish an article for which the demand will be, at least, more remunerative?" In other words, Wayland floated that if correctly designed, teaching reform might raise demand, easing rather than aggravating resource constraints.

In 1850 he proposed courses in applied science and agriculture, which he argued would appeal to future farmers, businessmen, mechanics, and manufacturers. Brown would offer such courses as electives, and students who took them would earn specific degrees—the Bachelor of Science and the Bachelor of Literature—thereby differentiating their trajectory from the classical curriculum leading to the Bachelor of Arts. In most cases, the new degrees could be completed in three rather than four years.

The key elements of this plan were not original. By 1850, other schools had noticed that subjects like engineering could attract students, and that many wished to take French and German given their usefulness in areas like business, math, and military science. In response, colleges created parallel courses and scientific schools.

Parallel courses were variants of those proposed by Wayland, essentially alternate (hence parallel) sequences leading to degrees like the BS. As at Brown, in many cases they could be completed in less than four years. For example, Miami University offered an English scientific course in which space created by eliminating Latin and Greek was devoted to applied mathematics, political economy, French, and German; similar programs appeared at Michigan, Princeton, Rochester, and West Point, among others.

Scientific schools went a step further and placed these endeavors in full-blown separate institutional structures with their own admission procedures and teaching staff. For example, at Dartmouth, Harvard, and Yale, such initiatives were located in the Chandler, Lawrence, and Sheffield scientific schools, respectively. Denison, Illinois, Missouri, and others set up similar outfits.[25]

The setup of these activities—particularly their segregation into degrees and even entirely separate academic units—was consistent with the sentiment that they were best kept at a distance from the traditional curriculum. For instance, a professor stated that the "spirit of science, while it is positive and affirmative in its appropriate sphere, becomes negative and contradictory, if not . . . blasphemous and scoffing, the moment it transcends the proper boundaries . . . ."[26]

But because schools serve a sorting purpose, segregation and boundaries can matter. For example, if a student were interested in one of these parallel programs, he or she might ask if its students mixed with and resembled those in the mainstream of the college that hosted it. In other words, while their teaching obviously differed, was their sorting similar?

Ample anecdotal evidence indicates this was often not the case. At Yale, for example, the Sheffield Scientific School students not only took separate classes, they sat separately at chapel services and were called "grinds" by their college peers; Brubacher and Rudy (1958) mention similar treatment at Lafayette and Wesleyan. At Brown, Wayland's new programs attracted less prepared students, leading his successor, Barnas Sears, to worry that they might develop a reputation for conferring degrees "upon the unfortunate rather than upon the elite."[27] Sinclair (2012, 41) reports that Harvard's Lawrence Scientific School had modest admission criteria, and Harvard's Eliot added, for good measure, that anybody, "no matter how ignorant," could enroll at Yale's Sheffield School.

Similarly, students who realized college can convey information might have wondered what a BS would say. Would a degree geared to farmers and mechanics transmit the same image as the traditional BA, which had historically gone to the elite? Would it put its holder on track to careers conferring upward mobility? Or would employers only consider parallel course graduates for certain types of roles? A student expressed such concerns more bluntly: "Why should anyone want to be a better hick?"[28]

The bottom line is that some early teaching reforms started with the left foot because they threatened colleges' sorting products. Consistent with this, Wayland's programs only temporarily stabilized enrollments at Brown, and failed to generate sufficient revenue to cover their incremental cost. In 1856, facing a renewed downturn in the school's finances, Wayland resigned, and soon most of his innovations were abandoned. This outcome was not unique—several similar programs ended similarly; for example, one at Princeton in 1806 and one at Amherst in 1829.[29]

To summarize, reforms aimed at teaching would require designs that considered how they affected sorting. In addition, there was no guarantee that teaching reforms would immediately produce net revenues; this necessitated financial provisions for a transition period.

Eliphalet Nott (Union)

We close this list of pre–Civil War attempts with a place that came close to getting various ingredients right: Union College. Union introduced several innovations discussed above and met with significant (if ultimately temporary) success. These happened under Eliphalet Nott, who led the school for more than sixty years beginning in 1804. Nott, an Albany clergyman and entrepreneur, was interested in the application of science to practical problems. His desire to heat churches and dormitories led him to file twenty-five patents, including one for the anthracite stove.[30]

Perhaps not surprisingly, therefore, Union implemented a parallel course similar to those mentioned above. The course attracted more demand than others, however. In 1830 Union graduated ninety-six students, while Yale, Harvard, and Princeton graduated seventy-one, forty-eight, and twenty, respectively. As late as 1861 it was among the three largest colleges, and like RPI, it developed a reputation for leading to jobs in railroad building.[31]

Four factors likely played a role in Union's relative success. First, it awarded the BA degree to all its students, and thus in at least this sense treated all equally. Second, since Nott took leadership of a recently created school, conservative constituencies were less of an obstacle to his ideas. Third, deeper pockets allowed Union to give its strategy some time to mature. Nott received substantial support from the New York legislature, which mostly paid for a campus close to Albany. Combined with private gifts and Nott's own contributions from his inventions' proceeds, Union had the highest college endowment at various points in the 1800s. Fourth, Union repeatedly advertised that it would engage in graduate instruction and research. Although it did not deliver on these promises under Nott, they might have temporarily helped attract enrollments.[32]

In sum, Union College was an early candidate to transform itself into the leading American university. Although this did not ultimately happen, its temporary success—along with all the failures listed—provided lessons for reformers. Daniel Gilman, founding president of Johns Hopkins, expressed that one could benefit from such experiences: "We begin our work after costly ventures of which we reap lessons, while others bear the loss."[33]

Post–Civil War Success

Lasting success at teaching reform came after the Civil War as some schools were able to: (i) overcome conservative resistance, (ii) design packages of teaching and sorting that appealed widely, and (iii) fund the transition to a new business model. This section discusses how the schools that first achieved this put together the requisite mix of ingredients.

We limit the discussion to four schools that arguably did this the earliest. These four suffice to illustrate key themes, even if later these schools were followed by many and eclipsed by some. Specifically, we begin with two entrants that were crucial to transforming American higher education: Cornell and Johns Hopkins. We then consider the two incumbents that most quickly and decisively responded: Harvard and Columbia. Later chapters will also make repeated references to other schools that appear in the top ranks of Table 1.3; for example, Berkeley, Chicago, Illinois, MIT, Michigan, Stanford, Princeton, and Yale.

More generally, for the remainder of Part I, we shift our focus from the whole college sector to the schools that most aggressively reformed and in many ways provided the models for American Research I universities.

Cornell

Cornell was the first American university to sustain many of the teaching reforms discussed above. It benefited from being an entrant, and thus lacking a deep bench of conservative stakeholders. At the same time, this intensified the need for a sound design and for money, since the experiment began without numerous potential donors or a long-standing reputation.

The ingredients came together through the collaboration of three actors. The first was Andrew White, Cornell's first president, who studied at Yale and later spent time at the University of Berlin. It was there he would later say, that he saw the ideal of a university "not only realized, but extended and glorified."[34] White taught history at Michigan, and later returned to his native Syracuse, where he was elected to the New York Senate. In Albany, he met a wealthy senator from Ithaca, Ezra Cornell, who had made a fortune working with Samuel Morse in the commercial implementation of the telegraph.[35] White and Cornell grew close, and White recounted that at some point Cornell casually asked: "I have about half a million dollars more than my family will need: what is the best thing I can do with it for the State?"[36]

The two immediately agreed on the desirability of bringing in a third actor: the federal government in the form of the Morrill Act. Signed into law by Abraham Lincoln, the Morrill Act provided for the sale of federal land holdings to benefit higher education. It transferred shares of mostly Western land to states, along with some control over the grants' location and sale. The proceeds were to benefit institutions whose objective was "without excluding other scientific or classical studies, to teach such branches of learning as are related to agriculture and the mechanic arts."[37] The act was silent on much else—for example, on whether the institutions funded had to be public.

Ezra Cornell announced that he would donate half a million dollars to a new school, along with a hilltop farm above lake Cayuga for a site, if New York committed its Morrill Act proceeds to the venture. The proposal faced an uphill battle as up to twenty other institutions, including Columbia and Union, had designs on the money.[38]

Thanks in part to Cornell and White's lobby, their school was promised about half of the land grant's proceeds. Ezra Cornell felt that the acreage came into a glutted market and took measures that later prompted an investigation by the legislature. He bought the State's shares himself, supervised the location of the land in Wisconsin, waited for an auspicious moment to sell, and only then gave the proceeds to the school. Curti and Nash (1965) calculate that this allowed the land to sell for about eight times the original value. In short, the first ingredient Cornell and White secured was a major amount of money.

The next question concerned the type of teaching the new school would offer. White argued for broad teaching that would simultaneously take on RPI and Yale. Specifically, he organized the university in two divisions: one had a technical orientation and featured departments of agriculture, mechanic arts, civil engineering, commerce, mining, medicine, law, education, and public service. The other had an academic orientation and offered: a classical course, classical courses emphasizing French, German, or the natural sciences, and an optional course featuring more electives. White envisioned equality of all courses "in position and privilege," with all leading to the BA; he also planned on an increasing role for electives.[39] Finally, from the start the school was coeducational and nonsectarian.

The package was altogether in keeping with the statement attributed to Ezra Cornell: "I would found an institution where any person can find instruction in any study."[40] This statement, which became Cornell's motto, may have been improved by White; Bishop (1962, 74) notes that the original may have been closer to "I'd like to start a school where anybody can study anything he's a mind to." Regardless, the pronouncement captures well that while no part of this design was truly new, the collection addressed drawbacks seen above–for example, it reformed teaching without creating second-class citizens, and it displayed deep pockets to fund a broad, multifaceted curriculum.[41] In addition, perhaps the project was simply better timed.

Whatever the reasons, upon opening in 1869, Cornell succeeded almost immediately. Only three years later, it had the largest freshman class in the country, and a few years after that Harper's Weekly wrote: "With a grip upon the best methods of education which is almost beyond the reach of [a school] weighted down by traditions. . . . Cornell University stands in the vantage-ground, if not at the head, of American educational institutions."[42] Cornell also quickly built up a stock of alumni and friends; Rudolph (1977, 127) observes that "So quickly did Cornell establish itself that an attack on Ezra Cornell's handling of the university's endowment resulted in an outpouring of gifts . . . ."[43]

Later, Cornell helped create the Ivy League, a collection of eight schools considered to be the guardians of tradition in American higher education. Seven of these schools were among the original nine colonial colleges; thus, if only due to age, they are the guardians of something. Cornell is the newcomer: if one went by age alone, hundreds of other schools have a stronger claim to membership. The key point is that by the time the Ivy League emerged for athletic purposes, the older schools considered Cornell a peer.

In short, Cornell's founders leveraged free entry and self-rule to offer an innovative teaching product. The school benefited from a sound design, one that featured substantial funding and avoided sorting-related drawbacks. Finally, as shown, the Cornell story can be told with little reference to graduate teaching or research. This would not be the case at Johns Hopkins.

Johns Hopkins

The Johns Hopkins University opened about a decade after Cornell and followed a different strategy. While Cornell's trademark was to offer a wide variety of courses ("any person, any study"), Hopkins's would be a focus on graduate instruction. Two key protagonists, in this case, were Andrew Gilman and Johns Hopkins.

Gilman had been a friend of Andrew White's at Yale and accompanied him to visit universities in Europe, where he took copious notes on educational organization. He later worked as a fundraiser at Yale's Sheffield Scientific School, where he commented that the colleges' lack of attention to individuals who wished to pursue science "for its own sake" was a drag on the country's economy.[44] Yale's Corporation considered Gilman for President in 1872 but opted instead for Noah Porter, widely regarded as the more conservative choice. Soon after, Gilman accepted the presidency of the University of California, but his vision never aligned the views of multiple members of the Board of Regents and state politicians, and he was soon looking to leave Berkeley.[45]

In 1874 he was contacted by a board that had received seven million dollars from the recently deceased Johns Hopkins. Hopkins's parents had been unable to fund a college education for him, and at age seventeen, he instead joined his uncle's wholesale grocery business in Baltimore. Soon he and his cousin, Elizabeth Hopkins, expressed a desire to marry, but encountered strong family opposition; neither ever entered matrimony nor had children. Hopkins went on to make a fortune, including through the early purchase of stock in the Baltimore and Ohio Railroad. Years later, he said he wished his money to go to "these two children of mine, a university and a hospital."[46] The result was the largest philanthropic gift the country had seen, likely exceeding the cumulative gifts received by Harvard up to then.[47]

From the start, some board members realized this vast sum might finally make full-fledged graduate teaching feasible at an American school. But they were also aware that this could be a risky departure and might limit enrollments on the part of Baltimore students.

For advice, the board turned to presidents James Angell of Michigan, Charles Eliot of Harvard, and Andrew White of Cornell (James McCosh

of Princeton and Noah Porter of Yale did not answer requests for input).[48]
Eliot doubted a focus on graduate teaching was desirable:

> I believe . . . that it is in the interest of the country to breed men thor-
> oughly instructed in something; that our institutions . . . confine them-
> selves too much to producing an average man . . . and that we want
> to . . . give more attention to the special capacities . . . of individual men
> and carry those . . . men to higher levels. But a university is not built in
> the air, so to speak. It is a growth and I should doubt . . . whether any
> institution, old or young, could cut loose from the educational founda-
> tions of the community . . . We are as well off at Harvard as any place
> in the country . . . , but we could not deliberately undertake to give only
> a high education for a few . . . even if we were starting from scratch.[49]

In short, Eliot advocated for slow growth such that for a long time Hopkins
would have emulated existing colleges. This advice was consistent with Eliot's early resistance toward teaching reform that would broaden colleges'
reach; he stated: "In our generation I hardly expect to see the institutions
founded which have produced such results in Europe . . . The Puritans
thought they must have trained ministers . . . and they supported Harvard
College; when the American people are convinced that they require more
competent chemists, engineers, artists, architects . . . they will somehow establish the institutions to train them."[50] White gave advice broadly consistent with Eliot's. Angell stated that at Michigan, postgraduate work was
growing but still almost incidental.[51] In short, the presidents were at least
ambivalent about graduate teaching.

On one count they were all enthusiastic: that the trustees appoint Daniel
Gilman as president. Upon interviewing him, the Board was won over by
Gilman's more daring vision. He had stated that the country did not need
another college or scientific school, but rather a university "to which young
men will resort for the highest sort of scholastic training, and to which they
should be refused admission, unless they have previously been well-
trained . . . in the institutions of the next lower or Collegiate grade."[52]

Gilman understood that staffing such a school called for professors with
a talent for research. Once inaugurated, he also showed himself to have a

good understanding of this activity, despite never having been a researcher himself. For example, he once stated:

> If you persist in taking the utilitarian view and ask me what is the good of Mr. Glaisher's determination of the least factors of the missing three out of the first nine million numbers . . . or if you put a much more comprehensive question, what is the use of the Abelian functions, I shall be forced to say that I do not know . . . but I know, and you know, and everybody may know, who will take the pains to inquire, that the progress of mathematics underlies and sustains all progress in exact knowledge.[53]

He added that research would benefit society, noting that applied math contributed to the creation of the steam engine, the telegraph, and the telephone. Gilman did not wish to prioritize research in one area over another, or to push only projects that would bear rapid fruit. He stated: "All sciences are worthy of promotion; it is useless to dispute whether literature or science should receive more attention . . . Remote utility is quite as worthy as immediate advantage. Those ventures are not always the most sagacious that expect a return on the morrow . . . So it is always in the promotion of science."[54] Similarly, he made it clear to graduate students and faculty that he valued their craft. One professor reported leaving Gilman's office "with a warm feeling that he appreciated . . . my work."[55] It bears emphasizing that this was somewhat of a novelty at the time. For instance, Gilman's friend, Cornell President Andrew White, said that as a student at Yale he "regarded the studies of my contemporaries in the Sheffield Scientific School with a sort of contempt, with wonder that human beings possessed of immortal souls should waste their time in work with blow pipes and test tubes."[56]

In addition, Gilman emphasized the publication of research and created the Johns Hopkins Press. Early in his presidency he hired James Sylvester, an English mathematician who founded the American Journal of Mathematics in 1878. Years later, in his retirement address, Sylvester qualified this:

> You have spoken of our Mathematical Journal. . . . Mr. Gilman is continually telling people that I founded it. . . . I assert that he is the

founder. Almost the first day I landed in Baltimore, . . . he began to plague me to found a Mathematical Journal on this side of the water . . . I said it was useless, there were no materials for it. Again and again he returned to the charge and again and again I threw the cold water I could on the scheme; nothing but obstinate persistence and perseverance brought his views to prevail.[57]

Not surprisingly, Gilman saw that the teaching he wished Hopkins to provide required choosing professors based only on expertise. He echoed Ruggles in stating:

> The institution we are about to organize would not be worthy the name of a University, if it were to be devoted to any other purpose than the discovery and promulgation of the truth; and it would be ignoble . . . if the resources . . . given by the Founder . . . should be limited to the maintenance of ecclesiastical differences or perverted to the promotion of political strife. . . . sectarian and partisan preferences should have no control in the selection of teachers. . . . [58]

Gilman began to aggressively hire faculty and wrote Eliot apologizing for upcoming raids on Harvard. Eliot responded graciously, saying he would have found it odd "if there had been no men here whom you cared to try for."[59] By 1884, Johns Hopkins had over fifty professors. The vast majority had spent time in Germany, and many had implemented a key component of the German seminar—the presentation of research for feedback from faculty and graduate students; some were calling the school "Göttingen at Baltimore."[60] The school was producing more PhDs than Harvard and Yale combined, and had taken control of the Johns Hopkins hospital and medical schools. The latter action began a trend of absorption of professional schools into universities, a move that would radically improve medical training and the status of the medical profession.[61]

Two final observations are relevant regarding Johns Hopkins. First, despite an initial desire to be essentially a graduate school of arts and sciences, it also established an undergraduate college. Several trustees argued that a college would create a feeder for the graduate school, and that beyond making the project more popular with Baltimoreans, a college would ac-knowledge that the youth of Baltimore had a claim on the Hopkins gift.[62] Second, in the following decades, financial difficulties caused the school to lose some steam. Johns Hopkins's benefaction came with what turned out to be a consequential constraint: he directed the trustees to keep the Balti-more and Ohio Railroad stock, and in the late 1880s the company stopped paying dividends.[63] For help, the school turned to the state of Maryland, which responded substantially but also sporadically. By the early 1900s Johns Hopkins was stabilized, although as Thelin (2004) points out, it was no longer as vital. One possibility this raises is that by focusing on graduate rather than college teaching, Gilman did not build as many steady streams of income as, say, Andrew White did in Ithaca. This is an issue we will re-turn to below.

Cornell and Johns Hopkins illustrate that free entry was crucial to changing American higher education. Gilman and White perceived that what the country demanded had changed. While offering denominational sorting might have been the best way to render a school viable early in the nine-teenth century, by the end specialized and advanced instruction could do the trick. There was even room for research—students and donors were willing to fund such activity. At this point, the incumbent colleges had to decide whether they too would engage in teaching reform. We now turn to the two that most quickly and aggressively responded: Harvard and Columbia.

Harvard

At Harvard, the key reformer was Charles Eliot. A Harvard graduate, he started his academic career there too, working first as a tutor and then an assistant professor of mathematics and chemistry at the Lawrence Scien-tific School. When the school did not renew his contract, he moved to MIT, where he developed a reputation for administration and thoughts on edu-cational reform. In 1868 he was elected to Harvard's Board of Overseers, and in 1869, aged 39, appointed to its presidency.

At this point Eliot confronted a situation quite different from that Gilman or White had faced. At the helm of the oldest and by many measures the wealthiest college, he did not need to produce a master plan to render viable a new school. That said, he wished to improve Harvard's medical school its and professional training more generally. He also aimed to enhance its college and recruit more students from beyond the Northeast, a dimension in which it had often lagged behind Princeton and Yale. To the extent that Eliot focused on one ingredient to achieve the latter, it was on electives; he wished to allow undergraduates to choose courses freely. He stated: "The elective system fosters scholarship, because it gives free play to natural preferences and inborn aptitudes, makes possible enthusiasm for chosen work, relieves the professor and the ardent . . . [student] of the presence of a body of students who are compelled to an unwelcome task, and enlarges instruction . . . ."[64] In short, electives would help focus faculty and students on academics and specialized instruction. Electives also dovetailed with Eliot's belief in freedom of choice—in this he advocated for a break with the colleges' *in loco parentis* tradition. Veysey (1965, 88) elaborates that Eliot believed in laissez-faire beyond the classroom: "[he] came perilously close to opposing free public primary education . . . looked with disfavor upon labor unions, exhibited a cheerful indifference toward poverty, and remained largely ignorant of the new world of social science . . . ."

Of course, electives were not a new idea; they had been discussed at Harvard since at least Ticknor, and Eliot himself mentioned that Thomas Jefferson had advocated for them at the University of Virginia.[65] In this sense, Eliot's challenge was not to devise a new path, but rather to overcome the resistance that had stopped other reformers. Electives had mixed support in Harvard's boards and faced strong opposition among many alumni and faculty. Given Harvard's national relevance, objections arose from outside too: eight New England college presidents wrote the Board of Overseers asking that Harvard keep its Greek requirement.[66]

To this situation, Eliot brought persistence and a strong personality. Publicly questioned by an influential professor as to the reason for so many sudden reforms, Eliot left time for some silence and stated: "I can answer . . . very easily; there is a new President."[67]

In 1869 the entire Harvard curriculum was prescribed, but from then on some courses became electives every year, and new ones automatically received that status. By 1886, students could earn a BA by taking any eighteen courses whatsoever.[68] Throughout this period, teaching reform continued to generate opposition. Morison (1936, 358) writes that particularly toward the end of this period, "one false step would have meant the end of [Eliot's] administration. College faculty and governing boards were boiling. The Corporation, it is said, at one point would have asked for his resignation if one of two fellows could have been persuaded to take the presidency." Neither did the external opposition abate; in these same years Princeton's President James McCosh admonished observers:

> Tell it not in Berlin . . . that the once most illustrious university in America no longer requires its graduates to know the most perfect language, the grandest literature. . . . Tell it not in Paris, tell it not in Cambridge . . . that Cambridge in America does not make mathematics obligatory. . . . Let not the Puritans in England know that a student may pass through the once Puritan college of America without having taken a single class . . . in religion.[69]

Eliot also introduced changes in instructional methods. In 1880 he reported that recitations had all but disappeared, giving way to lectures and discussions; he stated: "Formerly, the only business of a teacher was to hear recitations. . . . Now, he has the opportunity of teaching. This is one of the greatest educational discoveries of modern times, that the business of a teacher is to teach."[70]

Eliot also reorganized Harvard and broadened its teaching. In the 1880s, he oversaw the creation of divisions and departments within the Faculty of Arts and Sciences.[71] In 1889–1891, the Lawrence Scientific School was partially absorbed into the college and a recently created graduate school. Eliot also supported the establishment of a business school in 1908 and strengthened the medical school. These reforms found a receptive market: enrollments increased by 66 percent in the 1880s, and 89 percent in the 1890s; growth rates higher than those of all colleges except Cornell and Princeton.[72] During Eliot's four-decade presidency, the faculty grew from about sixty to six hundred members, and Keller and Keller (2001, 13) add that "major scholars began to be more than an occasional fluke."

In closing, it is useful to compare Eliot's approach with those of White at Cornell and Gilman at Hopkins. Like White, Eliot managed to broaden his college's teaching without creating second-class citizens. Indeed, their approaches had a fair bit in common, and this may be why some competition developed between them; for example, White claimed he was for mixing of scientific and other students before Eliot.[73] Eliot, however, went further and faster in the use of electives. Although both emphasized responsiveness to student demand, their schools ended up occupying slightly different places in the market, with Cornell emphasizing a more technical and Harvard a more academic approach. As Morison (1936, 121) puts it: "Students attracted to Cornell were so vocationally oriented that their pattern of course selections shoved Cornell more in the direction of an expanding technical curriculum than in the direction of a broad range of opportunities in the liberal arts and sciences. At Harvard a different clientele used the elective system to shove Harvard in the opposite direction."[74]

A greater contrast arises between Eliot and Gilman. Eliot did not share Gilman's focus on graduate instruction. As late as 1904, he was writing that "neither the serviceableness nor the prestige of the University is determined by the work of the Graduate School in Arts and Sciences."[75]

As a result, Eliot emphasized research talent less; early in his presidency he stated: "Experience teaches that the strongest . . . professors will contribute something to the patrimony of knowledge. . . . Nevertheless, the prime business of American professors in this generation must be regular and assiduous class teaching."[76] The contrast extended to their attitude toward research. In the 1870s, a young chemistry professor asked Eliot for a course release to pursue an investigation. Eliot asked what the end product would be, and when the professor named a German journal, Eliot answered: "I can't see that will serve any useful purpose here."[77] Eliot was also less disposed to hire only on expertise, vetoing one otherwise desirable candidate because his wife was thought "ill bred."[78] Indeed, to the extent that he eventually moved Harvard toward research, Eliot acknowledged his debt to the example of and perhaps most of all, to the pressure exerted by Johns Hopkins. At Gilman's farewell, Eliot stated:

President Gilman, your first achievement here . . . has been . . . the creation of a school of graduate studies, which not only has been in itself a strong and potent school, but which has lifted every other university in the country. . . . I want to testify that the [Harvard] graduate school . . . started feebly in 1870 and 1871, and did not thrive, until the example of Johns Hopkins forced our faculty to put their strength into the development of our instruction for graduates.[79]

Columbia

That Columbia would be among the first successful American research universities (Table 1.4) would have surprised many observers around 1850, as the school had seen real oscillations in its fortunes.[80] For the first decades after its creation in 1754, Columbia was a wealthy but small school. In 1774 it had the highest collegiate endowment, but only 36 students, while Harvard and Yale had four or five times as many.[81] Further, to the extent that Hofstadter's (1955) "great retrogression" indeed took place, Columbia was certainly one of its victims: while in 1797 the college had eight faculty members, during most of the 1800s it had four. In 1809, an inquiry warned that Columbia College "was fast becoming, if it has not become already, a mere Grammar School"; between 1800 and 1850, even as New York City grew, the school's enrollment stagnated, and even in 1850 the average entering age was 15.[82]

Several factors contributed to this state of affairs. First, Columbia historically catered mostly to the city's Anglican elite. It charged high tuition and did not apologize for it—in 1753 a spokesman said it aimed to serve those whose "fortunes enable[d] . . . to attend."[83] Second, into the 1800s much training for medicine and law was done by apprenticeship, with no college degree required; thus the city's numerous law and medical practices were a source of competition rather than demand.[84] Third, the city's college market also saw ample entry; by the 1870s City College, Cooper Union, NYU, Fordham, and St. John's provided lower-cost alternatives to Columbia. Fourth, historically, many Americans have felt that students are best kept far from temptations and therefore, from cities. To them New York was obviously unattractive; for example, Thomas Jefferson called it a cesspit of "all the depravities of human nature."[85] As a result, even wealthy Anglican families often preferred Princeton and Yale.

The bottom line is that the school generated little tuition, received few donations, and often appealed to the legislature for help. After this body relocated to Albany, however, it began to favor Union College. By 1851, interest payments absorbed a fifth of Columbia's budget. When the need came to respond to Cornell and Johns Hopkins, Columbia was in a much weaker position than Harvard, Princeton, Yale, and numerous historically stronger schools including Amherst and Dartmouth. How then did it achieve its early research prominence?

There are multiple actors in this case; a salient one is Frederick Barnard. After graduating from Yale, Barnard worked there as a tutor and began to develop hearing loss that would later be severe. In 1832 he moved to New York to teach at the Institute for the Instruction of the Deaf and Dumb, and later served as Chancellor of the University of Mississippi. In 1864 he assumed the presidency of Columbia.

Barnard benefited from public help in a somewhat unexpected way. Fifty years earlier, the legislature had allocated major funding to Union College. As a consolation, it had given Columbia a plot of land known as the Hosack property for the doctor who grew medicinal plants there. The school's trustees felt cheated: Union's grant would help it become the largest college, while Columbia got what one observer called a "rundown herb garden and lovers' lane."[86] The Hosack property, however, contained what we now know as Rockefeller Center.

By the late 1850s, Manhattan's growth allowed the trustees to sell Columbia's original campus and use the proceeds to develop the site. The lease of the resulting lots had a dramatic impact; McCaughey (2003, 133) states that "Within two decades Columbia had been financially transformed from one of a dozen budgetarily strapped . . . colleges into one of the country's richest academic institutions." Throughout the 1870s, it ran surpluses even as Harvard regularly ran deficits, and by 1899 it had the largest endowment again.

Barnard used the income to create new academic units. The first addition was the School of Mines, essentially an engineering school, which by the 1870s was graduating twice as many students as the college.[87]

In the social sciences, Columbia's ascent began with Samuel Ruggles's efforts to recruit John Burgess, a political scientist from Amherst. Burgess initially resisted the overtures; Amherst had long been a stronger school, and Burgess preferred rural life. In addition, he was a popular teacher there; in 1876, a month before commencement, several students requested to stay an extra year to study with him. The Amherst leadership realized this was "nothing more and nothing less" than a petition for Amherst to take on graduate training.[88] When it rejected the request, Burgess moved to Columbia. He did not give his new academic home a glowing review:

> I found the institution to consist of a small old-fashioned college, or rather school, for teaching Latin, Greek, and mathematics . . . , and a very little natural science . . . called the School of Arts; a School of Mines for teaching a little more natural science and educating mining and civil engineers; and a School of Law . . . loosely connected with the college . . . The qualifications for entrance to the first two schools were quite easy . . . , and for . . . Law nothing at all. . . . [89]

One of Columbia's senior professors, he added, had little understanding of educational systems, and another was a variation of the first "on a more pedantic pattern."[90]

Ruggles informed Burgess that Columbia had "one hundred thousand dollars more of income than of outgo, and we want you to tell us how best to expand it for the development of the college."[91] Burgess proposed the creation of a graduate faculty to prepare students for public life, a school along the lines of the *École Libre des Sciences Politiques*. Ruggles helped him secure leave time to visit Paris on a fact-finding mission; he also attempted to convince the trustees to create the school and authorize Burgess to search for faculty. While in Paris, Burgess received a 5 a.m. telegram from Ruggles: "Thank God, the University is born. Go ahead."[92] By 1900 each of Columbia's social science departments was providing some form of graduate instruction and was considered among the top three in the United States.[93]

Barnard also successfully advocated for greater electives, arguing this was necessary to compete with Cornell and Harvard. In contrast, he failed to convince trustees and faculty to follow Cornell in admitting women.

Burgess, for example, worried that parents had an even stronger demand for proximity when it came to their daughters, and given New York's growing Jewish population, implementing coeducation would turn Columbia into "a female seminary, and a Hebrew female seminary . . . at that."[94] Another professor appealed to seemingly pedagogical considerations: "you can't teach a man mathematics if there's a girl in the room and if you can, he is not worth teaching."[95] In the end, the outcome was to create a separate college with its own Board of Trustees. By the time this was approved in 1889, Barnard was terminally ill.

Columbia continued to develop under Seth Low, taking over the College of Physicians and Surgeons to match Harvard and Johns Hopkins in running a medical school. It also consolidated the law school and created a graduate school of arts and sciences. Columbia also began to receive gifts from men like Dodge, Havemeyer, Pulitzer, and Vanderbilt; and Low used the proceeds to leave midtown for a grand space in Morningside Heights, where he personally paid for a grand library.[96]

In the decade following 1889, the size of the faculty went up by a factor of five, and in some years in the early 1900s, Columbia had the highest output of journals and instructional expenditures per student.[97] To acknowledge the change in the school's size and scope, Columbia joined many schools over these years in changing its overall designation from college to university, while keeping the term college for its undergraduate school.

In short, Columbia experienced a more thorough transformation than Harvard, and some have pointed out that in this sense, Barnard may have added higher value than did Eliot. For instance, McCaughey (2003, 146) writes:

> Eliot inherited the largest, wealthiest, and most nationally recognized of American colleges, including law, divinity, medical, and scientific schools, and forty-one years later turned over to his successor all that he had begun with and one of America's two or three world-class universities to boot; Barnard inherited a small, potentially wealthy, and nationally negligible college (and law school) and twenty-five years later turned over to his successor an institution within a decade of being one of America's two or three world-class universities.

On the other hand, Eliot likely had to deal with greater opposition than Barnard, who might have paradoxically benefited from Columbia's historical relative weakness. McCaughey (2003, 175) adds: "Columbia became a world-class University as rapidly and as fully as it did because it was not held back by what Barnard . . . viewed as the dead weight of a collegiate past. . . . Columbia was simply freer than more successful antebellum colleges . . . to make itself over into a university . . . Columbia did not so much evolve into as it was reborn a university."

To summarize, after the Civil War some American schools were finally able to engage in successful teaching reform; their essential steps would be followed by several others (some of which we cover in later chapters). The final section of this chapter discusses how these reforms produced dynamics that allowed these universities to begin cornering more than their fair share of (research) talent.

Minds

As the universities reformed their teaching and responded to market demand, the academic areas they covered fragmented into specialized fields. For example, natural philosophy split into fields including astronomy, chemistry, and physics; political economy into economics, political science, and sociology, and so on. Universities began to supply advanced instruction in these fields, most importantly in doctoral programs of graduate schools of arts and sciences which, as Roberts and Turner (2000, 7) observe, "became the essential hallmark of the modern American university, perhaps even more than [an] array of professional schools . . . ."

These developments increased the need for faculty who could teach specialized courses at the highest level, and relatedly, could do some research. In other words, just as the antebellum curriculum demanded a certain type of teacher, the new teaching required a specific kind of professor. This development created a challenge because initially, such faculty were not easy to find. In 1872 Charles Eliot observed that "There is in this country a very considerable body of teachers who know how to teach Latin and Greek, and the elements of language; but if you are in search of teachers to teach botany, chemistry, physics and so on, you cannot find them. They do not exist."[98]

Universities had every incentive to address this problem since they are the ultimate source of supply and demand of people who can teach at the most advanced level.

Credentials and Measures of Research Output

To do so, the universities took two measures. First, they began to require that their professors have a PhD, the main credential certifying one is at the frontier of knowledge in a given area. This reform produced rapid change: as late as 1884, only 10 percent of Harvard faculty had a PhD; by 1900, this exceeded 50 percent at several schools, and by 1910 the University of Illinois required a doctoral degree of all faculty.[99] On the supply side, schools expanded their PhD programs to satisfy demand. Second, universities began to prefer professors who did research, as this is a central way to assess a person's expertise.

In response, the academic system began to provide more ways of measuring research quantity and quality. This happened in a decentralized fashion. For instance, as faculty members' affiliation with specific fields increased, they founded professional associations; for example, the American Chemical Society (1877) and the American Historical Association (1884).[100] Such groups also began to publish journals (e.g., the American Political Science Review) which, via the peer-review process, helped to certify research quality. University department journals supplemented these periodicals. For example, Harvard created the Quarterly Journal of Economics (1886), Clark the American Journal of Psychology (1887), and Chicago the American Journal of Sociology (1895). By 1900, Chicago was printing over 150,000 pages of journals a year, and Columbia was publishing thirty-five titles.[101]

In time some journals gained a reputation for publishing better papers. This development reflects that journals also serve a sorting function; for example, they transmit information on paper quality. If a journal is known for applying high standards and using expert referees, then seeing a paper appear there provides indication of its quality.[102] As better journals received more submissions, their editors made them even more selective and prestigious, thus attracting more papers: a virtuous circle for these periodicals, with corresponding losses for the publications that lost the race. The result was a relatively clear hierarchy of journals in each field: a consensus as to which were the very best, which were in a second tier, which came third, and so on.[103] This is the type of sorting dynamic that we will repeatedly see below.

In this case, one aspect facilitating sorting was that researchers could submit their work to any journal, and thus often preferred to send their best papers to the most prestigious outlets regardless of their location. For example, while Chicago or Harvard professors might have initially published in their home journals, they were soon willing to send their papers elsewhere; indeed, publishing elsewhere might help convey their papers' quality. The sorting dynamic was also aided by the existence of association journals that belonged to a profession rather than to a specific school.[104]

Another venue to assess research quality emerged as departments established seminars at which visiting faculty presented their work. Similarly, professional associations set up annual conferences that also took on the role of job fairs at which departments could observe and hunt for talent. Rudolph (1962, 407) indicates: "Here the professors . . . paraded their most promising students (and others as well), and sent them out into the market . . . That annual meeting . . . brought together groups of specialists who spoke in a language all their own, shared discoveries, and went back to their campuses with a renewed sense of belonging." In time, every field developed many curated meetings where those who might trust journals less could assess research quality for themselves.

Thanks to all these formal and informal institutions, by the early 1900s it was increasingly feasible to obtain useful if imperfect measures of (research) talent. Eliot reflected on how this happened over the course of his long presidency:

> The chief difficulty that I encountered was the procuring of teachers competent to give advanced instruction. There were really no guides to the discovery and invitation of the persons needed. Then none of the societies organized for the development and mutual support of learned and scientific men existed. By 1885 I could get some assistance . . . from the proceedings of the learned and scientific societies. At the beginning there was no such aid.[105]

Since then measures of research talent have become even more accessible. For example, today one can use a phone to count not just the papers a professor has published, but the number of citations they have received. But it must be noted (and will be relevant below) that the machinery that makes this possible is not costless. Senior professors spend multiple days a month in associated activities, including writing referee reports, tenure letters, and letters of recommendation.

Sorting of Minds

These developments also moved faculty hiring in the direction reformers like Ruggles had struggled to advance before the Civil War: gradually, expertise became the critical qualification for a professorship, with this mainly ascertained by research. For example, Geiger (1986, 35) mentions that while initially Eliot preferred candidates with Harvard connections, by 1880, "[a]ware of the competition from a vigorous Johns Hopkins, [he] now sought professors with distinguished scholarly attainments to their credit."

Similarly, Michigan President James Angell remarked that poaching talented professors had become common during his presidency. Perhaps the person most responsible for this development was William Harper, the first president of the University of Chicago and a serious academic in his own right.[106] Harper had an enormous amount of money at his disposal: a founding donation from John Rockefeller, then the richest man in the world. He also had help from people like Helen Culver, Charles Hutchinson, Martin Ryerson, and Marshall Field, who gave ten acres of land in the Hyde Park neighborhood of Chicago.[107] Harper set up his school at a pace that made Barnard's at Columbia seem slow, and he had raided multiple campuses even before Chicago opened. One of his victims was Clark University, which had made a notable but underfunded attempt to compete with Johns Hopkins at graduate teaching; Harper hired away fifteen of its professors. But he also targeted better-heeled institutions, taking five faculty members from Yale, and Alice Freeman Palmer from Wellesley. The result was that Chicago opened with about 120 distinguished professors. Later, Harper also focused on the humanities, hiring John Dewey from Michigan.[108]

Other schools had to rely on strategies other than monetary advantage. For example, at Berkeley President Benjamin Wheeler secured substantial funds from the state and donors like Phoebe Hearst, allowing him to create twenty new departments and a graduate division, beginning the school's move into the top tier of research universities.[109] Nevertheless, Wheeler often found it hard to recruit established scholars in open competition with wealthy private schools.

His successor, William Campbell, began emphasizing the careful hiring of less expensive but talented junior professors, for whom competition at the time was less overt. As Geiger (1986, 212) states: "The only alternative seemed to be to attract the most promising young scholars . . . and then to give them the best possible conditions in which to advance their research." To illustrate, in 1928 Campbell recruited the young Ernest Lawrence, then an assistant professor at Yale, and later on President Robert Sproul made sure to retain him. By the 1930s, Berkeley had leading chemistry and physics departments, and in 1939 Lawrence received the first Nobel Prize awarded to a sitting California faculty member.[110]

As it grew, Berkeley also resisted inbreeding—the practice of hiring one's students—which was still relatively common at other schools. For example, Karabel (2006) reports that between 1865 and 1916, 80 percent of Yale's professors were graduates of the college and had been members of one of its secret societies, and Geiger (1986) adds that the practice was also evident at Cornell and Wisconsin. In this sense, Berkeley exploited an early acceptance that a school that pursued the best researchers would be less able to ensure homogeneity along other dimensions. As Jencks and Riesman (1968, 21) put it:

> The professionalization of the faculty reduced the internal homogeneity of. . . . colleges. Upper-class colleges took on literary critics with working-class ancestors, Southern colleges hired more historians who had grown up in the North or even in Europe, women's colleges hired male psychologists, and Methodist colleges took on Unitarian philosophers. . . . It also put trustees and parents who opposed who opposed heterogeneity very much on the defensive.

One consequence of the demand for research talent was an improvement in professors' negotiating position. Salaries went up, and universities began to offer their faculty members time and money for research, not least because it would enhance their own reputation. By 1920, the most aggressive schools (e.g., Berkeley, Chicago) required only six to eight hours of teaching per week.[111] Here again, Chicago's Harper often led the way, creating consequences for schools lower down the research ladder. For example, Boyer (2015, 81) states he extended "overt or covert" promises that professors would not have to teach undergraduates. At Swarthmore, President Joseph Swain informed an astronomer he was recruiting that he would satisfy his nonnegotiable demand for a 24-inch telescope, adding a caveat: "remember, this is a Friend's College and thee should give up thy smoking."[112] In the event, Swain had to accommodate the candidate's tobacco habit too. Along similar lines, in these years universities began to offer sabbaticals (i.e., giving professors each seventh year free for research).

Note that improvements in compensation and working conditions were not equally shared. They disproportionately benefited the most research-oriented professors at the most research-oriented schools (inequality between professors and schools is a theme we will return to below).[113]

Beyond compensation, research-oriented professors gained status and power. Within each department, they gained control over hiring, and collectively they acquired quasi-veto power over major university decisions. This development is illustrated in an anecdote that professors hold dear and comes in multiple renditions, with one originating at Columbia. There, President Dwight Eisenhower once described a group of professors as employees of the university. He was politely interrupted by Isidor Rabi, a physics Nobel prize winner who explained, "Excuse me Mr. President. We are not employees of the university. We are the university."[114] In the antebellum college, everyone would have found this anecdote hard to understand; by the 1950s the consequences of teaching reform had rendered it comprehensible.

The result was that in addition to seeing papers begin to sort into journals according to quality, this period saw professors begin to sort into universities according to (research) talent. Faculty members at each university, and particularly at each department, became more similar in terms of talent, with a relatively clear ranking of schools emerging in each field. This sorting of minds happened for several reasons. First, research-talented professors became easier to identify, allowing the schools that most needed them (which the next chapter will show were often the ones who could most afford them) to recruit them. Second, this sorting process was facilitated by professors themselves, since many of them prefer to be at higher-ranked departments—for example, many believe that being close to smart colleagues improves the quality of their research.[115] In addition, professors may have informational concerns of their own: observers may infer a faculty member's research ability from the quality of her home department. This is one reason why departments often favor hiring from peer institutions; the fact that a prospective colleague is at a similar department certifies his quality and suggests that hiring him will maintain or raise quality. This can be particularly useful when convincing a dean or a provost, who will typically be less familiar with the candidate's work. All these reasons meant that the best minds were happy to congregate in a small fraction of schools.

Finally, note that although a couple of dozen universities dominate most rankings, their strengths are not perfectly correlated. Some schools invested more heavily in the humanities or pure science; in other cases, public universities invested in research relevant to their state, such as Colorado in areas related to mining, Texas to petroleum, and Wisconsin to agriculture.[116]

To summarize, while the free market helped keep the antebellum colleges short of research talent (Chapter 2), it later allowed some schools to lead in teaching reform, and to attract way more than their fair share of the best minds. The next chapter considers subsequent reforms that allowed these schools to attract substantial amounts of money.

CHAPTER 4

Sorting Reform

Universities found that despite its positive impacts, teaching reform also had unintended consequences, in part because it made their students more diverse. This chapter describes how they addressed these challenges by engaging in sorting reform. This second reform in time produced dynamics that also concentrated resources at these schools.

In short, together teaching and sorting reform produced a virtuous circle for the schools that moved early and aggressively—they benefited from dynamics that sent enormous amounts of minds and money their way. These developments help explain a key trait of the American university system: significant inequality, with a few dozen extremely well-provided-for schools at the top.

Enrollment Growth and Diversity

American schools had historically coveted greater demand; in Eliot's (1908, 79) words: "The American universities have always and everywhere been desirous of increasing the number of their students; and this is a true instinct of university governors in a democratic country." This attitude, combined with the teaching reform that improved their services, led to enrollment growth, including at private universities that today tend to be smaller than their public counterparts. For example, in the 1910s Harvard and Columbia were the largest American universities, and Chicago had higher enrollments than Wisconsin and Michigan.[1] This growth was also aided by the substantial expansion of the secondary education system: between 1870 and 1900, the number of students graduating from high school roughly quintupled;

from then until 1940 the high school movement produced another tenfold increase.[2]

The emerging universities were glad to accommodate these customers for several reasons. First, they needed revenue to fund the very reforms that were making them appealing, particularly since tuition grew little during this period.[3] For example, Morison (1936) reports that in the decades around 1900, Harvard faced deficits in years in which enrollment did not climb as much as projected. In addition, during these years, a school's size was still taken as a key sign of its quality. Rosenthal (2006, 146) points out that at Columbia, President Nicholas Butler "recognized that his ambitious building plans required equally ambitious plans to expand the student body—and only partly because tuition income was needed to defray the building costs. The public would use the size of Columbia's enrollment, Butler realized, as a means of assessing the University's health and influence . . . ."

In this environment, the emerging universities essentially practiced open admissions: any applicant above a minimum standard was welcome. Charles Eliot articulated this in 1869, stating that Harvard would never turn away a student with the capacity for college work.[4] This policy held for schools across the country, with variation only in how they measured this capacity. In the Midwest and West, the state universities increasingly accredited high schools, and in exchange, accepted any student with a degree from these in- stitutions, a practice called "admission by certificate."[5] In the East, "admis- sion by examination" was the norm, and featured institution-specific tests at schools like Princeton. These mostly dovetailed with preparation offered at elite preparatory schools; any student who did reasonably well at those schools could pass. Passing, however, was not required. In the early 1900s, for example, more than 50 percent of students at Harvard, Princeton, and Yale were accepted with conditions—that is, despite failing some part of the examination. Similar practices extended into schools' graduate depart- ments, which often accepted students without college degrees.[6]

Of course, one must add a major caveat to this image of openness. Some schools remained closed to women even as female enrollments grew substantially at coeducational schools like Oberlin; many ranged from unwelcoming to closed for blacks and some groups of immigrants.[7] Charles Eliot stated that Harvard should not have more than a few black students, and Yale received only a handful of exceptional transfer applicants from schools like Talladega and Tuskegee. And yet both were more open than Princeton, where Woodrow Wilson responded to a recommendation for a black applicant, writing: "Regret to say that it is altogether inadvisable for a colored man to enter Princeton. Appreciate his desire to do so, but strongly recommend his securing education in a Southern institution. . . ."[8]

Despite such policies, growth made the leading universities' student bodies more diverse. In other words, by reforming their teaching, these schools increased their appeal, and by simultaneously running open enrollment policies, they took on students they had typically not seen. This happened in part because schools continued to draw students mostly from their vicinity, and thus growth entailed enrolling less wealthy and college-ready students.

This development was most salient at urban schools like Columbia, Harvard, and Pennsylvania, whose host cities were relatively diverse and, by the late 1800s, centers of arrival for Catholic and Jewish immigrants from Eastern and Southern Europe. Consistent with this, Veysey (1965, 283) provides a categorization of universities by diversity circa 1900:

> On the basis of their undergraduate atmosphere, . . . three major kinds of . . . institutions may be distinguished . . . : (1) the homogeneous eastern college, internally cohesive and sharply isolated from the surrounding American society. Of this pattern were Princeton, Yale, the early-day Columbia, and most of the New England colleges. (2) The heterogeneous eastern university, containing a great variety of discordant elements . . . and mirroring, if in a top-heavy fashion, the social gamut of the area at large. Pennsylvania, the latter day Columbia, and above all, Harvard carried this stamp. (3) The heterogeneous western university, which better reflected the surrounding society, . . . but, because western society was less diverse, offered fewer internal contrasts in practice.

Diversity also increased along dimensions other than socioeconomic status. For example, by the late 1800s, many Americans were becoming less sensitive to theological disagreements—that is, more willing to mingle with other denominations than to open colleges to avoid them. Lemann (1999) points out that between 1860 and 1900, the membership of the Episcopal Church roughly tripled. This change was not owing to immigration, but rather to a merging of elites. Methodists and Baptists—many of them newly rich—and Congregationalists and Unitarians—many of them old money— switched their allegiance to the American branch of the Anglican Church. Lemann (1999, 13) observes that: "Episcopalianism had two main appealing features: to the new capitalists it offered an opulence of ritual and setting and to the old mercantilists it provided a link to England which—at a time when . . . uncontrolled migration from other places was changing the character of the United States—for them had gone from being the place where their ancestors had fled to the mother country."[9] Greater denominational mixing was also associated with the elimination of compulsory chapel services at many schools.

Growth and openness also meant that in the early 1900s, schools were much less differentiated by student ability than they are today (we return to this issue below). While this is hard to quantify precisely, Jencks and Riesman (1968, 280) state: "It has been said, for example, that the average IQ at CCNY [the City College of New York] in the 1920s and 1930s was about the same as at Harvard, and we are inclined to believe it. The average at Berkeley may well have been higher than at Stanford, and the average at Michigan probably not very different from Chicago."

Challenges

Increasing diversity created challenges surrounding universities' sorting, particularly in their undergraduate colleges. This section reviews some that arose because growing diversity: (i) led students to self-sort into clubs, (ii) was associated with a rise in bad academic outcomes, and (iii) partially originated with Jewish students.

To see how these challenges came to be, recall that for all their problems, the antebellum colleges delivered the sorting their customers desired: they provided educational spaces catering to denominationally homogeneous regional elites. This reflects that before the Civil War, college enrollment rates were low: about 1 percent.[10] Thus, enrolling at the antebellum Brown or Pennsylvania immediately provided one with the chance to mix with the children of wealthier Providence and Philadelphia families, respectively. Far from apologizing for catering to elites, many schools saw it as their mission. In 1772, Princeton's President John Witherspoon observed that:

> The children of persons in the higher ranks of life, and especially of those who by their own activity and diligence, rise to opulence, have . . . the greatest need of an early, prudent, and well-conducted education. The wealth to which they are born becomes often a dangerous temptation, and the station in which they enter upon life, requires such duties, as those of the finest talents can scarcely be supposed capable of, unless they have been improved and cultivated with the utmost care.[11]

This does not mean that the antebellum colleges contained no socioeconomic heterogeneity. Some students with little wealth—Alexander Hamilton provides a shining example—did enroll. And early in its history Harvard saw fit to emulate the distinction Cambridge made between "commoners"—students who could afford all fees and dined in the commons—and "servitors" who could not do so and worked in these dining facilities.[12] But despite such exceptions, the elite dominated. For instance, Rudolph (1962) notes that when NYU opened in 1832 it had, despite its stated democratic intentions, a student roster well populated with names of prominent New York families like Coit, Dodge, and Livingston.

The bottom line is that likely, many parents were satisfied with the antebellum colleges' sorting. Of course, we have seen that at the same time, many observers criticized the college teaching (Chapter 3). In fact, it is possible that these two aspects were related: that the antebellum colleges' socioeconomic exclusivity and their teaching deficiencies reinforced each other. For if as some claimed the colleges taught little of use, that would have further made their services an expensive indulgence only suitable for the wealthy.

In other terms, the antebellum colleges might have been providing a form of what economists call Spencian signaling. In Nobel-prize-winning work, Spence (1973) argued that if going to school conveys information, then it might make sense to do so even if one learns nothing there. To see the logic, suppose individuals are of either high or low ability. Employers would like to hire those of high ability but cannot easily identify them: individuals do not have their type stamped on their forehead, so to speak. To this add only two ingredients: (i) employers can observe if someone went to school, and (ii) school is easier to complete for people of high ability (e.g., they may find it easier to do homework). Spence's insight was that this can result in a situation in which only high-ability individuals go to school (their low-ability counterparts find it too costly), and by so doing they reveal their ability to employers. In this setting, the point of school is that it identifies the able, not that it teaches them. This provides one instance in which education is about sorting—separating people out—rather than about teaching.[13]

The setting Spence had in mind was one in which the more able go to school. The antebellum college was one in which the wealthy went to school, such that college would have signaled membership in an economic rather than an ability elite. But of course, many people might still have found that information useful, and wealth and ability are positively correlated.[14] To summarize, it is possible that the antebellum colleges provided their customers with valuable sorting in part *because* of their lackluster teaching.

With this background, one can see why increasing diversity posed a challenge for schools: they could no longer offer a student body as exclusive as they had before the war. This development may not have been an issue for the families that had not historically used them. For them, the colleges had improved their teaching, and they still provided valuable sorting—the 1 percent was still massively overrepresented on campus. For that 1 percent, however, things were more complicated: they may have felt that their educational "club" was becoming less exclusive.

To elaborate, economic models show that when students care about sorting, they will prefer schools in which their peers are close to or ideally better than themselves along traits like ability or wealth. For example, MacLeod and Urquiola (2015) consider a case in which employers cannot easily observe students' abilities. In contrast, employers can see which *specific school* each graduate attended, and thus being accepted to a selective school allows a student to transmit her ability.[15] For instance, Yale Law

School is the most selective in the United States, and if one meets a Yale lawyer one immediately knows that she is of very high ability (at least along the dimensions required to get into law school). The implication is that Yale lawyers will prefer to keep their school exclusive; they will not want lower-ability people "invading" the club. This idea was humorously captured by Groucho Marx, who on being admitted to the Friars Club is said to have sent it a telegram stating: "PLEASE ACCEPT MY RESIGNATION. I DON'T WANT TO BELONG TO ANY CLUB THAT WILL ACCEPT ME AS A MEMBER."[16]

In short, people often want to belong to the most exclusive clubs possible and will object to reforms that threaten their selectivity.

MacLeod and Urquiola (2015) also show that if it were inexpensive to open and run schools, then in the presence of sorting-related concerns there would be a large number of schools, each catering to individuals of very specific types. Of course, in real life there is never a school for every type of student, and it is hard for students who feel that their school is being invaded to pick up and move. This was essentially the situation in the leading universities around 1900: their traditional customers still wanted to use them, but many were becoming increasingly dissatisfied with their sorting services. Something had to give.

Clubs

One thing that gave was that students began to create their own sorting devices: clubs at which they controlled admissions. In other words, unable to create whole new schools, students devised "schools within a school." These schools produced no teaching—no academic instruction took place in the clubs. But they produced sorting: clubs selected specific types of students and provided settings where their members could associate with each other, segregated from the broader student body. Some clubs became well known and signaled membership in certain elites, much as going to college had done before.

For good measure, some of the clubs addressed another consequence of rapid enrollment growth: a shortage of dormitories and dining halls. To elaborate, historically American colleges had an Anglophile desire to provide sleeping and dining facilities for undergraduates (in the Oxford and

Cambridge manner). They seldom realized this ideal, however, and even wealthy schools like Princeton and Yale at times failed to house substantial shares of their students.[17] The decades after the Civil War saw further shortfalls, along with policies like those of Berkeley and Michigan, which abandoned dormitory provision altogether. In addition, it is not surprising that the clubs—institutions focused on sorting—were interested in providing food and lodging: a key way in which individuals form friendships is by eating and living together; this happens not just in colleges but in the military and in summer camps.

Different kinds of clubs emerged in universities, but they shared three characteristics. First, their goal was to select only a certain type of student. Thelin (2004, 6) states that the clubs wanted the college men, the "consummate 'insiders' who dominated the prestigious groups, whether literary societies or Greek-letter fraternities. Standing in sharp contrast to the college men and their extracurricular orbits were the 'outsiders'—students who usually were from modest economic backgrounds. . . . These low-income students were ridiculed as 'blue skins'—pious rubes who were often suspected of currying favor with instructors and officials." As Charles Eliot (1908, 221) put it, the clubs created a distinction between their members and the rest, who were "regarded as unfortunates." Second, as any institution that provides sorting (e.g., a journal or a school), clubs developed admissions procedures. Third, in most cases, the clubs were much more selective than the universities that housed them.[18] We illustrate these three traits by describing clubs at four schools at which they became relatively formalized: Harvard, Princeton, Yale, and Michigan (in the order presented).

At Harvard, a first type of club developed in the 1890s: luxurious private dormitories known as the "Gold Coast." These facilities, concentrated around Mount Auburn Street in Cambridge, were run for profit, and catered to wealthy students who did not use rooms supplied by the college. They provided steam heat and private bathrooms at a time when many college dormitories had limited plumbing. One, Claverly Hall, featured a ground floor swimming pool. Of course, such amenities came at a cost and due to this, renting a room in the Gold Coast immediately allowed one to mix with an economic elite.

For a recent example of how such amenities can drive sorting—one also involving swimming pools—consider a 2018 opinion piece written by James Koch, former president of the University of Montana. He observed that "in a competition to woo students, public universities are . . . offering lavish amenities that have nothing to do with education."[19] He criticized the construction of "lazy rivers," meandering relaxation swimming pools. If one conceives of schools as engaging only in teaching, it is hard to disagree with Koch; a lazy river is almost by definition a learning-free zone. On the other hand, if one conceives of schools as engaging in sorting, swimming pools have a lot to do with education—they can exclude those who cannot pay for them. As Koch himself hinted, flagship universities seem to realize that if they are to appeal to students wealthy enough to pay for such facilities, they need to allow their construction.[20]

Of course, the Gold Coast dormitories, in part because they were private investments, provided little selection beyond that based on income. They admitted any student who could afford the rent, and excess demand called forth more construction. For example, the owners of Claverly Hall also financed Westmorly, Apley Court, and Craigie halls.[21]

This fact left space for Harvard's finishing clubs to fill. The origin of this set of clubs may be traced to the College of William and Mary, where secret societies appeared in the 1770s. The two main ones were known by their initials, FHC (Flat Hat Club) and ΦBK (Phi Beta Kappa, the initials corresponding to the Greek motto "philosophy is the guide of life"). ΦBK provided a model for exclusivity and rituals like an annual dinner. While the Revolutionary War mostly finished these groups in Virginia, a visiting student had taken a "chapter" of ΦBK to Harvard, creating an "Alpha of Massachusetts" at Cambridge.[22] There, around 1791, the Porcellian or "Pig Club" emerged, with a ritual centered on a meal of roast pig. As its motto, *dum vivimus vivamus* (while we live, let us live) suggests, the group had fewer academic pretensions.[23] Some years later the Hasty Pudding Club was born with a similar orientation, and with a dinner involving a corn-based porridge (similar to polenta) known as a hasty pudding. By the time Eliot became president, Harvard had about ten finishing clubs enrolling about 15 percent of juniors and seniors. All collected dues, and several rented space and provided meals.

Their admissions procedures became formalized in the late 1800s, when they began to choose members from the "Institute of 1770," a group that provided a "first social sifting of sophomores."[24] About one hundred students chosen for the institute became eligible for consideration by the finishing clubs. As if to maximize suspense and sorting, the institute's membership was announced by sets of ten students and covered in Boston newspapers. The first group was the highest ranked, and the second contained the next most desirable ten, and so on. Making the ninth or tenth groups still conferred social distinction, but essentially ruled out eligibility for the most prestigious clubs like Porcellian.

Among factors that helped a student get into a final club were living in the Gold Coast and having attended an elite preparatory school. Things to avoid included "overcareful dress, . . . long hair, and grades above a C."[25] In the words of Morison (1934, 422): "You must say, do, wear, the right thing, avoid the company of ineligibles, and, above all, eschew originality. Athletic success, except possibly a place on the freshman crew, was not much help. Intellect was not a handicap, provided it was tactfully concealed, and all the social taboos observed. Once having 'made' a club, you could reassert your individuality; often by that time you had none." As we shall see below, the clubs also selected along ethnic lines.

Franklin Roosevelt's experience provides a sense of the clubs' potential impact on students. From the moment he arrived at the Gold Coast, FDR aimed to join Porcellian. As a sophomore, however, he did not appear in the Institute of 1770 until the sixth group. Karabel (2006, 16) reports that this was possibly related to FDR's association with nicknames that reflected poorly on his masculinity, including "'Miss Nancy,' because he allegedly 'pranced and fluttered' on the tennis court, and 'Feather Duster,' a pun . . . deriving from his supposed resemblance to the 'prettified boys' displayed on a well-known brand of hand-kerchief boxes." FDR failed to make Porcellian, an outcome he later described as the greatest disappointment of his life; Eleanor Roosevelt added that it was this experience that helped FDR "identify with life's outcasts."[26] This reaction might seem entirely out of proportion, and in that it is reminiscent of the disappointment some young students today feel about not getting into this or that elite college. It therefore shows that during this period it was the clubs rather than the colleges that were delivering the most valuable sorting.

For its part, Princeton developed eating clubs. At their core, these groups were also about sorting, but as their name suggests, their most visible function was the provision of meals for students who continued to live in dormitories. Slosson (1910, 103) asked a student to explain how the eating clubs differed from related outfits at other schools; he reports that the interviewee "explained to me the essential distinction, and I will quote his words because they show an admirable mastery of the language: 'you see, the frats eat you and sleep you; the Princeton Clubs eat you, but don't sleep you; and the Harvard clubs don't do either.'" To elaborate, while Princeton more successfully housed its students than most colleges, after the Civil War its leaders perceived that growth was producing demand for off-campus housing. To foreclose the rise of something like the Gold Coast, President James Mc-Cosh allowed some segregation within the college's facilities. For example, he oversaw the construction of Edwards Hall, a "modest residence [for] students of limited means, as well as Witherspoon Hall, the grandest dormitory in the country."[27] McCosh also mostly successfully resisted the growth of fraternities and secret societies.

Due to the lack of sufficient dining rooms, however, he permitted the rise of informal off-campus dining arrangements, the origin of the eating clubs. By 1902 there were eleven, with the oldest being Ivy (1879), Cottage (1886), Colonial (1891), Cap and Gown (1892), and Tiger Inn (1892). In part due to the cost of their services, these catered to wealthier students—for example, around 1920, about 70 percent and 100 percent of Tiger Inn and Ivy members, respectively, were private school graduates.[28]

On average, Princeton's eating clubs were easier to get into than their Harvard counterparts, perhaps because of the college's smaller size and its greater homogeneity. Nevertheless, they similarly induced admissions-related stress. One student reflected on learning he had not been chosen for one: "The news came like a thunderbolt. With a cold, sick feeling the bottom dropped out of my college life"; this reflected that the excluded were deemed to be "poor," "unlikable," "queer," or all of the above.[29]

Yale's entry into the club category were its senior societies, of which Skull and Bones was the most prestigious. The students learned of their selection into these societies on "Tap Day," and Karabel (2006, 20) states that "so great a public honor was election to a society that the question of who was (and was not) 'tapped' . . . was the subject of regular coverage in the New York Times." The press attention reflected that these societies were widely seen as a source of useful business and social contacts; again, a sign that these clubs had taken over part of their host institution's sorting function.

Of the clubs discussed so far, Yale's were arguably the most selective and had the strongest claim to using meritocratic criteria. They looked not only for social standing but also for athletic and extracurricular achievement. Averell Harriman, a member of one of the wealthiest families in the country, said of the tap system, "it gave me purpose. . . . I scoffed at Harvard's Porcellian club. It was too smug. But to get into Bones you had to do something for Yale."[30] That something, however, did not have to be academic: in most years the prevalence of students with academic honors was no higher in the secret societies than in the general student population; in many years it was lower.[31]

At Michigan, many instances of exclusion centered around fraternities, which by 1860 accounted for one third of wolverines, as the students were already known.[32] These groups prospered due to a lack of student housing at times explicitly engineered by university policy, such as under President Henry Tappan. In 1870 Michigan began admitting women, and soon after numerous sororities, led by Kappa Alpha Theta, had joined the scene.

As the university's enrollment grew, a distinction developed between the newer and older fraternities. The older had historically published the *Palladium,* a yearbook detailing fraternity and secret society membership. Fraternities founded after 1879 were not included in the publication, and hence the older clubs came to be known as the Palladium fraternities. The newer groups resented this and set up their own yearbook, the *Castalian.*[33]

The older fraternities gradually came to dominate the social scene. For instance, they organized the "junior hop," the principal social event of the year, and used their control to exclude some students. In 1897, when the university ruled that events held in school buildings had to be open to all, the Palladium fraternities organized their own hop in Toledo, reachable only by chartered train. In short, as Veysey (1965, 101) notes, these fraternities achieved prestige and power "almost comparable with that of the secret societies at Yale."[34]

Finally, it should be noted that not surprisingly, private dormitories, fraternities, and dining associations also arose elsewhere. For example, Graham (1974, 220) notes that at Wisconsin a handful of fraternities dominated the social scene and created resentment among the excluded, who they labeled "barbs" (barbarians). Similarly, Slosson (1910) discusses fraternities at Cornell, Leslie (1992) eating clubs at Franklin and Marshall, Brubacher and Rudy (1958) secret societies at Wesleyan, and Burgess (1934) boarding houses at Amherst.[35]

Self-sorting is not a priori problematic; in fact, initially many college leaders did not see the clubs as posing a challenge at all. In 1892 Charles Eliot wrote that while some might wish that the university not feature the contrasts in wealth evident in the world, this was inevitable; the clubs simply reflected the fact that: "Rich people cannot be made to associate comfortably with poor people, or poor with rich. They live, necessarily, in different ways, and each set will be uncomfortable in the habitual presence of the other. Their common interests are unlike, and their pleasures are as different as their more serious occupations."[36] The clubs merely illustrated, he later added, that birds of a feather flock together, "a principle which obtains in all human as well as bird society."[37]

However, in time observers like Morison (1935, 419) realized such attitudes constituted "un-salutary neglect." This is for several reasons, all related to the fact that sorting is among the key services a school provides, and like any firm a school will want to control the attributes of the goods it sells. First, the clubs could impact the student experience in a way that affected alumni generosity. The students a club accepted might be grateful to the club rather than to the college if, as stated, the clubs were the ones providing the valuable sorting. Eliot (1908, 222) himself observed that the clubs, "like the fraternities, are often helped pecuniarily by former members, who remember gratefully the pleasure their club gave them in their college days." Morison (1936) notes that every final club at Harvard had successfully "shaken down" its graduates for money for houses, and Zink (2017) reviews the remarkable architecture of some buildings still owned by the Princeton eating clubs, rather than by Princeton University. On the flipside, the individuals the clubs rejected were probably less likely to harbor warm feelings toward their *alma mater*. Some trustees worried about the demoralizing struggle that students experienced trying to get into the clubs, and at Princeton Woodrow Wilson expressed concern that the students who failed to make them were "thrust out of the best and the most enjoyable things which university life naturally offers—the best comradeships, the freest play of personal influence, the best chance of such social consideration as ought always to be won by natural gifts of force and character."[38] With the years even Eliot realized the risk, writing that it was "highly desirable that students of all sorts mix together" and, departing from his usual laissez-faire inclinations, floated regulation of students' ability to live in for-profit dormitories.[39]

Second, a loss of control over the student experience can entail a loss of control over admissions. If the clubs were not friendly to a certain group, then that group might avoid the school altogether. To be sure, at times this can play into the administration's hands. To illustrate (and as we will expand upon later in this chapter), the decades after 1900 saw significant antisemitism at American universities. While some colleges were looking for ways to repel Jewish applicants, a Princeton official noted that at his school the clubs did the job: "I hope the Alumni will tip us off to any Hebrew candidates. As a matter of fact, however, our strongest barrier is our club system. If the . . . clubs . . . make the admission of the Hebrew . . . the rarest sort of a thing, I do not think the Hebrew question will become serious."[40] But clubs' effects on admission need not align with the administration's desires, and ceding control to them is a risky game. For example, Karabel (2006) points out that in the early 1900s, many students chose Princeton or Harvard over Yale because getting into Yale's clubs was perceived as too difficult. Presumably Yale's administrators felt uneasy that secret societies were determining their school's relative attractiveness.

Third, clubs can induce undesirable student conduct. This reflects that when individuals covet membership in some group, they behave in ways they believe will render them attractive to its members.[41] Slosson (1910, 103) points out that some Princeton trustees worried about "the discouragement of the higher scholarship among . . . [freshmen and sophomores] through their conviction that scholarship is valueless and extra-curriculum activities of paramount importance in securing a club election." In other words, clubs and fraternities could produce an unscholarly ambiance. For example, at Cornell fraternities helped organize an annual book-burning ceremony, and at Yale the class of 1904 boasted of having "more gentlemen and fewer scholars" than any other.[42] In short, academic leaders realized that such attractions could produce a loss of control over student experiences and attitudes; in the words of Woodrow Wilson: "The side shows are so numerous, so diverting, so important, if you will, that they have swallowed up the circus."[43]

Academic Outcomes

The challenges created by increasing diversity also applied to universities' instruction, illustrating that sorting and teaching can interact. As schools enrolled students whose families had historically not used them, there were naturally some who arrived less prepared.

In addition, increasing diversity may have diminished universities' teaching effectiveness: many instructors claim that it is harder to teach groups of students who differ widely in their preparation, and there is rigorous evidence supporting this impression.[44] Further, Hoxby (2012; 2014) raises the interesting possibility that as universities invested in increasingly sophisticated professors, these became increasingly mismatched with students of low or heterogeneous ability.[45]

Consistent with all this, in the early 1900s many schools saw their graduation rates decline; for example, Amherst's fell from about 80 percent to 50 percent between 1885 and 1905, and there were similar declines at Brown, Chicago, and Harvard.[46]

Jewish Students

Finally, increasing diversity posed a challenge because it partially originated in growing Jewish enrollments during a period of significant antisemitism. To illustrate, at Harvard the proportion of Jewish undergraduates went from about 10 percent in 1909 to over 20 percent in the early 1920s; by that date at Columbia it was closer to 30 percent. These are estimates, since initially colleges kept little data on religious affiliation. At Harvard, in an exercise dreamed up for today's machine learning, President Abbott Lowell asked a committee to analyze extensive personal data to identify students who fit into three groups: J3 ("possibly, but not probably Jewish"), J2 ("indicatively Jewish"), and J1 ("conclusively Jewish").[47]

The growth of Jewish enrollments was particularly salient at Columbia, Harvard, NYU, and Pennsylvania. This did not merely reflect these schools' proximity to Jewish students; they had been quicker to liberalize religiously and had deliberately if unwittingly rendered themselves more accessible to them. For example, Harvard eliminated compulsory chapel forty years before Yale; it also began admitting students whose grades placed them in their schools' "highest seventh" without examination. Columbia improved its relations with public schools and assigned greater weight to the College Entrance Examination Board test.[48]

Soon these schools' leaders were expressing concern for various reasons. First, some were themselves clearly antisemitic; one trustee at Columbia complained that the law school would soon be filled with "little scrubs (German Jew boys mostly) whom the school now promotes from grocery counters on Avenue B."[49] Second, some expressed worries that antisemitic customers might be alienated. Harvard President Abbott Lowell stated: "The summer hotel that is ruined by admitting Jews meets its fate, not because the Jews it admits are of bad character, but because they drive away the Gentiles, and then after the Gentiles have left, they leave also . . ."[50] This was also a sensitive issue at Columbia, long wary of losing the children of the New York elite to Harvard, Princeton, and Yale. Third, some leaders like Lowell, worried that Jewish students helped drive segregation; for example, the same years that saw Harvard's Gold Coast appear saw the students designate one dormitory "little Jerusalem."[51]

To summarize, while teaching reform had brought the leading universities a welcome increase in enrollments, it created challenges related to their sorting product. We now turn to how the universities addressed these by implementing sorting reform.

Sorting Reform

Before listing the specific actions taken, it is worth noting that there was no consensus regarding what needed to be done. In part this reflected that developments like self-sorting were most relevant to the universities' undergraduate operations: their colleges.

One group of leaders took what one might describe as an "if thy right hand offend thee" position. They reminded observers that the college was the educational straitjacket teaching reform had endeavored to abandon in the first place. They suggested that at least part of its activities might be best cast off—transferred to high schools or junior colleges. William Harper and David Jordan, the first presidents of Chicago and Stanford, respectively, were leading proponents of this view, and even took actions in this direction. For example, Harper divided Chicago's four-year college curriculum into two segments—the first labeled junior or academic college, and the second senior or university college. The first was meant to be preparatory, and the second more advanced, with students focused on a major and a minor. In 1892, Harper expressed the hope that "The time will come when the Academy College work may be transferred to some other place, and the higher work be given all our strength. . . ."[52] For his part, Jordan added: "the American universities are not yet universities. They are destined to become such, but not until as a first step the first two years . . . of the junior college are relegated to the high school or the college. . . . so long as the institution tries to carry this double function of college and university in the same buildings, with the same staff, the present difficulties must persist."[53] Other influential reformers supported the spirit of these proposals, including James Angell at Michigan and Frederick Barnard at Columbia. The latter prioritized the graduate school and stated that next to it Columbia's "original function, as a school for the training of boys, shrinks into comparative insignificance."[54]

One question this raised is what would happen to colleges (e.g., Carleton or Smith) that had chosen not to become universities. Jordan predicted they would disappear in fact, if not in name, turning into academies. At Columbia John Burgess echoed this: "I am unable to divine what is ultimately the position of the Colleges which cannot become Universities and which will not be Gymnasia. I cannot see what reason they will have to exist. It will be largely a waste of capital to maintain them, and largely a waste of time to attend them."[55]

Opposing these views were people who saw in the college not a burden but an asset worthy of further investment. Harvard's Lawrence Lowell was a salient exponent of this view: "May we not feel that the most vital measure for saving the College is not to shorten its duration, but to ensure that it shall be worth saving."[56]

Perhaps not surprisingly given the centrality of colleges at their institutions, similar positions were held by Woodrow Wilson at Princeton, Noah Porter at Yale, and of course by presidents of liberal arts colleges. In addition, at most schools, substantial portions of professors, trustees, and alumni valued the colleges. Their view was likely buttressed by cultural and historical developments. Specifically, the desire to eliminate the colleges was often intertwined with an admiration of German universities, but World War I brought a resurgent preference for things English.

The pro-college position ultimately prevailed, and its advocates implemented three measures that can be described as sorting reform; that is, three measures that affected who students are exposed to or associate with at school:

1. Selective admissions, first at the college and eventually at the graduate level,
2. Investment into dormitories, and
3. Greater control over the undergraduate experience.

The remainder of this section discusses these elements.

Before proceeding, we note that while these three measures were not explicitly advertised as a package, they displayed coherence. For example, selective admissions allowed schools greater control over the types of students they enrolled, but also made enrollments much more predictable, making it easier to plan for the provision of dorms. Similarly, selectivity increased homogeneity in ability, facilitating changes to other aspects of student life. In short, sorting reform called for complementary measures. Few seem to have understood this as well as Harvard's Lowell; Morison (1936, 445) states that in discussing strengthening the college: "It was a favorite simile of Mr. Lowell's that you cannot lift a blanket by one corner. There must be effort at several points in order to lift the general standard."

Selective Admissions

Columbia led in the implementation of selective admissions, in large measure because it saw the greatest growth in Jewish enrollments. In the 1910s, discussions surrounded how the latter might be rolled back, with President Nicholas Butler himself floating one idea: requiring freshmen to live in dormitories (given that many Jewish students lived at home). This was rejected as too blunt an instrument, and suggestions to further emphasize the use of the Thorndike test were similarly dismissed. Calls for action increased after the United States entered World War I and Butler characterized the freshman class as depressing: the desirable students of old American stock had gone to fight, he claimed, and those left to enroll were "children of those but recently arrived in this country."[57]

In 1919 the office of admissions implemented three measures. First, it capped the size of the freshman class at 550 students. Second, it began to base admissions decisions on multiple criteria including an interview and student background, collected via forms asking for a photograph, religious affiliation, extracurricular activities, father's occupation, and so forth. Third, it implemented an explicit preference for students from outside New York City.[58]

In the years following, Columbia's share of Jewish students declined by ten to twenty percentage points. Soon the school was seen as a source of expertise in this area. In 1922 an MIT professor asked if the use of tests accounted for Columbia's success. He reported this was not the case; the key was to use multiple criteria and not share the reasons for rejection. This, he said, left officers free to discriminate "at their own sweet will against the

Jew."[59] He further asked Columbia's dean of the college for a written statement describing the admissions procedures, noting that it could be provided on blank paper. The Dean responded that Columbia had nothing to hide and no desire to exclude Jewish students. What he wrote makes interesting reading:

> We had 1200 applications . . . and could accommodate only 550. . . . We have not eliminated boys because they were Jews and do not propose to do so. We have honestly attempted to eliminate the lowest grade of applicant and it turns out that a good many of the low grade men are New York City Jews. It is a fact that boys of foreign parentage who have no background in many cases attempt to educate themselves beyond their intelligence. Their accomplishment is well over 100% of their ability on account of their tremendous energy and ambition. I do not believe that a College would do well to admit too many men of low mentality who have ambition but not brains.[60]

In addition, in 1928 Butler created Seth Low Junior College in Brooklyn, with the intention of placing Jewish and Italian students there. Its most famous alumnus was probably Isaac Asimov. Despite receiving a full scholarship offer at City College, Asimov wished to attend Columbia, but worried he would not make it past the interview; he feared his adolescent acne gave him away as "too Jewish to give at least the appearance of a gentleman."[61] The interviewer offered Asimov admission to Seth Low rather than Columbia, and it later came to light that his notes on Asimov read, "Very high Thorndike. Not too good an appearance due to bad complexion which may clear. A+ scholarship."[62]

Harvard largely followed Columbia in these measures, although perhaps with less finesse. Lowell initially sought quotas for Jewish and black students but met with open opposition from many professors. He abandoned the idea and formed committees that might propose a more palatable approach. In 1924, Harvard informally capped the size of the entering class at 1,000 students. In 1926 the faculty recommended that the dean interview applicants and collect their photographs, and the board of overseers directed that discretion apply to all admissions decisions, closing the automatic "top seventh" entryway. By 1930, Harvard's share of Jewish students had declined by about ten percentage points.[63]

At Yale the outcome was much the same. Based on recommendations from a 1923 "Committee on Limitation of Numbers," the school capped the entering class at 850 freshmen and put in place longer application forms and personal interviews. Between 1927 and 1934, the share of Jewish students fell by about five percentage points.[64] Some observers suggested that Yale had employed the best approach; it had not acted too late, like Columbia, or too overtly, like Harvard. This, they argued, had improved the school's competitive position. For instance, Karabel (2006) observes that at the start of the 1900s Harvard and Yale enrolled about equal numbers of students from New York City's upper class, the nation's largest; in the 1920s Yale had moved ahead.

In short, antisemitism was a key driver behind the implementation of selective admissions in the United States, and of a unique type of selective admissions largely still in place today. That said, antisemitism might not have been necessary to this development. Leaders like Lowell realized that heterogeneity along dimensions like ability—which would have existed with or without Jewish students—was at the root of several challenges. Similarly, providing housing required predictable enrollments, whether or not the students were Jewish.

Consistent with this, later in the 1920s Chicago and Cornell capped their entering classes without salient discussions of Jewish enrollment.[65] Of course, this might still have ultimately reflected antisemitism if these schools were looking to turn away Jewish students who would no longer use their competitors. More generally, to the extent that sorting matters, schools will have incentives to respond to competitors' selectivity so as not to be saddled with their rejected students. In this way, selectivity began extending to other American universities too, including essentially all in Table 1.3.

It is also worth highlighting that some schools took a different path to selectivity, including in the timing of its implementation. A salient case is that of Stanford, which in some respects followed the eastern schools. For example, it capped its freshman class slightly after Columbia, and at a level similar to Harvard's. However, by this time Stanford already had selective admissions for women, for historical reasons. In particular, Leland and Jane Stanford had created the Leland Stanford Jr. University as a memorial to their son, and under the charter they retained substantial control over the school. In 1893 Leland Stanford died, just as a recession and a federal investigation effectively froze the income the school derived from his assets. The university barely survived the next decade, largely thanks to Jane Stanford, who convinced the courts to allow her to draw a monthly income from the estate, and to let her consider the faculty as her personal employees. At one point she traveled to London to attempt the sale of jewelry that might bring a fortune but concluded that the prices offered were too low.[66]

In these years she also began to fear that excessive female enrollment might change the character of the school she saw as a monument to her son, and a ceiling of 500 women was set. By the 1910s this had created excess demand and a waiting list to which parents were adding their daughters at birth. The university gradually began to select women based on their "personality, physique, and other qualities."[67] By 1925 it was also considering high school grades, College Board examinations, and references. In short, what antisemitism did for eastern universities, sexism might have done for Stanford.

There were also research universities that implemented selective admissions relatively late. For example, Penn's delay may reflect that in the early 1920s it still had a limited pool of applicants, as well as a strong tradition of openness to students from Pennsylvania, as the state continued to provide funding. There would be analogous considerations at schools like Berkeley, Michigan, and Wisconsin.

Eventually, selective admissions also reached graduate schools. Princeton was an early mover in this area, in part because its investment into a gothic-style graduate college building imposed space constraints. But by the late 1930s most research universities had followed it. Interestingly, this development typically involved less drama. Perhaps for reasons related to their age, universities felt less of a need to manage graduate students' experience. There similarly was less of a desire to consider aspects like ethnicity or nationality at this level. Even Lowell, who stated that he had no desire "to see the undergraduate body become a Cosmopolitan Club," took pride in the "cosmopolitan character of our graduate school."[68]

Dormitories

A second type of sorting reform addressed infrastructure, particularly dormitories. It might seem that changing housing arrangements would be less controversial than imposing ethnic quotas, but both interventions affect sorting, and hence can involve high stakes. Woodrow Wilson realized this when he attempted to eliminate Princeton's eating clubs. He put forth a "Quadrangle Plan" that would have divided the students into a small number of colleges, self-contained units in which students would live and eat with faculty supervision—a model with a clear English inspiration. Wilson's plan displayed internal consistency: if selective admissions produced a more homogeneous student body, it would reduce the need for the mechanisms that students had used to self-sort. Put more poetically by Veysey (1965, 246), Wilson wished to abolish eating clubs so that Princeton might become a "single gigantic eating club."

Wilson initially enjoyed support from substantial portions of his trustees, faculty, and alumni, and received encouragement from Lowell, who had envisioned residential colleges as early as 1887.[69] But support quickly peeled away as the clubs realized the threat they faced. Despite offering compromises—for example, the clubs might be allowed to continue operations if they built dormitories and allowed unmarried supervising professors to live within them—Wilson was unable to change the status quo; this was a major factor in his departure from Princeton. Nevertheless, the school did engage in massive improvements to its dormitories during the 1920s, and at present these house essentially all its students.

Things proceeded more smoothly at Harvard and Yale, if only because their leaders benefited from Wilson's experience. At both schools, major proposals and financing for dormitories came from the same individual, Edward Harkness, an heir to a fortune in Standard Oil stock. Harkness, a Yale graduate, was troubled by the fact that men like himself had failed to make fraternities and secret societies, missing out on useful experiences.[70] His ideas were not far from Wilson's: he envisioned honors colleges in which students would be housed, fed, and supervised by a master in the English style.

Morison (1936, 477) reports that initially Harkness did not find an enthusiastic reception at Yale, whereas Lowell took seconds to accept. Few presidents understood sorting as well as Lowell, and he put energy into the project, involving himself directly in the design of student lounges and dormitory furniture. He opened two residential houses in 1930, and by 1945 Harvard had such facilities for all undergraduates. Yale began construction slightly later, but the end result was much the same, if the label different: ten residential colleges.[71]

While these developments were later mirrored elsewhere—particularly at Chicago where President Harper also moved to establish a house system—today only a distinct minority of mostly private colleges in the United States house all their students. In addition, some schools like Dartmouth and Duke not only require all freshmen to live in dormitories but randomize them into rooms. At such schools, private dormitories and freshman self-sorting are a thing of the past.[72]

Control of the Student Experience

Schools also moved to control aspects of student life that they had previously neglected. For example, into the 1900s many schools left athletics to students and alumni. While the resulting activity helped to fuel school pride, it created a "Wild West" in which alumni personally recruited and paid athletes—an environment that Brubacher and Rudy (1958, 132) note allowed the "tramp athlete" and his cousin, "the ringer," to appear. This was particularly the case in football, which developed quickly after an 1869 Princeton-Rutgers game, and grew aided by academic leaders like Charles Adams at Wisconsin and Vernon Parrington at Oklahoma.[73] Violence became increasingly problematic, with multiple player deaths in the 1905 season. That same year, a picture of an injured Swarthmore player—Robert "Tiny" Maxwell—allegedly reached President Theodore Roosevelt. Maxwell, who reportedly had a speech impediment and whose tuition was paid by a board member, had played a brutal game to completion; he was shown staggering off the field, his face dripping with blood, his eyes swollen shut. Whether that picture was the final straw or not, that year Roosevelt summoned a group of college presidents and told them to clean up their act.[74]

In 1906 new rules helped stem the violence, and in subsequent years, schools began to hire coaches and more formally recruit athletes. Such developments illustrate one aspect of free scope: today some research universities—for example, Florida, Georgia, Illinois, Northwestern, Ohio State, Penn State, Purdue, Southern California, Stanford, and Texas—run enormous athletic operations, some with stadiums seating more than one hundred thousand fans.

Along similar lines, artistic endeavors increasingly came under university control. Just as unsupervised athletics had been criticized for violence, unfettered theatricals were reported to contain "features offensive to good taste and propriety."[75] Illustrating the response, at Princeton McCosh accepted that drama could have redeeming qualities if supervised, and at Bucknell the President's wife helped organize and protect a drama club.[76] As Axtell (1971, 345) summarizes, whether applied to football or theater, such reforms signaled that after "an initial flirtation with the uncongenial German ideal of official unconcern for the student outside the classroom, the new universities returned to the distinctly American concern for the whole collegiate experience . . . ."

This preoccupation extended to teaching. Here inspiration came from England, where Cambridge and Oxford were known to have defined curricula, and to use tutors to lavish attention on undergraduates. Schools like Bryn Mawr and Johns Hopkins began to move away from Eliot's free election, and eventually Wilson's Princeton systematized the concentration and distribution requirements common today. Under these, students typically declare a major field by their junior year, and before that must sample courses from a variety of areas. Schools like Chicago and Notre Dame went further and put in place core curricula for the freshman year.[77]

Some also invested into individualized teaching. At Princeton, Wilson introduced preceptors, breaking down classes into sections with a more intimate feel. He also joined other schools in catering to the brighter undergraduates with an honors program; Slosson (1910, 94) states that after their sophomore year these had access to "special classes . . . that the [hoi polloi] may not enter, such as the Proseminary; they have a greater range of election and are not so strictly bound by the rules of compulsory attendance . . . , etc."[78]

Interestingly, such teaching reforms helped reinvigorate schools that had chosen not to become universities, but rather to remain pure colleges. At Swarthmore, President Frank Aydelotte created an honors program that placed stronger students in small seminars that met for discussion around weekly seminar papers. Rudolph (1962, 457) points out that this system "made much of such older collegiate values as close faculty-student relations, small classes, and attention to oral and written communication." The result was that, as Thelin (2004, 295) notes, "many faculty and presidents at the large research universities looked with envy at the teaching and learning environment offered by a Dartmouth, a Brown, a Pomona, a Swarthmore, a Carleton, a Davidson, or a Reed." These reforms also reflected that, thanks in part to the contemporaneous implementation of selective admissions, student ability and motivation improved. For instance, when Lowell introduced a pre-final exam reading period in 1927, he stated that Harvard students could be trusted to study; a decade earlier, he added, this would not have been the case.[79]

Student Sorting and Resources

These reforms, particularly the introduction of selectivity, set the stage for another massive sorting process—in this case, one involving students. To see this, a first thing to note is that where it happened, the imposition of enrollment caps did not go unnoticed. For example, Yale felt it necessary to publicly reassure alumni that: "limitations of numbers shall not operate to exclude any son of a Yale graduate who has satisfied all the requirements for admission."[80] Setting aside the fact that Yale would eventually renege on this promise, the fact it was made suggests that the caps had been noted by families that historically considered admission to the college all but a birthright. Students targeted for exclusion noticed too. McCaughey (2003, 257) points out that the Yale seal features a Hebrew inscription, and remarks that "among college-bound Jewish kids in Brooklyn in the late 1930s, [this] Hebrew inscription . . . translated as 'if you can read this, don't apply.'" In short, customers realized change was afoot.

Such individuals presumably pondered what effect selectivity would have on schools' sorting. For example, suppose that in 1920 a Yale alumnus had wanted his son to follow in his footsteps because he thought Yale provided valuable friends and a prestigious degree. Would this still be the case after the introduction of selectivity? Answering his question would not have been trivial, because the outcome ultimately depended on the decisions of numerous parents and schools, many making choices significantly later. This reflects that people typically attend college only once and carry whatever cachet their alma mater supplies forever. In short, this alumnus would have had to act on how he *expected* selectivity would affect Yale's student body and reputation in years to come.[81]

With the benefit of hindsight, it is clear that on average people like him expected—correctly, it would turn out—that with selectivity, the sorting service offered by schools like Yale would only improve. Far from turning off the children of successful alumni, "limitations of numbers" rendered them even more interested; far from running from essentially overt discrimination, bright Jewish students doubled down on their desire to enroll.

It is useful to consider why one might have expected this to happen. First, schools that face excess demand will generally on average choose applicants with high ability, where as a first pass we take ability to be simply the likelihood that a person has good outcomes—for example, that they have a good career in the arts, business, or politics, or that they make a good husband or wife. Schools desire that good outcomes be common among their graduates because this is an important part of their reputation. For example, if a given law school's graduates typically go on to jobs at good firms, prospective applicants might assume the school can also produce that for them.

Of course, such outcomes are a function of a number of students' attributes—ability is multidimensional—and different university stakeholders may prefer different ones. For example, professors usually prefer students who score well on tests and show deep interest in some subject. This affects admissions decisions, given that faculty quality also factors into school reputation. University presidents may additionally prefer students likely to be wealthy and donate. For example, the children of alumni—commonly known as "legacy" students—sometimes come from well-off, well-connected families that have shown a track record of generosity to their school. Such preferences affect admissions decisions too.[82]

The bottom line is that while ability is multidimensional, those who expected that selectivity would result in a sorting process on student ability saw this expectation fulfilled. In other words, just as happened with papers at journals and with professors at university departments, the most able students began to gravitate to the most selective, highest ranked schools. Even among the most prestigious set, a pecking order of selectivity emerged.

But it is possible that this process turned out to be even more thorough than early observers expected. This reflects that in this case too, further measures of ability came online, likely facilitating sorting. An early instance of this was the appearance of the College Entrance Examination Board (CEEB) test in 1901. While this test was not used widely for at least a decade, alert observers realized that its appearance was a high-stakes development. Such measures help elite schools identify able students and can thus accentuate sorting; they also can make it harder for schools to exercise discretion in admission decisions. Two leaders who understood this were presidents Ethelbert Warfield of Lafayette and Charles Eliot of Harvard. Rudolph (1962, 437) reports that Warfield and Eliot discussed the creation of the CEEB:

> "Lafayette College," said President Warfield, "does not intend to be told by any board whom to admit and whom not to admit. If we wish to admit the son of a benefactor, or of a trustee, or of a member of the faculty, and such action will benefit the institution, we are not going to be prevented from taking it." To which the president of Harvard responded in a way that must have been infuriating to all who knew how right he was but how much easier it was for Harvard to talk this way: "The President of Lafayette College has misunderstood . . . It will be perfectly practicable under this plan for Lafayette College to say, if it chooses, that it will admit only such students as cannot pass these examinations. No one proposes to deprive Lafayette . . . of that privilege."

Later, in 1937, Columbia, Harvard, Princeton, and Yale cooperated to develop the Graduate Record Examination (GRE).

Even later came the SAT, and it is not surprising that another Harvard president was instrumental in its creation: James Conant.[83] Conant criticized the CEEB test for its low "reliability"; that is, the fact that a student's score tended to be unstable over repeated administrations, owing in part to its use of essay questions that had to be graded by hand. Early indications were that a multiple-choice test like the SAT could perform better in this dimension.

In pushing for such improvement, Conant surely had Harvard's interests in mind. He wanted his school to become the most national university, and a reliable measure of ability would facilitate the recruitment of students from all over the country. But by all indications, Conant also had prosocial motives: he was concerned about what he perceived as decreasing social mobility, which he felt was turning the United States into a hereditary aristocracy. He wished to see schools like Harvard work toward a classless society by identifying low-income, high-ability students who could be attracted using generous scholarships.

So far so uncontroversial. But Conant went a step further in arguing that if a test could truly measure ability or aptitude, this would turn out to be unrelated to socioeconomic status—that is, wealthy students would not outperform their lower-income peers. Lemann (1999, 47) asks a reasonable if sharply worded question about Conant's position: "Was this touchingly naïve, or willfully naïve, or just unpardonably naïve?"

In Conant's defense, at the time there was less evidence that the correlation between measures of ability and parental background is strong and observed very early.[84] On the other hand, Eliot had intuited as much decades earlier when he stated: "The pecuniary capacity of parents is one valuable indication of the probable capacity of their son or their daughter . . . ."[85]

At any rate, the SAT was first administered in 1956 to about eight thousand high school students in the Northeast. It not only performed reasonably in terms of reliability; it was found to have validity—that is, it was useful in predicting future outcomes like college GPA. Its reach grew in the 1960s, particularly once Clark Kerr promoted its use in sorting students between the three tiers of California's public higher education system: the University of California, California State University, and the community colleges.[86]

Once this happened, the SAT likely intensified the sorting process and certainly rendered it more observable. The key illustration of this is due to Hoxby (2009), who shows that over the past fifty years American higher education institutions have increasingly diverged in terms of their students' average SAT scores.[87] In 1962, the most selective schools had average SAT scores at about the 90th percentile; the least selective schools at about the 50th. Thus, the difference in their average scores was about forty percentile points. As Hoxby (2009) points out, if one extrapolated back, the difference in 1940 would have been even smaller—about twenty percentage points. This illustrates why observers (cited above) stated that in the early 1900s the differences in ability between, say, Harvard and City College might have been hard to notice.

Over the following decades the schools at the top became more selective, and those at the bottom less so. By 2007 the schools at the 99th percent of selectivity (which likely includes all the American research universities in Table 1.3) had average scores close to the 99th percentile. By contrast, the average ability at the least selective schools had declined, such that the gap between the top and the bottom line had increased to more than seventy percentile points.

This student sorting is not exclusively due to the appearance of standardized measures like the SAT. The increasing availability of scholarships also played a role, and Hoxby (2009) emphasizes the role of reductions in transportation and communication costs that made it easier for students to attend college far from home. In addition, the benefits of going to the top schools (e.g., in peer quality and faculty quality—the latter at least as measured by research output) were increasing in this period.

An important note is that none of the measures or processes that American universities use to sort students is perfect—far from it. For example, any single measure, such as the SAT, is noisy and can be manipulated. Many talented lower-income children may fail to prepare for the SAT or to take it, or even having taken it and done well, they may not apply to colleges that their scores put them in range for.[88] This can deny them any advantages these schools confer. Further, the recent scandals around admissions-related corruption dramatize that subjective factors count. All this said, the nebulousness of American admissions can be an advantage too, as admissions procedures can be adjusted and competed over. For example, should corruption or prejudice drive school X to leave good students "on the table," school Y—which may not be ranked very differently—has incentives to pick them up (and collect their donations years later). Further, the American system avoids excessive attention on a single measure of performance, such as the single national exam accorded extraordinary importance by institutions and students in some countries.

Money

The sorting of students by ability helped the leading universities secure substantial resources. First, the fact that these universities often catered to wealthy students and experienced excess demand (and increasingly provided scholarships) meant that they could raise their tuitions. Over time, American universities became outliers in this dimension, and today well-off American parents are used to shocking their Canadian and European friends when they reveal how much they pay research universities like Caltech and Case Western Reserve. Because such parents often pay "full freight," they help these schools raise substantial revenue.[89] Second and at least as important, such schools were able to draw donations from increasingly successful alumni, particularly in periods in which wealth or inequality grew (Clotfelter 2017).

Here Harvard, Princeton, and Yale blazed a path that many followed later. Not only did these schools enter the 1920s with a significant stock of wealthy alumni, they grew this asset as measured by ability and satisfaction. Consider the case of Yale. In 1871, when the school asked alumni for money toward a memorial for President Woolsey, the result was widely considered a failure. Even twenty years later, President Timothy Dwight remarked: "Yale University, like all our collegiate institutions, must depend very largely for its success on the generosity of men who have not themselves participated in its undergraduate life . . . ."[90] Yet the same year, a group of New York-based graduates created the Yale Alumni Fund with the observation that while their initiative might not be a rousing success, it "could do no harm"; they were clearly onto something—thirteen years later Yale was reporting that "nearly all" gifts in recent years had "been made either by alumni . . . or by their immediate family connections."[91] By the 1920s, the school was engaging in fundraising campaigns with alumni accounting for over 90 percent of individual contributions. The often unrestricted and predictable flow of donations this produced proved enormously valuable to any number of efforts. Later on, newer schools gave their older counterparts a run for the money. For instance, in some recent years Stanford has received more alumni donations than any eastern school.

Aside from money, alumni contributed advice. For example, Oberdorfer (1995) reports that Dean Mathey, an investment banker and Princeton alumnus, helped his alma mater successfully time large movements into and out of equities around the 1929 crash. Such help also reflected that wealthy and influential alumni became increasingly well represented on boards of trustees.[92] In general, they also gained power as a group; for example, Yale's Noah Porter observed that "alumni retain and somewhat liberally exercise the traditional privilege of all children, freely to criticize the ways of the household."[93]

On a more speculative note, it is possible that schools like Princeton and Yale, which historically lavished attention on their colleges, benefited disproportionately from the increase in alumni giving.[94] My own impression is that on average, college alumni display particularly good will toward their school. This might be because college students spend a long time on campus, or because they do so at a more formative age. Or it might reflect that they live in dormitories, or that not allowed to specialize quickly, they form an attachment with their school rather than with a field or profession. Whatever the reason, my sense is that college graduates often exhibit what Gabriel García Marquez called the heart's memory: "the heart's memory eliminates the bad and magnifies the good; thanks to this artifice we manage to endure the burden of the past." It is likely this memory speaking when graduates say things like "My [student] life was so exquisitely happy that I should like to relive it in my son."[95]

If this is correct, then the reforms to improve the undergraduate experience were a smart investment. This point is made explicitly by Hoxby (2012), who considers many of the outcomes discussed in this book, including the concentration of resources in a few schools that emphasize research. Hoxby's model is not focused on how these outcomes came to be, but on the fact that they are consistent with a view of the university as a venture capitalist making investments into high-ability students. To survive, the university needs a return on these investments in the form of donations (or advice or political influence). A key issue therefore is how to build loyalty, and Hoxby (2014, 20) emphasizes that one means can be "creating athletic teams, clubs, traditions, songs, events, and special apparel." Similarly, Clotfelter (2011) notes that while big-time athletic university operations can generate financial losses, they also serve to generate loyalty and donations.

This also suggests that universities that took on a wide scope of activities— particularly those with a well-tended-to college in addition to a graduate school—may have been well positioned to marshal resources for research. Veysey (1965, 171) makes this point, arguing that institutions with colleges might have ironically been better equipped to branch out into research:

> During the 1890s graduate schools developed an important, autono-mous existence at a number of American campuses, most notably Har-vard [and] Columbia, ... The growth of graduate training in these in-stitutions was of greater future importance than the isolated experiments at Johns Hopkins and Clark. Research ultimately throve in a more luxuriant fashion at these larger universities because they could offer a broader and more dependable basis for its existence. A uni-versity which maintained a vigorous undergraduate tradition could at-tract continual endowments from wealthy alumni or alternatively, sup-port from a state legislature. Even the crumbs from such endowments would have seemed bountiful at hard-pressed Clark and Johns Hopkins. Precisely because Harvard and the others could offer this kind of finan-cial security, the story of the creation and expansion of their graduate schools is spiced with comparatively little sense of adventure. There was no risk. The men who led Harvard, Chicago, and Columbia were inter-ested in developing facilities for research largely as a means of gaining or retaining an up-to-date reputation for their institutions. But means here triumphed over singleness of motive.

In this passage, Veysey (1965) implicitly suggests that at some institutions a failure to aggressively invest in their colleges may have been a mistake. Jencks and Riesman (1968, 163) make this point even more forcefully:

> Locally oriented undergraduate programs provided recruits for the graduate school, alumni to support the university, teaching jobs for graduate students, tuition to help pay a scholarly faculty, and a link with

the local community that was both politically and economically useful. This kind of symbiosis arose even at the three universities that originally hoped to resist it by operating as national graduate schools: Catholic, Clark, and Hopkins. Perhaps one could even trace the relative decline of these three institutions at the graduate level to financial problems stemming from their failure to develop strong undergraduate programs and reputations.[96]

Of course, it must be noted that alumni participation is not an unmitigated blessing. For example, the heart's memory can make for conservative alumni, and this is perhaps why Harvard's Lowell once remarked, "sometimes I wish I were the head of a penitentiary. Then I should have no trouble . . . with the alumni."[97] Despite such normal frustration, alumni loyalty has been a crucial resource for American universities.

In closing, we note that as the 1900s progressed and admission caps kicked in, enrollment growth at most top research universities slowed substantially. In other words, since overall college attendance continued to grow, effectively many top universities—particularly private ones—let their market shares slip.[98] It is worth emphasizing that this stands in contrast with what happens in many non-educational markets in which firms prioritize market share. For example, the smartphone market is dominated by firms like Apple, Huawei, and Samsung, which every quarter strive to sell more than their rivals.

The reason that education is different again reflects sorting. Models like Epple and Romano (1998) and MacLeod and Urquiola (2015) suggest that when customers care about the quality of other customers, the top schools will be relatively small and cater to fine-grained segments of the population. For example, if peer effects exist then a large school may prove less attractive to very good students than a smaller one, which by virtue of having a smaller student body may be able to be more selective. When the mechanism is informational, a similar tendency arises, as encapsulated in the Groucho Marx anecdote cited above. Such models also predict a key feature of the American higher educational market: that selective schools may coexist with a nonselective sector that functions on an open enrollment basis.

It is also possible, if somewhat counterintuitive, that in obtaining donations, a smaller and therefore more prestigious school may, all else equal, do better than a larger one. For instance, Clotfelter (2001) considers fourteen private colleges and universities, and finds contributions to be quite concentrated, with more than half coming from the most generous 1 percent of alumni.

To summarize, the universities that aggressively pursued teaching reform eventually followed it up with sorting reform, introducing elements like selective admissions. The latter led the most able students to gravitate toward them—they sorted such that the identity of the school a student went to increasingly became a good predictor of her ability.

The end result was that these schools could sell a compelling package: they offered teachers who by virtue of their research talent were certified to deliver specialized and advanced instruction, and they offered the best peers and took care of the student experience. The package tended to produce satisfied customers who later turned around and donated to their *alma mater*.

The schools that put this package together enjoyed a virtuous circle: reforms brought large amounts of minds and money, which helped them procure more of each. The flipside was a vicious circle for some schools that lost good students or researchers. In short, these dynamics created inequality: a few dozen schools emerged as hugely wealthy research universities, while further down the food chain hundreds of others went less well provided for.[99]

These developments also tended to give the leading universities a substantial advantage, making it much harder for an entrant—even a well-heeled one—to compete for leadership. This point is made by Goldin and Katz (1998, 1): "something profoundly altered higher education around 1890 so that almost all of today's noteworthy U.S. universities and colleges were founded before 1900."[100] In other words, large private donations have gone to existing rather than new institutions, which may reflect factors like alumni allegiances and the reputational advantage of incumbent schools.

Chapters 3 and 4 have made the case that sorting dynamics unleashed by teaching and sorting reform concentrated minds and money in a few dozen schools. We now turn to why this arrangement works well for research.

CHAPTER 5

Productivity

T HE UNITED STATES SPENDS a lot on higher education—Figure 5.1 shows it is the highest spender, in per-student terms, among wealthy countries. Of course, throwing money at a sector does not guarantee that it will perform well; that additionally requires that the money be used productively. For example, the United States' lead in health spending is even greater than that in higher education, and yet the American health system underperforms in multiple dimensions; not surprisingly, studies suggest that up to a third of its expenditure is wasted.[1] More generally, any sector's productivity will depend on the quality of its top firms, and on whether they account for a large share of activity.[2]

In the case of the American university sector, this comes with a major wrinkle: sorting processes unleashed by the free market (Chapters 3 and 4), mean that Figure 5.1 substantially understates spending by "Research I" universities. For example, Hoxby (2016) estimates that the most selective American universities spend about $150,000 per student—roughly six times the U.S. average depicted in Figure 5.1, and about fifteen times as much as many of their less well-heeled American counterparts.

The key question, therefore, is whether the American system directs spending toward universities which use it productively. This chapter argues that *when it comes to research,* the answer is likely yes.[3] We note that making this case admittedly involves speculation—this is an area in which establishing definitive links is not easy.

The chapter begins by noting that in the United States, inequality between universities is exacerbated by federal research funding, which disproportionately benefits top-ranked, wealthier schools. It argues that if the objective is to enhance research output, this makes sense: given the

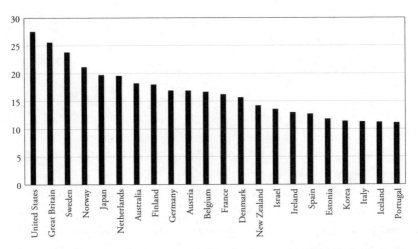

FIGURE 5.1 The figure uses OECD data to describe countries' total (public and private) expenditure on instruction and ancillary services provided through higher education institutions. It only includes countries spending above $11,000 (the minimum is below $5,000). (See https://data.oecd.org/eduresource/education-spending.htm, accessed October 2018).

existence of mechanisms that identify research talent, and of sorting processes that concentrate it at top schools, it is reasonable to direct funding there. A second section provides further justification for this allocation: not only do top schools have the best talent, they direct a disproportionate amount of their energy to research: to some extent they "cheat" their teaching mission. A third section points to another factor that improves U.S. universities' research productivity: the sorting of talent *interacts* with the tenure system to provide professors incentives to do research. Finally, the chapter explains that while at present the market mechanism enhances the production of research, that does not happen with respect to other educational outputs.

Federal Funding: Doubling Down on Inequality

Given that it mostly operates as a free market, it is not shocking that the American university system displays inequality: the sorting forces described earlier predict this outcome. For another example, Hoxby (2016b, 1) points out that there is often a correlation between a school's wealth and the average ability of its students; she adds: "moreover, my research shows, the more powerful the market forces, the stronger the correlation."

What is perhaps more surprising is that through its research expenditure, the federal government reinforces this tendency—one might say it doubles down on inequality. This matters because the federal government is a major source of research funding, particularly in the health area. Its distribution differs from that in many countries, where governments tend to equalize spending across universities. Indeed, it stands in contrast with other educational settings in the United States; for example, at the K-12 level most states are more generous to school districts that have fewer resources.[4] It is worth reviewing how this situation came to be.

The American government began providing research funding during World War I, when the military engaged professors in the war effort. After the war, the consensus returned that the government might best leave research alone. Geiger (1993, 4) states that during the 1920s the scientific leadership was

> of one mind concerning the proper organization of science. Direction, above all, had to be lodged with the most competent scientists. Scientific autonomy of this type was best guaranteed . . . by relying upon . . . private philanthropy to support basic research, preferably in universities. To permit government involvement in university research would only bring the intrusion of political considerations and the diminution of the effectiveness of science.

World War II brought renewed funding but through a different mechanism. The Office of Scientific Research and Development (OSRD) contracted with universities for professors' time, paying "overhead" to cover costs. This approach was used, for example, in the Manhattan Project, widely considered "display A" of successful government-university collaboration.[5]

As the war ended, a key question concerned what configuration further federal funding might take. Should universities receive public money for research, and if so, which ones? A wide-ranging debate ensued. On one side was a group of New Deal Democrats informally led by Senator Harley Kilgore, who advocated for an approach with three elements.[6] First, the managers of a new funding mechanism would be politically appointed and accountable to elected officials; Congress would help set broad research priorities. Second, this mechanism would distribute funding to reach most schools across the country. Here Kilgore's group cited an important precedent: the Morrill Act, which distributed support widely. Third, funding would grow to cover additional thematic areas, including the social sciences.

On the other side was a Republican-leaning group led by Vannevar Bush, head of the OSRD and former dean of engineering at MIT.[7] It argued that the government should continue to fund universities, which provided the best environment for science liberated from short-term goals. The support would be distributed by a single agency to avoid compartmentalization. While the president would appoint its board, the agency would avoid political control by supporting projects selected by panels of experts. The latter was key for our purposes, because such a process—given the sorting of research talent across schools—would likely yield an unequal distribution of funds.

The outcome was a compromise. Kilgore's side prevailed in that funding was extended to areas beyond pure science (e.g., area studies, engineering, social sciences) and came to be distributed through multiple funding agencies including the National Institutes of Health (NIH), the Department of Defense (DOD), the National Science Foundation (NSF), the Atomic Energy Commission (AEC), and the National Aeronautics and Space Administration (NASA).[8] Crucially for our purposes, Bush's side prevailed in that project selection came to be heavily guided by input from experts, many originating in universities themselves.

The result is in Table 5.1, which lists the thirty universities that received the most federal research funding in 1968 and 2018. Two observations arise. First, each year the schools listed easily account for more than half of all expenditures; that is, the top universities receive the lion's share of federal research funding.[9] Second, even within this set, the distribution is not equal, and a handful of schools do especially well. For example, in 1968 MIT was distinctly ahead, getting more than double the amount going to the

Table 5.1 Federal research funding by university, 2018 dollars

	1968			2018	
Rank	Institution	Federal funding (in millions)	Rank	Institution	Federal funding (in millions)
1	Massachusetts Inst. of Tech.	578	1	Johns Hopkins University	1,884
2	Stanford University	300	2	University of Washington	949
3	Harvard University	284	3	University of Michigan	820
4	University of Michigan	274	4	Columbia University	707
5	Univ. of Calif., Los Angeles	265	5	University of Pittsburgh	662
6	Columbia University	252	6	University of Pennsylvania	656
7	Univ. of Calif., Berkeley	247	7	Univ. of Calif., San Diego	645
8	University of Wisconsin	225	8	University of Wisconsin	637
9	University of Illinois	216	9	Univ. of Calif., San Francisco	594
10	University of Washington	203	10	Duke University	585
11	University of Chicago	195	11	Univ. of Calif., Los Angeles	570
12	University of Minnesota	191	12	Stanford University	564
13	New York University	176	13	Univ. of North Carolina, Chapel Hill	562
14	Univ. of Calif., San Diego	174	14	Univ. of Texas, Anderson Cancer Center	543
15	Cornell University	169	15	Univ of Florida	520
16	Johns Hopkins University	161	16	University of Arizona	493
17	Yale University	142	17	University of Minnesota	489
18	University of Pennsylvania	134	18	Cornell University	489
19	Ohio State University	119	19	Harvard University	477
20	Duke University	118	20	Ohio State University	469
21	Washington University	108	21	Univ. of Texas, Austin	469

(continued)

Table 5.1 (Continued)

	1968			2018	
Rank	Institution	Federal funding (in millions)	Rank	Institution	Federal funding (in millions)
22	Case Western Reserve	107	22	Penn State and Hershey Medical Center	428
23	University of Maryland	103	23	Northwestern University	400
24	University of Rochester	102	24	Univ. of Calif., Berkeley	363
25	Michigan State University	97	25	Massachusetts Inst. of Tech.	355
26	Yeshiva University	97	26	Yale University	336
27	California Inst. Of Tech.	96	27	Univ. of Calif., Davis	328
28	University of Colorado	95	28	Washington University	306
29	University of Miami	95	29	Texas A&M	292
30	University of Pittsburgh	94	30	Georgia Inst. of Tech	236

The table lists federal research funding by university. The data in the left column refer to 1968 and come from Graham and Diamond (1997) (based on data from the National Science Foundation). The right column draws on data from the National Center for Science and Engineering Statistics (https://www.nsf.gov/statistics /nsf19325/content.cfm?pub_id=4240&id=2, accessed November 2018). The figures are in 2018 dollars, adjusted using the Consumer Price Index.

4th ranked school (Michigan), and more than five times that going to the 25th ranked (Michigan State).

It is worth stopping for a moment to discuss MIT's and Stanford's early leadership in this dimension. Just as schools like Cornell and Harvard blazed certain types of paths in teaching and sorting reform, MIT and Stanford developed in a way that prepared them for externally funded research, providing a model that other major research universities later successfully emulated.

MIT's origins lie in the same impulses that created RPI. Namely, as the 1800s progressed, New England industrialists wished for a school training technicians and engineers, and felt that Harvard's Lawrence School did not fulfill this goal.[10] A group led by William Rogers, a former professor of natural philosophy at Virginia, discussed a prospective "Polytechnic School of the Useful Arts" inspired by French academies like the *École Centrale des Arts et Manufactures* and the *Conservatoire des Arts et Métiers*.[11] In 1861 the state granted the group a charter for the Massachusetts Institute of Technology which, with Rogers as president, began functioning in a few buildings in the Back Bay area of Boston. Aided by private donations and one-third of Massachusetts' Morrill Act proceeds, by 1897 MIT had about 1,200 students and was delivering undergraduate-level teaching in applied science, engineering, and architecture. It thus joined a successful group of schools including RPI, the Case School of Applied Science, the Carnegie Institute of Technology, and the Georgia Institute of Technology.

Around then, several MIT stakeholders pushed for complementary teaching and sorting reforms. Some argued that a greater focus on pure rather than applied science would better position the school to compete for foundation support, which was beginning to grow. Others suggested that MIT further strengthen its ties with industrial firms, which could fund research and provide jobs for the school's graduates. Yet others argued that the school needed to elevate its teaching and sorting to produce "captains" rather than "corporals" of industry.[12]

MIT created a graduate school of engineering in 1903, and awarded its first PhD in 1907. In a move reminiscent of Columbia's, it sold its Back Bay properties and combined the proceeds with donations from George

Eastman, the Du Pont family, and Massachusetts to begin building a grand space in Cambridge. By the 1930s MIT had transformed itself into a leading research university: its endowment was among the top five, it appointed Karl Compton (an experimental physicist) as president, and joined the Association of American Universities.[13]

In these years, MIT also pioneered the idea that a university could change its environment to suit its goals. Superficially, it helped dam the Charles River, creating a basin and eliminating the "ugly mudflats" that had extended into Cambridge.[14] More importantly, it deepened its cooperation with industry, a process that eventually led some of its collaborators to begin locating close to it. By the time MIT's own Vannevar Bush put in place extensive federal funding for science, the school was positioned to benefit from competitively allocated research money; through the 1950s and 60s, sponsored research accounted for more than half of its operating budget.[15]

Broadly similar impressions arise regarding Stanford, the second-ranked school in the first column of Table 5.1. As discussed above (Chapter 4), Stanford did not have the easiest start. For example, Cole (2009, 117) states that: "Stanford was never less than a good university within a few decades of its founding. But for generations it was better known for its undergraduate programs and could not be counted among the world's great centers of higher learning." Unusually, Stanford's ascent is generally credited to leadership from a provost rather than a president. For example, Wallace Sterling, the school's president from 1949 to 1968, stated somewhat undiplomatically: "My first appointee [as provost] was quite popular with the faculty, but, unfortunately, he was unable to take responsibility and make decisions . . . He was delightful company,—but he was not doing what I . . . needed him to do. . . . Then I struck it rich. In 1955, Fred Terman became Provost."[16] Terman, a Stanford graduate, had obtained a PhD at MIT and returned to Palo Alto where he eventually became the chair of electrical engineering. He was soon stating (also undiplomatically) that a period would soon close in which Stanford could either rise or take the path of schools like Dartmouth, "a well-thought of institution having about 2 percent as much influence on national life as Harvard."[17]

Once he was provost, Terman engaged in three key initiatives. First, he encouraged professors to work closely with industry, particularly if the projects were funded and fit into their research agendas. Terman's own students included William Hewlett and David Packard, who Terman encouraged to go into business and collaborate with the university. Hewlett often credited Terman with beginning the process that ended with parts of the Santa Clara Valley being known as Silicon Valley. In other words, Terman also understood that universities could productively work with external funding and shape their environment. He stated:

> Universities are rapidly becoming major economic influences in the nation's industrial life, affecting the location of industry, population growth, and the character of communities. Universities are in brief a natural resource just as are raw materials. . . . Industry is finding that, for activities involving a high level of . . . creativity, location in a center of brains is more important than location near markets, raw materials, transportation, or factory labor.[18]

Second, Terman worked to move Stanford's medical school from San Francisco to Palo Alto, where it could better connect with basic science and position itself to receive NIH funding. Third, because Stanford would be hard-pressed to expand everywhere at the same time, he focused on gradually building "steeples of excellence"—parts of the university equal to, for example, their Berkeley or Harvard counterparts.[19] The bottom line is that Stanford too was well-positioned to take advantage of federal funding, once it came online.

Broadly similar efforts took place elsewhere, as schools sought to leverage their locations to invest in research. For example, in North Carolina's Research Triangle Park, Duke, North Carolina State, and the University of North Carolina at Chapel Hill collaborated to create links with industry. Similarly, in some cases resource constraints and strategic considerations led schools to follow Terman in focusing their competitive energy on just a few areas.

The second column of Table 5.1 shows that these developments, along with the growing importance of health-related funding, changed universities' ranks in terms of federal funding. For example, at present Johns Hopkins, Washington, and Michigan occupy the positions that MIT, Stanford, and Harvard did before. It is still the case, however, that the lion's share of federal funding goes to less than 1 percent of institutions.

If the objective is to maximize the production of quality research, this lop-sided allocation makes sense. To elaborate, note that in any market, customers wish to buy from firms that supply the highest quality or value for money; those firms usually have access to talented workers. For example, companies like Apple and BMW make good phones and cars, respectively, likely because they use workers (e.g., designers, engineers, assemblers) who are good at what they do. When one buys from such firms, one can be confident that one is indirectly employing such people. Something similar happens when the NIH contracts with schools like Johns Hopkins, Michigan, or MIT—it can be confident that it is dealing with some of the best researchers. This is thanks to the machinery that identifies research talent, and to the sorting processes that concentrates it at top schools (Chapter 3).

In other words, concentrating funding at a few universities makes sense under the assumptions that the professors recruited by them do better research than others, and that a top-rate insight (e.g., one that leads to a Nobel prize) is more valuable than multiple lower quality ones. Hoxby (2012, 14) illustrates these assumptions by defining aptitude as an array of capacities a person needs to engage in activities like research, and then adding that "a person who has 99th percentile aptitude may generate returns that are an order of magnitude greater for given investment . . . than a person with 90th percentile aptitude."[20] While the precise advantage that top researchers have is impossible to quantify, that they have an advantage is a reasonable assumption. It was this assumption and its implications that Harvard's James Conant supported when he stated: "In the advance of science . . . there is no substitute for first-class men. Ten second-rate scientists or engineers cannot do the work of one who is in the first rank."[21]

To summarize, this section has argued that the American university system is productive at research because it matches minds and money; specifically:

1. The system has developed mechanisms to identify research talent,
2. Market dynamics (sorting) concentrate talent and resources in a fraction of schools,
3. Buyers (e.g., the NIH) can easily identify these schools and are willing to use them,
4. The nature of research is such that the highest quality output has outsize importance.

Note that we attribute the top schools' quality to their research talent rather than to their managerial talent. The latter is a factor that economists often argue is a key determinant of firm productivity.[22] The top American universities may be better managed than others (although I know numerous professors at numerous top schools who would beg to differ), but that is not central to the argument.

Diversion of Energy to Research

Another reason it makes sense to direct resources to the top universities—always assuming research output is the goal—is that these schools can divert energy toward this activity. In other words, they are able to "cheat" some of their other missions in favor of research.

To see this, set aside the NIH to think of another type of university customer: students who buy teaching and sorting. When it comes to teaching, can students be confident that the top research universities have the best employees for the job? This section reviews four reasons why the answer may be no: (i) teaching talent can be distinct from research talent, (ii) teaching talent is harder to identify than research talent, (iii) professors at top universities face strong incentives to focus on research, and (iv) prestigious universities can get away with, at times, prioritizing research over teaching.[23] We begin by reviewing these reasons, and then note their implications for research productivity.

Teaching Versus Research Talent

Teaching at an advanced level requires expertise; in that sense, researchers are natural university teachers. Indeed, in some cases, research talent is all that is required to teach well. For example, PhD students are training to advance the frontier of knowledge themselves, and they often learn best from observing others engaged in this craft.[24] Similarly, for a smart undergraduate highly motivated in chemistry, there is likely nothing better than joining a university laboratory. It is important to be clear that in cases like that, top universities clearly supply excellent teachers and environments. As Hoxby (2012) emphasizes, individuals with the greatest aptitude for research may benefit the most from the expertise and infrastructure available there.

But not all students are of this type; some take classes they are not captivated by, and some are just getting started in a discipline. Serving them well requires not only expertise but also effort and pedagogical technique. A good teacher must be organized, engaging, and able to simplify concepts. Not all good researchers have these talents. To illustrate, return to the case of James Sylvester, a leading mathematician Andrew Gilman hired at Johns Hopkins. Gilman found that Sylvester's research and teaching talents were not held in equally high esteem. Benjamin Pierce, a Harvard professor, wrote: "If you inquire about [Sylvester] you will hear his genius universally recognized, but his power of teaching will probably be said to be quite deficient."[25] It is interesting that Pierce nonetheless emphatically advised Gilman to hire Sylvester on the grounds that he was suited to teach the most advanced students: "Among your pupils, sooner or later, there must be one who has a genius for geometry. He will be Sylvester's special pupil, the one pupil who will derive from his master's knowledge and enthusiasm—and that one pupil will give more reputation to your institution than the ten thousand who will complain of the obscurity of Sylvester."[26] For another example, Gilman received a letter from Princeton's President McCosh, who stated that while he was sure about a certain candidate's qualities as a scholar, he did not know whether he was *also a lively teacher*."[27] For an even more extreme case, there is an anecdote that Isaac Newton's lectures were poorly attended: "So few went to hear Him, & fewer y^t understood him, y^{t}oftimes he did in a manner, for want of Hearers, read to ye walls."[28] The key point, for now, is that there is no guarantee that great researchers will always be great teachers—research and teaching talent can be distinct.

Teaching Talent Is Difficult to Identify

Since Gilman hired Sylvester, one might conclude that universities do not prioritize teaching talent. In their defense, teaching talent is hard to identify: even if delivering the best teaching were their sole objective, universities would be hard-pressed to know exactly who to recruit. To illustrate, suppose one asked the professors in a given department to list the ten people whose hiring would most improve their unit's research. In my experience, they could produce such a list within days, if not hours. This list would surely contain some noise, but it would also contain useful information, if only because academics are constantly investing real energy into evaluating colleagues' research performance (by reading and refereeing papers, seeing seminar and conference presentations, etc.).

Now suppose that instead one asked them to list the ten hires that would most improve their undergraduate teaching; I suspect they would find this much harder—there is less information on this front. This does not mean there is none; for example, some professors win teaching awards, and sometimes word gets around that this or that one's poor performance is off the charts. But in most cases, there is remarkably little to go on.

One might be tempted to think this reflects neglect on the part of professors, but this difficulty is not unique to higher education. A large literature on the K-12 sector grapples with a key fact that makes it difficult to identify teaching talent: students are not randomly assigned to teachers. To elaborate, suppose we compare two English teachers and notice that at the end of the year, teacher A's students read much better than teacher B's. This could indicate that teacher A is better, but it might merely reflect that teacher A gets better students. For example, he may be assigned wealthy students whose parents provide good literacy environments, whereas teacher B is assigned low-income students.

The only sure way to address this problem would be to assign students to schools and to teachers randomly. Lotteries could be used to ensure that on average all teachers had students who come from similar circumstances. If at the end of the year teacher A's students still displayed better literacy than teacher B's, we would know for sure that was due to his teaching ability.

Such a randomized assignment of students is all but impossible to achieve. It would require transporting children long distances and eliminating parental input on school assignment, both deeply unpopular policies.[29] Another way of saying this is that households care about sorting, and sorting is the negation of the random assignment of students. For an illustration, the Upper West Side of Manhattan contains many parents who are adamant that they value diversity. In effect, however, many of their neighborhood's schools are quite segregated. Some are heavily populated by children whose parents have high levels of education and income, and tend to be white; others just a few blocks away, cater to families in public housing who are low income and mainly black and Hispanic. In 2016 the city implemented expensive reforms (including moving schools to new buildings) to integrate a handful of the most egregious examples. The reform had at best limited success. Some wealthy parents, who found they no longer were in the school zone they desired, moved. Some low-income parents whose children could now attend a wealthier school opted not to—some stated they did not wish their kids to be among the few nonwhite students in the classroom. As a result, the city is considering other options, and this will likely not be the last chapter in this story: attempting to control sorting is like trying to lose weight—the battle is never over.[30]

The ubiquity of sorting might suggest that it is hopeless to measure K-12 teachers' talent. In recent years, however, economists have worked hard to derive "teacher value added" measures by observing the reading proficiency of students assigned to teachers like A and B at the beginning *and* the end of the year. The resulting *changes* in their performance—that is, how much progress students make—provide a measure of teacher effectiveness. This approach has been found to reasonably approximate the effects one finds in the rare situations in which one can argue that students were allocated to teachers close to randomly.[31]

This work yields three key conclusions. First, there is a lot of variation in teaching talent: some instructors are much more effective at raising scores than others. Second, and perhaps more surprising, it is hard to predict which teachers are better. Even if one gives researchers or educators a large amount of data on teachers A and B—for example, their age, experience, educational degrees, college attended, a filmed interview—they struggle to predict which has higher value added.[32] Third, not surprising given the above, it is not the case that a few schools corner the good teachers; good and bad teachers can be found at essentially all schools, whether they cater to wealthy or poor children.[33]

Identifying teaching talent might be arguably even harder at the university level. Calculating analogous value-added measures for professors would be difficult: the material they seek to teach is hard to capture via standardized tests administered at the beginning and end of a term. Further, the outcomes that colleges should target, and indeed that parents and students wish them to target, are not test scores, but rather preparedness for future career and life. It is impossible to observe these until several years after students have graduated, and there are no beginning and end of the year observations for such outcomes.[34]

The bottom line is that while students can be confident that top universities on average have excellent researchers, they cannot be certain that they offer excellent teachers; universities would be hard-pressed to ensure that. Ben-David (1977, 22) makes a similar point relative to university systems—one can be sure some are better at research, but that is much harder to ascertain with respect to teaching:

> Until about the 1870s, German universities were virtually the only institutions in the world in which a student could obtain training in how to do scientific or scholarly research. It was known that this superiority in research was not accompanied by equal superiority for training in professional practice . . . or in the education of those who did not intend to become scientists or professionals, but excellence in professional practice, or in education for its own sake, was much more difficult to measure than excellence in research.

Professors Face Incentives to Focus on Research

Of one thing students at research universities can be sure: many of their professors face stronger incentives to focus on research than on teaching. After all, it is research that earns professors tenure (discussed below) and pay increases. Their single-minded focus on it must come at the cost of something, and teaching—particularly teaching undergraduates—often loses out.

To illustrate, a professor at a leading department once told me that as a young faculty member, he received advice from a senior colleague and mentor on his teaching performance. The colleague said to him that he would be able to convince other senior professors to tenure him if his research were excellent. Good teaching evaluations were not necessary; in particular, the level of his teaching evaluation scores did not need to be high. It would suffice, he said in mathematical terms, that the scores somewhere display a relevant positive derivative. For example, they could be bad as long as they were improving. But even that was not necessary; they could be bad and getting worse, as long as they were getting worse less quickly. Any sign of improvement, however subtle, would allow an excellent research record to carry the day.

While that colleague may have been exaggerating or even joking, he captured a truth. In years as a faculty member, I have never heard of an excellent teacher receiving tenure at a top research university unless that person was also a good researcher. In contrast, excellent publications can outweigh distinctly weak teaching. The victim of this attitude is often the undergraduate student. In the words of California's Clark Kerr: "a superior faculty results in an inferior concern for undergraduate teaching."[35]

Universities Can Get Away with It

So far, we have argued that top universities shirk in delivering teaching: they do not always hire professors with the best teaching talent (in part because it is difficult to identify), and they incentivize those they hire to focus on research rather than teaching. What would happen if a firm like Apple shirked similarly—for example, if it encouraged its engineers to focus on something other than designing products? It would soon pay the price: its customers would drift away. Apple knows this: it only dominates the smartphone market, for example, because it displaced previous leaders like Nokia, BlackBerry, and Palm that somehow dropped the ball.

And yet the colleges associated with top research universities remain hugely popular. The list of the most selective colleges in the United States routinely includes those at Caltech, Chicago, Columbia, Harvard, MIT, Princeton, Stanford, and Yale. True, some liberal colleges that focus on teaching (e.g., Harvey Mudd, Pomona, Wellesley) also have very low admissions rates, but these have not displaced the research universities. In fact, the evidence suggests that a school like Harvard rarely loses an accepted student to a liberal arts college.[36]

Thus, the top research universities enjoy an unusual privilege: they can all but openly shirk their duties to a major set of customers, and yet these customers remain stubbornly loyal. *This situation enables these schools to privilege research, and hence to use minds and money productively in this activity.* How can they get away with this?

By now the reader will not be surprised to read that the answer involves sorting; namely, students are willing to buy from schools that offer good sorting, even if they do not offer the best teaching. This follows from three observations (formalized in MacLeod and Urquiola 2018). First, education is not a consumer good like a phone; it is rather an investment good: when households use schools, they purchase an *asset*—hence Becker's (1964) use of the term "human capital". This asset is only assigned value after a student graduates and enters subsequent arenas. For example, if she trained to be an actor or a banker, the student will only later discover if she can land auditions or Wall Street interviews. Similarly, parents choose high schools with the hope that they will one day place their children into good colleges or improve their marriage prospects. As a result, individuals choose schools based on their beliefs regarding how agents like employers will value their skills.[37] Second, students' outcomes after graduation vary with the quality of the matches they make. For example, despite having similar characteristics, some graduates may land jobs at firms that pay more than others.[38]

Third, particularly when there is sorting, not all agents like firms, colleges, or prospective spouses consider the graduates of all schools. For example, Weinstein (2017a; 2017b) shows that many firms interview only at selective or nearby campuses. Similarly, Hoxby and Avery (2013) point out that college admissions officers visit only a small percentage of high schools, focusing mainly on "feeders" known to produce many applicants. Along the same lines, some dating services cater only to graduates of certain schools.

These observations imply that when schools supply sorting, they can also provide match quality. If some schools are better at placing students into jobs, colleges, or marriages, then students will be willing to use these schools, *even if their teaching service is weak.*[39] In other words, students realize that while schools supply teaching, they also provide pathways to outcomes like jobs. Because they care about such outcomes, they are willing to trade off performance in one dimension for the other. In addition, agents like employers wish to hire skilled workers—they ultimately do not care whether workers' skill comes from their innate ability or from what they learned at school. Hence, they too are willing to hire from schools that offer good sorting, even if they do not offer the best teaching. This point was captured by Justice Antonin Scalia, who when asked how he selected his clerks, responded: "By and large, I'm going to be picking from the law schools that basically are the hardest to get into. They may not teach very well, but you can't make a sow's ear out of a silk purse. If they come in the best and brightest, they're probably going to leave the best and the brightest, ok?"[40]

In yet other words, selective schools can get away with weak teaching because sorting creates a coordination challenge for their customers. Suppose that a given college caters to high-ability students, and that these individuals are pleased with the job placements the school produces—good employers recruit at this school. Now suppose that the students come to realize that the school provides poor teaching. Any one of them could migrate to a school with better teachers, but if she does it alone, she may find that she no longer has an easy way to get noticed by good employers. Indeed, this would be a concern even if they all move: in time, employers will notice that the high-ability students have migrated, but a lag could prove very costly to the students who move first if they therefore miss landing the best jobs.[41] Similar considerations may apply to high schools sending children to colleges.

This helps explain why the benefits of incumbency are so marked in education; for example, why among universities or high schools, it is rare to see a Nokia obliterated by an Apple. Once a school establishes itself as a destination for certain types of students, it will tend to display inertia, staying in that position. In other words, there is a strong "first mover" advantage. For example, the schools that first introduced selective admissions, like Columbia, obtained an enduring edge that continues to pay off even if they later encounter difficulties. Similarly, schools that historically served the elite, like Princeton and Yale, could afford to more leisurely transform into research universities than entrants like Cornell or John Hopkins, which had no choice but to make aggressive moves.

The bottom line is that top universities' selectivity provides a further reason for why—if the goal is to increase research output—it makes sense to disproportionately direct resources toward them: their selectivity allows them to get away with diverting their professors' energy to research.

A separate but important implication of all this is that market-oriented educational systems need not always perform well. First, we have already seen that market forces hampered the production of research in the antebellum period and have enhanced it since. More generally, in education, market forces can have different effects in different dimensions. To see this, it is worth repeating, for reference, the reasons we have given for why the U.S. university system currently does well at research:

1. The system has developed mechanisms to identify talent,
2. Market dynamics (sorting) concentrate talent and resources in a fraction of schools,
3. Buyers (e.g., the NIH) can easily identify these schools and are willing to use them,
4. The nature of research is such that the highest-quality output has outsize importance.

There are areas where the market fails to generate these conditions. Consider, for example, whether each of them is satisfied in the context of K-12 schooling. First, as discussed, the market has not developed reliable ways of identifying teaching talent: good teachers are as likely to be in schools that experience excess demand as they are to be in those few parents seem to want to use. Second, sorting dynamics aggravate this problem—the whole teacher value added literature is an implicit acknowledgment of this. If the market readily identified teaching talent, economists would not be trying to measure it. Conversely, there is no "researcher value added" literature—universities can identify and recruit research talent without economists' help, even if they naturally sometimes make mistakes. Third, even if parents were able to observe schools' teaching quality perfectly, they might decide to buy from schools that offer good sorting rather than from those that offer good teaching.[42] This blunts all schools' incentives to invest in good teaching. Fourth, the nature of K-12 education is such that the performance of essentially every school matters. For example, a country with thousands of schools is unlikely to perform well in an international test if only one hundred teach well. In contrast, this can happen with universities because in research top-quality output is so important. The bottom line is that when it comes to education, the free market can at times work extremely well, but it is not a silver bullet. At present it allows the United States to perform well at research, but there is no guarantee that it will promote performance in other dimensions (or that it will help research forever, an issue we return to in Chapter 8).

In some sense, this conclusion contradicts the influential work by Friedman (1955; 1962), who argued that introducing market forces in education—particularly by giving parents more freedom to choose schools—would more or less automatically improve education.[43] Specifically, Friedman argued that school vouchers would allow parents to escape dysfunctional and underperforming public schools. This is a reasonable position to the extent that in many countries the public school sector is one in which it at least appears difficult to terminate transparently bad teachers, reduce rampant absenteeism, or introduce meaningful curricular experimentation.[44]

But fifty years after Friedman, we know that the impact of vouchers is mixed. For example, rigorous papers show a voucher program in Colombia was highly beneficial to students; one study suggests that it more than paid for itself.[45] In stark contrast, Abdulkadiroglu et al. (2018) suggest that a voucher program in Louisiana substantially reduced students' learning.[46] This evidence is consistent with what we stated above: in choosing a school, parents have multiple considerations, and there is no guarantee that they will always choose the one with the best teaching.[47]

This is also seen in the country of Chile, a laboratory for Friedman's voucher proposal since 1981. In that year Chile began offering all students vouchers usable at private schools, for-profit or otherwise, which were given freedom to select students and charge additional tuition. This led to massive entry by private schools, which came to dominate most markets: today more than 60 percent of all children use them. As data to evaluate the intervention came online, Hsieh and Urquiola (2006) argued that the first-order consequence of this reform had been massive sorting, with little change in average educational achievement.[48] The evidence suggested that the market had let people sort out along socioeconomic, geographic, or other lines, creating situations in which attributes other than teaching value added drove school choice. In other words, like the antebellum colleges, Chilean schools were creating value for their customers, but not necessarily in the dimension policymakers had envisioned they would.

At the time, this was a surprising result, as people still mainly expected that market forces would dramatically improve educational performance. If this had been the case, then Chile would have been done with educational reform. In fact, over the past twenty years and despite subsequent improvement in its international testing performance, Chile has been experimenting with extensive reforms to reduce sorting and make school productivity more transparent, such that it might drive parental choice.[49] The American charter school sector provides an interesting model in this regard. It allows choice, but by basing admissions on lotteries, comes closer to forcing schools to compete on the quality of their teaching rather than the quality of their sorting.[50]

The bottom line is that the mixed effects of the market on different dimensions of educational performance can help explain, for example, why American universities lead the world in the production of research even as U.S. K-12 schools trail in outcomes like PISA scores.

Sorting and Tenure

To close this chapter, we discuss a third factor that enhances the American university system's research productivity: the sorting of talent interacts with the tenure system to provide professors with incentives. This final section begins with some background on how tenure arose, and on its basic characteristics.[51]

Tenure: Its Origins and Rules

One can understand tenure as arising from two interrelated sets of demands. The first is a desire on the part of American professors for academic freedom and protection from arbitrary dismissal; aspects that many of them at least perceived had been relatively rare during the antebellum period (Chapter 2). This desire became more intense as the research universities developed and the faculty professionalized and gained power. Several events around which these issues came to the fore involve economists, in part because early in their field's development many of them saw themselves as reformers or activists in addition to researchers, and their actions provided opportunities for tension with the university administration.

A famous case was that of Richard Ely, who Andrew Gilman hired to teach at Johns Hopkins. Ely was active in the progressive movement, supported labor unions, and participated in the founding of the American Economic Association. He later moved to the University of Wisconsin at a time of labor tensions in that state's industrial sector. This set up Ely for conflict, in part because Wisconsin had historically expected its university to participate actively in the life of the state—the "Wisconsin Idea." Soon President Charles Adams and members of the Board of Regents were receiving complaints to the effect that Ely supported strikes, taught elements of socialism, and had "entertained a union organizer in his home."[52] Demands that he be removed received press coverage, and the board appointed a committee to investigate. In the end the board not only supported Ely, but made a broader statement:

> As Regents of a university with over a hundred instructors supported by nearly two millions of people who hold a vast diversity of views . . . we could not for a moment think of recommending the dismissal or even the criticism of a teacher even if some of his opinions should, in some quarters, be regarded as visionary. Such a course would be equivalent to saying that no professor should teach anything which is not accepted by everybody as true. . . . We cannot for a moment believe that knowledge has reached its final goal, or that the present condition of society is perfect. We must therefore welcome from our teachers such discussions as

shall suggest the means and prepare the way by which knowledge may be extended, present evils be removed and others prevented. . . . [53]

That the outcome could differ, however, is shown by the case of Edward Ross, one of Ely's students. Ross taught economics and sociology at Stanford, where he advocated for the municipal ownership of utilities, publicly defended socialist Eugene Debs, and like many of his Progressive contemporaries, opposed Asian immigration.[54] These positions were noted by Jane Stanford, whose fortune partially derived from her late husband's investment into railroads built partly by Chinese workers. In widely publicized events, she accused Ross of playing into the hands of the "lowest and vilest elements of socialism," and pressured President David Jordan to terminate him.[55] Jordan secured Ross's resignation, but at the cost of bad press and the departure of eight additional faculty members.

The case helped lead to the creation of the American Association of University Professors (AAUP), which stated a desire to formulate general principles "respecting the tenure of the professional office and the legitimate ground for the dismissal of professors."[56] In short, the AAUP formalized the desire for permanence and academic freedom.

A second set of demands arose because historically administrators and professors have desired mechanisms that would encourage able individuals to enter academia and work hard, and would allow for the termination of those unwilling to do so.[57] Harvard's early hiring practices illustrate several of the associated challenges. Early on, Harvard hired tutors using finite, renewable term contracts, a practice which likely reflected that if faculty are given indefinite contracts immediately, less productive ones may stay while their more talented peers leave. For example, in 1716 Harvard stated that permanent contracts raised the risk that the weaker might "be fixed on the college for life."[58] In addition, renewable contracts can provide incentives; in the words of Harvard's statutes, they could "excite tutors from time to time to greater care and fidelity in their work."[59] A further benefit of fixed terms is that if a professor fails to perform, the school does not have to state a cause for termination and can simply let his contract end quietly.

At the same time, term contracts are not a panacea. As any manager knows, terminating a worker can be costly even if it is contractually feasible. When renewals come up it is tempting to "kick the can" and postpone the issue. Metzger (1973, 119) states that a 1760 Harvard rule limiting appointments within a rank to eight years: "was to prevent incumbencies from being lengthened by reappointments given out of neglect or sympathy; it was intended to defeat the importance of kindness in the serious business of evaluating personnel."

It is not surprising that the two sets of demands—for permanence/freedom and performance/incentives—could become intertwined. Harvard, during the presidency of James Conant (1933–1953), provides an illustration. Conant wished to strengthen the school's social sciences, which at the time were widely perceived to have fallen behind Chicago and Columbia thanks to inbreeding and other hiring mistakes.[60] In other words, Conant emphasized that assembling a strong faculty requires constant vigilance; a truth that is often missed. There are presidents, deans, and professors who wonder why some colleagues scrutinize each hiring decision—could they not just let this or that case be? In contrast, Conant felt that faculty positions were precious and to fill one of these "with a second-rate person was to betray a trust—to be guilty of almost criminal negligence."[61]

It was in this environment that in 1937 two faculty members with somewhat limited publication records, Alan Sweezy and Raymond Walsh, came up for reappointment. For a change, both were economists associated with labor unions.[62] When they were terminated, some colleagues expressed suspicion that their political stance had been the cause. Conant insisted this was not the case, stating he did not even consider their positions particularly notable. A faculty committee later found no evidence of political bias, but did indicate that the two economists had not received a fair assessment, and raised questions regarding the timing of their review.[63] Cases like these made clear that it would be difficult to disentangle the desire for permanence/freedom and the desire to provide incentives. It is possible to see tenure as an imperfect means to address these two sets of demands.

The key feature of tenure is a fixed-term trial period followed by an "up or out" decision. At this point, the candidate is either asked to leave the university or allowed to stay, and in the latter case will not be terminated except for serious misconduct. It is worth elaborating briefly on these arrangements, noting that we describe a generic case—the details vary across schools.

First, tenure by and large applies only to research-oriented faculty. A young individual of this type enters the tenure track as an assistant professor. She is initially put on a three- or four-year contract that can be renewed once, for a trial period lasting a total of six to eight years. In preparation for the up or out decision, a review committee must determine if the candidate's research rises to the standard required. At the top schools, she must have published multiple articles in the very top journals, or books with the best university presses. But there is no explicit, mechanical listing of requirements; the broader expectation is that the candidate have established a strong research presence.

A key input into the deliberations are between five and twenty "outside" letters written by tenured professors at peer institutions. In some cases, these people are asked to write free form; in others, to address specific questions like: Are you familiar with the candidate? What are her main contributions? How do they compare to those of the attached list of individuals? Would you be in favor of tenuring her at your school? It is not unusual for the responses to run into multiple pages. The letters range from bad to good for the candidate. The worst possible outcome, of course, is a letter that explicitly recommends against tenure. More than one such letter, even among a dozen, will often end the case. The next worst is a referee who declines to write—this could mean that the writer wishes to avoid making a negative statement, or perhaps even worse, that she has not noticed the candidate's work. Next come letters that recommend tenure; even in this case, the text is scrutinized for subtle negative messages.

Based on these letters and its own assessment, the committee makes a recommendation. Its report is extensive and explicitly addresses disagreements with letter writers. The report is then voted on by the department's tenured members. If the vote is affirmative, the case will typically be considered by at least one more committee convened by the provost, one that includes members of other disciplines. The final decision is, *de facto,* in the hands of the provost; *de jure,* it still belongs to president and trustees. If the result is positive, the candidate is henceforth tenured, if negative, she is granted a grace year before leaving.

It is not entirely clear where these policies were formalized because, as many features of the American university system, they appeared gradually and without central planning. Salient parts of the package had emerged at Princeton by the 1920s, and at several schools by the 1930s; by 1950 the full package was commonplace.[64] It is also important that tenure is often a norm rather than a legal contract. Private universities, in particular, are under little if any legal obligation to respect anyone's tenure.[65] Finally, it is also worth noting that tenure has become less common over the years; it is increasingly available only to research professors at higher-ranked and wealthier universities.[66]

Tenure likely has mixed effects on research productivity. On the positive side, it leads young professors to work hard. My sense is that, relative to their counterparts elsewhere in the world, young professors in the United States are more likely to prioritize research and to display focus. Of course this may also reflect selection: these days, promising young PhD holders have opportunities all over the world; the ones who sign up for the grueling American tenure track may be more willing to take risks and sacrifice non-research aspects of their lives.[67] In addition, tenure may allow for better decision-making regarding faculty appointments. First, because of the long commitment it implies, tenure forces the faculty to take the "up or out" decision seriously. Second, by protecting incumbents, it may enhance the quality of recruits. To illustrate, suppose chemistry professors are the best at identifying talent in their area. They might be reluctant to help their university hire someone better than themselves if this could cost at least one of them his job; tenure provides them with the right incentives.[68]

On the negative side, tenure may lower effort among senior faculty.[69] The possibility that this hampers relative American research performance is mitigated by two considerations, however. First, the fact that on average older professors are likely to have job security does not set the United States apart from other countries. In addition, as discussed in Chapter 1, the incentives senior professors face do not go to zero simply because they gain tenure; pay, promotions, and prestige continue to depend on research output.

Interaction with Sorting

To the extent that tenure has positive impacts, these are likely reinforced by the fact that it interacts with the sorting of faculty by research talent (Chapter 3).[70] Sorting implies that each assistant professor is likely matched to a department at which she is not far, in expected output, from her colleagues; combined with a tenure goal, this will tend to raise effort.

To illustrate, consider a situation in which each individual's research output depends upon her innate ability and effort, and in which only the top half of candidates, ranked by output, receive tenure.[71] Now consider effort under two scenarios. In the first, everyone is put "in the same bag"—one could think of this as everyone trying to gain tenure in a single, huge university. In this case, individuals with very low innate ability would realize that their effort is unlikely to put them in the top half; in the extreme, they would give up.[72] Something analogous could happen at the top: if individuals with the highest ability felt sure that they would end up in the top half, they might exert less effort. The incentive to work hard would be the strongest in the middle of the distribution. Now consider a second scenario in which people are sorted by raw ability into a large number of schools. This would be more likely to elicit effort all along the distribution, since in this case every person would be competing against similar athletes, so to speak. Particularly if the sorting is finely grained (and if there is a role for some noise in outcome determination), the incentives will extend more broadly.

Part I has argued that the American university system's free-market orientation explains the unusual evolution of its research performance. This orientation made for a poorly funded antebellum college system that, while satisfying the demand for sorting, delivered weak teaching and little research. The same orientation allowed a few entrants and incumbents to introduce specialized and advanced instruction, thereby naturally extending their activities to research. It also allowed sorting reform that helped create inequality, yielding a few exceptionally wealthy schools. The result is a system that matches minds to money at a few dozen universities, which, due to sorting, can devote a disproportionate share of their energy to research.

In short, Part I has offered a story satisfying the requirements set out in Chapter 1: it explains the weakness of American schools into the 1800s, the onset of improvement decades before World War II, the outsize role of a few schools in leading that improvement, and the concentration of the highest quality research output in a fraction of institutions. Put otherwise, while in Europe states arguably prodded universities to seek talent and certainly gave them resources to do so, in the United States the free market set in motion dynamics that produced an ultimately more successful research machine.

Of course, Part I has not addressed *why* the American university system operates as a free market, while its European counterparts mainly do not. Part II turns to this question.

Self-Rule, Free Entry, Free Scope

CHAPTER 6

Europe

AMONG WEALTHY COUNTRIES, the United States is unusual in letting its university sector operate as a free market. Self-rule, free entry, and free scope are much less prevalent in Europe. In France, Germany, and the U.K. it has historically been harder to open new universities. In France and Germany, further, the vast majority of universities are publicly financed and controlled; they are by and large unable to unilaterally create new senior professorships or set faculty salaries. Ministries of education exert substantial control over such decisions, in part because most faculty members are essentially public servants.[1]

In some cases, European universities do not even control their own identity; for example, after 1789 the French state repeatedly fractured and reassembled the institutions of higher education. More recently, Gumbel (2013, 149) asks his readers to imagine

> If the government of the United States were to announce a program to merge Harvard, MIT, Boston University, the New England School of Law, and a dozen other higher education institutions in Massachusetts with the aim of creating one gigantic university. The reaction would be one of ridicule. Several of these institutions are already among the best in the world, and are fiercely proud of their independence. . . . . In France, such a scenario is not only thinkable, it is official policy.

European governments are also more likely to limit universities' scope; for example, in France some *grandes écoles* were given relatively narrow missions (like certain types of engineering instruction) and the *École Pratique des Hautes Études,* instructed to train scientists and scholars, was initially not allowed to grant degrees.[2] The bottom line is that among the countries we have focused on, in terms of free market orientation the United States is at one extreme, France and Germany are at the other, and the U.K. is somewhere in between.[3]

This book has claimed this has important consequences. For one, it allows the United States to better match minds and money at a few institutions. For example, German universities display much greater equality in per-student expenditures and prestige than their American counterparts, but at the same time there is no German university as well-heeled as Stanford. Similarly, Goastellec (2012) speaks of a French doctrine that pretends all universities are equal. Beyond this, minds and money may be less thoroughly matched in Europe because federal research funding often goes to institutions that operate at some distance from universities, such as the Max Planck Society in Germany and the National Committee for Scientific Research (CNRS) in France.[4] In the same vein, Ben-David (1977) raises that the French *grandes écoles* attract the best students, but do not necessarily match them with the best researchers.

Of course, the discussion has not yet addressed why free market rules tend to prevail in the United States, with this being much less the case in Europe.

Part II of the book argues that, ironically, Europe *invented* the expansive, unfettered university market. This happened because religious and political factors determined that as universities emerged there, they did so in a single university market that did not have a singular authority capable of controlling it. This situation ended with the Protestant Reformation, however, as the market fragmented and states became willing and able to rule over still religiously oriented educational systems.

Also ironically, the American colonies that first created colleges—Massachusetts, Connecticut, Virginia—generally adopted European-style control. In other words, if the United States had consisted only of such colonies, its university sector might not display self-rule or free entry either. However, once college founding moved into the Middle Atlantic—New Jersey, New York, and Pennsylvania—the system took on the market orientation it displays today.

Understanding the European side of this story requires reviewing the rise of the oldest universities. These are a handful of institutions like Bologna, Oxford, and Paris, that appeared in the High Middle Ages and do not have precise founding dates because they emerged spontaneously. Among these, we will focus on Paris not because it is the oldest—again, whether it is cannot be settled conclusively—but because it served as a central institutional model in France, Germany, the U.K., and the United States. For instance, as it developed, Paris directly influenced Oxford and thereby Cambridge and eventually, Harvard. Similarly, when the Elector of Palatine founded the first German university at Heidelberg, he stipulated that it be "ruled, disposed, and regulated according to the modes . . . accustomed . . . in the University of Paris, and that as a handmaid of Paris, a worthy one let us hope, it shall imitate the steps of Paris in every way possible."[5] Thus, all universities in the countries we have focused on trace their lineage quite directly to Paris. And yet they now exist in national systems that differ substantially in their market orientation. It is this differential evolution that this and the next chapter try to explain.

This chapter tackles the European side of the story (and Chapter 7 the American side). The first section covers how self-rule, free entry, and free scope arose; the second how the Reformation swept them away.

Rise of the Free Market

The context in which universities appeared is as follows. The decline of the Roman Empire fragmented Europe, disrupting trade and lowering living standards and urbanization rates. The world's religious and political center of gravity shifted east towards Constantinople. Despite this, Christianity continued to expand under the leadership of regional bishops, and scholarly activity took refuge in the rural monasteries they controlled.

Around the year 1000, roughly as the High Middle Ages started, the picture started to change. Trade grew again, and urban economies strengthened as tradesmen prospered and organized into guilds. The decline of Constantinople led the pope to shift his attention north toward a more or less fully Christianized Europe. Educational activity shifted out of monasteries and into urban areas, with many towns seeing growth in the number of active schools.[6] This growth reflected that urbanization and economic growth increased the rewards to education, leading more families to demand some formal schooling for their children.[7] In addition, schools had more to teach as trade and the Crusades brought Europeans into contact with places where classic works by scholars like Aristotle had survived.[8]

Each school was run by a master known as a *magister scholarum* in Latin, then the universal language of instruction. Guibert de Nogent, a Benedictine monk, commented on these changes in 1117: "formerly, including when I was young, the masters were not numerous; there were none in the towns and one barely found them in cities. And when one found them, their science was so weak that it would be hard to compare it . . . to that of today's . . . clerics."[9] His reference to clerics illustrates that these schools had a distinct religious character that would have seemed normal at the time. Scholarly activity, such as it was, had survived thanks to the church, and at this time literacy rates were so low that clerics were among the few people who could read and write. Indeed, earlier in the Middle Ages the term *clericus* essentially implied the ability to read and write; in contrast, a *laicus* or layman would have been highly likely to be illiterate.[10] In addition, theology, as the study of God and religious belief, was the ultimate objective of any educational enterprise.

In some cases, church officials directly operated town schools. For example, bishops often supported cathedral schools by allowing a cleric on their payroll to teach. In this they followed instructions from Rome, such as Pope Gregory VII's 1079 admonition: "let some sufficient benefice be set aside in every cathedral church for a master who shall teach the clergy. . . . and poor scholars gratis . . . ," where a benefice was a stipend paid out of church revenues.[11]

In addition, in many towns there were independently run schools, precursors of our private schools. The local bishop also exercised significant control even over these, however, as it was in his hands to grant the school master the license to teach, the *licentia docendi*. In larger, wealthier dioceses, the bishop delegated school supervision to an official known as the chancellor.

The schools were not elaborate affairs. A single master might have offered instruction in a rented room, funding his operation from student fees.

Particularly in smaller towns, he would have focused on basic teaching, conveying Latin literacy at a level suitable for liturgical tasks. Some schools would have gone further and covered parts of the *trivium* (grammar, logic, and rhetoric) and the *quadrivium* (arithmetic, geometry, music, and astronomy), the seven subjects descended from the Roman liberal arts. This curriculum provided preparation for religious careers, but also attracted sons of merchants and nobles looking to practice law and medicine.

The schools were not evenly spread across Europe: present-day Germany had relatively few, and northern Italy accounted for more than its fair share in places like Bologna and Salerno. They were also common in present-day France: by the 1100s Paris had many in the vicinity of the Cathedral of Notre-Dame.[12] Towns with more schools naturally had a larger number of masters and were more likely to offer more advanced instruction: lectures in law, theology, and medicine. These were usually designated as the higher faculties, since typically completing work in the arts would have been a prerequisite for such lectures.[13]

As collections of schools grew, they came to be known as *studia*. This was an informal designation: a *studium* was simply a place where masters and students congregated. A distinction emerged based on these locations' ability to attract students. A *studium particulare* served a particular area, mostly attracting students and scholars from its vicinity; by contrast, a *studium generale* attracted students from a larger, more general domain. The latter were more prestigious; the idea was that one could glean a *studium*'s quality from how far students and masters traveled to join it.[14]

This would have only made sense if medieval students were relatively mobile, and perhaps surprisingly, they were. To elaborate, we tend to think that travel has never been easier than it is at present. For example, today one can go from Brussels to Paris in under two hours by high speed train; medieval masters would have taken days—they would have struggled to understand how easy we have it. But in other ways, it is we who struggle to understand how easy they did. For example, as a college student I spent a term at the University of Grenoble, in France. The first leg of my journey there would have indeed baffled a medieval student: a direct flight between New York and Lyon. But I faced other costs. I did not speak French well, and found the lectures hard to follow; French economists' approach to teaching was quite different from that used in the United States. I had invested time in obtaining the necessary visa and documents. None of these would have bothered my medieval counterparts. Instruction at all schools was in Latin and followed essentially the same curriculum; in a real sense everyone was a citizen of Christendom.

The bottom line is that by the late 1100s, some *studia generalia* did their designation justice by attracting scholars from every corner of Europe.[15] Some even developed institutions to address the variety of students they hosted. In Paris there emerged four nations or associations of students: the French nation contained students from, roughly, central France, Italy, and Spain; the English nation those from England, Wales, Scotland, Ireland, Normandy, Germany, Scandinavia, Finland, and Hungary; the Picard nation those from the low countries and northern France; and the Norman nation those from Brittany.[16] By some measures a *studium* like Paris had more diversity than many of our vaunted "global" universities.

In time the masters and students in such places developed *esprit de corps* and began to behave like a guild, an association of tradesmen controlling commerce in a given location. Among medieval guilds' key activities was petitioning town councilors and kings for privileges and protection. What privileges interested the school masters? What challenges did they hope to address by obtaining them?

While their requests were varied, they are all legible to modern eyes. A first set fell under the heading of "town vs. gown" and arose because the *studia* needed to house and feed their students, but being informal institutions with little physical property, were not equipped to do so. As a result, masters and students generally made their own arrangements to rent rooms and buy meals. In some cases, their number was significant relative to the population of the town that hosted them, and their economic impact was substantial. For instance, a medieval Oxford worker observed that the town's population consisted of "them that lives off the young gentlemen, and them that lives off them that lives off the young gentlemen."[17]

Not surprisingly, such settings saw increases in the price of room and board. Beyond this, the students would have been easy to identify, allowing locals to target them for higher prices. Inevitably this led to claims of price gouging, and of grievances surrounding the quality of goods and services delivered. For instance, students complained of bad ale and rotting meat. While this might seem extreme, analogous impulses are still alive and well. Wealthy American colleges control related parts of the student experience by operating their own dining rooms, but food-related complaints have not disappeared—the standards merely change. In 2013 the New York Times reported that undergraduates at Columbia's dining halls had been consuming copious amounts of Nutella, and given the expense, the management removed the item. This caused, as the Times put it, a tempest in a jar, and the spread promptly returned. An undergraduate explained the controversy; it combined things students love: "Nutella and complaining about the dining halls."[18]

Safety was potentially a more serious issue for the *studia*, and again in some sense the root of the problem has not changed. In 2016 the New York Times reported that Harvard had fifty staff members dealing with issues related to sexual assault.[19] The expense would have astonished medieval scholars. On the other hand, they would have completely understood the need. Having no campus and hence no campus-based entertainments, medieval students frequented town taverns in which the use and abuse of alcohol was associated with sexual assault. Since virtually all the students were male, incidents mostly involved women from the town, making for an explosive mix. For example, in 1209 an Oxford scholar was involved in the death of a local woman, and townspeople attacked his hostel, leading to days of fighting and the death of several scholars. In Paris in 1200, the servant of a wealthy German student was expelled from a tavern, after which the student's friends assaulted the innkeeper, leading to fights and several student deaths.[20]

Such challenges led the scholars to seek privileges and protection. For example, in Paris they asked the king and bishop to criminalize attacks on their members, and to grant them forms of immunity if they themselves were accused of attacks. Regarding food and drink, they essentially petitioned for price and quality controls.[21]

In responding to such requests, the authorities began to address the scholars using the term *universitas*. This word was just a means to designate the group—that is, "the universe of" or "all of the" scholars. This is the origin of the term university, and it is worth underlining that initially the term was not specific to the scholars. For instance, *universitas vestra* (again, all of you) was used to address other corporations and guilds. Consistent with this, for years after it came into use, the term was modified to specify who was being addressed—for example, the pope addressed the Paris group as the "University of Masters and Scholars of Paris."[22]

Self-Rule

In addition to the above mundane requests, the scholars asked for something that would be worth an epic struggle at Dartmouth 700 years later (next chapter): self-rule. By self-rule we have understood the ability of a school to control its affairs; the medieval masters would have largely agreed with this definition. To be precise, the scholars wished to draft their own statutes, elect their own leaders, and have members swear an oath to their group (oaths were salient in the Middle Ages; breaking them could imperil one's admission to heaven).

Importantly, they also objected to the bishop's control over the license to teach. To begin, this raised issues of principle related to the fact that the *licentia* was the original university degree.[23] The masters felt that they alone were qualified to determine who should receive it; after all, the very designation, *magister,* suggests mastery of a body of knowledge, much as a member of a guild would have been expected to know a trade. The license also raised issues of interest because fees levied at graduation were a key source of revenue, and not surprisingly, there were allegations that corrupt bishops granted it to unqualified individuals.[24] More generally, like any guild, the masters in each location wished to exercise some control over their trade, including to protect themselves from competition.

Of course, it would have been surprising if bishops or their chancellors willingly gave up control of the license in their jurisdiction. In this case, however, the masters could address themselves to the pope, who at least in principle controlled the bishops.

What led the masters to expect that the authorities might grant their requests? The universities had three sources of leverage. A first had to do with their mobility. If the scholars behaved cohesively—if their *esprit de corps* were effective—their enterprise was mobile. Most of the students were young and already away from home, and many masters were single, given their clerical affiliation.[25] Regardless of where they went, the curriculum and language of instruction would be the same, the ultimate formal authority still the pope. Further, the early universities had next to nothing in the way of physical assets: no buildings or libraries a move would have required them to abandon. This was a time when the scholars truly were the university.[26] As a result, the scholars could threaten to leave *en masse,* an act variously known as a migration, a dispersion, or a cessation. When this happened, instruction stopped at the given location, some resuming in places the scholars had agreed upon. This might seem extreme, yet work stoppages and coordinated moves were not unheard of in the Middle Ages when, for example, an epidemic could lead to substantial numbers of people leaving town. Migrations were costly for the town the university left, as it lost the revenue associated with the scholars' activity. While not necessarily common, they did happen. To cite three, a migration from Oxford led to the creation of Cambridge in 1208, as some of the scholars that left never returned. In 1228 migrations from Paris led to growth at Orleans, Oxford, and Toulouse. In 1409 a migration from Prague led to the foundation of the University of Leipzig.[27]

A second source of leverage reflected that popes and kings had an interest in strengthening, controlling, and monitoring the university. After all, the faculty of arts trained priests, that of theology future church leaders, and that of law increasingly important bureaucrats.[28] Further, the material taught in the universities could be of direct importance; as we will see; any heresy—nonconformity with Catholic teaching—could have major political and military ramifications. In addition, the university could come between higher powers. For instance, in the early 1300s when tension arose between King Phillip the Fair and Pope Boniface VIII, each convened doctors of theology and canon law to condemn the other. Similarly, Henry VIII, unable to convince the pope to annul his marriage, asked university scholars for an opinion on the question.

Third, the medieval universities used a source of leverage we easily understand: well-placed alumni. By the 1200s many popes had studied at Paris or Bologna, and some had been masters themselves. In 1286 the Archbishop of Bourges told the students of Paris: "That which we are today you will be tomorrow. I do not believe, in fact, that there is today any prelate among us who did come out of this university."[29] Thus the masters knew that at least some who heard their requests understood where they were coming from.

In some scenarios these sources of leverage might not have been effective, but the late Middle Ages provided an auspicious setting for the universities' pursuit of self-rule. The key point is that the authority they faced was far from monolithic. Although the universities most immediately depended on local authorities—kings and bishops—they were also under the pope's jurisdiction. This reflected that by today's standards, there was a strong cultural consensus anchored around the church. As put by Eire (2016, viii):

> Religion was more than a social glue back then: because it linked [all individuals] in every village and kingdom, it . . . allowed them to transcend seemingly insurmountable social, political, cultural, linguistic, and ethnic boundaries. From Portugal in the southwest to Lithuania in the northeast, and from Sicily in the far south to Scandinavia in the extreme north, a common set of myths, rituals, symbols, and . . . norms linked all westerners, and so did one ancient . . . institution that mediated this religion: the Catholic Church . . . .

At the same time, the pope's power was constrained. To begin, he had little means to exert physical control beyond his immediate surroundings; for this he relied on rulers including not just kings, but dukes, princes, and so on. And yet these rulers were also weak by modern standards: they were sometimes unable to control even their nominal territories. The lack of monolithic authority is illustrated by the fact that neither side could always make appointments without interference. For example, throughout this period, bishops were not only chosen by the pope; local rulers often had ample input. On the other hand, kings and emperors drew legitimacy from the church, as illustrated by the pope's role in crowning emperors. The bottom line is that no single authority was able to everywhere and always control education, and when cleverly led, a university could also play off one power against the other.

Under these conditions, universities obtained various concessions. A first set related to physical protection. For instance, in 1194 Pope Celestine

III threatened all who attacked the Parisian scholars with excommunication. In 1200, King Philip II stipulated that all citizens were to protect them, and those who injured them would be dealt with by his forces.[30] Masters and students would not be arrested by lay authorities, and they would be subject to trial only in ecclesiastical courts—privileges usually reserved for ordained priests. The thought of drunken students with such immunity must have sent shivers down neighbors' spines. Similar events took place in Northern Italy. In 1158, in a document titled *Privilegium Scholasticum* (scholarly privileges), the Holy Roman Emperor extended his protection to anyone traveling into or out of Italy for purposes of study.[31]

A second set of concessions covered material goods. For instance, following a 1209 dispersion at Oxford, Innocent III issued a charter with instructions for the town authorities. For ten years, scholars were to be charged half the rents in effect before the dispersion, and the full amount for ten years after that. The townspeople were not to overcharge for food.[32] In 1217 the students at Bologna obtained similar concessions. Of course, one wonders how closely everyone adhered to these instructions, but the intention is revealing.

For our purposes, the most important concessions relate to self-rule, and they only arrived after significant conflict and reversals. For example, in 1215 Pope Innocent III's legate issued a set of university statutes that significantly blunted the chancellor's powers over the Parisian masters.[33] The scholars then moved to unilaterally amend these statutes and adopt a seal, major moves toward establishing an autonomous corporation. The bishop and his chancellor strongly opposed these measures. The latter stated:

> In the old days, when each master taught for himself and the name of university was unknown, lectures . . . were more frequent and there was more zeal for study. But now that you are united into a university, lectures are rare, things are hurried, and little is learned. . . . the time taken from lessons being spent in meetings and discussions. In these assemblies, while the older heads are deliberating . . . the younger spend their time hatching the most abominable schemes and planning their nocturnal raids.[34]

In 1219 the bishop excommunicated the entire university. This was reversed by Pope Honorius III, but the tension between the university and the chancellor continued, and in 1228 following further disorders, the university engaged in a major dispersion.[35] In 1229 Pope Gregory IX and King Louis IX essentially granted it self-rule. The masters returned to Paris thanks to a series of papal communications, the crucial being the 1231 bull *Parens scientiarum* (Mother of Sciences), which left the chancellor as only the nominal head of the university. In the words of Rudy (1984, 25) at this point, the University of Paris emerged as "a fully chartered corporate entity under papal protection, secure from various kinds of interference by local church authorities or civil government."[36] For their part, Oxford and Cambridge had a generally easier time obtaining autonomy, which, as we will see later, also ultimately proved more durable. One reason for this might have been that these universities were physically more distant from their bishop and his chancellor.[37]

To summarize, by the 1200s multiple universities had been able to secure a significant degree of self-rule, a crucial ingredient of a free market university system. We now discuss the emergence of two other ingredients: free entry and free scope.

Free Entry

A university system displays free entry when new institutions can be easily opened. Determining whether this holds first requires specifying what economists call the extent of the market: what is the market in question, for example, in geographical terms?[38] During this period the university market extended throughout Europe; several factors point to this expansive definition. Masters and students were able to move across this area, and at least formally, the pope claimed authority over all of it. This is underlined by another privilege the Pope granted graduates of some universities: the *ius ubique docendi*— that is, the right to teach anywhere in Christendom without need of further license from a bishop.[39] Nicholas IV granted this privilege to Bologna and Paris in 1292, thereby all but proclaiming a European-wide university market.

Within the market so defined, there were certainly agents who would have preferred to restrict entry. To begin, in seeking to control the license and in behaving as guilds, universities were asking, to some extent, for a local monopoly. Kings might have also wished to control entry in their territories. But all these agents had only limited reach; for example, the University of Paris or the King of France could not prevent an elector from opening a university in Heidelberg, especially if the pope were willing to endorse the creation with a charter.

In this environment, Europe experienced its own version of massive entry. To begin, in the decades following the appearance of the earliest universities, migrations led to the establishment of schools such as Cambridge. Later on, kings, nobles, and municipal authorities moved from being pleased to host universities to actively setting them up. This reflected that as states gradually strengthened, so did their need for trained officials and their desire for the prestige and economic activity that a university could bring. In addition, several cited the desirability of having instruction closer by, much as the founders of antebellum colleges would do centuries later.

The first wave of creations took place mostly around the 1300s.[40] In 1290, citing the long distance to Salamanca and Paris, King Diniz of Portugal created schools that eventually settled at Coimbra. With similar reasoning, the kings of Aragon created universities at Lérida (1300), Perpignan (1350), and Huesca (1354). Cities in Italy likewise provided alternatives to Bologna, creating Perugia (1308), Florence (1349), and Pavia (1361). Charles IV, King of Bohemia and Holy Roman Emperor created the University of Prague (1347), and Rudolph II founded Vienna (1365). The kings of Poland and Hungary created Cracow (1364) and Pécs (1367), respectively.

The popes could have restrained entry to some extent, but at times they themselves contributed to it by setting up universities close to their bases, such as Avignon (1303) and Cahors (1332). In addition, during this period the popes were weakened by the Great Schism. Specifically, in the early 1300s the popes moved to Avignon in southern France, driven from Rome by factors including lack of safety and French involvement in papal elections. In 1377 Gregory XI, the last of a line of French popes, returned to Rome. Following his death, the largely French cardinals made an Italian, Urban VI, his successor. Urban quickly alienated them, however, and they responded by electing another French pope, Clement VII, who returned to Avignon. Thus there came to be two popes, each of whom appointed cardinals who in turn elected pontiffs between 1378 and 1417. The schism divided Europe as different rulers took sides. At some universities, the resulting tensions produced an exodus of students. For example, Scottish students left Oxford, German students left Paris, and French students left Bologna.[41] Such movements increased the demand for local instruction, contributing to the creations of Heidelberg (1385), Cologne (1388), and Erfurt (1389) in the Holy Roman Empire, and Saint Andrews in Scotland (1410). Papal approval, further, became easier to secure with two popes competing for influence.

Another larger wave of creations came in the 1400s as counts, dukes, and dauphins joined the action, aided by municipal governments and wealthy townspeople. This period produced about thirty additional schools.[42]

To summarize, in this broad period Europe's expansive university market came to display free entry, in part because there was no single authority who could restrain it. In fact, echoing his assessment of the American antebellum college market, Hofstadter (155, 41) writes that the result was to "overbuild" the system "to a point at which the University of Paris begged the pope not to authorize any more foundations." Toward the end of the 1400s, university creation did indeed slow and the number of universities did not change significantly until the 1700s.

Widespread entry had several effects on the university system. For instance, it made attendance more local and democratic. While in the 1200s only wealthier young men could afford to leave Germany for Bologna or Paris, by the 1400s individuals of more modest means were enrolling locally. There were also related changes in organization and governance: given the reduced prevalence of foreign students, the system of nations declined in Paris and elsewhere; the reason for its existence had essentially left town.[43]

Free Scope

Free scope characterizes a university market when institutions are free to offer diverse products, particularly a variety of instruction. For example, many American universities offer PhD and professional degrees even as they provide relatively basic and nonspecialized teaching. The early European universities displayed analogous scope. One can illustrate this by describing the trajectory of a hypothetical student who remained in the university long enough to experience all the types of instruction it offered.

Particularly earlier in the period covered here, he could have arrived young; entering fourteen-year-olds were common.[44] He would have signed up with a lecturing master in the arts faculty and been labeled a *scholarius*. Despite his age, he would have immediately been considered a full member of the university and been expected to carry his weight. It was largely from such students, for example, that the university derived its muscle in confronting the town. In short, our student would have felt that he too was the university.[45] On a side note, today many American graduate students are asking to be recognized as employees—employees!—of their universities, and to be organized in that capacity by organizations like the United Auto Workers, which have little to do with education. Whatever the merits of this, the medieval students, aggressively protective of their full membership in a self-ruling community of scholars, must be turning in their graves.

After about three years in the arts, our student would have been designated a *bacalarius* (the origin of our bachelor's degree). At this point he essentially became an apprentice to his master, in another parallel to the medieval guilds. Verger (1973) estimates that only a fourth of entering students made it this far. This was in part because while this first credential was useful, it was not essential for almost any career. Even in the late 1400s, a large proportion of clergy had never attended university.[46] Gradually, however, and especially for higher clerical or civil positions, university credentials became important.

After about another three years, our student would have received the *magister artium* (the Master of Arts) and the license.[47] Over much of this period, less than one in ten entering students would have gotten to this point. If our student became a teaching master, he would not have been likely to remain one for long. Like the tutor positions in the antebellum college, these were not particularly attractive. The income from fees could be low, and celibacy was expected, particularly in northern Europe and if the master received a benefice.[48] In addition, teachers in the arts did not specialize but rather taught different books in different terms.

Our student would have then gone on to one of the higher faculties: law, medicine, or theology. Given that few reached this stage, these faculties were smaller and generally catered to wealthier students. After up to six additional years, he would have completed his doctorate.[49] This degree would have allowed him to teach in a higher faculty, but also opened opportunities in the service of king or church.

This illustrates that soon after they emerged, European universities achieved one hallmark of free scope: the simultaneous provision of basic and advanced / specialized instruction. A final note is that this development seems not to have attracted much interference from the authorities, who might not have seen universities' scope as a salient issue. The result was that as in the antebellum college, there was not always a tidy boundary between school and university.

In short, by the 1400s Europe had developed a university system that featured self-rule, free entry, and free scope. This reflected that due to religious, cultural, and political factors, there was a single European university market, and no single authority had the power to control it. In closing this section, we discuss one institutional innovation that arose in this period, is related to free scope, and will be relevant below: colleges.

In the early university, student economic background varied significantly across faculties. At one extreme, law faculties typically included wealthy students who rented houses and employed servants.[50] Their arrangements were the medieval equivalent of Harvard's Gold Coast. At the other extreme, the faculties of theology and arts—particularly north of the Alps—included students of modest means. One sees evidence of this diversity even among graduates who went on to stellar religious careers. There is Thomas Aquinas (the preeminent theologian of the High Middle Ages) born to one of the most powerful families of Sicily; but there is also Robert Grosseteste (Bishop of Lincoln and revered religious and academic leader in England) born to peasant parents.

The students of modest means often had trouble procuring food and lodging, and colleges emerged in response. Their original aim was not to provide instruction, but to keep students housed and fed. The typical model was for a wealthy individual to provide an endowment consisting of a building and a grant of land, the proceeds of which funded operations; this individual often also helped attract further support from influential friends. Multiple considerations motivated such benefactors. They might have wanted to support students including their relations: the terms of endowments could stipulate preferences for donors' blood relatives, an early version of American "legacy" students.[51] There were also religious motivations.

Salvation was a central concern in medieval times, and founding a college was not just a good deed that might help open the gates of heaven. It could be a source of prayers after death: college endowments could stipulate that students hold daily prayers for the benefactor's soul.[52] Of course, there were also considerations of prestige.

Today colleges are associated almost exclusively with England and the United States. But given that they addressed generalized challenges and motivations, it is not surprising that they appeared elsewhere. In fact, the first emerged in Paris, and up to about 1500 Paris had more than Cambridge and Oxford combined.[53] The early ones included: the *Collège des Dix-huit* (1180), so-called because it housed eighteen students; the *Collège de Sorbonne* (1257), founded by Robert de Sorbon, confessor to Louis IX; and the *Collège de Navarre* (1304), founded by Queen Jeanne of Navarre. As in other dimensions, Oxford was close to Paris in institutional development. Early colleges there included Balliòl (1263) founded by John de Balliol and supported by his wealthy widow, Devorguila of Halloway; and Merton (1264), which initially catered largely to the nephews of Walter de Merton, Lord Chancellor and Bishop of Rochester.[54] Colleges did not grow as much outside Paris and Oxford (and eventually Cambridge), although Toulouse had twelve by 1500. Italian universities had few in part because they often dealt with wealthier, older students.

The 1400s saw two further developments on the college front, both most pronounced in England. First, infrastructure improved greatly; it was at Cambridge and Oxford that universities' image first transitioned from that of capital-poor collections of scholars to wealthy schools housed in monumental buildings. Second, although initially the college fellows' only duty was to study, with time, some began to provide instruction. At first, older college members held recitations in the evenings, but eventually some of these developed reputations that attracted students beyond those living in the college. In Paris the colleges of Sorbonne and Navarre gradually took over the teaching of theology. In England, some which had focused on theology (and thus on older students) began taking in and tutoring younger men and charging them for lodging and instruction.[55] This strengthened the English colleges and they in some sense replaced the university. Specifically, although part of the larger university, which still was the sole source of degrees, the colleges became well-funded and essentially independent institutions.

Finally, colleges also experienced innovations in governance. Many developed leaders, usually a graduate elected from among the residents. In addition, at many a visitor was designated, often an ecclesiastical dignitary uninvolved in day-to-day management but ultimately responsible for the school's welfare. The visitor was typically empowered, for instance, to remove a master who misbehaved, or to settle disputes between members.[56]

Decline of the Free Market

The conditions that allowed for the rise of an unfettered European university market were reversed by events surrounding the Protestant Reformation. Although these would take centuries to play out, they essentially had two effects. First, by breaking down religious and linguistic uniformity, they fragmented the university market. For instance, they brought vernacular languages to the fore, gradually making it appropriate to speak of multiple educational markets. Second, within markets there emerged strong states willing and able to control universities, in part due to their continued religious relevance.

One way to summarize this is to say that the Reformation created what historians call *confessional* and *territorial* universities. As the religious consensus disintegrated, rulers demanded that their schools subscribe to statements of doctrine known as confessions; this turned the universities confessional. As the market fragmented, strengthening states moved to fund and control their schools; this turned the universities territorial. Together, these developments ended self-rule and free entry. Finally, states also moved to control the configuration of entire educational systems. For instance, they moved basic / general schooling out of the universities and into formalized secondary schools. In other cases, they assigned only specific forms of instruction to certain higher educational institutions. Such limitations eventually ended free scope.

Two remarks are important before reviewing these developments. First, these changes took centuries, but they accelerated in 1517, when Martin

Luther entered the scene and the Reformation began in earnest.[57] In the words of Metzger (1973, 104):

> the history of institutions, while it shuns the flawless age and the complete debacle, does sometimes tell of a decisive moment . . . For the medieval university, the Protestant Reformation was that kind of partitioning event. It did not strike the first blow against faculty immunity and autonomy. . . . . Long before Luther wrote his manifesto, the universities of Central Europe had given signs that they were heading toward a new era of state dependence. . . . But the Protestant Reformation did strike the blow that killed.

Second, from our vantage point it might seem strange that religious developments could affect university market configuration. But again, the importance of religion in this period cannot be overestimated. Recall Eire's (2016, viii) statement that in the High Middle Ages the church served as a sort of social glue; he adds a corollary: "To break with this church was to turn it from an adhesive into an explosive, to change it into social dynamite."

Given this, this section begins with some brief religious history that will also be relevant to the creation of American colleges covered in Chapter 7. This background can be useful because, to modern observers, it can be difficult to understand how intertwined universities and religion once were.

By the time universities were fully formed, the Catholic Church had defined its mission as one of intermediation between the faithful and God. The essential rites it celebrated were known as sacraments, and among these the Mass was salient because it featured transubstantiation: the bread and wine became the body and blood of Christ even as they retained their appearance—a phenomenon discussed by doctrine partially developed at universities.[58] Only ordained priests could celebrate the Mass, although many lacked thorough preparation for it. For instance, their Latin literacy might have been insufficient to engage the official fifth-century translation of the Bible. In their intermediation task, the clergy enjoyed the help of an army of saints whose presence was strongest where they had lived or appeared. These locations turned into pilgrimage sites, and visiting them was one way of gaining indulgences: reductions in the time one's soul would spend in purgatory waiting for potential admission to heaven.

While the High Middle Ages featured wide acceptance of these ideas, they also saw calls for reform to deal with the clergy's problematic behaviors. Some of their transgressions received specific names: absenteeism arose when bishops did not live in the seat of their diocese; pluralism when they simultaneously held two or more offices; nepotism when they placed nephews or other relations in clerical posts; simony when they sold offices like bishoprics (which often came with revenue from church-owned lands). Aside from these named offenses, many priests drank and broke their vows of celibacy, and in a gray but controversial practice, some bishops sold indulgences.

Such behaviors had produced resistance for centuries, usually dispatched quickly and violently enough to keep it at the fringes. But in time, the church faced stronger challenges due to three factors. First, its critics were bolstered by intellectual developments like humanism and a renewed interest in classical culture. These movements had as their motto the phrase *ad fontes*; Eire (2016, 65) elaborates on its meaning:

> Few slogans have captured the essence of an era so perfectly as "Ad fontes!" or "Return to the sources!" These words were much more than a trendy slogan in the fifteenth and sixteenth century: they were also a battle cry, a paradigm for genuine reform. *Ad fontes* became a mentality, a way of thinking beyond questioning: ancient languages, ancient wisdom, ancient arts, ancient piety—all became undisputed models to follow, blueprints for a brighter future.

In education, humanists advocated for a liberal arts curriculum centered on ancient texts.

In some sense none of this was new; universities were born as medieval schools rediscovered ancient books. But the impulse was taken in directions that threatened the church and rejected university conventions. For instance, humanists argued that ancient texts were best studied in the original languages (e.g., Greek or Hebrew) rather than in the available Latin translations. In the 1400s, Lorenzo Valla used philological methods to demonstrate that the Donation of Constantine—whereby the Emperor gave the Pope control over the western Roman empire—was a forgery. In 1518 Erasmus of Rotterdam published a new translation of the Bible and criticized university theology for an insufficient concern with scripture, which he believed contained revelation more than any sacrament. He added that pilgrimages were overemphasized.[59] Importantly, humanists like Erasmus and Valla did not break with the church—Valla ended his career in possession of multiple clerical offices and a mistress.[60] But their work strengthened arguments that would one day feed the Reformation and contribute to a growing defiance of the clergy. The bottom line is that as Moeller (1972, 36) put it: "One can state this pointedly: No humanism, no Reformation."

Second, states continued to strengthen in the run-up to the Reformation. The same urbanization processes that gave rise to universities shifted economic activity into towns and away from feudal lords. This increased kings' capacity to tax and fund armies, which along with changes in military technology, reinforced their power. Universities supplied these rulers with a more professional bureaucracy and, through the rediscovery of Roman law, with greater justification for control. These trends were relevant in large kingdoms like France or Spain, but also in smaller jurisdictions like duchies and Swiss cantons. They were also relevant in Central Europe in the Holy Roman Empire, a loose confederation of kingdoms (e.g., Bavaria, Hungary), principalities (e.g., Saxony), self-governing free cities (e.g., Augsburg), and territories ruled by archbishops.

Third, the emergence (around 1450) of movable-type printing in Germany made it easier for new texts and ideas to propagate. This, despite the intense interest in classical languages, helped fuel the growing importance of vernacular ones, such as English or French.

All this set the stage for Martin Luther, a Wittenberg theology professor who objected when his archbishop sold indulgences to fund the purchase of his latest religious office.[61] In the following years, Luther developed the core beliefs of Protestantism. He viewed scripture as the ultimate source of truth, as expressed in the maxim *sola scriptura* (only scripture). He believed that salvation originated in God's grace and human faith, rather than in good works, pilgrimages, or indulgences: *sola gratia, sola fide* (only grace, only faith). He held that lay people should engage the Bible directly, rejecting intercession by the church and saints.

Luther was obviously more successful than previous reformers. Humanism prepared his ground, and the printing press suited him as much as Twitter suits some modern personalities. Increasingly powerful rulers offered his movement protection. For instance, he himself was a subject of the Elector Frederick of Saxony, who took a liking to his "prize professor" and shielded him from the emperor.[62]

If Luther's German reformation had been the only one, perhaps Europe and its university market would have split into two. But importantly for our purposes, several more followed. Ulrich Zwingli and Jean Calvin led the Swiss reformation, and although their ideas had much in common with Luther, there were also salient differences. Zwingli placed greater emphasis on resistance to idolatry, and Calvin stressed predestination, the belief that God alone decides who is saved. Even more than Luther, Zwingli and Calvin emphasized that church and state should collaborate to create a society organized around religion. Their followers turned Zurich and Geneva, depending on one's view, into truly Christian or truly gloomy puritanical towns in which authorities attempted to stamp out any behavior religious leaders condemned.

Such collaboration between church and state earned the movements associated with Luther and Calvin the label "Magisterial Reformation." This reflects that, as Eire (2016, 251) states, this reformation "depended for its existence on magistrates or princes and other civil rulers, and employed *magisters* (university-trained masters or teachers) . . . to enforce its teachings and ritual among all who lived within particular jurisdictional boundaries." Moeller (1972) states that the view that civil authorities should be responsible for religious uniformity was particularly intense in German and Swiss municipalities.

Such church-state collaboration in creating a *civitas christiana*—a holy city—will also be important in the next chapter (on the founding of American colleges). For instance, Eire (2016, 246) states: "When John Winthrop admonished the New England-bound Mayflower Puritans, 'We must consider that we shall be as a City upon a Hill, . . . ,' Zwingli's Zurich was his paradigm, whether he knew it or not."

In addition, the Anglican church emerged in England in 1534, when Henry VIII severed ties to the pope. The Puritans emerged later out of a desire to purify this church, which they felt retained too many Catholic elements like a clear hierarchy. Close by, in 1559 John Knox established the Church of Scotland with a more Calvinist orientation, although it too retained some episcopal elements.

In addition, so-called radical reformations joined the action. In Switzerland, Felix Mantz led the Anabaptists, a group that practiced adult baptism on the grounds that the Bible contained scant reference to the infant version. Mantz was eventually executed by Calvinists who saw him as a grave threat: adult baptism implied that church membership could be voluntary, a notion at odds with the idea of a uniform religion imposed by church and state. Radical reformers also quickly displayed their ability to cause disorder. In the early 1520s, some preachers supplemented their religious message with calls for the redistribution of wealth. By 1524 this had led to a massive uprising called the Peasants' War, which involved parts of present-day Austria, Germany, and Switzerland. The nobility suppressed it only at the cost of tens of thousands of lives. Violence would also be a theme as Protestants and Catholics struggled for control in countries such as England and France.

In short, this period saw the emergence of religious diversity at a time when religion could scarcely have been higher stakes, and during which universities still played a major role in religious life. In time, many rulers attempted to handle the associated challenges by stipulating that each state—typically personified in a king—could choose a religion that then had to be followed by all in the jurisdiction. This notion was captured in maxims like: *cuius regio eius religio* (whose realm, his religion) and *un roi, une loi, une foi* (one king, one law, one faith). The reasoning was that political and social stability required religious uniformity. Illustrating this spirit, in 1525 the council of Berlingen (a German imperial free city) stated, "in order that in our city there be no disunion, no discord, no dissension . . . Rather we should always live united in peace, in the future as we have up to now."[63]

Such reasoning ended Europe's free university market, as it persuaded rulers to take control of schools that still had the training of clergy among their central functions. This change was not just encouraged by events; it was justified by religious leaders. For example, in a letter titled "To the Councilmen of all Cities of Germany that they Establish and Maintain Christian Schools," Martin Luther underlined the need for the state to provide and control schools, if only to ensure the literacy necessary to a faith based on scripture rather than sacrament. Illustrating what this implied, in 1527 the Landgrave of Hesse abolished Catholicism and established a Lutheran church with a University in Marburg to train its clergy. Similarly, Catholics were expelled from the University of Tubingen in 1535; Lutherans from the University of Leipzig in 1539.[64] More broadly, after the Peasants' War civil governments issued ordinances that determined many aspects of primary and secondary schooling, from curriculum development to the hiring and certifying of teachers.[65]

In short, what had been a single European-wide university market began to splinter into localized segments featuring state-controlled universities and schools, ending self-rule. As Hofstadter (1955, 71) states, "Under the territorial confessional States . . . the long process by which the secular State had been encroaching upon the university reached its climax." Not surprisingly, within each market free entry also ceased to exist.

It was also not long before states' educational authorities were also dictating universities' scope. The faculties of arts were forced to stop teaching a good part of the liberal arts, which were transferred to improved state-funded secondary schools. This reform seems to have reflected a perception that the universities' faculties of arts had declined during the 1400s, and especially at smaller universities had become essentially grammar schools that many students wished to skip altogether.[66] Further, there was a sense that liberal arts training should be accessible to privileged children before reaching university. Eire (2016, 89) points out that by the 1500s it was fashionable

> for the elites of Europe to send their children to schools where the curriculum was shaped by humanistic learning. This was the ultimate triumph of the humanists throughout Europe: the establishment of schools where successive generations of children would be educated in the *studia humanitatis,* the liberal arts, not necessarily as scholars-to-be, and much

less as churchmen, but as literate, well-rounded laymen who could engage in any profession or follow any calling. . . . Gone were the days
when literacy and erudition were reserved for the clergy.[67]

The adverse effects of the Reformation on university self-rule, free entry,
and free scope were probably the most acute in Germany, where Rudy (1984,
70) describes a pattern "of university subjugation to the will of the state." A
key aspect was increased state funding, a feature that had always existed to
some extent, since typically German universities did not develop spontaneously.[68] Some historians have also argued that German states' desire for
control was stronger due to their smaller average size; for example, Paulsen
(1906, 72) states "The smallness of the German territories favored the con-
ception of the state as a single great household under a 'paternal' government." Regardless, by the end of what historians label the early modern
period (around 1789), German universities were fully controlled by their
states, and professors were essentially public servants.

For our purposes, the outcome in France was qualitatively similar, with
the key difference being that control was even more centralized. Around
1500, Louis XII limited the universities' privileges, and local *parlements*
began to control them; by 1600 Henry IV had put the University of Paris
under civil rule.[69] Louis XIV further enhanced state control, and the Revolution completed the task, dissolving universities and confiscating college
endowments. The National Convention and the Napoleonic regime reassembled the system, with elements including limitations on scope; for example, they created and/or reinforced institutions with narrowly defined
missions. For instance, some of the *grandes écoles* were focused only on business or engineering, while standalone institutions like the *Collège de France*
(earlier known as the *Collège Royal*) received research-related tasks. The
academies, organized around the *Institut de France,* continued to have a large
role in intellectual life.[70] Through multiple subsequent reforms, the state
kept control.

The effects of the Reformation on universities were least acute in
England, among the countries we have focused on, particularly concerning the reduction in self-rule. Metzger (1973, 108) suggests that this
was not necessarily because the English crown had a different intent, but

because institutional development had better equipped English schools to resist:

> If anything, the academic policies of the English kings were even more [draconian], their spoliations of academic offices even more incessant, their assaults on academic autonomy even more far-reaching than anything accomplished by the Valois or Habsburgs or by the princelets of the German states. Yet the teachers of Oxford and Cambridge held to their corporate traditions more successfully than did their foreign counterparts. Fatefully for these universities and for the American colonial schools they sired, something else transpired in this period: the triumph of . . . the collegiate way.[71]

The English colleges' endowments made state support less essential / attractive and allowed them to invest in lavish buildings and expensive tutorial instruction. Catering to wealthy students provided some protection that mostly allowed them to keep their wealth and eventually reclaim some self-rule. Metzger (1973, 110) adds: "the prosperous condition of the colleges gave assurance that they could live with rampaging monarchs and ride out the Reformation storms."[72] Morison (1936, 42) similarly adds that for a time it seemed like the English colleges would lose their lands just like many monasteries had, but eventually the king declared that he had nowhere else in his realm seen "so many persons so honestly mayntayned in lyvying bi so little lond and rent." The colleges also derived strength from the fact that they had essentially taken over educational tasks from the university.

By contrast, on the Continent the Reformation ended the colleges' existence. This was both due to educational reforms and the fact that strengthening secondary schools meant that students arrived at universities older and in less need of supervision. Butts (1939, 46) summarizes the situation in Germany:

> as Protestantism destroyed in the universities the old ecclesiastical order with its celibacy and cloister life, the communal college with its dormitory life and monastic seclusion began to disappear. In the German commercial towns . . . the students began to live about the towns much

as other professional men lived. Much of the arts curriculum had been pushed down into secondary schools and thus made a longer secondary education necessary, so that most students were now older than students had been in previous centuries when they came to the university. Since the students were more mature (seventeen or eighteen years old) the college as an institution disappeared.

Verger (1986) discusses analogous developments in France.

The bottom line is that by the 1600s, the European university market displayed a much lower free-market orientation than it did in say the 1300s, or than the present-day United States. The next chapter describes how the United States followed the opposite trajectory: from low to high market orientation.

Before turning to that, and although this book's focus is on the United States, it is worth noting that state control did have positive impacts on European universities' research output. For example, between 1700 and 1850—years in which many American colleges were reaching their low point—European states encouraged (and provided funding for) universities to supply specialized and advanced instruction. They helped them incorporate scientific work that had been previously housed in non-university venues like learned societies. This development was most marked in Germany, where schools like Halle, Göttingen, and later Berlin became centers of academic activity, with the additional benefit of some competition between them; for example, some attempted to hire each other's professors. It was less the case in France, given greater centralization and the fact that research-focused institutions (e.g., the *Collège de France*) retained greater roles at the expense of universities.[73] In any case, it allowed European schools to lead in research, even if later on market dynamics emphasized in Part I would help the United States take the lead.

CHAPTER 7

The United States

AT INDEPENDENCE, the United States had nine colleges,
listed in Table 7.1 (including their original designation—this chapter mostly
uses their current designation). This chapter discusses how the creation
of seven of these reveals the origin of the free-market orientation of the
American university system, particularly of the prevalence of self-rule and
free entry.

The first three colleges were founded in Massachusetts, Virginia, and
Connecticut. This chapter will argue that these colonies did not provide a
setting conducive to the emergence of a free college market. The reason for
this is that they contained religiously homogeneous populations heavily influenced by the Magisterial Reformation (Chapter 6). Their leaders thus
wanted church and state to regulate society jointly; for instance, in New
England, to create a Calvinist "city upon a hill." As a result, they created
territorial-confessional colleges that civil and religious authorities controlled and helped finance.[1]

The second part of the chapter turns to the Middle Atlantic, where the
colonies of New Jersey, New York, and Pennsylvania provided a very different setting for college founding. They displayed much greater religious
heterogeneity, a trait that the authorities were unwilling to suppress, and
in some cases, even encouraged. This led college founders to begin envi-
sioning schools that might be left to their own devices; for example, in
terms of funding, this set the stage for self-rule to emerge. It also led authorities to envision that each denomination might create and pay for its own
college; this set the stage for free entry. In other words, while the Middle
Atlantic continued to produce confessional colleges, these ceased to be

Table 7.1   The colonial colleges

Year created	Current name	Original name, if different	Colony
1636	Harvard University	New College	Massachusetts
1693	College of William and Mary		Virginia
1701	Yale University	Collegiate School	Connecticut
1746	Princeton University	The College of New Jersey	New Jersey
1754	Columbia University in the City of New York	King's College	New York
1755	University of Pennsylvania	The College of Philadelphia	Pennsylvania
1764	Brown University	College of Rhode Island	Rhode Island
1766	Rutgers University	Queen's College	New Jersey
1769	Dartmouth College		New Hampshire

The table lists the nine colonial colleges by their date of founding, indicating their current and original designation.

territorial, and this prepared the way for the massive entry that followed independence (Chapter 2).

Finally, a third section of the chapter turns to post-independence events at Dartmouth College in New Hampshire, where a Supreme Court ruling ultimately cemented self-rule.

New England and the South

European colonists had not been in America long before their attention turned to providing higher education. This desire might have been particularly intense in Massachusetts and Connecticut, where Puritans—strict Calvinists with a scriptural rather than sacramental approach to religion—emphasized an educated clergy and a literate flock.[2] But it was also evident in Virginia, where Anglicans, members of the official English church, were the dominant group.

Founders in these three colonies faced broadly similar economic and legal constraints. Their incomes were low and their jurisdictions new; their immediate concerns surrounded not whether new colleges might afford lavish buildings in the English style, but whether they would survive. Legally, ambiguity surrounded their ability to create institutions of higher learning. Some observers contended that royal approval was necessary; that is, that the colonists should procure charters from Europe, as the Spanish colonists had done by petitioning the Holy Roman Emperor.[3] These concerns were perhaps more salient in Massachusetts and Connecticut, where the colonists' status as religious dissenters made them wary of contact with the English authorities. Even in Virginia, however, there was concern about proceeding in ways the authorities in London would tolerate.

These founders also desired religious uniformity. This sentiment was again perhaps most intense in New England where, in the words of Hofstadter (1955, 79): "the Puritans held [that] . . . anyone who was willing to tolerate the active propagation of a religion other than his own was simply not sincere in it. A state that would give liberty of conscience in matters of religion might just as well give liberty of conscience in its moral laws." We now describe how these conditions led to the creation of Harvard, William and Mary, and Yale. The governance that the colonists designed for each of these schools had two key traits. First, the founders sought to achieve joint state/church control by putting the colleges in the hands of external boards composed of civil and religious authorities. Associated with this came an expectation that colonial governments would play a key role in supervising and financially supporting their school. Second, and perhaps out of necessity, internally the founders placed power in the hands of a president rather than those of the faculty, as had been the practice in Europe.

Harvard

In 1636 the Massachusetts General Court allocated "400£ towards a schoale or colledge."[4] This was not spare change; Morison (1935) calculates it was equivalent to more than half the colony's tax revenue for 1635. The same act set up a committee to "take order for [the] college."[5] This body was the first Board of Overseers and consisted of equal numbers of civil and religious officials: the colony's governor, deputy governor, and treasurer, three magistrates, and six ministers. All of them had full time occupations and were thus outsiders. The Court implicitly gave this group only temporary status, as none of its members served *ex officio,* and there was no provision for their replacement.[6]

We remark on three aspects of this configuration. First, the board's membership envisioned joint state and church control. Second, the setup was in stark contrast with that in the original European universities. There the masters secured self-rule, and in the case of England, managed to retain a fair amount of it through the Reformation. At Harvard control was never in the hands of the faculty. Third, by this point the idea of placing ultimate control of a school in external hands was not new. Europe had already seen visitors at English colleges, *reformatores* in Italy, and *curatores* in Holland.[7] In Scotland the universities of Edinburgh and New Aberdeen had close connections with their town governments, and the non-university academies that arose in England in the wake of the Reformation had external boards too.[8]

In 1636 a group of colonists, including John Harvard and Nathaniel Eaton, arrived in Boston. Morison (1936, 8) explains that most of them continued south because, "[as] . . . Londoners and traders, . . . [they] wanted a good harbor . . . and after carefully examining the coastline they decided that Massachusetts had nothing so good to offer as Quinnipiac, which they purchased from the Indians and named New Haven." Eaton and Harvard remained in Boston, however, and the Board of Overseers hired Eaton, a graduate of Trinity College (Cambridge), as first master of the new college. John Harvard, who had been enthusiastic about the school, died of tuberculosis two years later, leaving it half of his estate; the Court renamed the school in his honor.

Eaton did not work out as well. Students and staff claimed that he beat them and that his wife provided poor food. A member of the Board remarked that Eaton was fitter to lead a bridewell than a college, a reference to the Bridewell Residence in London, which housed homeless children, petty criminals, and "disorderly women."[9] The General Court fired Eaton and suspended the college's operations. The fact that it took this action directly underlines that it did not see itself as having created a self-ruling institution from which it would remain at arm's length.

In 1640 the Board of Overseers hired Henry Dunster, another Cambridge graduate, and designated him president rather than master. The change in designation may have been an acknowledgment that in the colonies, survival would require strong leadership, and a bet that Dunster could provide it. This paid off: over fourteen years Dunster stabilized the school, implemented a Cambridge-inspired curriculum, and saw multiple graduating classes complete it. In part this was thanks to continued financial support from the Court: it granted Harvard the revenues of the Boston-Charlestown ferry, the tolls for the bridge that later replaced it, and about two thousand acres of land.[10]

In this period the Court also reconstituted the Board of Overseers as a permanent body with seventeen rather than six members: the governor and deputy governor, all assistants to the Court, pastors and teachers of adjoining towns, and the college president. The Board was empowered to draft statutes and administer operations. The absence of faculty participation on this body was noted by observers including Dunster; perhaps since at his alma mater, Emmanuel College, control still resided in a self-perpetuating collection of fellows, and the master elected from among them was seen as a *primus inter pares*.[11]

One can see some subsequent changes, likely proposed by Dunster himself, as attempting to move Harvard toward this English model. In particular, in 1650 the Court incorporated the President and Fellows of Harvard College, a body usually referred to as the Corporation. This entity's official designation suggests that Dunster had in mind a larger role for faculty, with the overseers, who retained the right to counsel and consent, assuming a visitatorial role.[12] Yet Metzger (1973, 111) points out that "the document was not without traces of ambiguity, or perhaps one should say evidence of double-mindedness."

Specifically, the statutes stipulated that the Corporation was to consist of the president, treasurer, and the five tutors who accounted for the entire teaching faculty at the time. But the statutes did not specify whether these tutors served *ex officio*—that is, whether the role was envisioned for every faculty member ever hired, or only for the five individuals named.

The question was relevant because at the time Harvard could not consistently afford a teaching staff of five, and at times pastors of neighboring congregations were appointed to the Corporation.[13] This created a precedent that the members of the Corporation, like those of the Board of Overseers, did not need to be faculty members; over time the two groups came to resemble each other in composition. In addition, the Overseers remained much more involved than would have been typical of English visitors, and the General Court continued its supervision too. Herbst (1982, 12) summarizes the situation: "Within the college the Overseers functioned as unincorporated trustees sharing authority with the Corporation and exercising implicit veto power over its major decisions. . . . As trustees and cogovernors, they could be said to be themselves under the visitatorial jurisdiction of the General Court." Whatever Dunster's true intent, over time tutors ceased to be automatically appointed to the Corporation—one complained of being treated "not as a colleague, but as an employé."[14] By the late 1700s, the Overseers effectively transferred control to the Corporation, but as Metzger (1973, 113) points out, "by that time the external board was deferring very largely to a mirror image of itself." The final result, *de facto,* was control by a single external board composed of colonial and church officials.

The end of Henry Dunster's presidency serves to underline the territorial/confessional nature of the college Massachusetts created. In the early 1650s, Dunster began to reveal his opposition to infant baptism publicly. For the authorities this was a grave matter; as stated above, a society in which people could choose when to get baptized could hardly claim to be a "city upon a hill." In a significant gesture, the Overseers offered to ignore the issue if Dunster promised to remain silent, but he resigned. Ironically, his successor Charles Chauncy turned out to raise related issues. He accepted infant baptism, but believed that it should feature total immersion, as was typical with adult baptism. The Governor decreed the colony could live with this, adding that the practice probably had a greater bearing "on infant mortality than infant immortality."[15]

The bottom line is that Massachusetts introduced innovations in college design, but it ultimately approached education as did many Calvinist jurisdictions in Europe. This was not a place where self-rule and free entry were likely to emerge.

William and Mary

Virginia took longer to sustain a college than Massachusetts, which may be somewhat surprising given that at the revolutionary war, the southern colonies were wealthier than their New England counterparts.[16] On the other hand, Herbst (1982) notes that Virginia's plantation-oriented economy featured fewer urban centers and large congregations that might have sustained schools.

The first successful effort there centered around the efforts of James Blair, the representative of the Bishop of London and head of the Anglican church in Virginia.[17] The work began in the 1690s, with the creation of a grammar school. As the Virginia Assembly sought to expand this investment, it asked Blair to go to London, obtain a charter, and define an institutional design. Its specific instructions were: "make it your business to peruse the best charters in England whereby free schools and colleges have been founded . . . having always regard to the constitution of this country and government."[18] Herbst (1982) indicates that the mention of schools and colleges may have reflected that a school typically did not require a charter, and hence it might have been easier to set up if the English authorities had reservations about college creation. Such reservations existed, apparently. The story goes that when Blair told the English Attorney-General that a college might help save the colonists' souls, he replied, "Souls! Damn your souls! Make tobacco!"[19]

In any event, Blair was advised that a royally chartered college would be less likely to turn into a center of religious dissent, and that a strong leader might give discipline to the masters.[20] In addition, some members of the Virginia Assembly considered that external governors would allow greater control than the incorporation of masters and fellows, and having studied in Scotland, Blair was presumably aware of such models.[21] Herbst (1982, 33) summarizes the consensus that emerged: "a provincial council could prevent the college from turning into a seatbed of dissenters. If, in addition, a trusted president, backed by a Chancellor in London, acted as liaison between the . . . board of control and the academic corporation . . . , joint secular and ecclesiastic government would be assured and both Royal and Anglican interests well represented." The end result was a second American territorial-confessional college ultimately controlled by an external board.

Specifically, Blair returned to Virginia with a charter authorizing eighteen "gentlemen" to act as trustees with the power to draft and modify statutes. He would be among them, as would the colony's lieutenant-governor, with the remaining members to be elected by the General Assembly. Masters and scholars were required to submit to this board, and to make an oath to the crown and the Anglican church.[22]

From here and for our purposes, the school's development parallels that of Harvard in key ways. First, like Harvard, it enjoyed public financial support. It was designated the College of William and Mary in honor of the sitting monarchs, received a 2,000 pound grant from King William, and the proceeds of taxes on tobacco, skins, and furs from the colony.[23] At a symbolic level, eventually the main street of colonial Williamsburg had the capitol at one end and the college at the other. Second, like at Harvard there was a strong foundational president: Blair not only participated in the design of the school, he later served in several of its leadership roles. Third, in Virginia there was also ambiguity regarding a role for the faculty in governance. The charter contemplated that once the masters were in place, they were to join the president to form a corporation that would manage the college, with the trustees supervising them as governors and visitors. This is roughly the formulation that Dunster seems to have wanted at Harvard, and it did work for a while in Virginia. But in time, the external visitors reasserted their power, effectively ending faculty control in the United States.[24]

The bottom line is that one can see Virginia as ultimately reaffirming the model that had come out of Cambridge: territorial / confessional control achieved through an external board that featured active participation from state officials, combined with a strong president.

Yale

Connecticut provided the third venue for college creation in the United States.[25] As early as 1647, six years after the creation of Harvard, the Puritans there were already entertaining such a venture. In that year the town court of New Haven created a committee "to consider and reserve what lot they shall see meet and most commodious for a college . . . ."[26] By 1700 this desire had grown more intense, in part due to a perception among Connecticut Puritans that Harvard was no longer sufficiently orthodox.[27] In 1701 the Connecticut General Court stated that:

> WHEREAS several well disposed, and Publick spirited Persons of their sincere Regard to & Zeal for upholding and propagating the Christian Protestant Religion by a succession of Learned & Orthodox men have expressed their earnest desires that fully Liberty and Priveledge be granted unto Certain Undertakers for the founding, suitably endowing & ordering a Collegiate School within his Majties Colony of Connecticot wherein Youth may be instructed in the Arts & Sciences . . . .[28]

and granted a charter to a board of trustees.

In this case the design went straight to a single board without faculty participation—this would henceforth become the standard issue design in the colonies.[29] Although the board was composed of twelve ministers and no colonial officials, the Court retained the right to review the college's bylaws, and in 1792 the charter was updated to include state officials *ex officio*. In addition, as in Massachusetts and Virginia, financial support from the colony was immediate and substantial. Kelley (1974) points out that during the 1700s, Connecticut's General Court contributed about half of Yale's total funding, and at times exempted its students from taxation. Writing about the college between 1701 and 1740, Warch (1973, 137) states, "Ministers created and shaped the collegiate school; legislators paid for it."

Like the College of William and Mary, Yale required a religious oath from teachers and students. Like both of its predecessors, it relied on strong executive leadership.[30]

To summarize, college creation in these three settings broadly followed a territorial-confessional model featuring elements like participation by civil authorities, religious oaths, and significant public support. Thus, these colonies did not provide an environment in which self-rule and free entry were likely to emerge.

In fact, Connecticut provides a concrete example of limitations on entry. The school that eventually gave rise to Dartmouth (Table 7.1) was originally in Connecticut rather than New Hampshire. It was created by Eleazar Wheelock, a Puritan himself, for the education of "Indian boys in the Christian Faith." In the early 1760s, Wheelock petitioned the Connecticut General Court to transform his school into a college. The Court turned down the request, in part out of fears that the school might eventually compete with Yale for white students.[31]

The Middle Atlantic

About fifty years after Yale opened, college creation began in the Middle Atlantic. The colonies in this region provided a different setting, in part because they contained significantly greater religious heterogeneity. Finke and Stark (2005) explain that this is hard to quantify precisely before 1890, but they provide estimates based on counts of congregations rather than individuals.[32] Table 7.2 uses their data to describe denominational prevalence in the New England and Middle Atlantic colonies that had colleges in 1776. In each case, the first column contains data for the whole region, and the remaining refer to individual colonies.

The rows contain the percentage share of each denomination, and the last row summarizes this information in a Herfindahl index, a measure that ranges between zero and one. An area with an index close to one is extremely homogeneous—effectively monopolized by a single denomination; one with an index close to zero is very diverse, with each denomination accounting for only a small share of the population.

Table 7.2 shows that in 1776, the Middle Atlantic colonies were much less homogeneous than their New England counterparts (the South, not listed, provides an intermediate case). By the summary measure (last row), Massachusetts was at one extreme, and New York at the other. Namely, in Massachusetts the Puritans (referred to as Congregationalists by Finke and Stark for reasons addressed below) accounted for 72 percent of congregations, and the next largest denomination, the Baptists, for only 14 percent. The Puritan share was likely even higher at the time Harvard was founded, because initially the Puritans expelled Baptists from Massachusetts (part of the reason for their high prevalence in neighboring Rhode Island). In contrast, in New York the denomination with the highest share, the Dutch

Table 7.2 Denominational shares by region and state, 1776

Denomination	New England					Middle Atlantic				South	
	Total	Conn.	Mass.	New Hamp.	Rhode Island	Total	New Jersey	New York	Penn.	Total	Virginia
Congregationalist	63.0	64.2	71.6	63.2	17.2	0.3	0.4	1.8		0.1	
Presbyterian	5.5	1.3	3.0	21.6	1.1	24.6	30.5	15.9	27.9	24.9	22.2
Baptist	15.3	9.4	14.3	8.8	57.5	7.6	18.3	8.2	4.9	28.0	29.9
Episcopal	8.4	17.7	3.7	1.6	6.9	12.9	11.5	15.5	6.0	27.8	34.6
Quaker	3.8	1.6	4.2	3.2	12.6	14.1	15.5	10.9	15.3	9.0	7.1
German Reformed						9.8	2.4	4.5	17.6	2.8	1.6
Lutheran						8.6	9.5	8.6	9.7	3.8	1.8
Dutch Reformed						8.9	3.2	26.4	8.6		
Methodist						3.8	6.0	3.2	0.2	1.4	2.0
Roman Catholic						4.2	2.0	0.5	1.9	0.1	0.2
Moravian					1.1	1.8	0.4	2.3	2.6	0.6	0.6
Other	3.6	5.8	3.0	1.6	3.4	3.1		2.3	5.4	1.2	0.6
Herfindahl index	0.43	0.46	0.54	0.46	0.38	0.13	0.18	0.15	0.16	0.23	0.26

This table presents descriptive statistics based on data in Finke and Stark (2005). The columns list the shares of different denominations for New England and the Middle Atlantic and, within each region, for the colonies that had colleges by 1776. "Other" includes Separatist and independent, Dunker, Mennonite, Huguenot, Sandemanian, and Jewish. The bottom row presents the Herfindahl index for each jurisdiction, given by <eq>Ch14_CAP_001.pdf</eq>, where s_i is the proportional share of each denomination.

Reformed, accounted for only 26 percent of congregations. While in New England three denominations (Congregationalist, Episcopalian, Baptist) had a share of at least 10 percent, in the Middle Atlantic there were six: Episcopalian (also known as Anglican), Baptist, Lutheran, Quaker, Dutch Reformed, and German Reformed.[33]

One can see each region's heterogeneity as an outcome of the objectives and attitudes that guided their settlement. As stated, European immigration into Boston began with English Puritans who wished to create a religious society and purify the English church, and who made it clear that they wished to be joined by those with a similar goal. Not surprisingly, historians suggest that early on New England was aptly named; for example, in the 1790 census, 82 percent of the Massachusetts population was of English descent.[34] By contrast, European settlement of New York City began after Giovanni da Verrazzano sailed into New York Bay and declared the surrounding harbor to be "not without some properties of value."[35] Many agreed, and by the 1600s Manhattan was receiving Dutch, English, and French (Huguenot) immigrants who often intended to make money rather than create a city upon a hill.[36] Archdeacon (1983) reports that as early as 1643, a French Jesuit priest reported eighteen languages being spoken in Manhattan.

These approaches naturally fostered different amounts of religious diversity. To illustrate, authorities in Boston and New Amsterdam reacted differently to the arrival of Quakers. This group posed a challenge because its members resisted assimilation and were prone to public displays of their faith; for example, neighbors reported they were liable "to quake and go into a frenzy."[37] In Boston, the authorities often detained them and asked them to move to Rhode Island, using the death penalty on four occasions in which they refused. In New Amsterdam, Governor Peter Stuyvesant also wished to exile them but was instructed by the Dutch East India Company to "shut your eyes" lest doing so scare away immigration.[38] Similarly, when a group of Jewish settlers arrived in 1654, Stuyvesant wrote to Amsterdam requesting "that these godless rascals. . . . may be sent away . . . ." The authorities declined, citing the "large amount of capital, which . . . [Dutch Jews] have invested in . . . this company."[39] In some dimensions, Philadelphia went even further; for example, William Penn's 1701 charter of privileges was explicit in granting protections to various religious groups, leading to large inflows of Mennonites and Quakers. Such attitudes likely contributed to the fact that during the 1700s New York and Philadelphia overtook Boston to become the largest cities in the colonies.

In addition to all this, college creation began later in the Middle Atlantic, perhaps better allowing the notion to develop that a successful society might be feasible without church and state working to impose a single religion.[40] Support for this principle would have reached the Middle Atlantic from places like the Netherlands and Scotland, sources of Dutch Reformed and Presbyterian immigrants into the region. While the Netherlands remained officially Calvinist, by 1648 the government allowed several rights for Catholics, Anabaptists, and Jews. Similarly, by the 1700s the Scottish Enlightenment was underway, with scholars like David Hume and Adam Smith influencing elite opinion.[41] More generally, by about 1650 the end of the Thirty Years' War and the Peace of Westphalia initiated an era in which religion lost its role as a salient driver of interstate conflict in Europe.[42]

All this does not mean that religion was less salient in the Middle Atlantic. While denominations may have been able to coexist, there was significant inter- and even intradenominational tension. For example, in the 1730s and 40s a conflict arose within Presbyterianism that was ultimately crucial to college creation. These years saw multiple "awakenings," periods of increased religious fervor expressed in mass meetings and conversions.[43] Charismatic itinerant preachers proliferated, the most notable being George Whitefield. Benjamin Franklin wrote of his performances:

> By hearing him often I came to distinguish easily between sermons newly composed and those which he had often preached. . . . His delivery of the latter was so improved by frequent repetition that every accent, every emphasis, every modulation of voice was so perfectly well turned and well-placed that, without being interested in the subject, one could not help being pleased with the discourse, the pleasure much the same kind with that received from an excellent piece of music. . . .[44]

Initially Presbyterian (and Puritan) ministers were sympathetic to preachers like Whitefield. But eventually a split emerged: those friendly to thcm were labeled new lights, and those skeptical of the new "enthusiasm" were called old lights. To see the source of this split, recall that being Calvinists, Presbyterians believed in predestination: one was either saved or not as determined by God, and one could not influence one's status in this dimension. Kelley (1974, 15) notes that a chosen individual, known as a visible saint, would become aware of his state "through the conversion experience, a moment when he felt absolutely dependent on God and suddenly knew that God had saved him." All one could do was lead a virtuous life in preparation for this moment of grace. Strictly speaking, further, only visible saints could be members of the Puritan church.

In time some of the itinerants began to suggest that the old light ministers were not visible saints, and thus were not suited to lead their congregations' preparation for conversion. This at least implicitly gave people license to leave these ministers' flocks.[45] The conflict also took on an educational dimension. Calvinists had historically emphasized schooling, but many of the itinerants had few educational credentials, and perhaps as a result began to claim that grace was more important than schooling, and that in the extreme, the latter could get in the way of the former.

Inevitably, colleges were dragged into this controversy. For instance, after visiting Harvard and Yale, Whitefield said both were places "where light is become darkness."[46] In response, in 1743 the Harvard faculty issued a "Testimony against the Reverend Mr. George Whitefield and his conduct," stating: "And we do . . . hereby declare, that we look upon his going about, in an Itinerant way, especially as he hath so much of an Enthusiastic Turn, utterly inconsistent with the Peace and Order, if not that very Being of the Churches of Christ."[47] Other parts of the Calvinist establishment responded too. In 1742 the Connecticut assembly began to require that all ministers have a college degree and granted incumbents the right to forbid itinerants from preaching in their parishes. In addition, it reaffirmed that Yale students and faculty had to swear whatever oaths the college required.[48]

With this background, we proceed to the emergence of Princeton, Columbia, Pennsylvania, and Rutgers. To preview some themes, we will note that the founders by and large kept the internal structure that had emerged at Yale: control in the hands of one external board, and managerial power vested in a president rather than the faculty. In contrast, they began to abandon the territorial-confessional model. Although no universal configuration emerged, in most cases colonial officials were no longer represented on boards or were no longer in the majority, and in general, there was less of an expectation of colonial financial support. As Rudolph (1962, 13) states, the colleges did receive public contributions, but on average "nothing so certain, nothing so regular, nothing so generous as the aid that owed into Cambridge, Williamsburg, and New Haven . . . ."

With these changes, the notion that colleges could be self-ruling began to emerge. In addition, the idea that even within one colony each denomination might have a school came to the fore, as New Jersey ended up with two colleges, each catering to a different religious group. With this development, the notion that there could be free entry similarly appeared.

Princeton

In the 1730s Presbyterians in New Jersey belonged to three presbyteries—supervising bodies that had oversight over local congregations and could conduct visitations and mediate in conflicts. The three presbyteries, in turn, belonged to the Synod of Philadelphia, an even higher court. When discussions surrounding the creation of a college began, ministers in these three groups generally took different positions.

One group of new light ministers working around Elizabeth and Newark (New Jersey) belonged to the Presbytery of New York (which included parts of both colonies) and favored the creation of a college. Another group, located further south in the Presbytery of New Brunswick, was more involved in the awakening and less concerned with educational activity; it considered the local schools and academies sufficient. A third group even further south in the Presbytery of Philadelphia, was distinctly old side; its members were suspicious of religious enthusiasm and were content to use Yale, which they viewed as a source of suitably orthodox training for ministers.[49]

Tensions came to a head with events surrounding William Tennent Sr., a Scotsman who ran a one-room schoolhouse in Bucks County, Pennsylvania. This school, known as the Log College, trained men for the ministry. The New Brunswick Presbytery approved the ministerial appointment of a Log College graduate, generating protests that reached the Synod of

Philadelphia. This body turned down the appointment on the grounds that Tennent and his students were "destroyers of good learning."[50] In 1738 the Synod ruled that henceforth, newly appointed ministers would need to have a degree from Harvard, Yale, or a European university. Not surprisingly, the new lights were upset, and Whitefield further raised the tension with a sermon titled "The danger of an unconverted ministry" in which Bonomi (1986, 143) notes he drew an analogy "between the opposers in the Philadelphia Synod who rejected experiential religion, and the legalistic Pharisees . . . who had rejected the radical teachings of Jesus." By 1745 the disagreement produced a formal split, with the presbyteries of New York and New Brunswick coalescing into a new Synod of New York.[51]

The Philadelphia Synod proceeded to make a more formal training arrangement with Yale, and the new lights continued to consider setting up a college. One later stated that the final straw came when Yale expelled a young evangelist, David Brainerd, for stating that one of Yale's tutors had "no more grace than the chair I am leaning upon."[52]

The new lights realized, however, that such a school would require colonial approval, possibly by charter, and that this would be difficult to obtain if their only goal was to train Presbyterian ministers. The group expected, further, that the survival of a new college would require that it appeal to students of different denominations. They therefore adopted a more general objective, with one of them stating: "Though our great intention was to erect a seminary for educating Ministers of the Gospel, yet we hope it will be useful in other learned professions—ornaments of the state as well as the church."[53]

Their initiative resulted in the creation of the College of New Jersey with a charter stating that the school was not to exclude any "Person of any religious Denomination whatsoever from free and Equal Liberty and Advantage of Education . . . on account of his or their speculative Sentiments in Religion and of his or their belonging to other Religious profession Different from the said Trustees of the College."[54] The founders followed Yale in placing control in a single external Board of Trustees that could draft and amend bylaws, and was empowered to appoint a president, faculty members, and staff.

In its first incarnation, the board had only seven members appointed as individuals rather than *ex officio*. All were Presbyterian, and none was a colonial official; three lived in New Jersey, and the other four in New York.

In other words, the governance of the college had a religious rather than political nature. Further, the understanding was that the college should not expect direct financial support from the colony, although it did receive authorizations to run lotteries.[55] In short, despite protestations to the contrary, the college had a clear confessional character; but importantly, it was, despite its designation, less of a territorial college than its predecessors; for example, the majority of board members lived in New York.

Later the board did see some colonial involvement. This happened because soon after the charter was authorized, Jonathan Belcher was installed as Royal Governor of New Jersey. He took an interest in the college, which he said he had adopted "for my daughter."[56] Belcher asked the trustees for *ex officio* membership for himself and four of his councilors. While they resisted the idea, they implemented a compromise by which the governor joined the board by virtue of his office, but the four councilors as individuals. These changes increased the number of trustees from nine ministers and three laymen to twelve ministers, ten laymen, and the governor. The new board retained its intercolonial character, now with members from New Jersey, New York, and Pennsylvania.

Like its predecessors, the college had a modest start. It enrolled ten students under President Jonathan Dickinson, who continued to serve as the pastor of the First Presbyterian Church in Elizabeth. Oberdorfer (1995, 16) states that in the first year, "The instructors were Dickinson and one of his divinity students, who served as a tutor; the dormitories, the spare rooms in the president's house or those of neighbors; the lecture hall, his parlor."

Columbia

The push for a New York college was led by Anglicans, who despite not being in the majority in the colony, enjoyed power and prestige in part because of their allegiance to the official Church of England. The group that led the charge viewed religious and educational developments with concern. The awakenings threatened established religion, and the creation of Princeton in their own backyard showed other denominations taking the educational lead.

In 1746 the Governor authorized a lottery to raise money for a college and created a board to oversee this activity. Anglican individuals and institutions began to support the initiative; for instance, Trinity Church, the leading congregation in Manhattan, offered a site for the school at the northern end of its property.[57]

In part due to New York's religious diversity, opposition emerged against the sectarian configuration the school seemed to be taking. This was led by William Livingston, a Presbyterian politician suspicious of the Anglican initiative. Livingston agreed with the Anglican promoters that a college would help counter religious enthusiasm, but although he did not put it in these terms, he advocated for a purely territorial college; that is, for placing the board of trustees under legislative control. It was in the legislature, he argued, where all denominational groups found representation.[58] Consistent with this, Livingston also opposed the use of the Trinity site.

In 1753 the lottery board chose Samuel Johnson, a former Yale tutor who had defected to Anglicanism and received a doctorate from Oxford, as president of the college. Johnston seems to have given indications that he was not interested in running a sectarian school, and Livingston's group did not oppose his election.[59]

That same year the lottery trustees obtained charters for King's College from both the Governor and the Crown. The statutes required that the president be Anglican, but otherwise the board had multidenominational representation. It consisted of forty-one members, twenty-four (mainly Anglican and Dutch Reformed) laymen named as individuals. The remaining seventeen, named *ex officio,* included the president of the college and the First Lord Commissioner of Trade and Plantations in London, the Archbishop of Canterbury, the rector of Trinity Church, the senior minister of the Dutch Reformed Church, and ministers of Lutheran, French, and Presbyterian churches in the city.[60] In addition, the Dutch Reformed Church was allowed to endow a chair of divinity. As in New Jersey, the charter was explicit that no one could be excluded for reason of religion and contained no provision for colonial financial support (although Columbia would later receive ample state support). The college also received the land donated by Trinity church.

Livingston's group made a last-ditch effort to stop the school by urging the assembly not to release the lottery funds, and in the end there was a compromise that split the proceeds between the college and New York City.

With this, Livingston gave up his struggle to prevent King's College from having a primarily denominational (Anglican and to a limited extent Dutch Reformed) governance. He stated "relative to the affair of the College, we stood as long as our legs would support us, and, I may add, even fought for some time on our stumps."[61]

Rutgers

Just as Anglicans had worried about Princeton's configuration, the Dutch Reformed had reservations about Columbia's, despite having some representation on its board. In particular, the Dutch Reformed group involved with Columbia was led by John Ritzema, senior minister of the Dutch Reformed Collegiate Church in New York City (Ritzema was a member of the first Columbia board).

A different group, more active upstate and in New Jersey, was led by Theodore Frelinghuysen. Its members felt that they would be ill-served by what they perceived to be a Presbyterian college in New Jersey and an Anglican one in New York, and that they should therefore attempt to sponsor their own school. At the same time, they were well aware that the prospects of colonial financial support were slim at best: by now both New Jersey and New York had colleges, and neither colony had promised much in the way of financial support even to the one it had.

With this in mind, they began to argue that they should be allowed to open another school, provided that they were willing to fund it. Frelinghuysen pseudonymously articulated this in a pamphlet that applied notions of American self-reliance to higher education. Not only did he break with the European territorial-confessional idea by advocating for a second college in New Jersey, he argued there was space for even more: "Let us Men, and Brethren, put our Trust in God, and be unanimous among ourselves, and not hearken to domineering parties who endeavor to divide us; we have no Business with their Colleges; they may erect as many as they please, and must expect to maintain them too themselves. Let every one provide for his own House . . ."[62]

In 1766, Frelinghuysen's wish became a reality when the colony of New Jersey granted Queen's College a charter. The school's board was intercolonial, including trustees from New Jersey, New York, and Pennsylvania. While two thirds of the seats were reserved for members of the Dutch Reformed Church, the board also included the Governor, Council President, Chief Justice, and Attorney General of New Jersey. As Herbst (1982) points out, the result was somewhat paradoxical: Queen's was arguably even more built to suit a single denomination than Princeton, and yet it ended up with a board that implied somewhat greater governmental supervision. Herbst speculates this might have been an insurance policy of sorts: the school was keen to garner protection from the authorities, particularly since it served an ethnic as well as a religious minority.

Regardless, from our point of view, the creation of Rutgers was momentous. It established the precedent that a colony or state could have multiple colleges, that these could be created to serve denominational ends, and that they could be expected to fend for themselves. These were the principles behind self-rule, free entry, and the massive creation of colleges that took place after independence (Chapter 2).

Pennsylvania

Finally, in 1744 a group of prominent Philadelphia laymen began to raise funds for what they termed an academy. In 1749, they signed the "Constitutions of the Public Academy in the City of Philadelphia" and elected Benjamin Franklin as President. That same year the school began to operate in a building that George Whitefield had acquired to house a charity school that never materialized.

The school's board consisted of the twenty-four individuals who had made the largest contributions. Of these, eight were merchants, four physicians, and the rest prominent individuals like Franklin. None were government officials. While the distinct majority were Anglican, their appointment originated in their wealth and prestige rather than their religious affiliation. Further, as at Princeton, there was a relatively low expectation of colonial support. In short, in the case of Pennsylvania the configuration moved away not only from a territorial but also from a confessional orientation. One might say that here again, the principles behind self-rule and free entry were crystallizing.

To summarize, the Middle Atlantic saw the territorial/confessional college model laid to rest, and the essential elements of self-rule and free entry put in place. One begins to see external boards with reduced colonial participation and lower expectations of public support. The creation of Rutgers, further, was an implicit acceptance of the rationale that would later produce massive entry.

The Dartmouth Case

Despite the developments that took place in the Middle Atlantic, after 1776 legal ambiguity still surrounded who ultimately controlled colleges. Would self-rule be a definitive trait of the American university system? To illustrate, having authorized the creation of Princeton, could New Jersey revise the charter it had granted? A legal case involving Dartmouth College ultimately settled such questions.

By way of background, recall that Eleazar Wheelock first attempted to create Dartmouth College out of a school that served "Indian boys" in Connecticut. The colony denied his request to transform the school into a college, and this reversal, along with declining enrollments as the frontier shifted west, convinced Wheelock to move. In 1769 he was able to secure a charter for an academy, along with land in which to place it, from Governor John Wentworth of New Hampshire. In communicating with the governor, Wheelock had mentioned, "Sir if you think proper to use the word college instead of academy I shall be pleased with it."[63] Wentworth agreed and the Indian Charity School became Dartmouth College of the Province of New Hampshire.

The charter gave Dartmouth the configuration that had become standard issue: a single external board of trustees. Consistent with its being a Puritan school in New England, the broader design looked roughly like that of Harvard and Yale: the board was composed of six magistrates and six ministers; that is, territorial-confessional control. In addition, New Hampshire provided the school with significant funds: grants of cash in 1773, the authorization of lotteries in 1784 and 1787, and further grants of land in 1791.

By 1815 Dartmouth was run by Eleazar Wheelock's son, John. Amid political tensions, the legislature attempted to take control of the school, elbowing out the board. This action was not without precedent; it had not been unheard of, after independence, for state legislatures to review charters granted in the colonial period. The trustees countered that any alteration of the original charter was a violation of law and took the issue to court. In our modern terminology, the essential issue concerned whether Dartmouth was a public or private corporation, although Herbst (1982) and Whitehead (1986) underline that it would take decades before that was the standard interpretation.

In 1817 the Superior Court of New Hampshire found in favor of the state: it deemed Dartmouth to be accountable, via the legislature, to New Hampshire's citizens. The ruling rejected the notion that the original charter had granted Dartmouth autonomy from the state. The trustees appealed, and in 1818 the case reached the U.S. Supreme Court. The trustees' case was presented to Chief Justice John Marshall's court by a then-unknown Dartmouth alum, Daniel Webster.

Webster clearly understood the implications of the case, and famously summarized it as follows:

> This, sir, is my case. It is the case, not merely of that humble institution, it is the case of every college in the land. It is more. It is the case of every eleemosynary institution throughout our country . . . the case of every man who has property of which he may be stripped—the question is simply this: Shall our state legislature be allowed to take that which is not their own, to turn it from its original use, and apply it to such ends or purposes as they, in their discretion shall see fit? Sir, you may destroy this little institution . . . , but if you do . . . you must extinguish, one after another, all those great lights of science, which, for more than a century, have thrown all their radiance over the land! It is, sir, as I have said, a small college, and yet there are those that love it.[64]

The Court found in favor of the trustees, ruling that the original charter was essentially a contract: while Dartmouth's mission was to serve the public, it was not under public control. It was therefore to be governed by its trustees—only they were responsible for the lands and funds that the colony had awarded the original institution. In short, the Supreme Court had affirmed that private universities in the United States would have a right to self-rule.

This was a major decision—one that limited states' ability to reconfigure educational systems in the French fashion. In response states began to create universities with charters including specific provisions to maintain state control. In this sense the Dartmouth case only applied to colleges founded without such stipulations.

To summarize, Chapters 6 and 7 have shown that religion had much to do with the development of university systems in Europe and the United States, and that in both cases it interacted with factors like political development. The end result was very different, however. In Europe it contributed to the appearance of a free university market, but also ultimately to its demise. In the United States, the trajectory was the opposite: while in New England and the South the country looked to develop a territorial-confessional configuration, the Middle Atlantic saw the emergence of self-rule, free entry, and free scope.

Finally, while these ingredients concern the rules under which universities compete, it is worth noting that history also endowed American universities with internal configurations that make them nimbler than their European counterparts. In particular, as explained in this chapter, in American universities power derives from the trustees and is channeled to the president, who has substantial latitude in setting the school's direction. This reflects the *de jure* configuration and two additional factors: (i) the president is the central agent in charge of obtaining funding, and hence is able to direct resources to areas of her preference, (ii) the president appoints deans, and hence can designate individuals willing to implement her vision. In short, despite the fact that professors' power increased after the Civil War, and although that they exert significant control over departments, American university presidents retain substantial discretion.

In contrast, particularly in Germany, the guild-type development experienced by European universities created powerful chaired professors who controlled seminars and eventually entire institutes.[65] These senior faculty members are typically less numerous and more powerful than their American counterparts (tenured full professors). For example, American professors exert collegial authority through their departments, but are ultimately subject to deans and presidents. By contrast, German chairs' funding often flows directly from ministries of education, in some sense by-passing university administrators. In addition, far from having a president imposed on them by a board of trustees, they choose a rector, typically from among themselves, and usually for a relatively short term. As Clark (1983, 112) notes, the rector is a "temporary chief representing the group, aware that his or her elevation is at their pleasure."[66] The basic structure is not too far from the medieval model, in which rectors served limited terms and enjoyed only powers delegated by the assembly of masters.[67]

While I know many American professors who would prefer the stronger faculty governance implied by the European model, it would make it harder for universities to change direction.[68] For example, in Europe creating a chair in a new field can be difficult; in many cases it must be approved by a ministry and a legislature, given that it involves public funding. Further, a decision to even propose a chair may require intricate internal negotiations with existing chaired professors. In contrast, subject to obtaining the funding for a new department, an American president faces few obstacles in its creation.

CHAPTER 8

The Future

THIS BOOK HAS ARGUED that the free market approach accounts for why American universities were weak at research into the 1800s, for why they improved, and for why they have managed to retain their lead. Among this argument's implications is that in education, "past performance does not guarantee future results." This final chapter therefore asks: What does the future hold for the American university system's research performance?

To address this question, recall that we have attributed the system's current strength to the fact that its component schools supply teaching and sorting in a competitive environment, and that this matches enormous amounts of talent and resources at a few dozen schools that prioritize research. The question for the future, therefore, is what developments could upset this arrangement.

To begin, we venture that it is not very likely that the system's market orientation—self-rule, free entry, and free scope—will change easily. These traits are embedded in norms and legal precedents in a way that would be difficult to reverse. This chapter therefore considers four factors that could threaten the system's research performance even in the absence of changes in its market orientation:

- A disruption of scope (a reduction in universities' ability to jointly produce research with outputs like teaching and sorting),
- An excessive resurgence of identity-related concerns,
- Political risks related to inequality, funding, and immigration, and
- Out of control cost increases.

Disruption of Scope

In the past century, American universities' broad scope has aided their research performance. This reflects that in general research is not a lucrative endeavor, and hence must rely on some subsidy. In the United States, this comes from university activities like undergraduate teaching and athletics, and crucially, from donations and political support these help generate (it also comes from federal funding, discussed below). It is not a coincidence that the first American PhD program emerged at Yale—historically a leading beneficiary of first public and later private largesse—or that research ultimately prospered most at universities with colleges. This implies that American research performance could be threatened by a reduction in universities' ability to jointly produce research with outputs like teaching and sorting, since that could dry up the revenues that cross-subsidize research.

The past few years have raised the possibility that such a reduction could originate in technological change, as illustrated by the appearance of massive open online courses known as MOOCs. These courses' original promise was that very high-quality, very low-cost teaching could be delivered to the bedrooms of students all over the world. Indeed, the mission statement of Coursera, one of the largest for-profit MOOC providers, states "we provide universal access to the world's best education."

Initially, observers expected this education would reach students via online lectures; today the expectation is for sophisticated combinations of lectures and content tailored to student ability by artificial intelligence. The lecture component, further, might feature star teachers (e.g., the most successful Harvard instructors) as well as other types of stars. For example, Cowen and Tabarrok (2014, 521) raise that the "package might be presented by a charismatic celebrity, perhaps in animated form, to generate student interest and involvement ('Lebron does Market Demand')." While such content would be expensive to produce, its use by massive numbers of students would keep average costs low. In time, technology (e.g., face and / or typing-pattern recognition) would allow providers to verify that an individual had mastered the content, allowing providers to award "mini" or full degrees.[1]

Taken at face value, MOOCs could indeed, to use the current term, "disrupt" American universities' ability to produce research. If families could get the world's best education essentially for free, they might very well resist forking over a quarter million dollars in tuition and fees, constraining universities' ability to procure resources for research. In other words, unable to sell teaching and cultivate alumni, top universities would find it increasingly hard to pay for research talent. Indeed, in time they might not even look for such talent—they would lose interest in minds capable of a great insight, and rather look for individuals capable of lecturing as well as an animated Lebron.

In short, although often sold as a means to improve and extend education as well as lower its cost, MOOCs could force universities to change in ways that would damage performance in some educational dimensions. As Hoxby (2014, 17) puts it, some enthusiasts of online education "foresee and look forward to the day" in which MOOCs destroy highly selective post-secondary (HSPE) institutions' financial

> virtuous cycle. Such enthusiasts apparently want to re-purpose the resources of HSPE institutions from advanced education (and research) to educating the masses. This would seem, however, to be a poorly thought-out scheme because HSPE institutions have no advantage in educating the masses, and their resources, though considerable for the narrow purposes they pursue, are negligible relative to the problem of mass post-secondary education. Destroying them in their current form would therefore destroy one type of education without adding appreciably to the other.

It is not clear that research university administrators always fully appreciate this threat. For example, Hoxby adds that universities engage in risky behavior when they give away MOOC content for free. Further, this book has made the case that research universities' vulnerability to technological change should not be dismissed. Top universities do indeed divert resources and energy towards research; for example, they carry some uninspiring courses by virtue of the types of professors they hire and the incentives they provide them (Chapter 5). Their exposure is therefore real.

All this said, the impact of MOOCs on research universities is likely to remain limited for four reasons. First, as Hoxby (2014) emphasizes, many elements of online instruction—for example, limited student-teacher inter-action and the use of distance learning—are much more prevalent at non-selective and for-profit colleges, making MOOCs a closer substitute for their services than for those of research universities (with the possible exception of teaching that takes place in some introductory courses). Consistent with this, research suggests that the impact of MOOCs has been substantial mostly in the nonselective, lower end of the postsecondary educational market.[2] Second, so far, there is little evidence that online courses are an educational silver bullet. Some rigorous studies suggest that students who take them learn more than students in regular classes, but others suggest they learn less; in addition, the majority of students who begin MOOCs do not finish them.[3] Third, top universities and colleges' attractiveness depends at least as much on their sorting as on their teaching services, and MOOCs have very little to offer in the former dimension—their students do not interact with almost anyone, and they are associated with essentially everyone. To the extent that education has to do with sorting, "universal access to the best education" is essentially a contradiction in terms. In other words, trying to destroy top schools without offering a sorting product is like attempting a major invasion without an air force. Fourth, as Hoxby (2014) and others have noted, questions remain as to MOOCs' financial model. For example, how will they pay for teaching talent once its price rises and universities no longer happily give it away? The bottom line is that as McPherson and Bacow (2015) point out, at this point it is not obvious that MOOCs present more of an existential threat for top universities than previous technologies that many predicted would close them, such as the printing press, radio, and television.[4]

Nevertheless, there could be further technological evolution in MOOCs, or other market participants may learn from MOOCs' shortcomings, much as university reformers in the 1800s learned from previous failures (Chapter 3). Indeed, Christensen and Eyring (2011) state that it is in the nature of disruptive technologies to need refinements and initially appear to only affect low-quality segments of the market.[5]

An example of an enterprise trying a different approach is Minerva Schools, a college run by the for-profit Minerva Project. Minerva delivers all its classes online, but otherwise is very different from a MOOC. Students earn college degrees and are required to live together; classes are live and never feature more than eighteen students (Minerva enrolled about 160 new students in 2018). In stark contrast to MOOCs, Minerva is extremely focused on sorting, with its CEO recently stating that "First and foremost, what the Minerva school is trying to do is become the most selective university in the western world."[6]

In this it is making progress: in 2018 it had 16,000 applicants and an admission rate below 3 percent. On the other hand, this low admission rate may reflect that Minerva makes applying easy: students need not supply letters of recommendation, application fees, or SAT scores. As a result, it is hard to ascertain how Minerva's students compare with those of the Ivy League schools it aims to displace. For an anecdote, this past year (because my daughter was a high school senior), I observed dozens of children from top New York City schools apply to college. These kids are part of the New York educational elite that schools like Harvard and Yale have competed over for centuries. They are extremely bright, and their schools reprimand them for excessively discussing each other's college applications. I worried that some of them might contemplate human sacrifice if it earned them a Stanford admission letter, but I never heard a single one mention Minerva. In part this may be because a school designed like Minerva cannot offer them world-class laboratories combined with athletic competition and a monumental campus teeming with thousands of highly able potential friends. This matters for Minerva because once a school develops a reputation for attracting (or not attracting) certain types of students, that can be difficult to change.

All this said, Minerva is clearly putting thought into its product, and its cost of attendance is only a fourth to a half of research universities' sticker price. Schools like it could multiply, eventually giving many universities and colleges stiff competition for at least some students. Again, if that happened at large scale, American research would likely suffer: Minerva is controlled by a for-profit organization, and not surprisingly makes no claim to doing research; for example, its website hardly advertises who its faculty members are. If such schools one day ruled the market, the American research advantage might evaporate.

The bottom line is that while the impact of MOOCs has been muted relative to huge expectations, a disruption of scope or a reduction in universities' ability to jointly produce multiple outputs could still happen. This would hamper American leadership in research and is something research university administrators and policymakers will have to keep an eye on.

Identity

Diversity along dimensions including religion and ethnicity has been a central theme in American history, and how the country has navigated diversity has been crucial to its development. For instance, Chapter 7 argued that religious diversity partially drove the emergence of self-rule and free entry in the American college sector, and hence helps account for American universities' research preeminence today.

At the same time, the salience of identity has not always helped research performance. For example, in the early 1800s religious diversity led colleges to hire professors with an eye to their denominational affiliation rather than their expertise. A reduction of such identity-related concerns was necessary to the sorting of faculty and students (and hence of minds and money) that took place in the 1900s.

Today there is renewed concern around identity in universities, particularly as groups like women and ethnic minorities appear in parts of the university where they have traditionally been underrepresented, such as the faculty. On the one hand, this is an overwhelmingly positive development; it can only help universities to access pools of talent that previously went largely untapped. To illustrate the impact of the changes it is producing, at my own institution the stock of tenure-track faculty is not very diverse, but the flow (e.g., newly hired professors) is. For example, in some recent cohorts roughly 50 percent of all assistant professors hired and eventually tenured have been women. In addition, anecdotally, I have seen the vast majority of those I know go on to very successful careers featuring offers from highly ranked departments. In part, this progress has been possible thanks to an explicit concern for identity; for instance, like the majority of its peers, Columbia has created formalized and funded initiatives to diversify hiring.[7]

On the other hand, some have argued that an excessive resurgence of identity-related concerns could blunt universities' ability to do things like measure talent and individual performance.

For example, Sullivan (2018) argues that

> the whole concept of an individual who exists apart from group identity is slipping. . . . The idea of individual merit—as opposed to various forms of unearned privilege—is increasingly suspect. The Enlightenment principles that formed the bedrock of the American experiment—untrammeled free speech, due process, individual (rather than group) rights—are now routinely understood as mere masks for white male power, code words for the oppression of women and nonwhites. Any differences in outcome for various groups must always be a function of hate, rather than a function of nature or choice or freedom or individual agency. And anyone who questions these assertions is obviously a white supremacist himself.

While this overstates the situation on campus, the point is worth keeping in mind. If identity-related concerns came to dominate decisions around hiring or promotion, or if they led to a complete questioning of criteria like publication, they would complicate top universities' ability to identify, recruit, and incentivize research talent.

In short, the United States has historically found ways to navigate diversity and draw strength from it. Ensuring this continues to hold with respect to research is another task for university leaders to keep in mind.

Political Risks Related to Inequality, Funding, and Immigration

Among wealthy countries, the United States displays a high level of (and tolerance for) inequality.[8] It is thus not surprising that its university system exhibits, has been shaped by, and contributes to inequality. Not only does the system feature its own 1 percent of schools, it would not have its present configuration were it not for gifts that inequality made possible, as personified in names like Bloomberg, Boalt, Carnegie, Cornell, Dornsife, Geffen, Hearst, Hewlett, Hopkins, Paulson, Pulitzer, Rockefeller, Stanford, Tulane, Van Rensselaer, and Vanderbilt—to begin a list that could go on for pages. In addition, when it comes to research funding, the federal government contributes to school-level inequality (Chapter 5). Further, prestigious American universities aggravate inequality to the extent that they produce large labor market returns that disproportionately benefit wealthier individuals, including legacy students.[9] The bottom line is that the concentration of minds and money at top schools is part and parcel of the broader American economic and social structure; an illustration of Charles Eliot's statement that "The institutions of . . . education in any nation are . . . a faithful mirror in which are sharply reflected the national history and character."[10]

And yet this equilibrium could change substantially, as recent years have seen inequality come increasingly under attack. This is clear from developments including President Obama's calling inequality the defining challenge of our time, the success of Thomas Picketty's (2014) *Capital in the Twenty-First Century,* and the positions of left-leaning politicians like Senator Bernard Sanders and Representative Alexandria Ocasio-Cortez. The policies some of these individuals advance could substantially impair universities' ability to attract large gifts. In addition, some of these politicians openly admire European systems, and might seek to move the United States toward a model much less tolerant of between-university inequality; for example, France, Germany, or Sanders' beloved Scandinavia.

Such moves could impact American university research output. This simply reflects that such fundamental changes are likely to have broad effects. This was illustrated in an exchange between Senator Sanders and Secretary of Health and Human Services Tom Price:

> SANDERS: . . . Do you believe that health care is a right of all Americans, whether they're rich or they're poor? Should all people, because they are Americans, be able to go to the doctor when they need to . . . ?
>
> PRICE: Yes. We are a compassionate society . . .
>
> SANDERS: No, we are not a compassionate society. In terms of our relationship to poor and working people, our record is worse than virtually any other country on Earth. We have the highest rate of childhood poverty of any other major country on Earth. And half of our senior older workers have nothing set aside for retirement. So I don't

think, compared to other countries, we are particularly compassionate. . . . . In Canada, in other countries, all people have the right to health care. Do you believe we should move in that direction?

PRICE: If you want to talk about other countries' health-care systems, there are consequences to the decisions that they've made, just as there are consequences to the decisions that we've made. . . . .[11]

Both Sanders and Price had good points. It is hard to argue that the United States is as averse to inequality as other wealthy countries; but it is also unlikely that major moves in a European direction would be a free lunch. For example, if it became unacceptable for one professor to make ten times as much as another, or for one university to spend ten times as much (per student) as another, then it would be harder to match minds and money at a few dozen schools.

Importantly, since research is to a large extent a global public good, such a development could hurt people all over the world. This is related to a point made by Acemoglu, Robinson, and Verdier (2012) in a paper titled "Can't we all be more like Scandinavians?" They begin from the frequent claim that due to lower inequality in their society, Scandinavians are better off than Americans (e.g., Krugman's (2018) op-ed, "Something not rotten in Denmark"). Presumably, therefore, average welfare would increase if Americans adopted the Scandinavian model—this is essentially the Sanders position. Acemoglu et al. warn, however, that this could reduce the incentives for innovation in the United States, a key point given the country's crucial role in expanding the technological frontier. Their model is focused on firms rather than universities, but a similar logic applies: inequality may well be tied to the mechanisms that give rise to innovation. In other words, if the medical advances that help keep Danes healthy originate disproportionately in American universities, then drastically attacking American inequality would affect them too. In a similar spirit, growing research explores whether taxation levels can affect innovation.[12]

It is also worth noting that for universities, inequality-related political risks come from the right as well as the left. For instance, in 2017 Republicans supported the introduction of an endowment tax for schools with more than 500 tuition-paying students and more than $500,000 in assets per student.[13]

This is analogous to the personal wealth taxes being proposed from the left. In addition, in 2019 President Donald Trump threatened to cut research funds to universities he claims do not allow conservatives free expression. The bottom line is that top universities could find themselves squeezed between right-leaning politicians with little sympathy for schools they perceive as aligned with leftist elites and left-leaning politicians who view them as privilege incorporated.

An additional set of threats to universities' research performance emerges from policy surrounding public funding and immigration. First, federal/state funding has been crucial to the development of American research universities. For example, state and Morrill Act support were central to the growth of schools including Berkeley, Cornell, Davis, Georgia, Michigan State, MIT, Pennsylvania, Purdue, Texas A&M, Washington, Wisconsin, and Yale. In addition, federal support has played a major role in the growth of research activity since the 1940s. Yet concern surrounds states' continued commitment to funding universities, and federal research funding has stagnated in recent years, particularly as a proportion of the economy.[14] Gruber and Johnson (2019) provide the salient facts: between 1938 and 1964, federal and state government expenditure on research went from 0.08 percent to 2.0 percent of national income; it has subsequently fallen back to 0.07 percent. Continued funding declines could deprive American universities of the resources they need to retain their research lead. Such reductions would be shortsighted at a time when innovation may be getting harder to produce, and the country's economy faces increasing competition.[15]

Second, while this book has argued that the seeds of American leadership lie in homegrown institutional structure, there is no question that once set in motion, American research universities' performance was enhanced by their ability to attract talent from around the world. In some sense they took on the role that German schools previously had, and which Paulsen (1906, 55) celebrated in 1906 when he wrote that, "just as in the Middle Ages students from every country sought the French and Italian institutions, so now strangers from the far west and the farthest east come to the German universities for scientific training." It follows that federal policy surrounding immigration could harm American performance. For example, if it became difficult for foreign professors and students to obtain visas, permanent residency, or citizenship, they might look for other shores. It is worth adding that limits to immigration might harm not just American but global research output. To illustrate, suppose that due to factors like a better match between minds and money the American university sector is more research-productive than others. Then it might be to the world's advantage to allow top talent to reach it. Relatedly, some of the most talented researchers in the world are attracted to American universities in part for the salaries they can pay; forced to remain in their own countries, they might enter other lines of work.

Out of Control Costs

Part of the enthusiasm behind MOOCs reflects the view that they may help control costs in higher education, which are often perceived to be rising so fast as to be out of control.[16] While research universities have been able to raise tuition to match cost increases, one cannot rule out that at some point that may no longer be feasible. Such a development would directly threaten their ability to engage in research.

I can personally provide one illustration of tuition increases' bite: as I worked on the final edits for this book, I received a bill for my daughter's first term in college, one that works out to $75,000 per year. This amount—granted at a private research university—exceeds the median household disposable income of any country. Further, although public research universities cost less, their tuitions have been rising just as quickly.

To some extent these increases are not a surprise, as they at least partially reflect Baumol's "cost disease": the relative costs of labor-intensive activities experiencing few productivity improvements will rise if other sectors of the economy see productivity gains.[17] In a common illustration, the technology to produce a given opera changes very little; if other sectors see productivity/wage increases, the cost of putting on the opera will rise (the people involved must be paid more). In recent work, Helland and Tabarrok (2019) illustrate this idea in higher education, showing that colleges' costs and prices have increased even as one measure of their output—college graduates' average literacy rates—has barely changed.

There are two reasons, however, why research universities' rising prices may not be as serious as commonly argued. First, in a real sense the quality of the services these schools provide has increased, despite Helland and Tabarrok's findings. To illustrate this, return to considering opera, which my daughter and I enjoy. Suppose that through time travel, one offered us the opportunity to see a 1919 rather than a 2019 Metropolitan Opera production of *Traviata*. I suspect we would jump at the opportunity, if only to see the stars of the early twentieth century. This illustrates that opera has not changed much, and it is indeed not obvious that the 2019 product surpasses that of a century ago.

Now suppose that one similarly offered us the chance to use the 1919 rather than 2019 version of my daughter's college (setting aside, or not, the fact that it did not then take women). I very much doubt we would choose the 1919 version, even at a much lower price. From a sorting perspective, American research universities today provide an arguably much better product than they did a century ago. Even more importantly, my daughter is very interested in chemistry in general, and in laboratories doing organometallics in particular. The 1919 version of her school had less of the former, and none of the latter—convincing her to go for the 1919 version would be an uphill proposition, to say the least. In short, part of the research universities' price increases reflects changes in their product, and hence may be less of a concern than is commonly supposed. Consistent with this, such schools face significant excess demand even at a $75,000 annual sticker price.

Second, as Hellman and Tabarrok explain, one must not forget that from a social perspective rising tuition can be seen as a blessing rather than a disease: Baumol's effect arises only if parts of the economy are experiencing productivity gains. In other words, prices are ultimately relative prices, and if some goods (e.g., computers, cellphones) become much cheaper due to technological change, others (e.g., college) will become relatively more expensive—that is not, a priori, a problem.

But in this case, there is a further important wrinkle. The productivity improvements in areas like computers and phones are to some extent due to universities themselves. As already noted, university research directly contributes to economic growth. In an extreme example, individuals like

Bill Hewlett credited Stanford University with a substantial role in developing Silicon Valley. And further, many university-based discoveries are behind the progress of technology-intensive sectors. In other words, some of the very productivity improvements that make schools like Stanford look relatively expensive may be a symptom of their success. In addition, selective research universities may further contribute to productivity by sorting bright students and matching them to productive employers. For example, Stanford may help identify good workers for Silicon Valley firms.[18]

The bottom line is that while research universities, like any enterprise, should avoid waste, rising costs need not imply an existential threat to their future, and it may still make good sense for families and governments to invest in their services.

The Massachusetts Puritans had a unique project: to create a religious beacon, a city on a hill the Christian world would admire. Four centuries later, it is hard to argue they succeeded. From this book's vantage point, however, they did set in motion a remarkable university system. The New England colonies drew the outlines of a college system that the Middle Atlantic colonies augmented with self-rule and free entry. This paved the way for the rise of hundreds of schools that aspired to be English colleges but struggled to produce quality teaching or research. After the Civil War, reformers changed some of these schools, aiming to create German universities. While some of them wished to dispose of the colleges, these were saved by sorting reform. The result was a truly American institution, unique in its broad scope and its amalgam of European elements—an institution, as put by Metzger (1955, 104), "not merely motley, but mongrel."[19] In time, as it concentrated minds and money in a few dozen schools, the American university system became the best at research. Despite this success, the future is not assured. While the U.S. university system's market orientation is unlikely to change, in education free markets do not guarantee good performance. University leaders and policy makers will have to remain vigilant if American research leadership is to endure.

APPENDIX

NOTES

REFERENCES

ACKNOWLEDGMENTS

INDEX

Appendix

1. The Nobel Prize-Based Measure

Our proxy for university research output originates in the 1901–2016 list of Nobel laureates in Chemistry, Economics, Medicine, and Physics. We exclude the Peace and Literature prizes because these are often awarded for work done outside universities. In addition, we note that the Economics prize, while awarded along with the others, was created more recently: the *Sveriges Riksbank* Prize in Economic Sciences in Memory of Alfred Nobel was created in 1969.

Our database initially consisted of the laureates' names, fields, and prize years. We then manually tagged each laureate with a list of his or her (postsecondary) affiliations. For each affiliation, we noted the name of the institution, the nature of the affiliation (faculty member, researcher, PhD student, BA student, etc.), and the years during which the laureate was at the institution. These data originate in a collection of sources: the Nobel Prize website's official biographies, the Dictionary of Scientific Biography, obituaries, and for more recent winners, laureates' self-authored CVs, as found online.

We built a separate database of institutions in which orthographic and historical variants of each institution's name are grouped under a single canonical name. To these records we added the name of the country in which each institution currently resides. Consider two examples for illustration. First, in our data Yale University is always referred to in the same way, and thus all references are easily grouped under the canonical "Yale University." The institution is in turn allocated to the United States. Second, the University of Strasbourg, the University of Strassburg, Louis

Pasteur University, Marc Bloch University, and Robert Schuman University are all grouped under the canonical "University of Strasbourg." We record this institution as being located in France, even though it was located in Germany at times. This also abstracts from the fact that in certain years it was composed of separate institutions. One exception to these rules concerns the University of Paris, which over the years has been repeatedly split and reassembled into different units. In this case we use the original more general designation.

The bottom line is that in many cases classifying institutions involves judgment calls, and some amount of noise surely remains in our data. Note, however, that the book's focus is on broad trends in country performance, and these are likely to be robust to these issues.

The majority of affiliations prize winners mention—about 92 percent—are with degree-granting institutions. We will call these universities, although they include schools that use other designations (e.g., colleges). Since this book's emphasis is on universities, we almost always focus on this set of affiliations. For completeness, a couple of appendix tables present results including nonuniversity affiliations.

To summarize, our procedure yields 639 prize winners whose biographies mention 446 universities 3,120 times. In addition, they mention 152 non-degree-granting organizations 286 times. The total number of mentions is 3,406.

2. Historical Coverage

Bibliographical databases could be used to produce data analogous to those in Figure 1.2 if information on articles, including on their authors' institutional affiliations, extended into the 1800s. Unfortunately, this is not the case. Figure A.1 illustrates this for the Web of Science data. The dotted line plots the number of articles that appear every year; the solid line the proportion that include institutional affiliations; that is, that specify that authors worked at a given university. Since the early 1970s, 80 percent to 95 percent of articles include such information. Before that, however, this proportion declines precipitously, to zero in many years. This makes it impossible to link papers to universities.

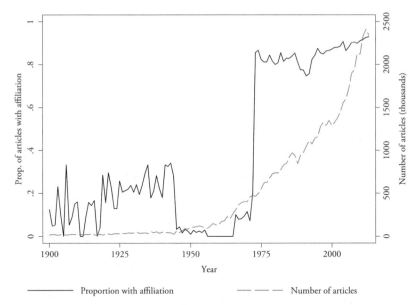

FIGURE A.1 The figure describes the number of articles that appear in the Web of Science (dotted line, right axis), and the proportion of these that include authors' institutional affiliation (solid line, left axis). The calculations are based on a 1/100th sample of all articles that have appeared in this bibliographic database.

3. Non-Degree-Granting Institutions

Table A.1 replicates Table 1.1 but also includes mentions of non-degree-granting institutions.

4. Controlling for Income and Population

Tables A.2 and A.3 present variants of Table 1.1 normalizing the results by income per capita and by population, respectively. In each case the tables present results only for the top ten countries (by cumulative mentions) and use more finely grained time periods.

Specifically, Table A.2 divides the mentions in Table 1.1 by each country's contemporaneous per capita income (in thousands of dollars). It thus provides a sense of the number of Nobel mentions generated by each country's universities per $1,000 in GDP per capita. The key findings remain: the

Table A.1 Country-level university mentions (including those going to non-degree-granting institutions)

Rank	Country	Total mentions	Mentions by period			
			1855–1900	1901–1940	1941–1980	1981–2016
1	United States	1,675	13	308	941	413
2	United Kingdom	472	22	159	236	55
3	Germany	421	90	198	107	26
4	France	171	34	56	58	23
5	Japan	83		7	41	35
6	Switzerland	82	9	30	30	13
7	Canada	58		10	39	9
8	Sweden	54	7	23	20	4
9	Denmark	39	6	19	12	2
10	Netherlands	39	10	13	11	5
11	Austria	36	9	25	2	
12	Russia	35	5	13	13	4
13	Australia	32		7	20	5
14	Italy	28	1	13	10	4
15	Israel	24			17	7
16	Belgium	17	2	7	7	1
17	Norway	17		4	7	6
18	China	14			6	8
19	India	13	1	5	6	1
20	Hungary	12		4	8	
21	Finland	11		6	3	2
22	Poland	10	2	8		
23	Argentina	9		3	6	
24	South Africa	8			8	
25	Spain	7	4	3		
26	Ireland	6		3	2	1
27	Czech Republic	5		5		
28	New Zealand	5	2		3	

The table lists the number of times Nobel winners' biographies mention institutions in different countries. This table is similar to Table 1.1 but includes mentions of non-degree-granting institutions as well. The table lists only countries with institutions accounting for five or more mentions. The countries with three mentions are Estonia, Pakistan, Portugal, and Ukraine. Egypt has two, and nine other countries have one each. The totals refer to all countries. For details on the data, see the text and Appendix Section 1.

Table A.2 Country-level university mentions normalized by per capita income

Rank	Country	Total mentions (normalized)	By period							
			1855–1880	1881–1900	1901–1920	1921–1940	1941–1960	1961–1980	1981–2000	2000–2016
1	United States	112.76	0.54	2.05	9.03	24.43	26.26	18.19	6.64	2.62
2	United Kingdom	56.75	1.38	3.54	8.06	14.04	11.00	5.87	1.42	0.30
3	Germany	33.60	11.87	16.76	17.11	20.80	6.60	2.93	0.49	0.07
4	France	41.07	6.84	4.64	6.01	4.57	3.42	1.60	0.37	0.23
5	Japan	7.84	0.00	0.00	0.00	2.52	4.86	1.81	0.68	0.37
6	Switzerland	4.61	1.07	1.40	2.67	2.63	1.41	0.59	0.11	0.04
7	Canada	3.53	0.00	0.00	0.80	0.68	2.08	0.46	0.17	0.07
8	Sweden	13.18	0.00	2.62	1.61	2.49	0.92	0.63	0.15	0.00
9	Netherlands	3.53	1.81	1.26	1.00	1.48	0.56	0.34	0.15	0.02
10	Denmark	3.28	0.00	1.68	1.56	1.53	1.00	0.06	0.04	0.02

The table lists the number of times Nobel winners' biographies mention universities in different countries, divided by each country's contemporaneous per capita income in dollars. For details on the Nobel data, see the text and Appendix Section 1. The data on per capita income come from the Angus Maddison historical data (https://www.rug.nl/ggdc/historicaldevelopment/maddison/).

Table A-3 Country-level university mentions normalized by population

Rank	Country	Total mentions (normalized)	By period							
			1855–1880	1881–1900	1901–1920	1921–1940	1941–1960	1961–1980	1981–2000	2000–2016
1	United States	12.82	0.05	0.17	0.74	1.87	2.70	2.15	0.96	0.43
2	United Kingdom	10.02	0.16	0.45	1.10	2.21	2.23	1.68	0.61	0.18
3	Germany	6.84	0.67	1.26	1.31	1.62	0.71	0.64	0.16	0.04
4	France	3.48	0.45	0.40	0.67	0.58	0.54	0.52	0.15	0.12
5	Japan	1.15	0.00	0.00	0.00	0.11	0.19	0.22	0.15	0.10
6	Switzerland	16.96	1.14	1.99	3.79	3.71	2.95	2.11	0.58	0.25
7	Canada	3.57	0.00	0.00	0.69	0.48	1.79	0.41	0.18	0.09
8	Sweden	8.66	0.00	1.46	1.27	2.11	1.15	1.38	0.47	0.00
9	Netherlands	4.81	1.41	1.09	0.83	1.01	0.39	0.46	0.27	0.06
10	Denmark	11.22	0.00	2.60	2.76	2.80	2.11	0.20	0.19	0.18

The table lists the number of times Nobel winners' biographies mention universities in different countries, divided by each country's contemporaneous population in millions. For details on the Nobel data, see the text and Appendix Section 1. The data on population come from the Angus Maddison historical data (https://www.rug .nl/ggdc/historicaldevelopment/maddison/).

United States had one of the lowest levels of this measure in the early periods, but later on became the leader (the timing of improvement is an important issue discussed later in the text).

Table A.3 replicates the exercise but normalizes by population (in millions) rather than by per capita income. It thus provides a measure of the number of Nobel mentions generated by each country's universities per million people. The evolution is the same: the United States goes from one of the lowest levels in the initial periods to the highest by the end.

One aspect in this second case is that the United States does not rank highest overall—Switzerland does, given its substantial early lead. This also illustrates that there is variation in performance among European countries, although that is not our focus here. It is worth mentioning that such variation in part reflects the relatively large number of countries Europe contains, and the associated relatively small size and peculiar characteristics of some of these. In particular, Switzerland has only about eight million people, is one of the wealthiest countries in Europe, and contains highly research-productive universities. That said, the United States contains jurisdictions which are obviously not countries but also produce a lot of research; for example, Massachusetts has about seven million people, is one of the richest states, and would be even more research-productive than Switzerland were it a country.

5. Additional Results on the Timing of American Improvement

This appendix presents two variants of Table 1.2. Both explore when American universities' research output overtook that of other countries. The key point is that under both, the United States was on an upward trajectory by 1930. Whether it had already overtaken all other countries by then depends on the measure used. Table A.4 considers only mentions that accrue to schools with which individuals were affiliated with as graduate or undergraduate students. This helps identify "up-and-coming" university systems to the extent those do well at training future prize winners. Using this measure, the United States had overtaken all countries by 1911–1920.

Table A.4 Mentions as doctoral and undergraduate students

Cum. rank	Country	Total number of mentions in						
		1855–1870	1871–1880	1881–1890	1891–1900	1901–1910	1911–1920	1921–1930
1	United States		1	3	6	15	30	52
2	United Kingdom	1	3	5	8	11	14	18
3	Germany	8	11	8	16	18	7	34
4	France	2	11	4	9	3	3	8
5	Japan							2
6	Canada						2	
7	Switzerland	2		3	2	2	2	5
8	Sweden			4	1	3	1	6
9	Netherlands		4	3		1	1	1
10	Russia	1	2				1	5

The table lists the number of times Nobel winners' biographies mention universities in different countries. The table considers only mentions of institutions with which winners were affiliated as graduate or undergraduate students. For details on the data, see the text and Appendix Section 1.

Table A.5 Mentions at award

Cum. rank	Country	Total number of mentions in						
		1901–1910	1911–1920	1921–1930	1931–1940	1941–1950	1951–1960	1961–1970
1	United States	1	2	3	8	12	27	27
2	United Kingdom	3	2	8	6	6	4	9
3	Germany	12	8	8	7	2	1	1
4	France	8	4	2	3		0	6
5	Sweden	1	1	3		1	1	3
6	Switzerland	0	2	0	2	2	0	0
7	Japan					1		1
8	Denmark	1	1	2	0	1		0
9	Canada	0		2		0		0
10	Austria		0	2	2	0		0

The table lists the number of times Nobel winners' biographies mention universities in different countries. The table considers only mentions of institutions with which the winner was affiliated at the time of award. For details on the data, see the text and Appendix Section 1.

Table A.6 Universities with two to six mentions

Institution	Mentions	Institution	Mentions	Institution	Mentions	Institution	Mentions
Australian National Univ.	6	Ohio State University	4	University of Lausanne	4	SM Kirov Mil. Med. Acad.	2
Brown University	6	Swarthmore College	4	University of Pavia	4	Saint Petersburg State Univ.	2
École Sup. Phys. et Chimie	6	Texas A&M University	4	University of Queensland	4	Scuola Normale Sup. di Pisa	2
Hokkaido University	6	Tufts University	4	University of Rostock	4	Stony Brook University	2
Indiana University	6	Univ. of Southern Calif.	4	University of Saskatchewan	4	Tsinghua University	2
King's College London	6	University of Aberdeen	4	University of Sussex	4	Tulane University	2
Rice University	6	University of Arizona	4	University of Tartu	4	Union College	2
Rutgers University	6	University of Giessen	4	University of Tennessee	4	United States Naval Academy	2
Stockholm University	6	University of Groningen	4	Virginia Tech	4	Univ. of Western Australia	2
Univ. of British Columbia	6	University of Halle	4	Wayne State University	4	University of Alberta	2
Univ. of Calif, Irvine	6	University of Lyons	4	Whitman College	4	University of Alexandria	2
Univ. of Calif, San Francisco	6	University of Madrid	4	Baylor University	3	University of Burgundy	2
University of Amsterdam	6	University of Missouri	4	Boston University	3	University of Coimbra	2
University of Budapest	6	University of Nebraska	4	Budapest Univ. Tech. Econ.	3	University of Delaware	2
University of Lund	6	University of Turin	4	Chapman University	3	University of Düsseldorf	2
University of Maryland	6	Chinese Univ. Hong Kong	3	Charles University in Prague	3	University of East Anglia	2
University of Nottingham	6	Dartmouth College	3	Colorado State University	3	University of Erlangen	2
University of Rochester	6	Delft Univ. of Technology	3	Czech Technical University	3	University of Essex	2
University of Sheffield	6	École des Ponts ParisTech	3	Dalhousie University	3	University of Gothenburg	2
University of St Andrews	6	GCU Lahore	3	Erasmus Univ. Rotterdam	3	University of Greifswald	2
University of Stockholm	6	Leningrad State University	3	George Mason University	3	University of Jena	2
Vanderbilt University	6	Michigan State University	3	Ghent University	3	University of Kentucky	2
Aachen University	5	Moscow State University	3	Haverford College	3	University of Leeds	2

(continued)

Table A.6 (Continued)

Institution	Mentions	Institution	Mentions	Institution	Mentions	Institution	Mentions
Amherst College	5	Norwegian School of Econ.	3	Illinois Inst. of Tech.	2	University of Miami	2
Ecole Polytechnique	5	Norwegian Univ. Sci. Tech.	3	Indian Institute of Science	2	University of Montana	2
University of Bern	5	Osaka City University	3	Lafayette College	2	University of Montreal	2
University of Bristol	5	Queen's University	3	MINES ParisTech	2	University of Munster	2
University of Cape Town	5	State University of New York	3	Manchester Mun. Coll. Tech.	2	University of New Zealand	2
University of Florida	5	Stevens Inst. of Tech.	3	McMaster University	2	University of Oregon	2
University of Glasgow	5	Stockholm School of Econ.	3	Meijo University	2	University of Pisa	2
University of Lyon	5	Technical Univ. of Darmstadt	3	Moscow Eng. Phys. Inst.	2	University of Rouen	2
University of Massachusetts	5	Technical Univ. of Denmark	3	Moscow Ins. of Phys. Tech.	2	University of Saint Petersburg	2
University of Melbourne	5	Technical Univ. of Stuttgart	3	Nagasaki University	2	University of Tokushima	2
University of North Carolina	5	Tokyo Inst. of Technology	3	National Tsing Hua Univ.	2	University of Tsukuba	2
University of Pittsburgh	5	Tokyo University of Science	3	Odessa University	2	University of Utah	2
University of Sydney	5	Trinity College Dublin	3	Osaka University	2	University of Warwick	2
Aarhus University	4	Univ. of the Witwatersrand	3	Peking University	2	University of the Punjab	2
Arizona State University	4	University of Adelaide	3	Penn. State University	2	Victoria Univ. Wellington	2
Florida State University	4	University of Bordeaux	3	Physikalisch-Tech. Bund.	2	Virginia Commonwealth Univ.	2
George Washington Univ.	4	University of Hannover	3	Presidency College	2	Wesleyan University	2
Iowa State University	4	University of Innsbruck	3	Radboud Univ. Nijmegen	2		
Lebedev Physical Institute	4	University of Kansas	3	Rensselaer Polytechnic Inst.	2		
Oberlin College	4	University of Karlsruhe	3	Royal Institute of Technology	2		

The table lists universities that received two to six mentions over the period covered by our data. For details on the data, see the text and Appendix Section 1.

Table A.7 Non-university institutions with two or more mentions

Institution	Mentions	Institution	Mentions
Nokia Bell Labs	18	Wellcome Trust	3
Francis Crick Institute	15	Atomic Energy of Canada	2
National Institutes of Health	14	Carnegie Institution of Washington	2
Max Planck Society	12	Cetus Corporation	2
College de France	10	DuPont	2
IBM	8	Hoffmann-La Roche AG	2
CERN	6	IG Farben	2
Institute for Advanced Study	6	ITT Inc.	2
Salk Institute for Biological Studies	6	Lebedev Physical Institute	2
Cold Spring Harbor Laboratory	5	Lister Institute of Preventive Medicine	2
GlaxoSmithKline	5	Mayo Clinic	2
Manhattan Project	4	NASA	2
United Kingdom Ministry of Defence	4	NIST	2
Boston Children's Hospital	3	National Bureau of Economic Research	2
Brookhaven National Laboratory	3	Royal Institution of Great Britain	2
CNRS	3	Royal Perth Hospital	2
Cancer Research UK	3	United States Department of Veterans Affairs	2
General Electric	3	Walter and Eliza Hall Institute	2
Kaiser Wilhelm Gesellschaft	3	Wool Industries Research Association	2
Novartis	3		

The table lists the non-degree-granting institutions mentioned at least twice in Nobel winners' biographies. For details on the data, see the text and Appendix Section 1.

The flip side is that American universities' progress is not seen as early if one considers only affiliations at the time of award (here each winner produces only one mention). Table A.5 shows that in this case the United States arrives at the top spot only in the 1930s.

6. Institutions with Three or Fewer Mentions

Table A.6 presents results supplementary to Table 1.3. It lists universities that received between six and two mentions over the period covered by

Chemistry

Table A.8 Country-level university mentions in chemistry

Rank	Country	Total	1855–1880	1881–1900	1901–1920	1921–1940	1941–1960	1961–1980	1981–2000	2000–2016
1	United States	365		3	15	61	86	113	61	26
2	Germany	157	9	28	37	36	20	19	6	2
3	United Kingdom	130	6	5	16	27	40	30	11	1
4	France	39		3	12	7	5	4	1	2
5	Switzerland	30		4	7	7	3	6	1	2
6	Japan	23					7	9	5	2
7	Israel	19						14	2	3
8	Sweden	17		3	4	4	1	4	1	
9	Canada	15			3	2	5	2	2	1
10	Austria	11		3	5	3				
11	Netherlands	8	3	1	1	1		1	1	
12	Denmark	6				2	3		1	
13	Belgium	4	1			1	1	1		
14	China	4						2	1	1
15	Finland	4			2		1		1	

16	New Zealand	4					2			
17	Estonia	3	2	1						
18	Hungary	3			1		2			
19	Norway	3			1	1				1
20	Poland	3			2	1				
21	South Africa	3					3			
22	Argentina	2				1		1		
23	Australia	2			1	1		1		
24	Czech Republic	2				2			2	
25	Egypt	2							2	
	Total	866	21	54	107	157	181	212	93	41

The table lists the number of times chemistry Nobel winners' biographies mention universities in different countries. For details on the data, see the text and Appendix Section 1.

Table A.9 Cumulative Nobel mentions by university in chemistry

Rank	Institution	Mentions	Rank	Institution	Mentions	Rank	Institution	Mentions
1	University of Cambridge	53		McGill University	5		University of Tartu	3
2	Harvard University	47		University of Edinburgh	5		University of Toronto	3
3	Univ. of Calif., Berkeley	33		University of Graz	5	21	Aachen University	2
4	Humboldt Univ. of Berlin	24		University of Texas	5		Aarhus University	2
5	University of Munich	23		University of Würzburg	5		Budapest Univ. Tech. Econ.	2
6	University of Oxford	20	19	Hebrew Univ. of Jerusalem	4		City University of New York	2
7	ETH Zurich	19		Purdue University	4		Czech Technical University	2
	University of Chicago	19		Univ. of Calif., Irvine	4		École Normale Supérieure	2
	University of Göttingen	19		University of Birmingham	4		Nagasaki University	2
8	Stanford University	17		University of Copenhagen	4		National Tsing Hua Univ.	2
9	Columbia University	16		University of Kiel	4		Queen's University	2
	Massachusetts Inst. of Tech.	16		University of London	4		Technical Univ. of Berlin	2
	University of Manchester	16		University of Lyon	4		Technical Univ. of Darmstadt	2
10	Technical Univ. of Munich	15		University of Michigan	4		Texas A&M University	2
11	California Inst. of Tech.	12		University of Minnesota	4		Tufts University	2
	Cornell University	12		University of Tubingen	4		Univ. of Calif., Santa Barbara	2
	University of Paris	12		Utrecht University	4		Univ. of Southern Calif.	2
12	University of Strasbourg	11		Washington Univ. in St. Louis	4		University of Alexandria	2
13	Univ. of Calif., Los Angeles	10	20	Case Western Reserve	3		University of Basel	2
	Uppsala University	10		Duke University	3		University of Buenos Aires	2
	Yale University	10		École Sup. Phys. et Chimie	3		University of Cape Town	2

Rank	University	n	University	n	University	n
14	University of Illinois	9	Free University of Brussels	3	University of Erlangen	2
	University of Marburg	9	Karolinska Institute	3	University of Florida	2
15	Imperial College London	8	Nagoya University	3	University of Halle	2
	Johns Hopkins University	8	New York University	3	University of Innsbruck	2
	Technion	8	Northwestern University	3	University of Kansas	2
	Univ. of Calif., San Diego	8	Rice University	3	University of Karlsruhe	2
	University of Freiburg	8	Technical Univ. of Stuttgart	3	University of Lausanne	2
	University of Wisconsin	8	Tokyo Inst. of Technology	3	University of Montana	2
16	Princeton University	7	University College London	3	University of Nebraska	2
	University of Pennsylvania	7	University of Bonn	3	University of New Zealand	2
	University of Zurich	7	University of Colorado	3	University of Oslo	2
	Weizmann Inst. of Science	7	University of Frankfurt	3	University of Stockholm	2
17	Heidelberg University	6	University of Glasgow	3	University of Sydney	2
	Rockefeller University	6	University of Helsinki	3	University of Vienna	2
18	Carnegie Mellon University	5	University of North Carolina	3	University of Wrocław	2
	Hokkaido University	5	University of Saskatchewan	3	Vanderbilt University	2
	Kyoto University	5	University of Sheffield	3	Victoria Univ. Wellington	2
	Leipzig University	5	University of St. Andrews	3		

The table lists the number of times chemistry Nobel prize winners' biographies mention specific universities. For details on the data, see the text and Appendix Section 1.

Table A.10 University-level mentions in given time periods in chemistry

Total number of mentions in:

1855–1900	1901–1940	1941–1980	1981–2016
10 Humboldt Univ. of Berlin	15 University of Cambridge	32 Harvard University	6 Yale University
6 University of Munich	13 Humboldt Univ. of Berlin	32 University of Cambridge	5 California Inst. of Tech.
3 University of Bonn	13 University of Munich	22 Univ. of Calif, Berkeley	5 Harvard University
3 University of Paris	12 University of Göttingen	14 University of Chicago	5 Stanford University
3 University of Tartu	9 ETH Zurich	12 Stanford University	5 University of Cambridge
3 Uppsala University	9 University of Manchester	12 University of Oxford	4 Cornell University
2 ETH Zurich	9 University of Marburg	11 Technical Univ. of Munich	4 Johns Hopkins University
2 Harvard University	8 Harvard University	8 Columbia University	4 Massachusetts Inst. of Tech.
2 Leipzig University	8 Univ. of Calif, Berkeley	8 Massachusetts Inst. of Tech.	4 Univ. of Calif, San Diego
2 University of Erlangen	7 Columbia University	7 University of Wisconsin	3 Duke University
2 University of Göttingen	7 University of Paris	6 Cornell University	3 Northwestern University
2 University of Graz	6 University of Illinois	6 ETH Zurich	3 Technion
2 University of Manchester	6 Uppsala University	6 Imperial College London	3 Univ. of Calif, Berkeley
2 University of New Zealand	5 University of Zurich	5 Univ. of Calif, Los Angeles	3 Univ. of Calif, Irvine
2 University of Oxford	4 Massachusetts Inst. of Tech.	4 University of Strasbourg	3 Univ. of Calif, Los Angeles
2 University of Strasbourg	4 University of Chicago	4 Princeton University	3 ETH Zurich
2 University of Würzburg	4 University of Freiburg	4 Technion	2 Heidelberg University
1 Agricultural College in Berlin	4 University of Oxford	4 University of Göttingen	2 Rice University
1 Delft Univ. of Technology	3 California Inst. of Tech.	3 University of Manchester	2 Rockefeller University
1 École Normale Supérieure	3 École Sup. Phys. et Chimie	3 Weizmann Inst. of Science	2 Technical Univ. of Munich
1 École Sup. Phys. et Chimie	3 Leipzig University	3 California Inst. of Tech.	2 Texas A&M University
1 École Pratique Hautes Etudes	3 McGill University	3 Carnegie Mellon University	2 Tufts University
1 Haverford College			

University	n	University	n	University	n	University	n
Heidelberg University	1	University College London	3	Hebrew Univ. of Jerusalem	4	Univ. of Calif., Santa Barbara	2
Leiden University	1	University of Birmingham	3	Hokkaido University	4	Univ. of Southern Calif.	2
Munich Academy of Painting	1	University of Graz	3	Kyoto University	4	University of Colorado	2
Riga Technical University	1	University of Lyon	3	Rockefeller University	4	University of North Carolina	2
Royal Trade Academy	1	Aachen University	2	Univ. of Calif., San Diego	4	University of Oxford	2
Tech. Univ. of Vienna	1	City University of New York	2	University of Freiburg	4	University of Pennsylvania	2
Technical Univ. of Berlin	1	Cornell University	2	Washington Univ. in St. Louis	4	University of Strasbourg	2
Technical Univ. of Stuttgart	1	Czech Technical University	2	Case Western Reserve	3	University of Texas	2
University of Amsterdam	1	Heidelberg University	2	Karolinska Institute	3	Weizmann Inst. of Science	2
University of Bordeaux	1	Imperial College London	2	Purdue University	3	Aarhus University	1
University of Cambridge	1	Johns Hopkins University	2	Tokyo Inst. of Technology	3	Academia Sinica	1
University of Ghent	1	Technical Univ. of Darmstadt	2	University of Edinburgh	3	Boston University	1
University of Jena	1	Technical Univ. of Munich	2	University of Illinois	3	Carnegie Mellon University	1

The table lists the number of times chemistry Nobel prize winners' biographies mention specific universities in given time periods. For details on the data, see the text and Appendix Section 1.

Economics

Table A.11   Country-level university mentions in economics

| Rank | Country | Total | Years | | | | |
			1917–1940	1941–1960	1961–1980	1981–2000	2001–2016
1	United States	347	25	82	129	66	45
2	United Kingdom	60	12	15	23	8	2
3	Germany	13	5	1	5	2	
4	France	11	2	1	3	4	1
5	Norway	7	2		5		
6	Sweden	5	3	1	1		
7	Austria	4	3		1		
8	Canada	4		1	1	2	
9	Netherlands	4	3		1		
10	Australia	3		2	1		
11	China	3					3
12	Denmark	3	2				1
13	Finland	3			2	1	
14	Hungary	3		3			
15	India	3		2	1		
16	Israel	3		1	1		1
17	Russia	3	2	1			
	Total	484	61	111	174	83	55

The table lists the number of times economics Nobel winners' biographies mention universities in different countries. For details on the data, see the text and Appendix Section 1.

our data. In addition, Table A.7 lists nonuniversity organizations with which Nobel laureates cite affiliations. It includes only those organizations with two or more mentions.

7. Results by Field

Tables A.8 through A.19 present field-specific results, with three tables for each of four fields. The structure of these tables roughly follows that of Tables 1.1, 1.3, and 1.4 in the main text.

Table A.12 Cumulative Nobel mentions by university in economics

Rank	Institution	Mentions	Rank	Institution	Mentions
1	University of Chicago	43		Leiden University	3
2	Harvard University	36		Norwegian School of Econ.	3
3	Massachusetts Inst. of Tech.	31		Stockholm School of Econ.	3
4	Univ. of Calif., Berkeley	24		Univ. of Calif., San Diego	3
5	Stanford University	22		University of Budapest	3
6	Columbia University	21		University of Frankfurt	3
	Princeton University	21		University of Nottingham	3
	Yale University	21		University of Paris	3
7	University of Cambridge	19		University of Virginia	3
8	London School of Economics	17		University of Washington	3
9	Carnegie Mellon University	13	18	Aarhus University	2
10	University of Oxford	10		Amherst College	2
	University of Pennsylvania	10		Arizona State University	2
11	University of Minnesota	9		Brown University	2
12	Univ. of Calif., Los Angeles	8		George Mason University	2
13	Northwestern University	6		Leningrad State University	2
15	New York University	5		Rutgers University	2
16	City University of New York	4		Univ. of British Columbia	2
	Johns Hopkins University	4		University of Essex	2
	Stockholm University	4		University of Freiburg	2
	University of Oslo	4		University of Illinois	2
17	California Inst. of Tech.	3		University of Manchester	2
	Cornell University	3		University of Michigan	2
	École Polytechnique	3		University of Pittsburgh	2
	Hebrew Univ. of Jerusalem	3		University of Tennessee	2
	Iowa State University	3		University of Vienna	2

The table lists the number of times economics Nobel prize winners' biographies mention specific universities. For details on the data, see the text and Appendix Section 1.

Table A.13 University-level mentions in given time periods in economics

Total number of mentions in:

University	1855–1900	University	1901–1940	University	1941–1980	University	1981–2016
Columbia University	5	University of Chicago	13	Harvard University	14	University of Chicago	13
University of Chicago	5	Columbia University	8	Massachusetts Inst. of Tech.	13	Massachusetts Inst. of Tech.	12
Harvard University	4	Harvard University	8	Stanford University	12	Harvard University	10
London School of Economics	4	Princeton University	7	University of Chicago	12	Univ. of Calif., Berkeley	9
University of Oxford	4	London School of Economics	6	University of Cambridge	11	Yale University	8
Leiden University	3	Massachusetts Inst. of Tech.	6	Carnegie Mellon University	10	Princeton University	7
Stockholm University	2	Univ. of Calif., Berkeley	5	Univ. of Calif., Berkeley	10	Stanford University	7
Univ. of Calif., Berkeley	2	Yale University	5	Princeton University	10	Columbia University	4
Yale University	2	Stanford University	3	Yale University	7	Northwestern University	4
University of Cambridge	2	Univ. of Calif., Los Angeles	3	University of Pennsylvania	7	University of Minnesota	4
University of Oslo	2	University of Budapest	3	Columbia University	6	London School of Economics	3
University of Vienna	2	University of Cambridge	3	London School of Economics	4	Univ. of Calif., San Diego	3
Univ. of Calif., Los Angeles	2	Iowa State University	2	Univ. of Calif., Los Angeles	4	University of Cambridge	3
Aarhus University	1	Johns Hopkins University	2	Norwegian School of Econ.	4	University of Pennsylvania	3
Austrian Inst. Bus. Cycle	1	University of Manchester	2	University of Minnesota	3	Arizona State University	2
City University of New York	1	University of Minnesota	2	University of Oxford	3	Carnegie Mellon University	2
École Polytechnique	1	University of Nottingham	2	California Inst. of Tech.	2	City University of New York	2
Erasmus School of Econ.	1	University of Tennessee	2	Cornell University	2	George Mason University	2
Humboldt Univ. of Berlin	1						
Iowa State University	1						
Leningrad State University	1						

University	n	University	n	University	n	University	n
Lund University	1	Amherst College	1	New York University	2	New York University	2
Middle Tennessee State Univ.	1	Brown University	1	University of Essex	2	University of Oxford	2
New York University	1	California Inst. of Tech.	1	University of Frankfurt	2	Aarhus University	1
Northwestern University	1	Carnegie Mellon University	1	University of Freiburg	2	Chapman University	1
Rutgers University	1	City University of New York	1	University of Oslo	2	Chinese Univ. Hong Kong	1
South Dakota State Univ.	1	Cornell University	1	University of Paris	2	EHESS	1
Stockholm School of Econ.	1	École Normale Supérieure	1	University of Virginia	2	École Polytechnique	1
University of Amsterdam	1	Florida State University	1	Amherst College	1	École des Ponts ParisTech	1
University of Copenhagen	1	Hebrew Univ. of Jerusalem	1	Australian National Univ.	1	Hebrew Univ. of Jerusalem	1
University of Dundee	1	Illinois Inst. of Tech.	1	Brown University	1	Helsinki School of Economics	1
University of Kiel	1	Jadavpur University	1	Case Western Reserve	1	Hong Kong Univ. Sci. Tech.	1
University of Leningrad	1	Leningrad State University	1	Colorado College	1	Indiana University	1
University of Liverpool	1	Stockholm University	1	Delhi School of Economics	1	Johns Hopkins University	1
University of Lyon	1	The New School	1	École Polytechnique	1	MINES ParisTech	1
University of Rome	1	Tufts University	1	Erasmus Univ. Rotterdam	1	McGill University	1
University of Warsaw	1	Univ. of British Columbia	1	Free University of Berlin	1	Peking University	1
University of Washington	1	University of Buffalo	1	Hanken School of Economics	1	RAND Corporation	1

The table lists the number of times economics Nobel prize winners' biographies mention specific universities in given time periods. For details on the data, see the text and Appendix Section 1.

Medicine

Table A.14 Country-level university mentions in medicine

Rank	Country	Total	1855–1880	1881–1900	1901–1920	1921–1940	1941–1960	1961–1980	1981–2000	2000–2016
1	United States	426		4	38	73	122	102	56	31
2	United Kingdom	118	1	4	13	26	31	27	12	4
3	Germany	70	5	9	11	22	10	11	2	
4	France	43	5	6	5	5	11	9		2
5	Switzerland	22			2	5	7	7	1	
6	Sweden	20		3	2	4	4	5	2	
7	Australia	17				3	3	9	1	1
8	Denmark	17		6	4	3	4			
9	Canada	16			2	3	7	4		
10	Austria	12	1	5	2	3	1			
11	Japan	12				4		5	3	
12	Italy	9	1			3	1			4
13	Belgium	8		1	2	3		2		
14	Spain	7	2	2	1	2				

15	Netherlands	6				3		3		
16	Norway	6							4	2
17	Argentina	5			1		4			
18	Russia	5	4	1			5			
19	South Africa	5					5			
20	Hungary	4			1	2	1			
21	Finland	3				3				
22	Portugal	3		1	1		1			
23	Ukraine	3	2	1			1			
24	India	2					2			
25	Poland	2	1		1					
	Total	846	22	47	87	165	217	183	81	44

The table lists the number of times medicine Nobel winners' biographies mention universities in different countries. For details on the data, see the text and Appendix Section 1.

Table A.15 Cumulative Nobel mentions by university in medicine

Rank	Institution	Mentions	Rank	Institution	Mentions	Rank	Institution	Mentions
1	Harvard University	44	20	Australian National Univ.	4		Brown University	2
2	University of Cambridge	42		Heidelberg University	4		Ghent University	2
3	Columbia University	28		Indiana University	4		Kyoto University	2
4	Johns Hopkins University	25		Univ. of Calif., San Diego	4		Lafayette College	2
5	Rockefeller University	24		University of Birmingham	4		Leiden University	2
6	University of Oxford	21		University of Gottingen	4		Leipzig University	2
7	University of Paris	20		University of Graz	4		Michigan State University	2
8	California Inst. of Tech.	17		University of Lyons	4		Northwestern University	2
9	Cornell University	16		University of Madrid	4		Norwegian Univ. Sci. Tech.	2
10	University of Copenhagen	14		University of Marburg	4		Odessa University	2
11	University College London	13		University of Oslo	4		Osaka City University	2
	University of Wisconsin	13		University of Toronto	4		SM Kirov Mil. Med. Acad.	2
	Washington Univ. in St. Louis	13		University of Turin	4		Tulane University	2
	Yale University	13		University of Würzburg	4		Union College	2
12	Karolinska Institute	12		University of Zurich	4		Univ. of Calif., Los Angeles	2
	University of Pennsylvania	12		Utrecht University	4		Univ. of Western Australia	2
	University of Texas	12		Vanderbilt University	4		Univ. of the Witwatersrand	2
13	New York University	11	21	Duke University	3		University of Aberdeen	2
	Stanford University	11		Free University of Brussels	3		University of Budapest	2
14	Massachusetts Inst. of Tech.	10		George Washington Univ.	3		University of Burgundy	2
	University of Chicago	10		King's College London	3		University of Coimbra	2
	University of Illinois	10		Oberlin College	3		University of Colorado	2
	University of Washington	10		Princeton University	3		University of Düsseldorf	2
15	Humboldt Univ. of Berlin	9		Rutgers University	3		University of Florida	2

Rank	University	Count
16	City University of New York	8
	Univ. of Calif., Berkeley	8
17	University of Munich	8
	University of Vienna	8
	McGill University	7
	Pasteur Institute	7
	University of Geneva	7
	University of London	7
18	University of Strasbourg	7
	Case Western Reserve	6
	Univ. of Calif., San Francisco	6
	University of Michigan	6
19	ETH Zurich	5
	Imperial College London	5
	University of Basel	5
	University of Buenos Aires	5
	University of Edinburgh	5
	University of Freiburg	5
	University of Melbourne	5

Rank	University	Count
	State University of New York	3
	Technical Univ. of Denmark	3
	Tokyo University of Science	3
	University of Bern	3
	University of Cape Town	3
	University of Helsinki	3
	University of Kiel	3
	University of Lund	3
	University of Missouri	3
	University of Pittsburgh	3
	University of Rochester	3
	University of Sheffield	3
	University of St. Andrews	3
	University of Stockholm	3
	University of Tübingen	3
	University of Virginia	3
	Uppsala University	3
22	Amherst College	2
	Baylor University	2

Rank	University	Count
	University of Frankfurt	2
	University of Glasgow	2
	University of Hamburg	2
	University of Liverpool	2
	University of Minnesota	2
	University of Montreal	2
	University of Nebraska	2
	University of North Carolina	2
	University of Pavia	2
	University of Queensland	2
	University of Rome	2
	University of Rostock	2
	University of Rouen	2
	University of Saint Petersburg	2
	University of Sydney	2
	University of Wrocław	2
	University of the Punjab	2
	Wesleyan University	2

The table lists the number of times medicine Nobel prize winners' biographies mention specific universities. For details on the data, see the text and Appendix Section 1.

Table A.16 University-level mentions in given time periods in medicine

Total number of mentions in:

1855–1900		1901–1940		1941–1980		1981–2016	
University of Copenhagen	6	Harvard University	15	Harvard University	23	University of Texas	8
Humboldt Univ. of Berlin	5	University of Cambridge	15	University of Cambridge	20	Rockefeller University	7
University of Vienna	5	Columbia University	10	Columbia University	14	Harvard University	6
University of Strasbourg	4	Johns Hopkins University	10	California Inst. of Tech.	12	University of Cambridge	5
University of Lyons	3	University of Oxford	7	University of Oxford	12	Columbia University	4
University of Stockholm	3	University of Paris	7	Rockefeller University	11	Massachusetts Inst. of Tech.	4
Johns Hopkins University	2	Rockefeller University	6	University of Paris	11	Stanford University	4
Odessa University	2	Washington Univ. in St. Louis	6	Johns Hopkins University	10	Univ. of Calif, San Francisco	4
SM Kirov Mil. Med. Acad.	2	Cornell University	5	Washington Univ. in St. Louis	10	University of Oslo	4
University of Cambridge	2	Karolinska Institute	5	Cornell University	8	University of Washington	4
University of Gottingen	2	New York University	5	Karolinska Institute	8	Duke University	3
University of Paris	2	Yale University	4	New York University	8	Johns Hopkins University	3
University of Saint Petersburg	2	McGill University	3	Yale University	8	Univ. of Calif, Berkeley	3
University of Würzburg	2	Stanford University	3	McGill University	7	University of Virginia	3
Utrecht University	2	University of Illinois	3	Stanford University	7	California Inst. of Tech.	2
École du Val-de-Grâce	1	University of Pennsylvania	3	University of Illinois	7	Norwegian Univ. Sci. Tech.	2
ETH Zurich	1	Massachusetts Inst. of Tech.	3	University of Pennsylvania	7	Osaka City University	2
Heidelberg University	1	University College London	3	Massachusetts Inst. of Tech.	6	Pasteur Institute	2
Free University of Brussels	1			University College London	6	Princeton University	2
Imperial College London	1						
Heidelberg University	1						
Kharkiv University	1						
Karolinska Institute	1						

University	n	University	n	University	n	University	n
Leipzig University	1	New York University	3	University of Chicago	6	State University of New York	2
Saint Petersburg State Univ.	1	University of Chicago	3	University of Wisconsin	6	University of Edinburgh	2
St Bartholomew's Hosp. Coll.	1	University of Helsinki	3	Case Western Reserve	5	University of Oxford	2
Univ. of Calif., Berkeley	1	University of Kiel	3	University of Geneva	5	University of Pennsylvania	2
University College London	1	University of Madrid	3	University of London	5	Yale University	2
University of Aberdeen	1	University of Marburg	3	City University of New York	4	Arizona State University	1
University of Amsterdam	1	University of Michigan	3	Indiana University	4	Australian National Univ.	1
University of Barcelona	1	University of Pennsylvania	3	Pasteur Institute	4	Brown University	1
University of Bern	1	University of Toronto	3	Univ. of Calif., San Diego	4	Cardiff University	1
University of Coimbra	1	University of Turin	3	University of Basel	4	City University of New York	1
University of Giessen	1	University of Vienna	3	University of Birmingham	4	Cornell University	1
University of Graz	1	Uppsala University	3	University of Buenos Aires	4	Drew University	1
University of Halle	1	Washington Univ. in St. Louis	3	University of Washington	4	Florida State University	1
University of Indonesia	1	Ghent University	2	Australian National Univ.	3	George Washington Univ.	1
University of Madrid	1	Lafayette College	2	Univ. of Calif., Berkeley	3	Karolinska Institute	1
University of Pavia	1	Leiden University	2	University of Cape Town	3	King's College London	1

The table lists the number of times medicine Nobel prize winners' biographies mention specific universities in given time periods. For details on the data see the text and Appendix Section 1.

Physics

Table A.17 Country-level university mentions in physics

Rank	Country	Total	Years							
			1855–1880	1881–1900	1901–1920	1921–1940	1941–1960	1961–1980	1981–2000	2000–2016
1	United States	410	2	4	15	71	128	100	62	28
2	Germany	148	12	24	33	43	18	14	3	1
3	United Kingdom	116	4	8	20	37	26	13	4	4
4	France	58	6	7	10	10	6	11	5	3
5	Japan	42				7	9	9	10	7
6	Russia	21			1	9	5	2	4	
7	Netherlands	20	2	1	4	1	4	4	3	1
8	Switzerland	19	3	2	5	3	4		2	
9	Canada	18					13	2	1	2
10	Italy	13				7	3	1	2	
11	Denmark	10			4	3	2	1		
12	Austria	8			4	4				
13	Sweden	8		1		3	2	1	1	
14	China	6					2	1	2	1
15	India	6			2	3			1	
16	Belgium	4					3			
17	Poland	4		1	2	1			1	
18	Australia	3			2					1
19	Ireland	3				2	1			
20	Pakistan	3					3			
21	Israel	2						1		1
	Total	924	29	48	103	204	230	160	100	50

The table lists the number of times physics Nobel winners' biographies mention universities in different countries. For details on the data, see the text and Appendix Section 1.

Table A.18 Cumulative Nobel mentions by university in physics

Rank	Institution	Mentions	Rank	Institution	Mentions	Rank	Institution	Mentions
1	University of Cambridge	56	19	Imperial College London	5	24	Dalhousie University	2
2	Harvard University	43		McGill University	5		Delft Univ. of Technology	2
3	Columbia University	41		University of Graz	5		École Polytechnique	2
4	Univ. of Calif., Berkeley	30		University of Rome	5		École des Ponts ParisTech	2
	University of Chicago	30		Uppsala University	5		Florida State University	2
5	Princeton University	28		Case Western Reserve	4		Indian Institute of Science	2
6	Massachusetts Inst. of Tech.	24		City University of New York	4		King's College London	2
	Stanford University	24	20	Johns Hopkins University	4		Manchester Mun. Coll. Tech.	2
7	California Inst. of Tech.	21		Lebedev Physical Institute	4		Meijo University	2
	University of Göttingen	21		Leipzig University	4		Moscow Eng. Phys. Inst.	2
8	University of Paris	19		University College London	4		Moscow Ins. of Phys. Tech.	2
9	École Normale Supérieure	18		University of Bristol	4		Osaka University	2
	Humboldt Univ. of Berlin	18		University of Colorado	4		Physikalisch-Tech. Bund.	2
10	University of Manchester	14		University of Groningen	4		Presidency College	2
11	University of Munich	13		University of Hamburg	4		Radboud Univ. Nijmegen	2
12	ETH Zurich	12		University of Liverpool	4		Rensselaer Polytechnic Inst.	2
	Leiden University	12		University of London	4		Royal Institute of Technology	2
	Nagoya University	12		University of Maryland	4		Scuola Normale Sup. di Pisa	2
	University of Illinois	12		University of Pennsylvania	4		Stevens Inst. of Tech.	2
13	Cornell University	11		University of Toronto	4		Texas A&M University	2
14	Heidelberg University	10		University of Wrocław	4		Tsinghua University	2
	University of Copenhagen	10	21	Aachen University	3		United States Naval Academy	2
	University of Tokyo	10		Duke University	3		Univ. of British Columbia	2
15	Utrecht University	9		École Sup. Phys. et Chimie	3		Univ. of Calif., San Diego	2

(continued)

Table A.18 (Continued)

Rank	Institution	Mentions	Rank	Institution	Mentions	Rank	Institution	Mentions
16	Kyoto University	8		Free University of Brussels	3		University of Adelaide	2
	Technical Univ. of Berlin	8		GCU Lahore	3		University of Alberta	2
	Technical Univ. of Munich	8		Moscow State University	3		University of Bordeaux	2
	University of Michigan	8		New York University	3		University of Hannover	2
	University of Oxford	8		Ohio State University	3		University of Kiel	2
	University of Strasbourg	8		Purdue University	3		University of Marburg	2
	University of Wisconsin	8		Trinity College Dublin	3		University of Massachusetts	2
17	University of Frankfurt	7		University of Amsterdam	3		University of Nottingham	2
	University of Minnesota	7		University of Arizona	3		University of Pisa	2
	University of Würzburg	7		University of Bonn	3		University of Rochester	2
	University of Zurich	7		University of Giessen	3		University of Tokushima	2
	Yale University	7		University of Lund	3		University of Tübingen	2
18	Carnegie Mellon University	6		University of Texas	3		University of Vienna	2
	Univ. of Calif., Santa Barbara	6		Whitman College	3		University of Washington	2
	University of Edinburgh	6	22	Chinese Univ. Hong Kong	2		Virginia Tech	2
							Washington Univ. in St. Louis	2

The table lists the number of times physics Nobel prize winners' biographies mention specific universities. For details on the data, see the text and Appendix Section 1.

Table *A.19* University-level mentions in given time periods in physics

			Total number of mentions in:				
	1855–1900		1901–1940		1941–1980		1981–2016
University of Cambridge	8	University of Cambridge	31	Columbia University	30	Stanford University	12
Leiden University	7	University of Göttingen	14	Harvard University	24	Harvard University	11
Heidelberg University	4	Humboldt Univ. of Berlin	13	Univ. of Calif., Berkeley	22	Massachusetts Inst. of Tech.	7
Humboldt Univ. of Berlin	4	Princeton University	10	University of Chicago	19	Nagoya University	7
University of Munich	4	California Inst. of Tech.	9	University of Cambridge	17	Princeton University	6
University of Paris	4	Harvard University	8	Massachusetts Inst. of Tech.	15	Univ. of Calif., Berkeley	5
University of Strasbourg	4	University of Chicago	8	Princeton University	12	Univ. of Calif., Santa Barbara	4
ETH Zurich	3	University of Manchester	8	Stanford University	12	Columbia University	3
École Normale Supérieure	3	Columbia University	7	California Inst. of Tech.	10	Cornell University	3
University of Würzburg	3	Technical Univ. of Berlin	7	University of Illinois	9	École Normale Supérieure	3
Aachen University	2	University of Copenhagen	7	École Normale Supérieure	8	University of Chicago	3
United States Naval Academy	2	University of Munich	7	University of Tokyo	7	University of Colorado	3
University of Bonn	2	University of Paris	7	Cornell University	6	University of Manchester	3
University of Giessen	2	University of Wisconsin	7	Utrecht University	6	University of Michigan	3
University of Göttingen	2	University of Graz	5	McGill University	5	University of Paris	3
University of Groningen	2	University of Minnesota	5	Nagoya University	5	California Inst. of Tech.	2
University of Liverpool	2	ETH Zurich	4	University of Göttingen	5	École Sup. Phys. et Chimie	2

(continued)

Table A.19 (Continued)

Total number of mentions in:

University	1855–1900	University	1901–1940	University	1941–1980	University	1981–2016
University of Manchester	2	École Normale Supérieure	4	University of Michigan	5	Johns Hopkins University	2
University of Marburg	2	Kyoto University	4	University of Oxford	5	Meiji University	2
University of Zurich	2	University of Rome	4	University of Paris	5	Moscow Ins. of Phys. Tech.	2
Case Western Reserve	1	University of Zurich	4	Carnegie Mellon University	4	Radboud Univ. Nijmegen	2
Chalmers Univ. of Tech.	1	Leiden University	3	ETH Zurich	4	Technical Univ. of Munich	2
Clark University	1	Leipzig University	3	Heidelberg University	4	Texas A&M University	2
Columbia University	1	Univ. of Calif., Berkeley	3	Imperial College London	4	University of Arizona	2
Delft Univ. of Technology	1	University of Amsterdam	3	Lebedev Physical Institute	4	University of Nottingham	2
École Polytechnique	1	University of Frankfurt	3	Technical Univ. of Munich	4	University of Texas	2
École des Ponts ParisTech	1	University of Hamburg	3	University of Frankfurt	4	University of Tokyo	2
Oberlin College	1	University of Lund	3	University of Toronto	4	Utrecht University	2
University of Hohenheim	1	University of Strasbourg	3	Yale University	4	Arizona State University	1
University of Karlsruhe	1	University of Wrocław	3	GCU Lahore	3	Australian National Univ.	1
University of Kiel	1	Uppsala University	3	Kyoto University	3	Boston University	1
University of Tübingen	1	Carnegie Mellon University	3	New York University	3	Chapman University	1
University of Wrocław	1	City University of New York	2	University College London	3	Chinese Univ. Hong Kong	1
		Cornell University	2	University of Copenhagen	3	Colorado State University	1
		Heidelberg University	2	University of Edinburgh	3	ETH Zurich	1

The table lists the number of times physics Nobel prize winners' biographies mention specific universities in given time periods. For details on the data, see the text and Appendix Section 1.

Notes

CHAPTER 1 • A Puzzle

1. The first quote is due to Hacker and Pierson (2016, 14). "Endangering prosperity" is the title of Hanushek et al. (2013). The characterization of test scores is due to Aghion et al. (2010, 10); that of institutions to Acemoglu and Autor (2012, 427).

2. For discussions on how international test score comparisons inform American educational performance, see Carnoy and Rothstein (2013) and Carnoy et al. (2015). On PISA and international tests more generally, see Schmidt et al. (2019).

3. Metzger (1955, 101). See also Shils (1978) and Werner (2013).

4. The Shanghai ranking is formally known as the Academic Ranking of World Universities and is largely based on research-related indicators (the statement in the text concerns the 2016 ranking). See Clotfelter (2010) for related discussion.

5. This list is partially due to Romer (1990), Cole (2009; 2016), and Gruber and Johnson (2019). More generally, the idea that innovation can drive growth is central to growth theory; see Solow (1956), Romer (1986; 1990), Aghion and Howitt (1997), Jones (2005), and Lucas (2009). For some recent empirical evidence, see Dittmar (2011). Universities can also contribute to innovation by training highly skilled human capital; see Mokyr (2002; 2005), Mokyr and Voth (2010), Squicciarini and Voigtlander (2015), Akcigit et al. (2017), and Bianchi and Giorcelli (2019). Research is also consistent with these channels—innovation and training—being simultaneously active. For instance, Valero and Van Reenen (2016) suggest that increases in the number of universities at the country level accelerate GDP growth, and Toivanen and Vaananen (2016) that expanding engineering training can enhance innovation. See Cantoni and Yuchtman (2014) for contributions of universities to institutional quality.

6. For discussions on the possibility that producing innovations is becoming harder, see Jones (2009), Cowen (2011), Gordon (2016), and Bloom et al. (2017).

7. Databases like the *Web of Science* and *Scopus* provide records for a massive number of publications, including information on authors' names and institutional affiliations. Such data allows one to assess universities' research performance even relative

to specific areas (e.g., Williams et al. 2014) or types of academic units (e.g., Ash and Urquiola 2018). One could also use such data to produce a figure like 1.2 if these records extended into the 1800s and additionally featured authors' institutional affiliations. Appendix Section 2 discusses that this is not the case.

8. Azoulay et al. (2010) study the premature and sudden death of academic "superstars," and find that their loss lowers their colleagues' research output. In further evidence that exposure to colleagues can matter, Ilaria et al. (2017) consider the interruption of scientific exchange that followed World War I. They compare the impact this had on scientists who were building on frontier research from abroad versus the effect on those building on frontier research from home. They find that the former became less likely to publish in top journals. See also Moser et al. (2014), Waldinger (2016), Catalani et al. (2018), and Akcigit et al. (2018a). Not all research finds evidence of such spillovers. For example, Waldinger (2010; 2012) considers the dismissal of scientists in Nazi Germany and finds that this affected the productivity of PhD students, but not that of professors. Borjas and Doran (2012) consider the arrival of Soviet mathematicians to the United States after the Cold War. They find this *lowered* incumbents' output and raised the likelihood that they eventually moved to lower-ranked schools.

9. Nobel Media. Willem Conrad Rontgen—Biographical. Unpublished paper. 2019 <https://www.nobelprize.org/prizes/physics/1901/rontgen/biographical/>

10. ETH Zurich was then known as the Federal Polytechnic Institute; we address name changes below.

11. This issue sometimes comes under the heading of the "forty-first chair," in reference to the fact that the French Academy historically limited its membership to forty. Inevitably, at any given time there were distinguished academics not included (Merton 1968; Zuckerman 1977).

12. Table 1.1 provides an alternative representation of the data in Figure 1.2. Note that Figure 1.2 describes the shares rather than the absolute number of mentions that accrue to universities in different countries. One reason the shares are relevant is that the total number of mentions varies somewhat across decades. This could reflect factors like changes in: norms surrounding affiliation reporting, the prevalence of shared prizes, and faculty mobility. Note also that being mentioned in a winner's biography is a rare occurrence for most universities, making for "noisy" data. Figure 1.2 deals with this by presenting "smoothed" values (the figure presents fitted values of locally weighted regressions using a bandwidth of 0.5). This can conceal variation, however, and in Table 1.1 and below we therefore rather use raw counts of mentions. Finally, Table 1.1 covers only mentions of universities; Table A.1 in

Appendix Section 3 presents country-level results, including non-degree-granting institutions as well.

13. In physics alone, more than one hundred academics moved to the United States between 1933 and 1941 (Cole 2009). Five of them were already Nobel Prize winners, and several others went on to make fundamental contributions (Zuckerman 1977; Fermi 1968).

14. For other work placing turning points relatively early, see Hofstadter (1963) and McCaughey (1974).

15. Werner (2013).

16. This is consistent with the discussion in Goldin and Katz (1999b, 37), who point out that salient features of the American university system are often described "as having been the outgrowth of post–World War II developments." They focus, rather, on the fifty years after 1890; this book's argument will begin with even earlier events.

17. We will generally refer to universities by shorter designations (e.g., Yale rather than Yale University), except where there might be ambiguity. The tables generally list longer designations, space permitting.

18. This number includes two- and four-year institutions (based on data from the National Center for Education Statistics for 2017).

19. For Table 1.4 we sorted schools first by mentions and then alphabetically, and include only the top twenty five in each period.

20. While free entry is a well-established term in economics, free scope is not. The term "economies of scope" refers to situations in which average costs decline when firms produce multiple products. I use free scope to combine the idea of free entry and scope. The closest term I am aware of that captures this is the (lack of) "line of business restrictions." These regulations precluded the Regional Bell Operating Companies from providing services other than those related to local exchange; for example, these firms were not allowed to manufacture telecommunications equipment (Sappington 1995).

21. Free scope does not imply that all institutions engage in diverse activities (e.g., many American liberal arts colleges offer only BA degrees). The point is that in a system with free scope, schools can do so if they wish. Note also that a system that displays self-rule need not display free scope, as regulations may restrict the activities universities can take part in. Self-rule is about universities' freedom to make decisions; free scope is about that freedom extending to the markets for multiple goods.

22. Countries' reliance on market mechanisms is an attribute that tends to transcend sectors—for example, a country with an unregulated airline industry is more likely to have an unfettered retail sector. Our discussion will naturally focus on university sectors; for broader assessments, see Engerman and Sokoloff (2002) and Acemoglu and Robinson (2012).

CHAPTER 2 · The Antebellum College

1. Historians often refer to the years 1789–1861 or 1812–1861 as the antebellum period.

2. Rudolph (1962, 172). See also Handlin and Handlin (1970) and Leslie (1992).

3. Rudolph (1962). Leslie (1992) notes that in part the prevalence of ministers reflects that at the time seminaries were one of the few natural destinations for individuals desiring intellectually oriented training.

4. Hofstadter (1955).

5. Rudolph (1962) points out that Edward Wigglesworth only joined Harvard after deafness prevented him from leading a congregation; loss of voice similarly led Albert Shipp to Wofford College.

6. Leslie (1992, 66).

7. Flexner (1946, 14). Thelin (2004, 63) adds that in the 1850s Harvard faculty enjoyed prestige in the Boston area, "yet were not especially well paid," and Veysey (1965) that professors often needed independent means to supplement their nominal salaries. Of course, in part due to their own or their spouses' inherited wealth, faculty could live well; for instance, Leslie (1992) presents evidence that many had live-in servants.

8. See Flexner (1946), Storr (1953), and Leslie (1992).

9. Rudolph (1962, 196).

10. Burke (1982) adds that most colleges in the West and South had between four and six faculty members. See also Cohen and Kisker (2010).

11. Hofstadter (1955).

12. These numbers are from each school's office of institutional research and reporting (June 2018).

13. See Paulsen (1906), Snow (1907), Butts (1939), and Rudolph (1977). In the High Middle Ages, some of these subjects were included in the *trivium* (grammar, logic, and rhetoric) and the *quadrivium* (arithmetic, geometry, music, and astronomy).

14. Broome (1903, 18).

15. Kelley (1974, 156). On the college curriculum see also Broome (1903), Hofstadter (1955), Rudolph (1977), Reuben (1996), Roberts and Turner (2000), and Cohen and Kisker (2010).

16. Kelley (1974, 157).

17. We set aside the disputation (*disputatio*), another common exercise in the Middle Ages; see Verger (1973) and Clark (2006).

18. Kelley (1974, 159). See also Brubacher and Rudy (1958), Bishop (1962), Rudolph (1977), and Cohen and Kisker (2010).

19. Veysey (1965, 38). Rudolph (1977, 89) adds that at Princeton in 1846, "Professor Everett Topping made the mistake of discovering that if he interspersed commentary on Greek literature with the study of the Greek language he could elicit a gratifying improvement in student interest. For this heresy he was called before the president, and a few days later his resignation was accepted."

20. Rudolph (1962, 158).

21. Brubacher and Rudy (1958).

22. Veysey (1965, 6).

23. For brevity, this section treats the higher educational systems of France, Germany, and the U.K. as if they were fairly homogenous. This sets aside important differences, some of which we return to later. For example, the discussion refers only to universities; these had a central role in Germany, while in France other types of specialized institutions (e.g., the *grandes écoles*) are more important (D'Irsay 1935; Ben-David 1977; Fox and Weisz 1980; Clark 1983; Verger 1986; Clark 2006).

24. See Paulsen (1906), Morison (1935), Ringer (1979), and Frijhoff (1996).

25. Having masters teach courses or books interchangeably was common in European arts faculties into the 1600s, but the practice ended in the 1700s. For instance, Sloan (1971) notes that the Scottish universities had left behind the so-called "rotating regency" by the early 1700s. Clark (2006, 171) adds that by 1768 the Prussian Ministry of Education required the University of Halle to list its courses organized by disciplines; this helped eliminate the game of "musical chairs," whereby faculty members jumped from teaching in one area to another. See also Porter (1996). For further discussion on the impact of humanism on the universities, see D'Irsay (1935), Butts (1939), Rudy (1984), Rüegg (1992), and Clark (2006).

26. This is the prevalent arrangement, although there are exceptions. Some concern entire countries, such as Scotland, and some subsets of institutions. Economic analyses of when students choose a field highlight the tradeoff between: (i) the amount of time students have to acquire specialized knowledge, and (ii) the mismatch that

might occur if they choose specializations too early. See Clark (1983), Malamud (2010; 2011) and Bordon and Fu (2015).

27. Vandermeersch (1996), Clark (2006). For example, Ben-David (1971) highlights that funding for science in France increased significantly between 1800 and 1830. Of course, such increases did not begin at the same time everywhere in Europe, nor were they always uniformly sustained (Ringer 1979). Further, the Enlightenment affected universities in England and France somewhat later than in Germany, the Netherlands, and Scotland, and French non-university academies and societies accounted for a large share of scientific activity for longer (Rudy 1984; D'Irsay 1935).

28. Morison (1936), Butts (1939), Hofstadter (1955), Curti and Nash (1965).

29. Rudolph (1962).

30. Kelley (1974, 137).

31. Butts (1939).

32. Brubacher and Rudy (1958, 17).

33. Brubacher and Rudy (1958).

34. Curti and Nash (1965, 65).

35. See Curti and Nash (1965), Rudolph (1977), Roberts and Turner (2000), and Thelin (2004). Later on, institutions like the Case School of Applied Science and the Carnegie Technical School also served this market.

36. Rudolph (1962, 271).

37. For example, some charter schools stipulate that children must be willing to attend school on Saturdays, or that their parents must attend meetings with teachers or parent associations. See Angrist et al. (2010). See also Bergman and McFarlin Jr. (2018) for evidence on more explicit selection on the part of charter schools.

38. For example, employers may prefer to recruit at selective colleges because they infer that individuals admitted to them are of high ability. This channel is formalized in MacLeod and Urquiola (2015), and MacLeod et al. (2017) provide rigorous evidence that it is active. The network channel has proven harder to isolate, but there is clear evidence consistent with it. For example, Hoekstra (2009), Saavedra (2009), and Oyer and Schaefer (2015) show that going to a more selective college raises wage income, and Zimmerman (2016) that it raises the probability of making it onto corporate leadership teams; see also Schmutte (2015) and Ioannides and Loury (2004). Sociologists have also discussed the impact of schools on networks; see for instance Kahn (2011) and Rivera (2015). In addition, some of the networks emphasized by Granovetter (1973) may be formed in school or through school friends.

39. Kaufmann et al. (2013) show that in Chile, admission to a higher ranked university has substantial returns in terms of partner quality for women.

40. For example, Hoxby (2012; 2014) presents a framework in which instructors at top universities are better at teaching high- than low-ability students, and Riehl (2018) provides causal evidence that may be the case. There is also a large literature covering peer effects, including models in Rothschild and White (1995), Epple and Romano (1998), and Epple et al. (2006). On the empirical front, there is evidence that going to a better school (as measured by peer quality) can improve one's outcomes (Jackson 2010; Pop-Eleches and Urquiola 2013), but it is difficult to attribute this exclusively to peer effects. In addition, such improvements are not always observed (e.g., Cullen et al. 2006; Clark 2010; Bui et al. 2014; Barrow et al. 2017). There is also evidence that such effects may be complicated and not robust to changes in the manner in which peer groups are formed (Carrell et al. 2013). For a review, see also Epple and Romano (2011). We return to the impact of peer homogeneity on learning below.

41. Hoxby and Avery (2013) and Chetty et al. (2017b) highlight the relative absence of low-income students at selective colleges, and Macartney and Singleton (2017) consider the impact of school board elections on K-12 racial segregation. These concerns certainly affect policy too; for example, the New York City Schools Chancellor has stated a desire for more racially integrated schools, and the 2019 Democratic primaries feature debates surrounding mandatory busing.

42. The colonial college missing in this list is Pennsylvania, which had the least defined religious affiliation. We return to it in Part II.

43. The literature provides ample evidence of a preference for school proximity. See for example Card (1995) and Hoxby (2009) on higher education, and more generally Bayer et al. (2007), Gallego and Hernando (2009), Hastings et al. (2009), Abdulkadiroglu et al. (2017b), Neilson (2017), and Walters (2018).

44. Curti and Nash (1965, 51).

45. Curti and Nash (1965), Dorn (2017).

46. See Burke (1982), Naylor((1973), and Cohen and Kisker (2010) for discussions; we return to this issue below.

47. Ringer (1979).

48. Tewksbury (1932, 4). See also Douglass (2000) and Handlin and Handlin (1970).

49. Thelin (2004, 50). Burke (1982, 38) adds that in almost every case, the new colleges were a product of an interaction between a local denominational organization's willingness to help "a college and a town's desire for education for its sons and

daughters." Similarly, Leslie (1992, 1) characterizes colleges in the late 1800s as "agents of ethnoreligious subcultures and local boosterism." This statement raises the fact that in some cases denominational affiliation and ethnic origin could overlap; for instance, he cites the case of the German Reformed population that supported Franklin and Marshall.

50. Butts (1939, 117).

51. In part because of its urban location, from early on Harvard was perceived as being on a liberalizing trajectory; see Morison (1936), Butts (1939), Jencks and Riesman (1968), and Kelley (1974).

52. Brubacher and Rudy (1958). Initially, states' role in college founding was strongest in the South, beginning in Georgia and North Carolina. Later, the Midwest and West were central to state university creation (e.g., the universities of Michigan, Minnesota, Wisconsin, and California eventually provided leadership for entire systems of public education). In the United States, essentially no university-creation activity concerned the federal government, despite proposals from influential leaders like George Washington, Thomas Jefferson, and James Madison. Brubacher and Rudy suggest this partially reflected the denominations' suspicion of a national, secular school, and more generally the suspicion of centralized governmental power. The federal government did create specialized institutions like the United States Military Academy at West Point, and the United States Naval Academy at Annapolis.

53. See also Morison (1936), Burke (1982), and Potts (2000).

54. Rudolph (1962, 198). Brubacher and Rudy (1958) add that in 1806 more than four-fifths of Dartmouth's graduating class left owing the college money.

55. Rutgers was initially designated Queen's College, as discussed further in Part II. The second time it reopened it received Colonel Henry Rutgers' name; see Frusciano (2006).

56. Rudolph (1962, 187).

57. Goldin and Katz (2011a) note that localities had a major role in expanding schooling in the United States. In time, these local entities coalesced into thousands of school districts. See Tiebout (1956) for seminal work on sorting at the district level, and for related empirical work see Kenny and Schmidt (1992), Hoxby (2000), and Urquiola (2005). On the motivations for educational expansion, see Goldin and Katz (2000), Goldin (2001), Graham (2005), and Bandiera et al. (2017).

58. For instance, Goldin and Katz (2008, 28) state that Great Britain, France, and Germany all tested children, generally before their twelfth birthday, to see who would be tracked to enter secondary school. See also Goldin (1998) and Clark (2006).

59. Cole (2009, 22).

60. The first quote is from Geiger (2015, 1). The quote for William and Mary comes from Herbst (1982, 31); the one for Yale from The President and Fellows of Yale University. The Yale Corportation: Charter and Legislation. New Haven: Yale University. 1976. https://www.yale.edu/sites/default/files/files/University-Charter.pdf

61. Hamilton's exact age upon entering King's is not entirely clear; see Chernow (2004) and McCaughey (2004). Here we use Princeton and Columbia's later designations; see Part II.

62. James (1930).

63. For further illustration, Leslie (1992) presents a comparative history of Bucknell, Franklin and Marshall, Princeton, and Swarthmore. He notes that of these only Princeton systematically avoided preparatory instruction. See also Henderson (1912).

64. See Brubacher and Rudy (1958) and Dorn (2017), respectively. See also Allmendinger Jr. (1975).

65. For example, Leslie (1992) notes that Swarthmore found it hard for its preparatory services to compete with the lower-cost public schools that appealed to Hicksite Quakers; once Swarthmore ended its preparatory program, it took years for enrollments to rise enough to compensate. Further illustrating the interaction between both sectors, Graham (1974) indicates that one reason Wisconsin's preparatory department was abolished was as an inducement to the development of public high schools in the state.

66. Kelley (1974, 115).

67. Storr (1953), Brubacher and Rudy (1958), Werner (2013).

68. For related discussions see Hanushek and Zhang (2009), Goldin (2016), and Woessmann (2016), as well as Eble and Hu (2017) in the context of China. Speculating further, if an international exam like that on the right panel of Figure 1.1 had been administered in 1800, the United States might have already placed relatively low.

69. See Committee of the Corporation, and the Academical Faculty (1828) for the full text. On the report's implications see also Butts (1939), Storr (1953), Brubacher and Rudy (1958), Veysey (1965), Rudolph (1977), Cohen and Kisker (2010), and Reuben (1996).

70. Veysey (1965, 23).

71. Rudolph (1977, 69).

72. Butts (1939, 120). Interestingly, Fermi (1968, 34) notes that the classical curriculum of the European secondary schools was defended along similar lines; those who

"questioned the wisdom of so much classical education were told that dead lan-guages were an excellent mental gymnastic . . . ."

73. Veysey (1965, 34).

74. Oberdorfer (1995, 83).

75. Walton (1986, 7). See also Clark (1970).

76. This illustrates that entry can have countervailing effects on welfare. In economic jargon, these are analogous to the "business stealing" and "product diversity" effects highlighted by Mankiw and Whinston (1986). In this case, the business stealing ef-fect originates in that entering colleges capture enrollments others lose. The product diversity effect originates in that consumers prefer variety; while a Congregation-alist household might be willing to use a Presbyterian college, it might prefer one of its own denomination. See also Spence (1976), Dixit and Stiglitz (1977), and Hsieh and Moretti (2003).

CHAPTER 3 · Teaching Reform

1. See also Kevles (1979), Rossiter (1979), and Labaree (2017).

2. Veysey (1965, 13).

3. Adams (1876, 13). Veysey (1965) suggests that college enrollments grew less than the overall population. Burke (1982) points to more significant growth, if from a very low base.

4. "Research University-I" was a category in the taxonomy of American colleges and universities developed by the Carnegie Commission on Higher Education. This cat-egory contained the schools most active in research based on criteria including the number of doctoral degrees they offered, and their research expenditure. The cate-gory designations began to change in 2005; this group is now labeled "Doctoral Uni-versities: Highest Research Activity." The number of schools in the highest category has trended up. In 1994 there were 88; in 2018 there are 115.

5. For further instances, see Butts (1939) and Rudolph (1962).

6. The institutional origins of boards and presidents will be covered in Part II.

7. Storr (1953, 18).

8. Butts (1939, 105).

9. There is rigorous evidence (discussed in the next chapter) that this can raise learning.

10. Butts (1939, 105).

11. Butts (1939, 105).

12. Reuben (1996, 24).

13. Storr (1953, 16).

14. Storr (1953, 23).

15. Butts (1939, 107). Ticknor wrote this in a communication to Thomas Jefferson, who was then pondering the configuration of higher education in Virginia.

16. McCaughey (2003, 117) indicates that in these years "it was not unusual for a son to be elected at the point of his father's retirement or death."

17. Ruggles had attended Yale and taken classes with Benjamin Silliman before going into law. He was involved in the construction of the Croton aqueduct and the expansion of the Erie Canal. Through his real estate investments, he was largely responsible for the creation of Gramercy Park. Hamilton Fish, a Columbia trustee and a noted Secretary of State, once stated that "Ruggles can throw off more brilliant and pregnant ideas in a given moment than any man I ever saw" (Burgess 1934, 184).

18. Thompson (1946, 80).

19. McCaughey (2003, 123).

20. Alexandar Bache, quoted by Storr (1953, 68).

21. Storr (1953, 78).

22. Storr (1953, 54).

23. Storr (1953, 58).

24. Butts (1939) notes that Brown's enrollment fell by about 25 percent between 1835 and 1849.

25. Rudolph (1962) notes these existed at more than thirty colleges. Butts (1939) adds that these two paths—scientific schools and parallel programs—were not mutually exclusive; some schools attempted both. See also Brubacher and Rudy (1958), Leslie (1992), Roberts and Turner (2000), and Cohen and Kisker (2010).

26. Veysey (1965, 41).

27. Butts (1939, 149). Leslie (1992) makes analogous observations regarding the BS programs at Bucknell and Princeton.

28. Rudolph (1962, 258).

29. Butts (1939).

30. Storr (1953).

31. Rudolph (1997), Cohen and Kisker (2010).

32. Storr (1953) mentions that Union's 1852 catalog announced forthcoming graduate departments in applied chemistry, mining and metallurgy, and higher mathematics and astronomy. It also advertised that the college would begin to emphasize the advancement rather than the diffusion of knowledge.

33. Storr (1953, 134).

34. Cole (2009, 19).

35. Becker (1943), Bishop (1962).

36. Bishop (1962, 63).

37. This quote is from Section 4 of the act itself; see National Research Council (1995, 2).

38. Curti and Nash (1965).

39. Veysey (1965, 85). Initially students were required to take one of the offered courses, but by 1896 there was free election in the entire curriculum (Butts 1939).

40. Bishop (1962, 74).

41. White acknowledged his debts to previous reformers. He particularly cited Henry Tappan, president of Michigan, who had earlier led unsuccessful university-oriented reforms there (Brubacher and Rudy, 1958).

42. Rudolph (1977, 127).

43. There were substantial early gifts for infrastructure from John McGraw, and for various purposes from Henry Sage (Becker 1943).

44. Flexner (1946, 9).

45. See Flexner (1946), Hawkins (1960), Douglass (2000), and Pelfrey (2004).

46. Flexner (1946, 34).

47. The first observation is due to Thelin (2004), the second to Curti and Nash (1965).

48. Hawkins (1960), Veysey (1965).

49. Flexner (1946, 40). See also James (1930) and Veysey (1965). Eliot was not alone in this position. For example, in 1866 Frederick Barnard (future president of Columbia, covered below) asserted that universities could not be created suddenly, but rather had to grow by gradual accretion continued through a long series of years (Curti and Nash 1965, 112).

50. Flexner (1946, 47).

51. Angell stated that graduate work was "supported warmly by the professors. We have organized a specific postgraduate course, and generally have from ten to twenty

persons and hope to increase that number. Our students fall into the habit of remaining, among them one or two young ladies" (Flexner 1946, 45).

52. Hawkins (1960, 65).

53. Gilman (1885, 31).

54. The passage is from Gilman's inaugural address (Flexner 1946, 58).

55. Hawkins (1960, 100).

56. Veysey (1965, 83).

57. Flexner (1946, 68).

58. Hawkins (1960, 22). While Gilman thought that academic ability should be the main criterion, he seems to not have totally abandoned other considerations regarding faculty behavior. For example, Veysey (1965) reports he once reprimanded a professor for smoking in public.

59. Hawkins (1960, 77).

60. Cole (2009, 21).

61. Starr (1982). Up to this period in most cases, professional (e.g., law and medicine) schools operated outside universities and often for profit; see discussions in Goldin and Katz (1998) and Thelin (2004). Further, into the 1900s professional schools rarely required a BA degree. Universities began to absorb these schools. For example, Yale took over the Litchfield Law School and Columbia the College of Physicians and Surgeons (Brubacher and Rudy, 1958).

62. Hawkins (1960).

63. Hawkins (1960).

64. Rudolph (1962, 293).

65. Kerr (1963), Werner (2013).

66. Morison (1936).

67. Starr (1982, 114). See also Kerr (1963).

68. Patton and Field (1927), Morison (1936), Butts (1939).

69. Oberdorfer (1995, 77). The quote is from an 1885 meeting of the Century Club in New York City, at which Eliot and McCosh debated educational reform. It is worth mentioning that McCosh mixed conservative tendencies with reforms that would eventually help place Princeton in the top rank of research universities as well; see Graham (1974).

70. Morison (1936, 347).

71. Morison (1936). This broadly implemented another of Ticknor's wishes.

72. Eliot (1908). It is worth noting that not all schools saw immediate increases in enrollments. The imposition of standards in the medical school, for example, initially caused lower enrollments there (Starr, 1982).

73. Veysey (1965).

74. Morison (1936, 342) notes, at the same time, that Eliot considered election should be limited to subjects "cultural in character, non-vocational, and therefore properly comprehended under the nineteenth-century definition of the liberal arts and sciences."

75. Veysey (1965, 96).

76. James (1930, 18).

77. James (1930, 19).

78. Veysey (1965, 97).

79. Flexner (1946, 336).

80. Columbia's early leadership is not only a feature of our Nobel-based ranking. Cole (2009, 33) mentions that the Carnegie Foundation produced a ranking of universities in 1908. He states: "It evaluated universities by their total income, allocation of resources to instruction, total number of students, size of the instructional staff, student faculty ratio, average expenditures for instruction per student, and expenditures for instruction per student in excess of tuition. Columbia led the list followed by Harvard, Chicago, . . . and Johns Hopkins."

81. McCaughey (2003).

82. McCaughey (2003, 67).

83. Rudolph (1977, 29).

84. See Morison (1936), Rudolph (1977), and McCaughey (2003).

85. McCaughey (2003, 77). More precisely, Jefferson called it a *cloacina* (for the Roman goddess of sewers).

86. Sovern (2014, 141).

87. See McCaughey (2014) for a history of Columbia's School of Engineering and Applied Science.

88. Burgess (1934, 141). See also Rosenthal (2006).

89. Burgess (1934, 161).

90. Burgess (1934, 164).

91. Burgess (1934, 178).

92. McCaughey (2003, 161).

93. McCaughey (2003).

94. McCaughey (2003, 164).

95. McCaughey (2003, 165).

96. Curti and Nash (1965).

97. Geiger (1986), McCaughey (2003).

98. Flexner (1946, 41). This observation came up in Eliot's comments to the Johns Hopkins trustees.

99. Rudolph (1962). It is possible that a part of this increase was illusory, as for a while there was a minor industry in fake PhDs. Rudolph (1962, 396) reports that "some institutions . . . covered their own embarrassment and that of others by trafficking in honorary Ph.D. degrees." See also Leslie (1992).

100. See Goldin and Katz (1998) for further data on the creation of learned societies in the United States, and Clark (1983) for international comparisons.

101. Berkeley, Cornell, and Harvard also stood out in this dimension; see Goldin and Katz (1999b) and Cole (2009).

102. This measure certainly still contains noise in the sense that some papers at a lower-ranked journal end up being more successful (by measures like citations) than some papers at a higher-ranked journal. The point is that on average, the papers at a higher-ranked journal will tend to have higher impact.

103. This illustrates the type of sorting dynamic explored for students and colleges in MacLeod and Urquiola (2015). We discuss it in further detail below. Note also that the emergence of a strict hierarchy of units like journals is more likely to happen when there is free entry, as there was in this case. For data on top journals in economics, see Card and Della Vigna (2017). Note also that the hierarchy of journal quality can be criticized; see Heckman and Moktan (2018).

104. A side note is that because research activity grew more suddenly in the United States, the development of professional associations and hierarchies of journals might have been more immediate than in Europe. There the tendency of professors to submit their work to their institute's or department's publications lasted longer. As Geiger (1986, 34) puts it, "in the U.S., Departmental publications for a time served an important function. . . . But the persistence of such publications, had it occurred, would probably have proved harmful to the development of effective disciplines. It would very likely have produced the kind of fragmentation that seemed to

accompany the chair system in certain European countries. In university systems where each chair-holding professor has an institute, and each institute publishes its own journal, strong disciplinary organizations have found it difficult to take root." See also Clark (2006).

105. James (1930, 12).

106. Harper was sought out by John Rockefeller and other Baptists to lead the re-founded University of Chicago, after the first had been forced to close by financial troubles. He had a BA from Muskingum College by age fourteen, and a PhD from Yale by nineteen. He taught divinity and Semitic languages at the original University of Chicago before returning to Yale, where he made an impression by his scholarship and by marrying the president's daughter. Harper studied the Bible with a linguistic approach and remained an active scholar during his entire life. At Chicago he edited the journal *Hebraica* (Thelin 2004; Boyer 2015).

107. Boyer (2015).

108. Rudolph (1962), Martin (2002).

109. Douglass (2000).

110. Pelfrey (2004).

111. Geiger (1986).

112. Leslie (1992, 166).

113. These developments are analogous to the impact Dittmar (2019) shows the printing press had on universities' ability to evaluate academics' performance, and hence on the salaries they paid. More recently, inequality has been shown to be related to research performance. For example, De Fraja et al. (2016) illustrate this in the U.K., where, as in the United States, faculty salaries are unregulated. Their findings are consistent with universities using salaries to recruit academics that improve their research-related reputation. Courant and Turner (2017) explore analogous issues in the United States and find evidence consistent with salaries being determined primarily by research output and associated reputation.

114. Rabi would go on to be Eisenhower's science advisor. It is also worth noting that the power Rabi personified is de facto rather than de jure. For example, from a legal standpoint all decisions including on faculty hiring remain in the hands of president and trustees. In essence, the increasing faculty power and compensation described in this chapter corresponds to aspects of the transition from a collegiate to a professorial university discussed by Clark (2006, 16).

115. There is rigorous evidence consistent with this, as noted in Chapter 1.

116. Consider, for example, the famous introduction of the Babcock test to determine the fat content of milk in Wisconsin (due to Stephen Babcock, a Wisconsin professor and graduate of Tufts, Cornell, and Göttingen). In addition, Goldin and Katz (2008) note that public universities were initially also disproportionately active in engineering.

CHAPTER 4 · Sorting Reform

1. This is consistent with data presented by Goldin and Katz (1998), who show that fourteen of the largest twenty universities were private in 1897, with the corresponding number being ten in 1924. Nonetheless, they also note that on average public schools were larger and less numerous: there was only one public school for every four private (this may have reflected that the public sector was less subject to the denominational concerns that propelled private college creation in the 1800s). Goldin and Katz also note that college enrollments expanded substantially between 1890 and 1910, and their growth accelerated further after that. See also Slosson (1910), Peckham (1967), and Graham and Diamond (1997).

2. This reflected greater enrollment rates as well as improving graduation probabilities. On net, the high school graduation rate went from 2 percent in 1870 to 7 percent and 51 percent in 1900 and 1940, respectively, with women outnumbering men throughout the whole period (National Center for Education Statistics 1993). See also Ayres (1909), Graham (1974), and Goldin and Katz (1999).

3. In other words, economies of scale intensified for universities in this period (Goldin and Katz, 1998), and funding had to originate in enrollment growth because prices increased only slowly. For instance, Thelin (2004) reports that between 1880 and 1920 tuition was relatively stable, with real increases beginning only in the 1930s. On related issues, see Gordon and Hedlund (2016) and Hoxby (1997).

4. Cohen and Kisker (2010).

5. See Slosson (1910), Jencks and Riesman (1968), and Graham (2005). In some cases, the inspiration for these articulations seems to have been the Napoleonic, centralized arrangements in France; see Henderson (1912) and Peckham (1967).

6. Eliot (1908), Karabel (2006).

7. By about 1900, about 40 percent of college students were female. See National Center for Education Statistics (1993) for further data, and Goldin and Katz (2011) for a discussion of patterns in the growth of coeducational institutions.

8. Oberdorfer (1995, 174). See also Synnott (1979) and Thelin (2004).

9. See Leslie (1992) for related discussion.

10. National Center for Education Statistics (1993) reports a 1.3 percent college enrollment rate for 18–24-year-olds for 1869–1870. This is in line with Burke's (1982) estimate of 1.2 for 1860.

11. Miller (1990, 103).

12. Thelin (2004, 23).

13. For an extensive review of the Spence model, see Caplan (2018).

14. What is less clear is why this correlation arises. It may be that wealthy children inherit good genes from their parents, or that they enjoy better environments (e.g., good nutrition, good schools) thanks to those parents. See for example Black et al. (2007) and Black et al. (2017).

15. Thus, in contrast to Spence (1973), the question here is "which school" rather than "whether school." In addition, in Spence's model different students face different costs of going to school, and some opt not to go; in MacLeod and Urquiola (2015) everyone has the same cost and attends. In this case it is the identity of the school that transmits information. MacLeod et al. (2017) provide causal evidence that school identity can convey information.

16. There are variants of this anecdote, see https://quoteinvestigator.com/2011/04/18/groucho-resigns/.

17. Slosson (1910), Morison (1936), Kelley (1974). Leslie (1992) adds that Swarthmore was highly unusual in having made a decision to not begin operations until it had a building large enough to house all students. In part, this reflected its commitment to acting *in loco parentis,* enforcing strict supervision of its male and female students.

18. This description of the clubs is consistent with the economic definition of a club good. Club goods are excludable and nonrival. As we will see, the university clubs clearly provided an excludable service—that was the whole point. To the extent that the clubs had reputational dimensions, they also had a partially nonrival element. In addition, since the clubs were selective, they also had attributes of what economists call positional goods (Frank 1985; 2005).

19. Koch (2018).

20. On competition-induced university infrastructure investment, see Jacob et al. (2018).

21. Morison (1936).

22. Morison (1936, 180).

23. Morison (1936, 181).

24. Morison (1936, 423). See also Karabel (2006).

25. Synnott (1979, 23).

26. Karabel (2006, 17).

27. Oberdorfer (1995, 80).

28. Synnott (1979), Oberdorfer (1995), Karabel (2006).

29. Karabel (2006, 59).

30. Karabel (2006, 54).

31. Such outcomes could have also reflected the impact of club participation itself. For instance, Even and Smith (2018) find that participation in fraternities lowers grades. See also Carrell et al. (2011) and Lindo et al. (2013).

32. Peckham (1967).

33. Shaw (1942).

34. See also Shaw (1942) and Peckham (1967).

35. Burgess (1934, 39) observes that the Amherst boarding houses were typically run by a widow with an unmarried daughter. Of the women who ran one house, he writes: "The widow was a kindly old lady . . . who moved herself around in a wheelchair, and the daughter was one of the prettiest, most refined, and genial of women. She was just turning forty, and threads of grey were beginning to appear in her lovely hair. It was said that she had had a great disappointment as a young girl, having been cruelly treated by a student. . . . He must have been an unconscionable brute. . . . I can remember to this day the sad, appealing look in her beautiful gray eyes as she went uncomplainingly about her duties, . . . preparing . . . with the help of a single girl the meals for a dozen voracious, inconsiderate youths. . . . she died twenty years later . . . If there are any in paradise, she certainly is among them."

36. Veysey (1965, 91).

37. Eliot (1908, 222).

38. Synnott (1979, 166). See also Slosson (1910).

39. Eliot (1908, 217). Eliot added that regulation could make the private dorms "bad investments" (p. 218).

40. Oberdorfer (1995, 119). In addition, despite the claim that Yale's secret societies were relatively meritocratic, for decades they excluded Jewish students (Karabel 2006).

41. For example, in settings in which admission to top schools depends only on a test, families spend energy and money on test preparation; see Dang and Rogers (2008) and Jayachandran (2014).

42. The quote on Yale comes from Thelin (2004, 189); the information on Cornell from Veysey (1965).

43. Brubacher and Rudy (1958, 121).

44. This was essentially the point George Ticknor made (Chapter 3). Duflo et al. (2011) provide evidence that segregation by ability can affect learning. Other research illuminates what mechanisms may account for this. For example, Banerjee et al. (2017) and Muralidharan et al. (2017) provide evidence that tailoring instruction to students' ability levels raises learning, and Pritchett and Beatty (2012) similarly argue that curricula can be poorly matched to student ability.

45. Riehl (2018) provides rigorous evidence of such mechanisms. His findings are consistent with different colleges' teaching styles becoming adapted to different types of students. They suggest that major changes to the student-college match can diminish schools' effectiveness. Arcidiacono et al. (2016) present evidence consistent with this from California, although of a more partial equilibrium nature. See also Arcidiacono et al. (2011) and Arcidiacono and Lovenheim (2016). In addition, Ellison and Swanson (2016) provide evidence that some K-12 schools are much more effective at helping high-ability children reach their math potential.

46. Thelin (2004), Boyer (2015).

47. Synnott (1979, 95).

48. Synnott (1979).

49. McCaughey (2003, 184). Avenue B extends along part of New York's East Village and Lower East Side, neighborhoods that historically had significant Eastern European and Jewish populations.

50. Karabel (2006, 88). This type of statement refers to "tipping" behavior, in which a share of a minority, once it climbs over a threshold, causes the majority population to abandon the scene. For a more recent treatment, see Card et al. (2008).

51. Karabel (2006, 51).

52. Boyer (2015, 80). Ambiguity as to the future of the college remained for a long time at Chicago. Boyer (2015, 197) adds a 1925 proposal by the president of Johns Hopkins University, "to abolish the first two years of undergraduate work in Baltimore was fuel for the fire of those who wished to do likewise in Chicago."

53. Slosson (1910, 118). See also Rosenthal (2006).

54. Rosenthal (2006, 79). Barnard added that it would therefore not be a misfortune if Columbia College ceased to exist. McCaughey (2003, 182) notes that Seth Low, Barnard's successor, broadly agreed: "The college is . . . the seed out of which has grown

the University, but the tree, which is the university, does not exist for the sake of the seed, but the seed for the sake of the tree."

55. Rudolph (1962, 330).

56. James (1930, 181). See also Yeomans (1948) and Kerr (1963).

57. Rosenthal (2006, 337).

58. In addition, the implicit preference for students from private schools continued. For further detail, see Synnott (1979), McCaughey (2003), and Rosenthal (2006).

59. Rosenthal (2006, 342).

60. Rosenthal (2006, 343).

61. Rosenthal (2006, 349).

62. Rosenthal (2006, 350).

63. Synnott (1979), Keller and Keller (2001), Karabel (2006).

64. Synnott (1979), Karabel (2006).

65. Synnott (1979), Oberdorfer (1995).

66. Curti and Nash (1965). See also Douglass (2000).

67. Geiger (1986, 136).

68. Synnott (1979, 68).

69. Wilson and Lowell agreed on this and several points. Wilson described Lowell as "of an absolutely different type from Mr. Eliot, cordial, natural, friendly, open to all ideas, and very democratic indeed" (Synnot 1979, 33).

70. Synnott (1979), Kelley (1974).

71. Yeomans (1948).

72. The implementation of randomized assignments at Duke is recent and seems to be a response to self-sorting based on social media connections students make before arriving on campus; see Bauer-Wolf (2018).

73. Brubacher and Rudy (1958).

74. Peckham (1967), Walton (1986), Leslie (1992). See Clotfelter (2011) for an extensive and interesting analysis of "big-time" athletics in American universities.

75. Slosson (1910, 196).

76. Leslie (1992).

77. Leslie (1992).

78. See Hoxby (2014) for a discussion on the fact that selectivity has led professors at top American universities to specialize in teaching advanced and relatively homogeneous students. See also Riehl (2018) for research on what can happen when such equilibria break down.

79. Geiger (1986).

80. Geiger (1986, 136).

81. Expectations are important in education because things like a college education are not repeat purchases. When one buys a sandwich for lunch, one can evaluate it, and if it is not good, shop elsewhere the next day. A college education, in contrast, is almost always only bought once, and one has to live with the institution's reputation in the long term. For discussion on how expectations affect educational choices, see MacLeod and Urquiola (2013; 2018).

82. Henry Rosovsky (1990), a Harvard dean, stated that his school gave special treatment to legacy students and faculty children, mentioning that these are two constituencies the university needs. Meer and Rosen (2018) suggest that about half of giving by alumni at a specific private, selective university is driven by hopes of reciprocity for their children. Meer and Rosen (2010) suggest that alumni and their families form bonds with a specific university, that alumni whose children, nieces or nephews attend it donate substantially more than alumni who do not have a member of the younger generation attend. Finally, Meer and Rosen (2009) and Butcher et al. (2013) find that alumni are more likely to give when they have children than when they do not, and that this giving drops if their children do not apply, and particularly if they are rejected. See also Clotfelter (2003), Espenshade et al. (2004), Marr et al. (2005), and Holmes (2009).

83. See Lemann (1999) for an extensive and interesting treatment of the history of the SAT.

84. It likely reflects genetic factors but also conditions, including *in utero,* that reflect parental circumstances; see Almond and Currie (2011). For discussion on the correlation of standardized test scores and socioeconomic status, see Riehl (2018).

85. Veysey (1965, 91).

86. Lemann (1999), Hoxby (2009).

87. See also Cook and Frank (1993).

88. See, for instance, Goodman (2016) and Goodman et al. (2018).

89. In recent years the percentage of students paying full tuition has been about 30 percent at Harvard and 50 percent at Johns Hopkins (data retrieved from the two schools' financial aid websites in 2018). This percentage is likely to drop at Hopkins

after Michael Bloomberg's recent massive donation, part of which is explicitly designated for financial aid. See also Ehrenberg (2000).

90. Geiger (1986, 49).

91. Geiger (1986, 49).

92. See Metzger (1955), Curti and Nash (1965), Synnott (1979), and Leslie (1992). See also Lerner et al. (2008) on returns to university endowments.

93. Rudolph (1962, 429).

94. Curti and Nash (1965). Along similar lines, Leslie (1992) notes that Princeton President James McCosh went out of his way to encourage the development of community among alumni.

95. Rufus Choate, quoted by Rudolph (1962, 428).

96. In the case of Catholic University, for instance, the resistance to offering undergraduate instruction seems to have stemmed from a reluctance to compete with earlier Catholic foundations, such as Georgetown and Notre Dame (Brubacher and Rudy 1958).

97. Yeomans (1948, 328).

98. Goldin and Katz (1998) note that fourteen of the largest twenty universities were private in 1897. This number fell to ten, eight, and zero by 1924, 1934, and 1994, respectively. Nationally the share of the public sector increased; Goldin and Katz note that it went from 22 percent in 1897 to 45 and 67 percent in 1940 and 1990, respectively. This differential evolution may reflect that public institutions' objectives may emphasize enrollment size to a greater extent than the reputational concerns that emerge in a market setting, as in MacLeod and Urquiola (2015). This may also help explain why the few schools that abandoned big-time sports tended to be private, such as Chicago, which dropped football under President Hutchins, or those that went on to form the Ivy League in 1954 (Clotfelter 2011).

99. Such dynamics have been emphasized in the sociology of science too. Merton (1968) referred to the Matthew effect, whereby well-known scientists are given disproportionate credit for shared discoveries; in other words, for a tendency toward increasing inequality. Zuckerman (1977, 63) notes that "Much the same processes of accumulative advantage apply to organizations as to individuals." For work in economics see also Clotfelter (2017).

100. They note that the two key exceptions are Carnegie Mellon (descended from the Carnegie Institute of Technology, established in 1900), and Brandeis University (established in 1948). The latter's creation is in fact related to the sorting dynamics

emphasized in this chapter, since it was partially a response to the exclusion Jewish professors and students were experiencing elsewhere in the system.

CHAPTER 5 · Productivity

1. Doyle et al. (2015) state that there is a consensus that the U.S. healthcare system wastes as much as 30 percent of expenditure; see also Fisher et al. (2009). There is also evidence consistent with waste in education. Hanushek (1986; 1997) showed that the American K-12 school system can increase spending with little to show for it in terms of testing improvements. Pritchett (2003) presents analogous data for other OECD countries. More recent studies measuring the causal impact of resources produce mixed results. Jackson et al. (2016) and Lafortune et al. (2018) find that spending improves outcomes, while de Ree et al. (2018) find no impact; see also Hyman (2017).

2. A central issue in growth concerns whether resources flow to the most productive parts of the economy. For discussions in the context of firms, see Hsieh and Klenow (2009), Syverson (2011), and Hsieh and Olken (2014), and for applications to policy see Levy (2018). For discussions in the context of education and health, see Hoxby (2016) and Chandra et al. (2016), respectively.

3. In Merton and Zuckerman's (1977, 60) terminology from the sociology of science, the hypothesis is that resources are concentrated on "functionally relevant criteria." That is, they are at least partially matched to those most likely to make productive use of them.

4. This in part reflects court-mandated equalization; see Murray et al. (1998). The situation also stands in contrast with Federal expenditure on financial aid, which benefits mainly lower-income households; see McPherson and Schapiro (1991), Dynarski and Scott-Clayton (2013), and Turner (2017).

5. Graham and Diamond (1997).

6. Cole (2009), Graham and Diamond (1997).

7. Bush's advisors at the OSRD included Karl Compton, president of MIT, Frank Jewett, director of Bell Telephone Laboratories, and Richard Tolman, dean at Caltech. Bush (1945) articulated their position in a paper titled "Science the Endless Frontier." See Gruber and Johnson (2019) for detailed and interesting discussion of Bush's contributions.

8. Graham and Diamond (1997). The agencies are listed according to their financial importance in 1963.

9. See discussions in Kerr (1963), Geiger (1993), and Thelin (2004). In addition,

Graham and Diamond (1997) mention that particularly during the Kennedy and Johnson administrations, efforts were made to reduce the concentration of grants to a reduced number of schools, but the main result did not change radically.

10. Incidentally, it seems the Lawrence School's activities might have also been out of step with its donor, who had envisioned a school training chemists and engineers, "who intend to enter upon an active life applying their attainments to practical purposes" (Sinclair 2012, 37). Sinclair (2012, 37) adds: "It would be difficult to imagine a more explicit set of directions or a more complete and instant disregard of them."

11. Smith (2012). Rogers had visited these schools in France, and more generally was interested in European training and work in science.

12. Geiger (1986).

13. Lecuyer (2012), Sinclair (2012).

14. Sinclair (2012, 49).

15. Kaiser (2012).

16. Gillmor (2004, 335).

17. Gillmor (2004, 254).

18. Cole (2009, 128). See Gruber and Johnson (2019) for related discussion applied to the current American context.

19. Cole (2009, 120). See also Gillmor (2004).

20. In Hoxby (2012), aptitude includes things like being intelligent, original, or having the drive to develop research and new products. Finally, we repeat that whether concentrating research funding at top schools makes sense is ultimately an empirical question, and it is hard to determine what the appropriate counterfactual to Table 5.1 is. Payne and Siow (2003) present causal evidence that increased funding results in more, but not necessarily higher quality research, and Wahls (2018) argues that less concentration might be optimal. Some of these results refer to changes at the margin—it is harder to make definitive statements regarding the desirability of the overall patterns.

21. Graham and Diamond (1997, 35).

22. See, for example, Bloom and Van Reenen (2007) and Bloom et al. (2013).

23. These points are formalized and/or discussed in Hsieh and Urquiola (2006), MacLeod and Urquiola (2009; 2015; 2018), Riehl et al. (2016), and Urquiola (2016).

24. For example, Zuckerman (1977) notes that a large proportion of Nobel prize winners were trained in the laboratories of previous winners, or among other highly

distinguished scientists. Waldinger (2010) considers the expulsion of Jewish math professors from Germany and shows this had an adverse effect on PhD students.

25. Flexner (1946, 68).

26. Flexner (1946, 68).

27. Leslie (1992, 67).

28. Clark (2006, 82).

29. One robust finding in the economics of education is that parents care about distance to school. This emerges from analyses of preferences and from quasi-experimental work. See Bayer et al. (2007), Gallego and Hernando (2009), Hastings et al. (2009), Abdulkadiroglu et al. (2017a), Herskovic (2017), Neilson (2017), and Walters (2018).

30. See Taylor (2017) and Hu (2018).

31. Kane and Staiger (2008), Chetty et al. (2014), Araujo et al. (2016), Ainsworth et al. (2017). Note also that there is not yet consensus on this approach (Rothstein 2017; Chetty et al. 2017a).

32. The main exception to this second conclusion concerns the fact that teachers with very little experience do not perform very well, but of course that soon wears out as a predictive factor (Rockoff 2004; Rivkin et al. 2005; Jackson et al. 2014). In recent work, Araujo et al. (2016) show that some more progress in identifying effective teachers is possible if one additionally videotapes classrooms and uses fairly sophisticated methods to analyze teacher behavior; see also Bruns et al. (2016).

33. In the jargon, the majority of the variation in teacher value added is within rather than between schools (Chetty et al. 2014).

34. That said, universities do collect information on teaching performance in the form of student evaluations. These provide useful data in that student satisfaction is a relevant outcome. As professors frequently point out, however, evaluations are far from a perfect measure of teaching quality. For example, a faculty member looking for good evaluations might be tempted to make the class easy. See Carrell and West (2010).

35. Kerr (1963, 65); see also Ehrenberg (1997). Bok (2013, 329) notes that from 1969 to 1997 the overall share of faculty members reporting that "it is hard to get appointed or promoted in my university without a strong record of research" rose from 40 percent to 65 percent.

36. Avery et al. (2013).

37. In other words, beliefs as to other agents' valuations matter; see Browning et al.

(2014). Related to this, Nelson (1970) made a distinction between inspection and experience goods. The quality of an inspection good can be determined before purchase; that of an experience good like education can only be determined after. In addition, research in industrial organization observes that with experience goods the reputation of the seller can affect the price (Hubbard 2002; Melnik and Alm 2002; Jin and Leslie 2003; Cabral and Hortacsu 2010; Dranove and Jin 2010). MacLeod et al. (2017) show that a similar effect arises in education: employers are sensitive to college reputation, and this sensitivity is reduced when better information becomes available.

38. Labor economists have long suggested that some firms may pay higher wages than others even for equally skilled workers. For example, Card et al. (2013) build upon Abowd et al. (1999) to suggest that employee matches can matter for compensation. Other authors have emphasized mechanisms like efficiency wages and rent-sharing (Krueger and Summers 1988; Van Reenen 1996; Card et al. 2014).

39. More generally, people will be willing to make tradeoffs whenever schools provide more than one service. See, for instance, Riehl et al. (2016), Beuermann and Jackson (2018), and Kraft (2018).

40. See Liptak (2009). Incidentally, Scalia might as well have been speaking for all his colleagues on the Supreme Court because the other justices similarly privilege top schools.

41. All this relates to what economists call labor market frictions. For example, von Wachter and Bender (2006) and Oreopoulos et al. (2012) show that starting wages can have long-term consequences. Lags in hiring decisions could reflect firms' attachment to specific locations reflecting the geographic distribution of economic activity; see Moretti (2004; 2012) and Davis and Dingel (2014). See also the literature on employer learning; for example, Farber and Gibbons (1996), Altonji and Pierret (2001), and Lange (2007).

42. The importance of what actually drives parental choice has been consistently noted over the years (Hanushek 1981; Rothstein 2006; Abdulkadiroglu et al. 2017).

43. This has been an influential viewpoint in academic and popular discussions alike (Hoxby 2002; Chubb and Moe 1990).

44. See, for example, Chaudhury et al. (2005), Duflo et al. (2012), and Urquiola (2016).

45. See Angrist et al. (2002), Angrist et al. (2006), Bettinger et al. (2010), and Bettinger et al. (2017).

46. A large number of studies lie in between these two, with the majority suggesting that vouchers have modest effects. See Muralidharan and Sundararaman (2015) for

an example and Epple et al. (2017) for a review. This conclusion also generally applies to charter schools, where some are found to substantially outperform public alternatives, and some to do worse; see Epple et al. (2016) and Cohodes (2018).

47. Recent work provides two explicit illustrations of this. In New York City, Abdulkadiroglu et al. (2017b) find that peer quality rather than value added is the key driver of parental preferences for public high schools. Ainsworth et al. (2017) consider high schools in Romania, where households are free to request any public school. They find that while parents systematically prefer the more selective schools, these often have lower teaching value added than the alternatives. Note also that the evidence is similar with respect to admission to elite public schools that many households covet. In some cases, these allow students to do better, but in others there are zero or negative effects. To illustrate, some papers find positive effects of access to a higher-ranked school (Jackson 2010; Pop-Eleches and Urquiola 2013) and some find negative effects at least for certain subgroups (Barrow et al. 2017; Beuermann and Jackson 2017; Angrist et al. 2019). In between, several point to modest, or mixed effects (Park et al. 2008; Clark 2010; Abdulkadiroglu et al. 2014; Ajayi 2014; Bui et al 2014; Dobbie and Fryer 2014; Lucas and Mbiti 2014).

48. Hsieh and Urquiola (2003; 2006).

49. The Chilean voucher scheme has been studied extensively. See, for example, McEwan and Carnoy (2000), Mizala et al. (2007), Urquiola and Verhoogen (2009), Gallego (2013), Mizala and Urquiola (2013), Valenzuela et al. (2013), Feigenberg et al. (2014), Navarro-Palau (2017), Neilson (2017), Aguirre (2018), and Allende Santa-Cruz et al. (2019). Another salient voucher reform is that of Sweden; see Ahlin (2003), Sandstrom and Bergstrom (2005), Bohlmark et al. (2016), Bohlmark and Lindahl (2015), and Hinnerich and Vlachos (2017).

50. MacLeod and Urquiola (2015) make this point theoretically. For related empirical evidence on charter schools, see Epple et al. (2016), Cohodes (2018), and Cohodes et al. (2018). For work on making teachers' quality more transparent, see Bergman and Hill (2018).

51. There are many possible rationales for tenure and interesting work on the subject; see for instance Ito and Kahn (1986), Carmichael (1988), Siow (1998), and Brogaard et al. (2018).

52. Schrecker (1986, 15).

53. Scott (2018, 17).

54. See Curti and Nash (1965) and Samuels (1991). Archdeacon (1983) and Douglass (2000) note that anti-Chinese platforms were observed among pro-labor groups in California.

55. Dorn (2017, 129).

56. Metzger (1973, 136). See also Schrecker (1986).

57. Of course, these concerns are not entirely separate from those surrounding academic freedom, because such freedom can make the academic profession attractive.

58. Metzger (1973, 117).

59. Metzger (1973, 118).

60. Geiger (1986). See also Keller and Keller (2001) and Karabel (2006).

61. Karabel (2006, 149).

62. Keller and Keller (2001, 66) observe that their publication records were slim but not embarrassing.

63. Keller and Keller (2001).

64. Geiger (1986).

65. See McPherson and Schapiro (1999). Rosovsky (1990, 1818) indicates that in 1990 the following was "all" that the Harvard statutes said with respect to tenure: "Professors . . . are appointed without express limitation of time unless otherwise specified. All other officers are appointed for a specified term or for terms of unspecified duration subject to the right of the university to fix at any time the term of such an appointment. All officers who hold teaching appointments, as defined from time to time by the Corporation with the consent of the Overseers, are subject to removal from such appointments by the Corporation only for grave misconduct or neglect of duty."

66. Lecturers and adjunct instructors mostly work on renewable contracts. The proportion of college instructors who are tenured or on the tenure track declined from 57 percent in 1975 to 29 percent in 2007 (Wilson 2010). Figlio et al. (2015) predict that this proportion may stabilize between 15 and 20 percent, at which point it would largely be a feature of only flagship public and private research universities, as well as the wealthiest liberal arts colleges. See also Baldwin and Chronister (2002), Bettinger and Long (2006), and Antecol et al. (2018).

67. Relatedly, Ito and Kahn (1986) suggest that tenure provides a way in which universities share some of the risk individuals take on when they invest in very specialized human capital. They note that similar considerations arise in accounting or law firms, which offer long-term rewards like partnerships. In addition, Manso (2011) observes that when firms wish to encourage innovation, contracts should exhibit high tolerance for early failure and significant rewards for long-term success. For work on intrinsic motivation among judges, who often also enjoy tenure, see Ash and MacLeod (2015).

68. Carmichael (1988) explores this mechanism. See also Waldman (1990), Siow (1998), and Friebel and Raith (2004). In addition, Brown Jr. (1997) suggests that by giving professors a long-term stake in the university, tenure encourages them to monitor the leadership's decisions.

69. Brogaard et al. (2018) find that economists' individual productivity peaks at about the time of tenure both in terms of total publications and home runs defined as highly cited papers. See also discussions in McPherson and Schapiro (1999), who note that this concern has increased with the removal of mandatory retirement for faculty in the United States. Consistent with this, Figlio et al. (2015) note that the declining prevalence of tenure accelerated after January 1, 1994, when mandatory retirement for faculty members was abolished by federal law.

70. I am indebted to Bentley MacLeod for this observation.

71. Tenure probabilities can vary substantially across departments and over time. Kaminski and Geisler (2012) report a tenure probability of about 50 percent at fourteen science departments.

72. This would require some assumptions on the distribution of ability, the cost of effort, and so forth. For example, it requires ruling out that achievement is determined by innate ability alone. We suppose sorting is on raw ability for simplicity. More generally, the sorting could be based on an early realization of research output, such as the research demonstrated by candidates at the time they complete their PhD degree.

CHAPTER 6 · Europe

1. See Noll (1998), Goastellec (2012), and Herzog and Kehm (2012).

2. Ben-David (1971).

3. For example, at present British universities have greater flexibility to set faculty pay than their French and German counterparts. See Ben-David (1977), Clark (1983), Goastellec (2012), Herzog and Kehm (2012), and Kitagawa (2012).

4. See Ringer (1979) and Noll (1998). That said, as Paulsen (1906) notes, the integration of research into universities' work has been more thorough in Germany since about 1700. Indeed, recent French efforts to create so-called *Pôles de recherche et d'enseignement supérieure* can be seen as an attempt to expand universities' scope to enhance their research performance (Goastellec 2010; Musselin 2017).

5. Haskins (1923, 20). Haskins adds that Heidelberg's imitation of Paris was a generalized phenomenon in Germany; see also Curtis (1959). Finally, note that Bologna also

served as a model institution, particularly in Spain and Latin America (Gieysztor 1992).

6. Activity shifted from "internal" to "external" schools, where the former served young men housed within a monastery and the latter operated in towns. See Rashdall (1895a), Baldwin (1971), Verger (1973), and Charle and Verger (1994).

7. This is analogous to the impact of urbanization under the Muslim caliphates. Botticini and Eckstein (2012) explain how this raised the economic returns to schooling in activities undertaken by merchants, shopkeepers, moneymen, scholars, and physicians. See also Haskins (1923).

8. Verger (1973; 1986).

9. Translated from Verger (1973, 2). See also Rashdall (1895a).

10. Baldwin (1971).

11. Lucas (2006, 37). See also Paulsen (1906).

12. Other towns with concentrations of schools included Reims, Orléans, and Chartres. See Leff (1968), Baldwin (1971), Verger (1973), and Rudy (1984).

13. Rudy (1984). Faculty comes from the Latin *facultas,* meaning the ability or power to do certain things. For instance, a member of the law faculty would have been able to practice or teach in his field.

14. Kibre (1948). In some cases, the distinction was also based on whether *studia* had at least one of the higher faculties; see Rashdall (1895a), Paulsen (1906), and Robertson (1930).

15. See De Ridder-Symoens (1992) for discussions on mobility-related issues.

16. Bologna also developed such associations; see Haskins (1923), Kibre (1948), and Charle and Verger (1994).

17. Morison (1935, 19). See also Baldwin (1971).

18. Barron (2013).

19. Hartocollis (2016).

20. Rashdall (1895c), Rudy (1984).

21. Rudy (1984). For details on analogous petitions at Oxford, see Rashdall (1895c).

22. Rashdall (1895a), Haskins (1923), Robertson (1930), Leff (1968), Baldwin (1971). In addition, the term university did not initially describe an institution featuring the universe of faculties or branches of knowledge. This meaning, captured in the term *universitas facultatum,* emerged later.

23. Some countries still use related designations for degrees; for example, the *licence* in France or the *licenciatura* in Spain.

24. Rashdall (1895a). As we discuss below, the sale of offices was a recurring problem during this period. More generally, the *licentia* raised issues related to licensing. For recent work, see Anderson et al. (2016) and Blair and Chung (2018).

25. This was particularly true north of the Alps.

26. It was said the university was built of men: "bâtie en hommes" (Haskins 1923, 2).

27. Verger (1973).

28. As ecclesiastical courts developed, the church also had increasing use for trained lawyers, including among its cardinals and popes (Baldwin, 1971).

29. Translated from Verger (1973, 82).

30. Leff (1968).

31. Kibre (1962), Rudy (1984), Nardi (1992).

32. Leff (1968). There is also the case of the 1355 St. Scholastica's Day riots at Oxford. A tavern dispute led to fights in which neighbors tortured and killed scholars. After a cessation lasting months, the king and the Bishop of Lincoln intervened. Their remedy involved a new charter for the town, one which gave the university greater control over commerce. In addition, a regulation obligated municipal officers to attend Mass in memory of the murdered scholars each anniversary day (Hofstadter, 1955).

33. Leff (1968).

34. Haskins (1929, 61).

35. Verger (1973).

36. See also Leff (1968), Baldwin (1971), Verger (1986), and Gieysztor (1992).

37. Rashdall (1895c).

38. Stigler and Rosen (1985).

39. Rashdall (1895a), Verger (1986). In practice, graduation from a university enjoying this prerogative was neither necessary nor sufficient to transfer across institutions. On the one hand, universities were to some extent guilds after all, and they typically did not allow new masters to enter entirely unimpeded. On the other hand, Oxford never received the *ius ubique docendi,* yet its prestige ensured that its masters were often well received.

40. Our goal here is not to provide an exhaustive accounting, but to review the relevant trends. That significant entry occurred is illustrated by the fact that even

organizing this list has presented historians with a challenge. Verger (1973) does so by describing three waves of creations, a useful division we heavily draw on here. See also Rashdall (1895b) and D'Irsay (1933).

41. Verger (1973), Nardi (1992).

42. The English kings founded universities in parts of France they held: Caen (1432), Bordeaux (1441), and Poitiers (1431). The counts of Provence created the University of Aix (1409), and the dukes of Bourgogne that of Dôle (1422). The Dauphin of France created Valence (1452) and the Duke of Brittany Nantes (1460); the Duke of Berry founded the University of Bourges (1464). In the Holy Roman Empire, new creations included Leipzig (1409), Louvain (1425), and Greifswald (1456). Others in this wave were Würzburg (1402), Rockstock (1419), Trèves (1454), Fribourg-en-Brisgau (1455), Bâle (1459), Ingolstadt (1459–1472), Mayence (1476), and Tübingen (1476–1477). In Scotland, Glasgow (1450) and Aberdeen (1494) appeared, while Castille saw the emergence of Alcalá (1499). In Aragon the creations were Barcelona (1450), Saragosa (1474), and Valencia (1500). In Italy the Count of Piedmont created Turin (1405). In Scandinavia Upsala (1477) and Copenhagen (1478) appeared.

43. De Ridder-Symoens (1996).

44. Verger (1973).

45. This was even more the case at Bologna, where historically the students were older, wealthier, and had the upper hand in the university. For instance, Haskins (1923) mentions that they imposed requirements on professors, like having to make a deposit to leave town.

46. Paulsen (1906).

47. It is worth noting that the university was informal and masters enjoyed discretion in promoting their charges. Thus, many of these periods were notional (Paulsen 1906; Verger 1992).

48. Baldwin (1971).

49. The doctoral degree seems to have spread slower than the MA; Clark (2006) notes it was not granted by German universities until around 1800. See also Baldwin (1971).

50. Verger (1973) points out that at Bologna, where law was the main activity, it was common to find German nobles among the students. See also Charle and Verger (1994).

51. In addition, Kearney (1970) notes that in some cases bishops contributed to colleges to fund accommodation for their clergy.

52. Rashdall (1895c).

53. Rashdall (1895a; 1895c), Verger (1973), Clark (2006).

54. Leff (1968). We note that some ambiguity surrounds these dates of creation; see Baldwin (1971), Leedham-Green (1996), Jones (1997), Gabriel (1992), Gieysztor (1992), and Martin and Highfield (1997).

55. De Ridder-Symoens (1996), Clark (2006), Delbanco (2012).

56. Verger (1973).

57. Intimations of the end of self-rule can be seen much before 1517; for example, in the controversy over the mendicant orders in Paris in the 1200s, the suppression of the Wycliffites at Oxford in the 1300s, or events surrounding Jan Hus at Prague in the 1400s. We leave aside these interesting episodes for the sake of brevity. See Rashdall (1895a; 1895c), Hofstadter (1955), Metzger (1973), Verger (1973; 1986), and Eire (2016) for discussions.

58. Rashdall (1895a).

59. In Spain, Francisco Jiménez de Cisneros published another translation soon after (Rummel 1999). Humanist activity was similarly in evidence in all major countries. In England, for example, Thomas More became chancellor and was eventually executed by Henry VIII. In France, Jacques Lefevre D'Etaples translated the Bible into French, and Guillaume Budé helped establish the *Collège des Lecteurs Royaux,* which would eventually become the *Collège de France* (Rüegg, 1992).

60. Eire (2016).

61. Eire (2016). The archbishop was Albrecht von Brandenburg, son of one of the imperial electors. By his early twenties, von Brandenburg held two bishoprics and desired the Archbishopric of Mainz, which had just become available. At the time Pope Julius II was in need of revenue for the rebuilding of St. Peter's Basilica, and he essentially auctioned off the seat at Mainz. Von Brandenburg offered ten thousand ducats; an additional ten thousand, he was informed, would produce a dispensation such that he could keep his two other bishoprics. He did not have the sum, and while he could secure a loan, he would need to generate revenue to pay it. The lending house involved arranged for him to be permitted, once he was archbishop, to sell plenary indulgences (allowing a remission of all sins). The stage was thus set for what economists call a Pareto improvement—everyone would be better off: Albrecht would be archbishop, the pope would have his revenue, the bank would get paid, and the faithful would see Saint Peter.

62. Eire (2016, 152).

63. Moeller (1972, 61).

64. Metzger (1973).

65. See Paulsen (1906), Moeller (1972), Frijhoff (1996), Eire (2016), and Dittmar and Meisenzahl (2018).

66. See Verger (1973). In this period the German universities by and large ceased to award the equivalent of the BA degree (Clark 2006). See also Paulsen (1906), Morison (1935), Ringer (1979), and Frijhoff (1996).

67. This emphasis was seen in Catholic jurisdictions too; as for example the Jesuits' schools adopted a similar approach, in part as they competed with Protestant establishments.

68. Rashdall (1895b), Gieysztor (1992), Verger (1992). Clark (2006) notes that state funding responded in part to states' desire to influence the curriculum; for example, the topics humanists taught were not part of examinations and hence difficult to fund without direct state support.

69. Butts (1939), Rudy (1984), Verger (1986).

70. D'Irsay (1935), Ringer (1979), Weisz (1983), Rudy (1984).

71. See also D'Irsay (1935).

72. See also Ringer (1979), Rudy (1984), Vandermeersch (1996), and Clark (2006). Note that Kearney (1970) places at least some of the growth in colleges' wealth as happening after rather than before the Reformation.

73. See D'Irsay (1935), Ben-David (1977), Ringer (1979), Clark (1983), Verger (1986), Fox and Weisz (1980), Clark (2006).

CHAPTER 7 · The United States

1. I use the term territorial-confessional to underline the parallel with European practices; Herbst (1982) calls them provincial, and Hofstadter (1955, 144) speaks of them being governed by a church-state complex.

2. Becker and Woessmann (2009) suggest that Protestant areas displayed greater investment in education than Catholic ones, and argue that this accounted for their later higher economic growth. This contrasts with Weber (1930), who attributed the effect to the Protestant work ethic. Dittmar and Meisenzahl (2018) provide further detail on the mechanisms that allowed greater educational investment.

3. In 1551 Charles V issued charters creating the University of San Marcos in Lima, and the Royal and Pontifical University in Mexico City.

4. Officers of the Harvard Club of New York City (1878, 5).

5. Morison (1936, 6).

6. Reisner (1931), Herbst (1982).

7. D'Irsay (1935), Brubacher and Rudy (1958), Nardi (1992), De Ridder-Symoens (1996).

8. At Edinburgh the charter allowed the Town Council to intervene directly in areas such as faculty appointments; see Sloan (1971) and Anderson et al. (2003).

9. Cotton Mather, cited in Doyle (1887, 115).

10. The toll and ferry revenue mainly came in the form of wampum, the shell beads native American tribes manufactured, and which by 1620 were already in use as currency in the Hudson River area. Wampum varied in quality and hence in value; in some cases, dye was applied to white shells to approximate the color of more valuable natural purple shells. Dunster observed that "all the fake wampum in the colonies found its way into the college treasury" (Morison 1936, 15).

11. Herbst (1982).

12. There were precedents for such shifts in control; see Morison (1935) for an example involving Trinity College in Ireland. See also Brubacher and Rudy (1958) regarding Dunster's intent.

13. Morison (1936).

14. Morison (1936, 70).

15. Hofstadter (1955, 89).

16. Engerman and Sokoloff (2002).

17. Thelin (2004) notes that unsuccessful attempts began as early as 1619, when the Virginia Company ceded ten thousand acres of land toward a college, and helped to secure commitments for an endowment of 1,500 pounds—about three times Harvard's original appropriation—for a university and Indian school to be set near Henrico. This plan was abandoned after the so-called Indian Massacre resulted in the death of more than three hundred settlers and wiped out the settlement in this area.

18. Herbst (1982, 31).

19. Curti and Nash (1965, 31).

20. Herbst (1982) notes that at the time vice-chancellors in England were gaining power.

21. Blair had a Master's degree from Edinburgh, which as indicated had an external board (Pryde 1957).

22. Hofstadter (1955), Thelin (2004).

23. Thelin (2004).

24. Brubacher and Rudy (1958), Herbst (1982).

25. Hofstadter (1955) indicates that in fact there is no evidence that the College of William and Mary actually operated before 1729. Hence from the point of view of actual operation, Yale preceded William and Mary.

26. Broome (1903, 27).

27. Thelin (2004).

28. The President and Fellows of Yale University. 1976. The Yale Corportation: Charter and Legislation. New Haven: Yale University. https://www.yale.edu/sites /default/files/files/University-Charter.pdf

29. Specifically, in 1745 the board of trustees was incorporated by the colony with the designation of the President and Fellows of Yale College, although in this case the fellows did not refer to faculty.

30. Rudolph (1962).

31. Herbst (1982).

32. In particular, they point out that these data are based on an effort to locate every church congregation in the United States, as led by the Chicago historian M.W. Jernegan (Jernegan 1929; 1932). They suggest their data may indicate greater religious diversity than existed in each colony prior to 1776—the key for our purposes is that such biases not differ across regions. Consistent with this, their calculated rates of adherence do not vary across the regions we focus on here; see page 31 in Finke and Stark (2005).

33. The Anglicans are referred to as Episcopalians to reflect the fact that they have bishops and archbishops, much as Catholics.

34. See Archdeacon (1983) and Finke and Stark (2005). Archdeacon presents a version of Table 1.2 that concerns ethnic origin rather than denominational identity; the bottom line is similar—significantly greater heterogeneity in the Middle Atlantic than in New England.

35. McCaughey (2003, 4).

36. Bonomi (1986).

37. Bonomi (1986, 25).

38. Bonomi (1986, 26).

39. Bonomi (1986, 25).

40. See discussions in Broome (1903) and Johnson and Koyama (2019).

41. Rasmussen (2017). In addition, Sloan (1971, 11) notes that in these years the Scottish

government came to be mostly controlled by a faction of Presbyterians who generally "espoused toleration and avoided fine points of religious controversy."

42. Eire (2016).

43. Bonomi (1986, 131) characterizes the Great Awakening as the intense period of revivalist tumult from about 1739 to 1745. There is some controversy among historians about the awakenings' true intensity.

44. Finke and Stark (2005, 51). See Cheyney (1940) for related discussion.

45. Kelley (1974).

46. Finke and Stark (2005, 53). See also Bonomi (1986).

47. Finke and Stark (2005, 61).

48. Finke and Stark (2005).

49. Herbst (1982).

50. Bonomi (1986, 141). See also Wertenbaker (1946).

51. Oberdorfer (1995) states that they were rather expelled from the Philadelphia Synod, although the end result is the same. The schism would last until 1758 (Bonomi, 1986).

52. Wertenbaker (1946, 17).

53. Oberdorfer (1995, 12).

54. Hofstadter (1955, 142).

55. Leslie (1992).

56. Oberdorfer (1995, 14).

57. McCaughey (2003).

58. Brubacher and Rudy (1958).

59. Herbst (1982).

60. Herbst (1982). The trustees residing in London had the right to name representatives.

61. McCaughey (2003, 22).

62. Smith (1889, 191). This was written under the name David Marin Ben Jesse in a document titled "A remark on the disputes and contentions in this province." McAnear (1950, 327) states that "The author almost certainly was Theodore Frelinghuysen, the domine of the Albany Church . . . ." See also Herbst (1982).

63. Herbst (1982, 130).

64. Rudolph (1962, 209).

65. Clark (1983) notes these are most prevalent in Germany and Italy but notes that they also have a presence in England, France, Portugal, and Spain; for example, the chaired professors in the *Collège de France;* see also Ben-David (1971) and Clark (2006).

66. Paulsen (1906) remarks that at many German institutions the position lasts one year and, when compared with the position of a president of an American university, is rather of an ornamental character. Clark (2006, 464) adds that, "The departmental structure in the United States, even with its various ranks of professor, effectively inhibited a Germanic professorial oligarchy of chair holders and institute directors."

67. Gieysztor (1992).

68. The implications of this and other sections are broadly consistent with recommendations made in the "Aghion Report" to the French Ministry of Higher Education and Research (Aghion, 2010a; 2010b). For example, the report highlights that university autonomy is desirable, and mentions boards of trustees as a relevant governance tool in achieving it. In addition, it underlines the role of resources in the production of research.

CHAPTER 8 · The Future

1. Straumsheim (2016) and Ubell (2017) note that in a bid to increase revenue, MOOC providers have increasingly shifted from free open access to charging for "mini certifications." The idea is to package some courses into thematic areas that confer partial or full degrees. In addition, providers have developed links with universities. For example, Coursera has partnerships with business schools at the University of Illinois and the *Ecole des Hautes Études Comerciales;* edX has programs with Georgia Tech.

2. For example, Deming et al. (2016a) find that 2006 regulatory changes that increased the number of online institutions reduced enrollments among private nonselective schools. See also Deming et al. (2015), Deming et al. (2016b), and Hoxby (2016).

3. Rigorous research has grown in this area and increasingly features randomized evaluations. On learning effects see Bowen (2013), Figlio et al. (2013), Bowen et al. (2014), Joyce et al. (2015), Alpert et al. (2016), Bettinger et al. (2017), and Goodman et al. (2019). On persistence, see Perna et al. (2014) and Banerjee and Duflo (2014).

4. Christensen and Eyring (2011, 18) state that "Another reason for the lack of disruption in higher education has been the absence of a disruptive technology. Since the time that universities first gathered students into classrooms, the learning technologies . . . have remained largely the same." Yet as Chapter 6 discussed, one

can certainly think of the printing press as having been a disruptive technology, since an early objective of the lecture was to let students copy otherwise very expensive books. McPherson and Bacow (2015) discuss that radio and television-delivered lectures were also seen as clear and very inexpensive substitutes for universities' services.

5. See also Christensen (1997).

6. Young (2017).

7. For work on such initiatives' effectiveness, see Bradley et al. (2018).

8. See Alvaredo et al. (2017) for recent discussion on the level and evolution of American inequality.

9. There is evidence consistent with this, but it is not unanimous. See, for example, Dale and Krueger (2002; 2017), Chetty et al. (2017b), MacLeod et al. (2017), and MacLeod and Urquiola (2018). See also an extended discussion of inequality among institutions of higher education in McPherson and Schapiro (1990).

10. Graham (2005, 37).

11. Jones (2017).

12. See Akcigit et al. (2016), Lockwood et al. (2017), Moretti and Wilson (2017), Akcigit et al. (2018b), and Jones (2018). One aspect these papers review is how considerations related to innovation affect results like those in Saez (2001) and Diamond and Saez (2011).

13. Lorin (2018). See also previous calls for such taxation, including Weissmann (2015).

14. Mervis (2017).

15. For discussions on the possibility that producing innovation is becoming harder, see Jones (2009), Cowen (2011), Gordon (2016), and Bloom et al. (2017). On declining public university funding see also Bound et al. (2019). In addition, there have been concerns that the federal funding mechanisms themselves need reform. For example, Alberts and Narayanamurti (2019) note that the proportion of NIH funding going to researchers younger than thirty-six declined from 6 percent to 2 percent between 1980 and 2017, and they ask whether this limits the system's ability to identify innovative thinking.

16. Helland and Tabarrok (2019) cite numerous instances of such perceptions. Caplan (2018) essentially argues that the education sector is a waste of money.

17. See Baumol and Bowen (1943) and Baumol (1967).

18. See MacLeod et al. (2017) and Riehl (2018).

19. This is in the same spirit as Kerr's (1963, 18) use of the term multiversity.

References

Abdulkadiroglu, Atila, Joshua Angrist, and Parag Pathak. 2014. The elite illusion: achievement effects at Boston and New York Exam Schools. *Econometrica* 82 (1): 137–196.

Abdulkadiroglu, Atila, Nikil Agarwal, and Parag Pathak. 2017a. The welfare effects of coordinated assignment: evidence from the New York City high school match. *American Economic Review* 107 (12): 3635–3689.

Abdulkadiroglu, Atila, Parag Pathak, Jonathan Schellenberg, and Christopher Walters 2017b. Do parents value school effectiveness? Unpublished paper. Duke University.

Abdulkadiroglu, Atila, Parag Pathak, and Christopher R. Walters. 2018. Free to choose: can school choice reduce student achievement? *American Economic Journal: Applied Economics* 10 (1): 175–206.

Abowd, John M., Francis Kramarz, and David N. Margolis. 1999. High wage workers and high wage firms. *Econometrica* 67 (2): 251–333.

Acemoglu, Daron and David Autor. 2012. What does human capital do? A review of Goldin and Katz's "The Race Between Education and Technology." *Journal of Economic Literature* 50 (2): 426–463.

Acemoglu, Daron and James A. Robinson. 2012. *Why Nations Fail: The Origins of Power, Prosperity, and Poverty.* New York: Crown Business.

Acemoglu, Daron, James A. Robinson, and Thierry Verdier. 2012. Can't we all be more like Scandinavians? Asymmetric growth and institutions in an interdependent world. National Bureau of Economic Research Working Paper No. 18441.

Adams, Charles Kendall. 1876. The relations of higher education to national prosperity: an oration delivered before the Phi Beta Kappa Society of the University of Vermont. Burlington: Free Press Print.

Aghion, Phillipe. 2010a. L'excellence universitaire et l'insertion professionelle: leçons des expériences internationales. Unpublished paper. Harvard University.

———. 2010b. L'excellence universitaire: leçons des expériences internationales. Unpublished paper. Harvard University.

Aghion, Philippe and Peter W. Howitt. 1997. *Endogenous Growth Theory*. Cambridge, MA: MIT Press.

Aghion, Phillipe, Matthias Dewatripont, Caroline Hoxby, Andreu Mas-Collel, and André Sapir. 2010. The governance and performance of universities: evidence from Europe and the US. *Economic Policy* 25 (61): 7–59.

Aguirre, Josefa. 2018. How can progressive vouchers help the poor benefit from school choice? Evidence from the Chilean voucher system. Unpublished paper. Teachers College, Columbia University.

Ahlin, Asa. 2003. Does school competition matter? Effects of a large-scale school choice reform on student performance. Working paper. Uppsala University Department of Economics.

Ainsworth, Robert, Rajeev Dehejia, Cristian Pop-Eleches, and Miguel Urquiola. 2019. What drives school choice? Implications from 350 markets. Unpublished paper. Columbia University.

Ajayi, Kehinde. 2014. Does school quality improve student performance? New evidence from Ghana. Unpublished paper. Boston University.

Akcigit, Ufuk, Salome Baslandze, and Stefanie Stantcheva. 2016. Taxation and the international mobility of inventors. *American Economic Review* 106 (10): 2930–2981.

Akcigit, Ufuk, John Grigsby, and Tom Nicholas. 2017. The rise of American ingenuity: innovation and inventors of the golden age. National Bureau of Economic Research Working Paper No. 23047.

Akcigit, Ufuk, Santiago Caicedo, Ernst Miguelez, and Stefanie Stantcheva, and Valerio Sterzi. 2018a. Dancing with the stars: innovation through interactions. National Bureau of Economic Research Working Paper No. 24466.

Akcigit, Ufuk, John Grigsby, Tom Nicholas, and Stefaie Stantcheva. 2018b. Taxation and innovation in the 20th century. National Bureau of Economic Research Working Paper No. 24982.

Alberts, Bruce and Venkatesh Narayanamurti. 2019. Two threats to U.S. science. *Science* 364 (6441): 613.

Allende Santa-Cruz, Claudia, and Francisco Gallego and Christopher Neilson. 2019. Towards the equilibrium effects of information interventions. Unpublished paper. Princeton University.

Allmendinger Jr., David F. 1975. *Paupers and Scholars: The Transformation of Student Life in Nineteenth-Century New England.* New York: St. Martin's Press.

Almond, Douglas and Janet Currie. 2011. Killing me softly: the fetal origins hypothesis. *Journal of Economic Perspectives* 25 (3): 153–172.

Alpert, William T., Kenneth A. Couch, and Oskar R. Harmon. 2016. A randomized assessment of online learning. *American Economic Review* 106 (5): 378–382.

Altonji, Joseph G. and Charles R. Pierret. 2001. Employer learning and statistical discrimination. *The Quarterly Journal of Economics* 116 (1): 313–350.

Alvaredo, Facundo, Lucas Chancel, Thomas Piketty, Emmanuel Saez, and Gabriel Zucman. 2017. Global inequality dynamics: new findings from WID.world. *American Economic Review* 107 (5): 404–409.

Anderson, D. Mark, Ryan Brown, Kerwin Kofi Charles, and Daniel I. Rees. 2016. The effect of occupational licensing on consumer welfare: early midwifery laws and maternal mortality. National Bureau of Economic Research Working Paper No. 22456.

Anderson, Robert D., Michael Lynch, and Nicholas Phillipson. 2003. *The University of Edinburgh: An Illustrated History.* Edinburgh: Edinburgh University Press.

Angrist, Joshua, Eric Bettinger, Erik Bloom, Michael Kremer, and Elizabeth King. 2002. The effect of school vouchers on students: evidence from Colombia. *American Economic Review* 92 (5): 1535–1558.

Angrist, Joshua, Eric Bettinger, and Michael Kremer. 2006. Long-term consequences of secondary school vouchers: evidence from administrative records in Colombia. *American Economic Review* 96 (3): 847–862.

Angrist, Joshua, Susan Dynarski, Thomas Kane, Parag Pathak, and Christopher Walters. 2010. Inputs and impacts in charter schools: KIPP Lynn. *American Economic Review: Papers and proceedings* 100 (2): 1-5.

Angrist, Joshua, Parag Pathak, and Roman A. Zárate. 2019. Choice and consequence: assessing mismatch at Chicago exam schools. National Bureau of Economic Research Working Paper No. 26137.

Antecol, Heather, Kelly Bedard, and Jenna Stearns. 2018. Equal but inequitable: who benefits from gender-neutral tenure clock stopping policies? *American Economic Review* 108 (9): 2420–2441.

Araujo, M. Caridad, Pedro Carneiro, Yyannú Cruz-Aguayo, and Norbert Schady. 2016. Teacher quality and learning outcomes in kindergarten. *The Quarterly Journal of Economics* 131 (3): 1415–1453.

Archdeacon, Thomas J. 1983. *Becoming American: An Ethnic History.* New York: The Free Press.

Arcidiacono, Peter, Esteban M. Aucejo, Hanming Fang, and Kenneth I. Spenner. 2011. Does affirmative action lead to mismatch? A new test and evidence. *Quantitative Economics* 2 (3): 303–333.

Arcidiacono, Peter, Esteban M. Aucejo, and V. Joseph Hotz. 2016. University differences in the graduation of minorities in STEM fields: evidence from California. *American Economic Review* 106 (3): 525–562.

Arcidiacono, Peter and Michael Lovenheim. 2016. Affirmative action and the quality-fit tradeoff. *Journal of Economic Literature* 54 (1): 3–51.

Ash, Elliott and Bentley MacLeod. 2015. Intrinsic motivation in public service: theory and evidence from state supreme courts. *The Journal of Law and Economics* 58 (4): 863–913.

Ash, Eliot and Miguel Urquiola. 2018. A research-based ranking of public policy schools. Working Paper. Social Science Research Network.

Avery, Christopher N., Mark E. Glickman, Caroline M. Hoxby, and Andrew Metrick. 2013. A revealed preference ranking of US colleges and universities. *The Quarterly Journal of Economics* 128 (1): 425–467.

Axtell, James.1971. The death of the liberal arts college. *History of Education Quarterly* 11 (4): 339–352.

Ayres, Leonard P. 1909. *Laggards in our Schools: A Study of Retardation and Elimination in School Systems.* New York: Russell Sage Foundation.

Azoulay, Pierre, Joshua Graff-Zivin, and Jialan Wang. 2010. Superstar extinction. *The Quarterly Journal of Economics* 125 (2): 549–589.

Baldwin, John W. 1971. *The Scholastic Culture of the Middle Ages, 1000–1300.* Long Grove, IL: Waveland Press, 1997.

Baldwin, Roger G. and Jay L. Chronister. 2002. What happened to the tenure track? In *The Questions of Tenure.* Edited by Richard P. Chait. Cambridge, MA: Harvard University Press.

Bandiera, Oriana, Myra Mohnen, Imran Rasul, and Martina Viarengo. 2017. Nation-building through compulsory schooling during the age of mass migration. Unpublished paper. London School of Economics.

Banerjee, Abhijit and Esther Duflo. 2014. (Dis)organization and success in an economics MOOC. *American Economic Review* 104 (5): 514–518.

Banerjee, Abhijit, Rukmini Banerji, James Berry, Esther Duflo, Harini Kannan, Shobini Mukerji, Marc Shotland, and Michael Walton. 2017. From proof of concept to scalable policies: challenges and solutions, with an application. *Journal of Economic Perspectives* 31 (4): 73–102.

Barro, Robert J. and Jong Wha Lee. 2013. A new data set of educational attainment in the world, 1950–2010. *Journal of Development Economics* 104: 184–198.

Barron, James (March 6, 2013). On campus, costly target of brazen thefts: Nutella. New York Times.

Barrow, Lisa, Laura Sartain, and Marisa de la Torre. 2017. The role of selective high schools in equalizing educational outcomes: using place-based affirmative action to estimate heterogeneous effect by neighborhood socioeconomic status. Unpublished paper. Federal Reserve Bank of Chicago.

Bauer-Wolf, Jeremy (March 2, 2018). Random roommates only. Inside Higher Ed.

Baumol, William J. 1967. Macroeconomics of unbalanced growth: the anatomy of urban crisis. *American Economic Review* 57 (3): 415–426.

Baumol, William J. and William G. Bowen. 1943. *Performing Arts, The Economic Dilemma: A Study of Problems Common to Theater, Opera, Music, and Dance.* Cambridge, MA: MIT Press.

Bayer, Patrick, Fernando Ferreira, and Robert McMillan. 2007. A unified framework for measuring preferences for schools and neighborhoods. *Journal of Political Economy* 115 (4): 588–638.

Becker, Carl L. 1943. *Cornell University: Founders and the Founding.* Ithaca, NY: Cornell University.

Becker, Gary 1964. *Human Capital: A Theoretical and Empirical Analysis, with Special Reference to Education.* Chicago: University of Chicago Press.

Becker, Sascha O. and Ludger Woessmann. 2009. Was Weber wrong? A human capital theory of Protestant economic history. *The Quarterly Journal of Economics* 124 (2): 531–596.

Ben-David, Joseph. 1971. *The Scientist's Role in Society: A Comparative Study.* Englewood Cliffs, NJ: Prentice-Hall.

———. 1977. *Centers of Learning: Britain, France, Germany, and the United States.* New Brunswick, NJ: Transaction Publishers, 2009.

Bergman, Peter and Matthew J. Hill. 2018. The effects of making performance information public: regression discontinuity evidence from Los Angeles teachers. *Economics of Education Review* 66: 104–113.

Bergman, Peter and Isaac McFarlin Jr. 2018. Education for all? A nationwide audit study of schools of choice. Unpublished paper. Columbia University.

Bettinger, Eric P. and Bridget T. Long. 2006. The increasing use of adjunct instructors at public institutions: are we hurting students? In

What's Happening to Public Higher Education? The Shifting Financial Burden. Edited by Ronald G. Ehrenberg. Baltimore, MD: Johns Hopkins University Press.

Bettinger, Eric, Michael Kremer, and Juan Esteban Saavedra. 2010. Are educational vouchers only redistributive? *Economic Journal* 120 (546): F204–F228.

Bettinger, Eric P., Lindsay Fox, Susanna Loeb, and Eric S. Taylor. 2017a. Virtual classrooms: how online college courses affect student success. *American Economic Review* 107 (9): 2855–2875.

Bettinger, Eric, Michael Kremer, Maurice Kugler, Carlos Medina, Christian Posso, Christian and Juan Esteban Saavedra. 2017b. Can educational voucher programs pay for themselves? Unpublished paper. Harvard University.

Beuermann, Diether W. and C. Kirabo Jackson. 2018. Do parents know best? The short and long-run effects of attending the schools that parents prefer. National Bureau of Economic Research Working Paper No. 24920.

Bianchi, Nicola and Michela Giorcelli. 2019. Scientific education and innovation: from technical diplomas to university STEM degrees. National Bureau of Economic Research Working Paper No. 25928.

Bishop, Morris. 1962. *A History of Cornell.* Ithaca, NY: Cornell University Press.

Black, Sandra E., Paul J. Devereux, Petter Lundborg, and Kaveh Majlesi. 2017. Poor little rich kids? The determinants of the intergenerational transmission of wealth. National Bureau of Economic Research Working Paper No. 21409.

Black, Sandra, Paul Devereux, and Kjell Salvanes. 2007. From the cradle to the labor market? The effect of birth weight on adult outcomes. *The Quarterly Journal of Economics* 122 (1): 409–439.

Blackburn, Robert T. and Clinton F. Conrad. 1986. The new revisionists and the history of U.S. Higher Education. *Higher Education* 15: 211–230.

Blair, Peter Q. and Bobby W. Chung. 2018. Job market signaling through occupational licensing. National Bureau of Economic Research Working Paper No. 24791.

Bloom, Nicholas and John Van Reenen. 2007. Measuring and explaining management practices across firms and countries. *The Quarterly Journal of Economics* 122 (4): 1351–1408.

Bloom, Nicholas, Benn Eifert, Aprajit Mahajan, David McKenzie, and John Roberts. 2013. Does management matter? Evidence from India. *The Quarterly Journal of Economics* 128 (1): 1-51.

Bloom, Nicholas, Charles I. Jones, John Van Reenen, and Michael Webb. 2017. Are ideas getting harder to find? National Bureau of Economic Research Working Paper No. 23782.

Bohlmark, Anders, Helena Holmlund, and Mikael Lindahl. 2016. Parental choice, neighbourhood segregation or cream skimming? An analysis of school segregation after a generalized choice reform. *Journal of Population Economics* 29 (4): 1155–1190.

Bohlmark, Anders and Mikael Lindahl. 2015. Independent schools and long-run educational outcomes: evidence from Sweden's large scale voucher reform. *Economica* 82 (327): 508–551.

Bok, Derek. 2013. *Higher Education in America*. Princeton, NJ: Princeton University Press.

Bonomi, Patricia U. 1986. *Under the Cope of Heaven: Religion, Society, and Politics in Colonial America*. New York: Oxford University Press.

Bordon, Paola and Chao Fu. 2015. College-major choice to college-then-major choice. *Review of Economic Studies* 82 (4): 1247–1288.

Borjas, George J. and Kirk B. Doran. 2012. The collapse of the Soviet Union and the productivity of American mathematicians. *The Quarterly Journal of Economics* 127 (3): 1143–1203.

Botticini, Maristella and Zvi Eckstein. 2012. *The Chosen Few: How Education Shaped Jewish History*. Princeton, NJ: Princeton University Press.

Bound, John, Breno Braga, Gaurav Khanna, and Sarah Turner. 2019. Public universities: the supply side of building a skilled workforce. National Bureau of Economic Research Working Paper No. 25945.

Bowen, William G. 2010. *Lessons Learned: Reflections of a University President*. Princeton, NJ: Princeton University Press.

———. 2013. *Higher Education in the Digital Age*. Princeton, NJ: Princeton University Press.

Bowen, William G., Matthew Chingos, Kelly A. Lack, and Thomas I. Nygren. 2014. Interactive learning online at public universities: evidence from a six-campus randomized trial. *Journal of Policy Analysis and Management* 33 (1): 94–111.

Boyer, John W. 2015. *The University of Chicago: A History*. Chicago: The University of Chicago Press.

Bradley, Steven W., James R. Garven, Wilson W. Law, and James E. West. 2018. The impact of chief diversity officers on diverse faculty hiring. National Bureau of Economic Research Working Paper No. 24969.

Brogaard, Jonathan, Joseph Engelberg, and Edward Van Wesep. 2018. Do economists swing for the fences after tenure? *Journal of Economic Perspectives* 32 (1): 179–194.

Broome, Edwin Cornelius. 1903. *A Historical and Critical Discussion of College Admission Requirements*. New York: The Macmillan Company.

Brown Jr., William O. 1997. University governance and academic tenure: a property rights explanation. *Journal of Institutional and Theoretical Economics* 153 (3): 441–461.

Browning, Martin, Pierre-Andre Chiappori, and Yoram Weiss. 2014. *Economics of the Family*. Cambridge: Cambridge University Press.

Brubacher, John S. and Willis Rudy. 1958. *Higher Education in Transition*. New York: Harper & Row.

Bruns, Barbara, Soledad De Gregorio, and Sandy Taut. 2016. Measures of effective teaching in developing countries. Research on Improving Systems of Education Working Paper No. 16–009.

Bui, Sa A., Steven G. Craig, and Scott A. Imberman. 2014. Is gifted education a bright idea? Assessing the impact of gifted and talented programs on students. *American Economic Journal: Economic Policy* 6 (3): 3–62.

Burgess, John W. 1934. *Reminiscences of an American Scholar: The Beginnings of Columbia University.* New York: Columbia University Press.

Burke, Colin B. 1982. *American Collegiate Populations: A Test of the Traditional View.* New York: New York University Press.

Bush, Vannevar. 1945. Science—the endless frontier. Unpublished paper. United States Government Printing Office.

Butcher, Kristin, Caitlin Kearns, and Patrick McEwan. 2013. Giving 'til it helps? Alumnae giving and children's college options. *Research in Higher Education* 54 (5): 481–498.

Butts, R. Freeman. 1939. *The College Charts Its Course: Historical Conceptions and Current Proposals.* New York: McGraw-Hill.

Cabral, Luis and Ali Hortacsu. 2010. The dynamics of seller reputation: evidence from Ebay. *The Journal of Industrial Economics* 58 (1): 54–78.

Cantoni, Davide and Noam Yuchtman. 2014. Medieval universities, legal institutions, and the commercial revolution. *The Quarterly Journal of Economics* 129 (2): 823–887.

Caplan, Bryan. 2018. *The Case Against Education: Why the Education System is a Waste of Time and Money.* Princeton, NJ: Princeton University Press.

Card, David. 1995. Using geographic variation in college proximity to estimate the return to schooling. In *Aspects of Labor Market Behaviour: Essays in Honour of John Vanderkamp.* Edited by Louis N. Christofides, E. Kenneth Grant and Robert Swidinsky. Toronto: University of Toronto Press.

Card, D., Fracesco Devicienti, and Agata Maida. 2014. Rent-sharing, holdup, and wages: evidence from matched panel data. *Review of Economic Studies* 81 (1): 84–111.

Card, David and Stefano Della Vigna. 2017. What do editors maximize? Evidence from four leading economics journals. National Bureau of Economic Research Working Paper No. 23282.

Card, David, Jorg Heining, and Patrick Kline. 2013. Workplace heterogeneity and the rise of West German wage inequality. *The Quarterly Journal of Economics* 128 (3): 967–1015.

Card, David, Alexandre Mas, and Jesse Rothstein. 2008. Tipping and the dynamics of segregation. *The Quarterly Journal of Economics* 123 (1): 177–218.

Carmichael, H. Lorne. 1988. Incentives in academia: why is there tenure? *Journal of Political Economy* 96 (3): 453–472.

Carnoy, Martin, Emma García, and Tatiana Khavenson. 2015. Bringing it back home: why state comparisons are more useful than international comparisons for improving U.S. educational policy. Briefing Paper. Economic Policy Institute.

Carnoy, Martin and Richard Rothstein. 2013. What do international tests really show about U.S. student performance? Report. Economic Policy Institute.

Carrell, Scott E., Mark Hoekstra, and James E. West. 2011. Does drinking impair college performance? Evidence from a regression discontinuity approach. *Journal of Public Economics* 95 (1–2): 54–62.

Carrell, Scott E., Bruce I. Sacerdote, and James E. West. 2013. From natural variation to optimal policy? The importance of endogenous peer group formation. *Econometrica* 81 (3): 855–882.

Carrell, Scott E. and James E. West 2010. Does professor quality matter? Evidence from random assignment of students to professors. *Journal of Political Economy* 118 (3): 409–432.

Catalani, Christian, Christian Fons-Rosen, and Patrick Gaulé. 2018. How do travel costs shape collaboration? National Bureau of Economic Research Working Paper No. 24780.

Chandra, Amitabh, Amy Finkelstein, Adam Sacarny, and Chad Syverson. 2016. Health care exceptionalism? Performance and allocation in the U.S. health care sector. *American Economic Review* 106 (8): 2110–2144.

Charle, Christophe and Jacques Verger. 1994. *Histoire des Universités*. Paris: Presses Universitaires de France.

Chaudhury, Nazmul, Jeffrey Hammer, Michael Kremer, Karthik Muralidharan, and Halsey Rogers. 2005. Missing in action: teacher and health worker absence in developing countries. *Journal of Economic Perspectives* 20 (1): 92–116.

Chernow, Ron. 2004. *Alexander Hamilton*. New York: Penguin Books.

Chetty, Raj, John N. Friedman, and Jonah Rockoff. 2014. Measuring the impacts of teachers I: evaluating bias in teacher value-added estimates. *American Economic Review* 104 (9): 2593–2632.

——— 2017a. Measuring the impacts of teachers: reply. *American Economic Review* 107 (6): 1685–1717.

Chetty, Raj, John N. Friedman, Emmanuel Saez, Nicholas Turner, and Danny Yagan. 2017b. Mobility report cards: the role of colleges in intergenerational mobility. National Bureau of Economics Research Working Paper No. 23618.

Cheyney, Edward Potts. 1940. *History of the University of Pennsylvania*. Philadelphia: University of Pennsylvania Press.

Christensen, Clayton M. 1997. *The Innovator's Dilemma: When New Technologies Cause Great Firms to Fail*. Cambridge, MA: Harvard Business Review Press.

Christensen, Clayton M. and Henry J. Eyring. 2011. *The Innovative University: Changing the DNA of Higher Education from the Inside Out*. San Francisco: Jossey-Bass.

Chubb, John E. and Terry M. Moe. 1990. *Politics, Markets, and America's Schools*. Washington, DC: Brookings Institution Press.

Clark, Burton R. 1970. *The Distinctive College*. New Brunswick, NJ: Transaction Publishers, 1992.

———. 1983. *The Higher Education System: Academic Organization in Cross-National Perspective*. Berkeley: University of California Press.

Clark, Damon. 2010. Selective schools and academic achievement. *B.E. Journal of Economic Analysis and Policy:* Advances 10 (1): 1–40.

Clark, William. 2006. *Academic Charisma and the Origins of the Research University*. Chicago: The University of Chicago Press.

Clotfelter, Charles T. 2001. Who are the alumni donors? Giving by two generations of alumni from selective colleges. *Nonprofit Management and Leadership* 12: 119–138.

———. 2003. Alumni giving to elite private colleges and universities. *Economics of Education Review* 22: 109–120.

———. 2010. Introduction. In *American Universities in a Global Market*. Edited by Charles T. Clotfelter. Chicago: The University of Chicago Press.

———. 2011. *Big-Time Sports in American Universities*. New York: Cambridge University Press.

———. 2017. *Unequal Colleges in the Age of Disparity*. Cambridge, MA: The Belknap Press of Harvard University Press.

Cohen, Arthur M. and Carrie B. Kisker. 2010. *The Shaping of American Higher Education: Emergence and Growth of the Contemporary System*. San Francisco: Jossey-Bass.

Cohodes, Sarah R. 2018. Charter schools and the achievement gap. *The Future of Children Policy Issue*, 1–16.

Cohodes, Sarah R., Elizabeth Setren, and Christopher Walters. 2018. Can successful schools replicate? Scaling up Boston's charter sector. School Effectiveness and Inequality Initiative Working Paper No. 2016.06.

Cole, Jonathan R. 2009. *The Great American University: Its Rise to Preeminence, Its Indispensable National Role, Why It Must Be Protected*. New York: Public Affairs.

———. 2016. *Toward a More Perfect University*. New York: Public Affairs.

Committee of the Corporation, and the Academical Faculty. 1828. Reports on the Course of Instruction in Yale College. Unpublished paper. Yale College.

Cook, Philip J. and Robert H. Frank. 1993. The growing concentration of top students at elite schools. In *Studies of Supply and Demand in Higher Education*. Edited by Charles T. Clotfelter. Chicago: The University of Chicago Press.

Courant, Paul N. and Sarah Turner. 2017. Faculty deployment in research universities. National Bureau of Economic Research Working Paper No. 23025.

Cowen, Tyler. 2011. *The Great Stagnation: How America Ate All the Low-Hanging Fruit of Modern History, Got Sick, and Will (Eventually) Feel Better.* London: Penguin Books.

Cowen, Tyler and Alex Tabarrok. 2014. The industrial organization of online education. *American Economic Review* 104 (5): 519–522.

Cullen, Julie Berry, Brian A. Jacob, and Steven D. Levitt. 2006. The effect of school choice on student outcomes: Evidence from randomized lotteries. *Econometrica* 74 (5): 1191–1230.

Curti, Merle and Roderick Nash. 1965. *Philanthropy in the Shaping of American Higher Education.* New Brunswick, NJ: Rutgers University Press.

Curtis, Mark H. 1959. *Oxford and Cambridge in Transition, 1558–1642: An Essay on Changing Relations between English Universities and English Society.* Oxford: Oxford University Press.

Dale, Stacy Berg and Alan B. Krueger. 2002. Estimating the payoff to attending a more selective college: An application of selection on observables and unobservables. *The Quarterly Journal of Economics* 117 (4): 1491–1527.

———. 2014. Estimating the effects of college characteristics over the career using administrative earnings data. *The Journal of Human Resources* 49 (2): 323–358.

Dang, Hai-Anh and Halsey Rogers. 2008. The growing phenomenon of private tutoring: does it deepen human capital, widen inequalities, or waste resources? *The World Bank Research Observer* 23 (2): 161–200.

Davis, Donald R. and Jonathan I. Dingel. 2014. The comparative advantage of cities. National Bureau of Economic Research Working Paper No. 20602.

De Fraja, Gianni, Giovanni Facchini, and John Gathergood. 2016. How much is that star in the window? Professorial salaries and research performance in U.K. universities. University of Nottingham Discussion Paper No. 11638.

de Ree, Joppe, Karthik Muralidharan, Menno Pradhan, and Halsey Rogers. 2018. Double for nothing? Experimental evidence on an unconditional teacher salary increase in Indonesia. *The Quarterly Journal of Economics* 133 (2): 993–1039.

De Ridder-Symoens, Hilde. 1992. Mobility. In *A History of the University in Europe: Volume I, Universities in the Middle Ages.* Edited by Hilde De Ridder-Symoens. Cambridge: Cambridge University Press, 2003.

———. 1996. Management and Resources. In *A History of the University in Europe: Volume I, Universities in the Middle Ages.* Edited by Hilde De Ridder-Symoens. Cambridge: Cambridge University Press, 2003.

Delbanco, Andrew. 2012. *College: What It Was, Is, and Should Be.* Princeton, NJ: Princeton University Press.

Deming, David J., Claudia Goldin, Lawrence F. Katz and Noam Yuchtman. 2015. Can online learning bend the higher education cost curve? *American Economic Review* 105 (5): 496–501.

Deming, David J., Michael Lovenheim, and Richard W. Patterson. 2016a. The competitive effects of online education. National Bureau of Economic Research Working Paper No. 22749.

Deming, David J., Noam Yuchtman, Amira Abulafi, Claudia Goldin, and Lawrence F. Katz. 2016b. The value of postsecondary credentials in the labor market: an experimental study. *American Economic Review* 106 (3): 778–806.

Diamond, Peter and Emmanuel Saez. 2011. The case for a progressive tax: from basic research to policy recommendations. *Journal of Economic Perspectives* 25 (4): 165–190.

D'Irsay, Stephen. 1933. *Histoire des Universités Françaises et Étrangères des Origines a Nos Jours: Tome I, Moyen Age et Renaissance.* Paris: Editions August Picard.

———. 1935. *Histoire des Universités Françaises et Étrangères des Origines a Nos Jours: Tome II, du XVIe Siècle a 1860.* Paris: Editions August Picard.

Dittmar, Jeremiah E. 2011. Information technology and economic change: the impact of the printing press. *The Quarterly Journal of Economics* 126 (3): 1133–1172.

———. 2019. Economic origins of modern science: technology, institutions, and the market for ideas. Unpublished paper. London School of Economics.

Dittmar, Jeremiah E. and Ralf Meisenzahl. 2018. Public goods institutions, human capital, and growth: evidence from German history. *Review of Economic Studies* 0: 1–37.

Dixit, Avinash K. and Joseph E. Stiglitz. 1977. Monopolistic competition and optimal product diversity. *American Economic Review* 67 (3), 297–308.

Dobbie, Will and Roland Fryer. 2014. The impact of attending a school with high-achieving peers: evidence from New York City exam schools. *American Economics Journal: Applied Economics* 6 (3): 58–75.

Dorn, Charles. 2017. *For the common good: a new history of higher education in America.* Ithaca, NY: Cornell University Press.

Douglass, John Aubrey. 2000. *The California Idea and American Higher Education: 1850 to the Master Plan.* Stanford, CA: Stanford University Press.

Doyle, Joseph, John Graves, and Jonathan Gruber. 2015. Uncovering waste in U.S. healthcare. National Bureau of Economic Research Working Paper No. 21050.

Doyle, John Andrew. 1887. *The English in America: The Puritan Colonies.* London: Longmans, Green, & Co.

Dranove, David and Ginger Zhe Jin. 2010. Quality disclosure and certification: theory and practice. *Journal of Economic Literature* 48 (4): 935–963.

Duflo, Esther, Pascaline Dupas, and Michael Kremer. 2011. Peer effects, teacher incentives, and the impact of tracking: evidence from a randomized evaluation in Kenya. *American Economic Review.* 101 (5): 1739–1774.

Duflo, Esther, Rema Hanna, and Stephen Ryan. 2012. Incentives work: getting teachers to come to school. *American Economic Review* 102 (4): 1241–1278.

Dynarski, Susan and Judith Scott-Clayton. 2013. Financial aid policy: lessons from research. *The Future of Children*. 23 (1): 67–91.

Eble, Alex and Feng Hu. 2017. The power of credential length policy: schooling decisions and returns in modern China. Unpublished paper. Columbia University.

Ehrenberg, Ronald G. 1997. The American university: dilemmas and directions. In *The American University: National Treasure or Endangered Species?* Edited by Ronald G. Ehrenberg. Ithaca, NY: Cornell University Press.

———. 2000. *Tutition Rising: Why College Costs So Much*. Cambridge, MA: Harvard University Press.

Eire, Carlos M. N. 2016. *Reformations: The Early Modern World, 1450–1650*. New Haven, CT: Yale University Press.

Eliot, Charles W. 1908. *University Administration*. Boston, MA: Houghton Mifflin.

Ellison, Glenn and Ashley Swanson. 2016. Do schools matter for high math achievement? Evidence from the American mathematics competitions. *American Economic Review* 106 (6): 1244–1277.

Engerman, Stanley L. and Kenneth L. Sokoloff. 2002. Factor endowments, inequality, and paths of development among new world economies. National Bureau of Economic Research Working Paper No. 9259.

Epple, Dennis and Richard E. Romano. 1998. Competition between private and public schools, vouchers, and peer-group effects. *American Economic Review* 88 (1): 33–62.

———. 2011. Peer effects in education: a survey of the theory and evidence. In *Handbook of Social Economics*. Edited by Jess Benhabib, Alberto Bisin, and Matthew Jackson. Amsterdam: Elsevier Science, North Holland.

Epple, Dennis, Richard E. Romano, and Holger Sieg. 2006. Admission, tuition, and financial aid policies in the market for higher education. *Econometrica* 74 (4): 885–928.

Epple, Dennis, Richard E. Romano, and Miguel Urquiola. 2017. School vouchers: a survey of the economics literature. *Journal of Economic Literature* 55 (2): 441–492.

Epple, Dennis, Richard E. Romano, and Ron Zimmer. 2016. Charter schools: a survey of research on their characteristics and effectiveness. In *Handbook of the Economics of Education*. Edited by Eric A. Hanushek, Stephen Machin, and Ludger Woessmann. Amsterdam: Elsevier.

Espenshade, Thomas J., Chang Y. Chung, and Joan L. Walling. 2004. Admission preferences for minority students, athletes, and legacies at elite universities. *Social Science Quarterly* 85 (5): 1422–1446.

Even, William E. and Austin C. Smith. 2018. Greek life, academics, and earnings. IZA Discussion Paper No. 11841.

Farber, Henry S. and Robert Gibbons. 1996. Learning and wage dynamics. *The Quarterly Journal of Economics* 111 (4): 1007–1047.

Feigenberg, Benjamin, Steven Rivkin, and Rui Yan. 2014. Illusory gains from Chile's targeted school voucher experiment. National Bureau of Economic Research Working Paper No. 23178.

Fermi, Laura. 1968. *Illustrious Immigrants: The Intellectual Migration from Europe, 1930–41.* Chicago: The University of Chicago Press.

Figlio, David, Mark Rush, and Lu Yin. 2013. Is it live or is it internet? Experimental estimates of the effects of online instruction on student learning. *Journal of Labor Economics* 31 (4): 763–784.

Figlio, David N., Morton O. Schapiro, and Kevin B. Soter. 2015. Are tenure track professors better teachers? *The Review of Economics and Statistics* 97 (4): 715–724.

Finke, Roger and Rodney Stark. 2005. *The Churching of America, 1776–2005: Winners and Losers in our Religious Economy.* New Brunswick, NJ: Rutgers University Press, 2014.

Fisher, Elliott S., Julie P. Bynum, and Jonathan S. Skinner. 2009. Slowing the growth of health care costs: lessons from regional variation. *The New England Journal of Medicine* 360 (9): 849–852.

Flexner, Abraham. 1946. *Daniel Coit Gilman: Creator of the American Type of University*. New York: Harcourt, Brace and Company.

Fox, Robert and George Weisz. 1980. Introduction: the institutional basis of French science in the nineteenth century. In *The Organization of Science and Technology in France 1808–1914*. Edited by Robert Fox and George Weisz. Cambridge: Cambridge University Press.

Frank, Robert H. 1985. *Choosing the Right Pond: Human Behavior and the Quest for Status*. New York: Oxford University Press.

———. 2005. Positional externalities cause large and preventable welfare losses. *American Economic Review* 95 (2): 137–145.

Friebel, Guido and Michael Raith. 2004. Abuse of authority and hierarchical communication. *RAND Journal of Economics* 35 (2): 224–244.

Friedman, Milton. 1955. The role of government in education. In *Economics and the Public Interest*. Edited by Robert Solow. New Brunswick, NJ: Rutgers University Press.

Frijhoff, Willem. 1996. Patterns. In *A History of the University in Europe: Volume II, Universities in Early Modern Europe*. Edited by Hilde De Ridder-Symoens. Cambridge: Cambridge University Press, 2003.

Frusciano, Thomas J. 2006. From "seminary of learning" to public research university: a historical sketch of Rutgers University. Unpublished paper. Rutgers University.

Gabriel, Astrik L. 1992. *The Paris Studium: Robert of Sorbonne and his Legacy*. Frankfurt, Germany: Verlag Josef Knecht.

Gallego, Francisco. 2013. When does inter-school competition matter? Evidence from the Chilean "voucher" system. *Advances in Economic Analysis & Policy* 13 (2): 525–562.

Gallego, Francisco and A. Hernando. 2009. School choice in Chile: looking at the demand side. Unpublished paper. Pontificia Universidad Católica de Chile.

Geiger, Roger L. 1986. *To Advance Knowledge: The Growth of American Research Universities, 1900–1940*. New Brunswick, NJ: Transaction Publishers.

———. 1993. *American Research Universities Since World War II: Research and Relevant Knowledge.* New Brunswick, NJ: Transaction Publishers, 2009.

———. 2015. *The History of American Higher Education: Learning and Culture from the Founding to World War II.* Princeton, NJ: Princeton University Press.

Gieysztor, Aleksander. 1992. Management and resources. In *A History of the University in Europe: Volume I, Universities in the Middle Ages.* Edited by Hilde De Ridder-Symoens. Cambridge: Cambridge University Press, 2003.

Gillmor, C. Stewart 2004. *Fred Terman at Stanford: Building a Discipline, a University, and Silicon Valley.* Stanford, CA: Stanford University Press.

Gilman, Daniel C. 1885. *The Benefits Which Society Derives from Universities.* Baltimore, MD: Publication Agency of the Johns Hopkins University.

Goastellec, Gaële. 2012. Changing the rules of the French academic market. In *Paying the Professoriate: A Global Comparison of Compensation and Contracts.* Edited by Philip G. Altbach Liz Reisberg, Maria Yudkevich, Gregory Androushchak, and Iván F. Pacheco. New York: Routledge.

Goldin, Claudia. 1998. America's graduation from high school: the evolution and spread of secondary schooling in the twentieth century. *The Journal of Economic History* 58 (2): 345–374.

———. 2001. The human capital century and American leadership: virtues of the past. *The Journal of Economic History* 61 (2): 263–292.

———. 2016. Human capital. In: *Handbook of Cliometrics.* Edited by Claude Diebolt and Michael Haupert. Berlin, Germany: Springer Verlag.

Goldin, Claudia and Lawrence F. Katz. 1998. The shaping of higher education: the formative years in the United States, 1890–1940. National Bureau of Economic Research Working Paper No. 6537.

———. 1999a. Human capital and social capital: The rise of secondary schooling in America, 1910–1940. *Journal of Interdisciplinary History* XXIX (4): 683–723.

———. 1999b. The shaping of higher education: the formative years in the United States, 1890–1940. *Journal of Economic Perspectives* 13 (1): 37–62.

———. 2000. Education and income in the early twentieth century: evidence from the prairies. *Journal of Economic History* 60 (3): 782–818.

———. 2008. *The Race Between Education and Technology.* Cambridge, MA: The Belknap Press of Harvard University Press.

———. 2011a. Mass secondary schooling and the state: the role of state compulsion in the high school movement. In *Understanding Long Run Economic Growth.* Edited by Dora Costa and Naomi Lamoreaux. Cambridge: Cambridge University Press.

———. 2011b. Putting the "co" in education: timing, reasons, and consequences of college education from 1835 to the Present. *Journal of Human Capital* 5 (4): 377–417.

Goodman, Joshua, Oded Gurantz and Jonathan Smith. 2018. Take Two! SAT Retaking and College Enrollment Gaps. National Bureau of Economic Research Working Paper No. 2494.

Goodman, Joshua, Julia Melkers, and Amanda Pallais. 2019. Can online delivery increase access to education? *Journal of Labor Economics* 37 (1): 1–34.

Goodman, Sarena. 2016. Learning from the test: raising selective college enrollment by providing information. *The Review of Economics and Statistics* 98 (4): 671–684.

Gordon, Grey and Aaron Hedlund. 2016. Accounting for the rise in college tuition. National Bureau of Economic Research Working Paper No. 21967.

Gordon, Robert J. 2016. *The Rise and Fall of American Growth: The U.S. Standard of Living since the Civil War.* Princeton, NJ: Princeton University Press.

Graham, Hugh Davis and Nancy Diamond. 1997. *The Rise of American Research Universities: Elites and Challenges in the Postwar Era.* Baltimore, MD: The Johns Hopkins University Press.

Graham, Patricia Albjerg. 1974. *Community & Class in American Education, 1865–1918*. New York: John Wiley & Sons.

——. 2005. *Schooling America: How the Public Schools Meet the Nation's Changing Needs*. Oxford: Oxford University Press.

Granovetter, Mark S. 1973. The strength of weak ties. *American Journal of Sociology* 78 (6): 1360–1380.

Gruber, Jonathan and Simon Johnson. 2019. *Jump-Starting America: How Breakthrough Science Can Revive Economic Growth and the American Dream*. New York: Public Affairs.

Gumbel, Peter. 2013. *Elite Academy: Enquête sur la France Malade de ses Grandes Ecoles*. Paris: Editions Denöel.

Hacker, Jacob S. and Paul Pierson. 2016. *American Amnesia: How the War on Government Led Us to Forget What Made America Prosper*. New York: Simon and Schuster.

Handlin, Oscar and Mary F. Handlin. 1970. *The American College and American Culture*. New York: Mc Graw-Hill Book Company.

Hanushek, Eric A. 1981. Throwing money at schools. *Journal of Policy Analysis and Management* 1 (1): 19–41.

——. 1986. The economics of schooling: production and efficiency in public schools. *Journal of Economic Literature* 24 (3): 1141–1177.

——. 1997. The productivity collapse in schools. In *Developments in School Finance*. Edited by William Fowler. Washington, DC: National Center for Education Statistics.

Hanushek, Eric A., Paul E. Peterson, and Ludger Woessmann. 2013. *Endangering Prosperity: A Global View of the American School*. Washington, DC: Brookings Institution Press.

Hanushek, Eric and Lei Zhang. 2009. Quality-consistent estimates of international schooling and skill gradients. *Journal of Human Resources* 3 (2): 107–143.

Hartocollis, Anemona (March 29, 2016). Colleges spending millions to deal with sexual misconduct complaints. New York Times.

Haskins, Charles Homer. 1923. *The Rise of Universities.* Ithaca, NY: Cornell University Press, 1957.

———. (1929). *Studies in Mediaeval Culture.* New York: Frederick Ungar Publishing, 1965.

Hastings, Justine, Thomas Kane, and Douglas Staiger. 2009. Heterogeneous preferences and the efficacy of public school choice. Unpublished paper. Brown University.

Hawkins, Hugh (1960). *Pioneer: A History of the Johns Hopkins University, 1874–1889.* Baltimore, ,MD: The Johns Hopkins University Press, 2002.

Heckman, James J. and Sidarth Moktan. 2018. Publishing and promotion in economics: the tyranny of the top five. National Bureau of Economic Research Working Paper No. 25093.

Helland, Eric and Alex Tabarrok. 2019. *Why Are the Prices So Damn High?* Arlington: Mercatus Center, George Mason University.

Henderson, Joseph Lindsey. 1912. *Admission to College by Certificate.* New York: Teachers College, Columbia University.

Herbst, Jurgen. 1982. *From Crisis to Crisis: American College Government, 1636–1819.* Cambridge, MA: Harvard University Press.

Herskovic, Luis. 2017. The effect of subway access on school choice. Unpublished paper, University of Chicago.

Herzog, Marius and Barbara M. Kehm. 2012. The income situation in the German system of higher education: a rag tag. In *Paying the Professoriate: A Global Comparison of Compensation and Contracts.* Edited by Philip G. Altbach, Liz Reisberg, Maria Yudkevich, Gregory Androushchak, and Iván F. Pacheco. New York: Routledge.

Hinnerich, Björn Tyrefors and Jonas Vlachos. 2017. The impact of upper-secondary voucher school attendance on student achievement: Swedish evidence using external and internal evaluations. *Labour Economics* 47: 1–14.

Hoekstra, Mark. 2009. The effect of attending the flagship state university on earnings: a discontinuity-based approach. *Review of Economics and Statistics* 91 (4): 717–724.

Hofstadter, Richard. 1955. *Academic Freedom in the Age of the College.* New Brunswick and London: Transaction Publishers, 1996.

———. 1963. The revolution in higher education. In *Paths of American Thought.* Edited by Arthur M. Schlesinger and Morton White. New York: Houghton Mifflin.

Holmes, Jessica. 2009. Prestige, charitable deductions, and other determinants of alumni giving: evidence from a highly selective liberal arts college. *Economics of Education Review* 28: 18–28.

Hoxby, Caroline M. 1997. How the changing market structure of U.S. higher education explains college tuition. National Bureau of Economic Research Working Paper No. 6323.

———. 2000. Does competition among public schools benefit students and taxpayers? *American Economic Review* 90 (5): 1209–1238.

———. 2002. School choice and school productivity (or could school choice be a tide that lifts all boats?) NBER Working Paper No. 8873.

———. 2009. The Changing Selectivity of American Colleges. *Journal of Economic Perspectives* 23 (4): 95–118.

———. 2012. Endowment management based on a positive model of the university. National Bureau of Economic Research Working Paper No. 18626.

———. 2014. The economics of online postsecondary education: MOOCs, nonselective education, and highly selective education. National Bureau of Economic Research Working Paper No. 19816.

———. 2016a. The dramatic economics of the U.S. market for higher education: The 2016 Martin Feldstein Lecture. National Bureau of Economic Research Reporter, 2016 Number 3.

———. 2016b. The productivity of U.S. postsecondary institutions. Unpublished paper. Stanford University.

Hoxby, Caroline and Christopher Avery. 2013. The missing "one-offs": the hidden supply of high-achieving, low income students. *Brookings Papers on Economic Activity* Spring: 1-65.

Hsieh, Chang-Tai and Peter J. Klenow. 2009. Misallocation and manufacturing TFP in China and India. *The Quarterly Journal of Economics* 124 (4): 1403–1448.

Hsieh, Chang-Tai and Enrico Moretti. 2003. Can free entry be inefficient? fixed commissions and social waste in the real estate industry. *Journal of Political Economy* 111 (5): 1076–1122.

Hsieh, Chang-Tai and Benjamin A. Olken. 2014. The missing "missing middle". *Journal of Economic Perspectives* 28 (3): 89–108.

Hsieh, Chang-Tai and Miguel Urquiola. 2003. When schools compete, how do they compete? An assessment of Chile's nationwide school voucher program. National Bureau of Economic Research Working Paper No. 10008.

———. 2006. The Effects of Generalized School Choice on Achievement and Stratification: Evidence from Chile's School Voucher Program. *Journal of Public Economics* 90: 1477–1503.

Hu, Winnie (June 6, 2018). In a twist, low scores would earn admission to select schools. New York Times.

Hubbard, Thomas N. 2002. How do consumers motivate experts? Reputational incentives in an auto repair market. *Journal of Law & Economics* 45 (2): 437–468.

Hyman, Joshua. 2017. Does money matter in the long run? Effects of school spending on educational attainment. *American Economic Journal: Economic Policy* 9 (4): 256–280.

Ilaria, Alessandro, Carlo Schwarz, and Fabian Waldinger. 2017. Frontier knowledge and scientific production: evidence from the collapse of international science. *The Quarterly Journal of Economics* 133 (2): 927–991.

Ioannides, Yannis M. and Linda Datcher Loury. 2004. Job information networks, neighborhood effects, and inequality. *Journal of Economic Literature* 42 (4): 1056–2093.

Ito, Takatoshi and Charles Kahn. 1986. Why is there tenure? Hoover Institution, Working Paper No. E-86-3.

Jackson, C. Kirabo. 2010. Do students benefit from attending better schools? Evidence from rule-based student assignments in Trinidad and Tobago. *The Economic Journal* 120 (549): 1399–1429.

Jackson, C. Kirabo, Rucker C. Johnson, and Claudia Persico. 2016. The effects of school spending on educational and economic outcomes: evidence from school finance reforms. *The Quarterly Journal of Economics* 131 (1): 157–218.

Jackson, C. Kirabo, Jonah Rockoff, and Douglas O. Staiger. 2014. Teacher effects and teacher-related policies. *Annual Review of Economics* 6: 801–825.

Jacob, Brian, Brian McCall, and Kevin Stange. 2018. College as country club: do colleges cater to students' preferences for consumption? *Journal of Labor Economics* 36 (2): 309–348.

James, Henry. 1930. *Charles W. Eliot: President of Harvard University, 1869–1909, Volume I.* Boston, MA: Houghton Mifflin.

Jayachandran, Seema. 2014. Incentives to teach badly? After school tutoring in developing countries. *Journal of Development Economics* 108: 190–205.

Jencks, Christopher and David Riesman. 1968. *The Academic Revolution.* Garden City, NY: Doubleday.

Jernegan, Marcus Wilson. 1929. *The American Colonies, 1492–1750.* New York: Frederick Ungar Publishing.

—— 1932. Colleges, universities, and churches, 1775–1890. In *Atlas of Historical Geography of the United States.* Edited by Charles O. Paullin. Washington, DC: Carnegie Institution.

Jin, Ginger Zhe and Phillip Leslie. 2003. The effect of information on product quality. *The Quarterly Journal of Economics* 118 (2): 409–451.

Johnson, Noel D. and Mark Koyama. 2019. *Persecution & Toleration: The Long Road to Religious Freedom.* New York: Cambridge University Press.

Jones, Benjamin F. 2009. The burden of knowledge and the death of the renaissance man: is innovation getting harder? *Review of Economic Studies* 76 (1): 283–317.

Jones, Charles I. 2005. Growth and ideas. In *Handbook of Economic Growth*. Edited by Phillipe Aghion and Steven Durlauf. Washington, DC: Elsevier.

———. 2018. Taxing top incomes in a world of ideas. Unpublished paper. Stanford University.

Jones, John 1997. *Balliol College: A History*. Oxford: Oxford University Press, 1988.

Jones, Susan (January 18, 2017). Bernie Sanders lecture HHS nominee on USA: 'No, we're not a compassionate society! Cnsnews.

Joyce, Ted, Sean Crockett, and David A. Jaeger. 2015. Does classroom time matter? *Economics of Education Review* 46: 64–77.

Kahn, Shamus R. 2011. *Privilege: The Making of an Adolescent Elite at St. Paul's School*. Princeton, NJ: Princeton University Press.

Kaiser, David. 2012. Elephant on the Charles: postwar growing pains. In *Becoming MIT: Moments of Decision*. Edited by David Kaiser. Cambridge, MA: MIT Press.

Kaminski, Deborah and Cheryl Geisler. 2012. Survival analysis of faculty retention in science and engineering by gender. *Science* 337 (6070): 864–866.

Kane, Thomas and Douglas Staiger. 2008. Estimating teacher impacts on student achievement: an experimental evaluation. National Bureau of Economic Research Working Paper No. 14607.

Karabel, Jerome. 2006. *The Chosen: The Hidden History of Admission and Exclusion at Harvard, Yale, and Princeton*. Boston, MA: Mariner Books, Houghton Mifflin Company.

Kaufmann, Katja M., Matthias Messner, and Alex Solis. 2013. Returns to elite higher education in the marriage market: evidence from Chile. Unpublished paper. SSRN Working Paper http://dx.doi.org/10.2139/ssrn.2313369.

Kearney, Hugh. 1970. *Scholars and Gentlemen: Universities and Society in Pre-industrial Britain, 1500–1700*. Ithaca, NY: Cornell University Press.

Keller, Morton and Phyllis Keller. 2001. *Making Harvard Modern: The Rise of America's University*. New York: Oxford University Press.

Kelley, Brooks Mather. 1974. *Yale: A History*. New Haven and London: Yale University Press.

Kenny, Lawrence W. and Amy B. Schmidt. 1992. The decline in the number of school districts in the United States: 1950–1980. *Public Choice* 79 (1–2): 1–18.

Kerr, Clark. 1963. *The Uses of the University*. New York: Harper.

Kevles, Daniel. 1979. The Physics, Mathematics, and Chemistry Communities: A Comparative Analysis. In *The Organization of Knowledge in Modern America*. Edited by Alexandra Oleson and John Voss. Baltimore, MD: Johns Hopkins University Press.

Kibre, Pearl. 1948. *The Nations in the Mediaeval Universities*. Cambridge, MA: The Mediaeval Academy of America.

——. 1962. *Scholarly Privileges in the Middle Ages*. Cambridge, MA: The Mediaeval Academy of America.

Kitagawa, Fumi. 2012. Academic salary in the United Kingdom: marketization and national policy development. In *Paying the Professoriate: A Global Comparison of Compensation and Contracts*. Edited by Philip G. Altbach, Liz Reisberg, Maria Yudkevich, Gregory Androushchak, and Iván F. Pacheco. New York: Routledge

Koch, James V. (January 9, 2018). No college kid needs a water park to study. New York Times.

Kraft, Matthew. 2018. Teacher effects on complex cognitive skills and socio-emotional competencies. *Journal of Human Resources*. 53 (4): 1–36.

Krueger, Alan B. and Lawrence H. Summers. 1988. Efficiency wages and the inter-industry wage structure. *Econometrica* 56 (2): 259–294.

Krugman, Paul (August 16, 2018). Something not rotten in Denmark. New York Times.

Labaree, David F. 2017. *A Perfect Mess: The Unlikely Ascendancy of American Higher Education*. Chicago: The University of Chicago Press.

Lafortune, Julien, Jesse Rothstein, and Diane Schanzenbach. 2018. School finance reform and the distribution of student achievement. *American Economic Journal: Applied Economics* 10 (2): 1–26.

Lange, Fabian. 2007. The speed of employer learning. *Journal of Labor Economics* 25: 497–532.

Lécuyer, Cristophe. 2012. Patrons and a plan. In *Becoming MIT: Moments of Decision*. Edited by David Kaiser. Cambridge, MA: MIT Press.

Leedham-Green, Elisabeth. 1996. *A Concise History of the University of Cambridge*. Cambridge: Cambridge University Press, 2011.

Leff, Gordon. 1968. *Paris and Oxford Universities in the Thirteenth and Fourteenth Centuries: An Institutional and Intellectual History*. New York: John Wiley & Sons.

Lemann, Nicholas. 1999. *The Big Test: The Secret History of American Meritocracy*. New York: Farrar, Strauss, and Giroux.

Lerner, Josh, Antoinette Schoar, and Jialan Wang. 2008. Secrets of the academy: the drivers of university endowment success. *Journal of Economic Perspectives* 22 (3): 207–222.

Leslie, W. Bruce. 1992. *Gentlemen and Scholars: College and Community in the "Age of the University," 1865–1917*. University Park: Pennsylvania State University Press.

Levy, Santiago. 2018. *Under-Rewarded Efforts: The Elusive Quest for Prosperity in Mexico*. Washington, DC: Inter-American Development Bank.

Lindo, Jason M., Isaac D. Swensen, and Glen R. Waddell. 2013. Alcohol and student performance: estimating the effect of legal access. *Journal of Health Economics* 32: 22–32.

Liptak, Adam (May 11, 2009). On the bench and off, the eminently quotable Justice Scalia. New York Times.

Lockwood, Benjamin B., Charles G. Nathanson, and E. Glen Weyl. 2017. Taxation and the allocation of talent. *Journal of Political Economy* 125 (5): 1635–1682.

Lorin, Janet (June 8, 2018). Colleges get tax reprieve in push to value endowment assets. Bloomberg.

Lucas, Adrienne and Isaac Mbiti. 2014. Effects of school quality on student achievement: discontinuity evidence from Kenya. *American Economic Journal: Applied Economics* 6 (3): 234–263.

Lucas, Christopher J. 2006. *American Higher Education: A History.* New York: Palgrave McMillan.

Lucas, Robert E. 2009. Ideas and growth. *Economica* 76 (301): 1–19.

Macartney, Hugh and John D. Singleton. 2017. School boards and student segregation. National Bureau of Economic Research Working Paper No. 23619.

MacLeod, W. Bentley and Miguel Urquiola. 2009. Anti-lemons: school reputation and educational quality. National Bureau of Economic Research Working Paper No. 15112.

———. 2013. Competition and educational productivity: incentives writ large. In *Education Policy in Developing Countries.* Edited by Paul Glewwe. Chicago: University of Chicago Press.

———. 2015. Reputation and school competition. *American Economic Review* 105 (11): 3471–3488.

———. 2018. Is education consumption or investment? Implications for the effects of school competition. National Bureau of Economic Research Working Paper No. 25117.

MacLeod, W. Bentley, Evan Riehl, Juan E. Saavedra, and Miguel Urquiola. 2017. The big sort: college reputation and labor market outcomes. *American Economic Journal: Applied Economics* 9 (3): 223–261.

Malamud, Ofer. 2010. The structure of European higher education in the wake of the Bologna reforms. In *American Universities in a Global Market.* Edited by Charles T. Clotfelter. Chicago and London: The University of Chicago Press.

———. 2011. Discovering one's talent: learning from academic specialization. Industrial and Labor Relations Review 64 (2) 375–405.

Mankiw, N. Gregory and Michael D. Whinston. 1986. Free entry and social inefficiency. *Rand Journal of Economics* 17 (1): 48–58.

Manso, Gustavo. 2011. Motivating innovation. *Journal of Finance* 66 (5): 1823–1860.

Marr, Kelly A., Charles H. Mullin, and John J. Siegfried. 2005. Undergraduate financial aid and subsequent alumni giving behavior. *The Quarterly Review of Economics and Finance* 45: 123–143.

Martin, G. H. and J. R. L. Highfield. 1997. *A History of Merton College, Oxford.* Oxford: Oxford University Press.

Martin, Jay 2002. *The Education of John Dewey: A Biography.* New York: Columbia University Press.

McAnear, Beverly. 1950. American imprints concerning King's College. *The Papers of the Bibliographical Society of America* 44 (4): 301–339.

McCaughey, Robert A. 1974. The transformation of American academic life: Harvard University 1821–1892. *Perspectives in American History* 8: 239–332.

———. 2003. *Stand, Columbia: A History of Columbia University in the City of New York, 1754–2004.* New York: Columbia University Press.

———. 2004. The education of Alexander Hamilton. *The New York Journal of American History* Fall (25–31): 1593–1660.

———. 2014. *A Lever Long Enough: A History of Columbia's School of Engineering and Applied Science Since 1864.* New York: Columbia University Press.

McEwan, Patrick and Martin Carnoy. 2000. The effectiveness and efficiency of private schools in Chile's voucher system. *Educational Evaluation and Policy Analysis* 22 (3): 213–239.

McPherson, Michael S. and Lawrence S. Bacow. 2015. Online higher education: beyond the hype cycle. *Journal of Economic Perspectives* 29 (4): 135–154.

McPherson, Michael S. and Morton Owen Schapiro. 1990. *Selective Admission and the Public Interest.* New York: The College Entrance Examination Board.

———. 1991. *Keeping College Affordable: Government and Educational Opportunity.* Washington, DC: The Brookings Institution.

———. 1999. Tenure issues in higher education. *Journal of Economic Perspectives* 13 (1): 85–98.

Meer, Jonathan and Harvey Rosen. 2009. Altruism and the child cycle of alumni donations. *American Economic Journal: Economic Policy* 1 (1): 258–286.

———. 2010. Family bonding with universities. *Research in Higher Education* 51 (7): 641–658.

———. 2018. Measuring the motives for charitable giving. National Bureau of Economic Research Reporter, Number 1.

Melnik, Mikhail I. and James Alm. 2002. Does a seller's ecommerce reputation matter? Evidence from eBay auctions. *Journal of Industrial Economics* 50 (3): 337–349.

Merton, Robert K. 1968. The Matthew effect in science. *Science* 159 (3810): 56–63.

Mervis, Jeffrey (March 9, 2017). Data check: U.S. government share of basic research funding falls below 50%. Science Magazine.

Metzger, Walter P. 1955. *Academic Freedom in the Age of the University.* New York: Columbia University Press, 1961.

———. 1973. Academic tenure in America: a historical essay. *Faculty Tenure: A Report and Recommendations* by the Commission on Academic Tenure in Higher Education. San Francisco: Josey-Bass, Inc.

Miller, Thomas P. 1990. *The Selected Writings of John Witherspoon.* Carbondale: Southern Illinois University Press.

Mizala, Alejandra, Pilar Romaguera, and Miguel Urquiola. 2007. Socioeconomic status or noise? Tradeoffs in the generation of school quality information. *Journal of Development Economics* 84 (1): 61–75.

Mizala, Alejandra and Miguel Urquiola. 2013. Parental choice and school markets: The impact of information on school effectiveness. *Journal of Development Economics* 103: 313–335.

Moeller, Bernd. 1972. *Imperial Cities and the Reformation: Three Essays.* Durham, NC: The Labyrinth Press, 1982.

Mokyr, Joel. 2002. *The Gifts of Athena: Historical Origins of the Knowledge Economy.* Princeton, NJ: Princeton University Press.

———. 2005. Long-term economic growth and the history of technology. In *Handbook of Economic Growth.* Edited by Philippe Aghion and Steven N. Durlauf. Amsterdam: Elsevier.

Mokyr, Joel. and Hans-Joachim Voth. 2010. Understanding growth in Europe, 1700–1870: theory and evidence, in *The Cambridge Economic History of Europe.* Edited by Stephen Broadberry and Kevin H. O'Rourke. Cambridge: Cambridge University Press.

Moretti, Enrico. 2004. Workers' education, spillovers and productivity: evidence from plant-level production functions. *American Economic Review* 94 (3): 656–690.

———. 2012. *The New Geography of Jobs.* Boston and New York: Houghton Mifflin Harcourt.

Moretti, Enrico and Daniel J. Wilson. 2017. The effect of state taxes on the geographical location of top earners: evidence from star scientists. *American Economic Review* 107 (7): 1858–1903.

Morison, Samuel Eliot. 1935. *The Founding of Harvard College.* Cambridge, MA: Harvard University Press, 1995.

———. 1936. *Three Centuries of Harvard: 1636–1936.* Cambridge, MA: The Belknap Press of Harvard University Press, 1964.

Moser, Petra, Alessandra Voena, and Fabian Waldinger. 2014. German-Jewish émigrés and U.S. invention. *American Economic Review* 104 (10): 3222–3255.

Muralidharan, Karthik, Abhijeet Singh, and Alejandro J. Ganimian. 2017. Disrupting education? Experimental evidence on technology-aided instruction in India. National Bureau of Economic Research Working Paper No. 22923.

Muralidharan, Karthik and Venkatesh Sundararaman. 2015. The aggregate effect of school choice: evidence from a two-stage experiment in India. *The Quarterly Journal of Economics* 130 (3): 1011–1066.

Murray, Sheila E., William N. Evans, and Robert M. Schwab. 1998. Education-finance reform and the distribution of education resources. *American Economic Review* 88 (4): 789–812.

Musselin, Christine. 2017. *La Grande Course des Universités*. Paris: SciencePo: Les Presses.

Nardi, Paolo. 1992. Relations with authority, In *A History of the University in Europe: Volume I, Universities in the Middle Ages*. Edited by Hilde De Ridder-Symoens. Cambridge: Cambridge University Press, 2003.

National Center for Education Statistics. 1993. *120 Years of American Education: A Statistical Portrait*. Unpublished paper. U.S. Department of Education Office of Educational Research and Improvement.

National Research Council. 1995. *Colleges of Agriculture at the Land Grant Universities: A Profile*. Washington, DC: The National Academies Press.

Navarro-Palau, Patricia. 2017. Effects of differentiated school vouchers: evidence from a policy change and date of birth cutoffs. *Economics of Education Review* 58, 86–107.

Naylor, Natalie. 1973. The Ante-bellum college movement: a reappraisal of Tewksbury's "Founding of American colleges and universities." *History of Education Quarterly* 260: 261–274.

Neilson, Christopher. 2017. Targeted vouchers, competition among schools, and the academic achievement of poor students. Unpublished paper. Princeton University.

Nelson, Phillip. 1970. Information and consumer behavior. *Journal of Political Economy* 78 (2): 311–329.

Noll, Roger G. 1998. The American research university: an introduction. In *Challenges to Research Universities*. Edited by Roger G. Noll. Washington, DC: The Brookings Institution.

Oberdorfer, Don. 1995. *Princeton University: The First 250 Years*. Princeton, NJ: The Trustees of Princeton University.

Officers of the Harvard Club of New York City. 1878. *Proceedings of the Harvard Club of New York City, 1878*. New York: G. P. Putnam's Sons.

Oreopoulos, Philip, Till von Wachter, and Andrew Heisz. 2012. The
short- and long-term career effects of graduating in a recession.
American Economic Journal: Applied Economics 4 (1): 1-29.

Oyer, Paul and Scott Schaefer. 2015. Firm / employee matching: an
industry study of U.S. lawyers. *ILR Review* 69 (2): 378–404.

Park, Albert, Xinzheng Shi, Chang-Tai Hsieh, and Xuehui An. 2008.
Does school quality matter? Evidence from a natural experiment in
rural China. Unpublished paper. University of Chicago.

Patton, Cornelius Howard and Walter Taylor Field. 1927. *Eight O'clock
Chapel: A Study of New England College Life in the Eighties.* Boston, MA:
Houghton Mifflin Company.

Paulsen, Friedrich. 1906. *The German Universities and University Study.*
New York: Charles Scribner's Sons.

Payne, Abigail and Aloysius Siow. 2003. Does federal research funding
increase university research output? *The B.E. Journal of Economic
Analysis and Policy* 3 (1) 1–24.

Peckham, Howard H. 1967. *The Making of the University of Michigan:
1817–1967.* Ann Arbor: The University of Michigan Press.

Pelfrey, Patricia. 2004. *A Brief History of the University of California.*
Berkeley: University of California Press.

Perna, Laura W., Alan Ruby, Robert F. Boruch, Nicole Wang, Janie Scull,
Seher Ahmad, and Chad Evans. 2014. Moving through MOOCs:
understanding the progression of users through massive open online
courses. *Educational Researcher* 43 (9): 421–432.

Picketty, Thomas. 2014. *Capital in the Twenty-First Century.* Cambridge,
MA: The Belknap Press of Harvard University Press.

Pop-Eleches, Cristian and Miguel Urquiola. 2013. Going to a better
school: effects and behavioral responses. *American Economic Review*
103 (4): 1289–1324.

Porter, Roy. 1996. The scientific revolution and universities. In *A History
of the University in Europe: Volume II, Universities in Early Modern
Europe.* Edited by Hilde De Ridder-Symoens. Cambridge: Cambridge
University Press, 2003.

Potts, David B. 2000. Curriculum and enrollment: assessing the popularity of antebellum colleges. In *The American College in the Nineteenth Century*. Edited by Roger L. Geiger. Nashville, TN: Vanderbilt University Press.

Pritchett, Lant. 2003. Educational quality and costs: a big puzzle and five possible pieces. Unpublished paper. Harvard University.

Pritchett, Lant and Amanda Beatty. 2012. The negative consequences of overambitious curricula in developing countries. Center for Global Development Working Paper 293.

Pryde, George S. 1957. *The Scottish Universities and the Colleges of Colonial America*. Glasgow: Jackson, Son and Company.

Rashdall, Hastings. 1895a. *The Universities of Europe in the Middle Ages, Volume 1: Salerno, Bologna, and Paris*. Cambridge: Cambridge University Press, 2010.

———. 1895b. *The Universities of Europe in the Middle Ages, Volume 2, Part 1: Italy, Spain, France, Germany, Scotland, etc.* Cambridge: Cambridge University Press, 2010.

———. 1895c. *The Universities of Europe in the Middle Ages, Volume 2, Part 2: English Universities, Student Life*. Cambridge: Cambridge University Press, 2010.

Rasmussen, Dennis C. 2017. *The Infidel and the Professor: David Hume, Adam Smith, and the Friendship that Shaped Modern Thought*. Princeton, NJ: Princeton University Press.

Reisner, Edward Hartman. 1931. The origin of lay university boards of control in the United States. *Columbia University Quarterly*. March: 63–69.

Reuben, Julie A. 1996. *The Making of the Modern University: Intellectual Transformation and the Marginalization of Morality*. Chicago: The University of Chicago Press.

Riehl, Evan. 2018. Fairness in college admission exams: From test score gaps to earnings inequality. Unpublished paper. Cornell University.

Riehl, Evan, Juan E. Saavedra, and Miguel Urquiola. 2016. Learning and earning: an approximation to college value added in two dimensions. National Bureau of Economic Research Working Paper No. 22725.

Ringer, Fritz K. 1979. *Education and Society in Modern Europe.* Bloomington: Indiana University Press.

Rivera, Lauren A. 2015. *Pedigree: How Elite Students Get Elite Jobs.* Princeton, NJ: Princeton University Press.

Rivkin, Steven G., Eric A. Hanushek, and John F. Kain. 2005. Teachers, schools, and academic achievement. *Econometrica* 73 (2): 417–458.

Roberts, John H. and James Turner. 2000. *The Sacred and the Secular University.* Princeton, NJ: Princeton University Press.

Robertson, Sir Charles Grant. 1930. *The British Universities.* London: Ernest Benn.

Rockoff, Jonah. 2004. The impact of individual teachers on student achievement: evidence from panel data. *American Economic Review* 94 (2): 247–252.

Romer, Paul M. 1986. Increasing returns and long-run growth. *Journal of Political Economy* 94 (5): 10002–10037.

———. 1990. Endogenous technological change. *Journal of Political Economy* 98 (5): S71–S102.

Rosenthal, Michael. 2006. *Nicholas Miraculous: The Amazing Career of the Redoubtable Dr. Nicholas Murray Butler.* New York: Farrar, Straus, and Giroux.

Rosovsky, Henry. 1990. *The University: An Owner's Manual.* New York: W. W. Norton.

Rossiter, Margaret W. 1979. The organization of the agricultural sciences. In *The Organization of Knowledge in Modern America.* Edited by Alexandra Oleson and John Voss. Baltimore, MD: Johns Hopkins University Press.

Rothschild, Michael and Lawrence J. White. 1995. The analytics of the pricing of higher education and other services in which the customers are inputs. *Journal of Political Economy* 103 (3): 573–586.

Rothstein, Jesse. 2006. Good principals or good peers: parental valuation of school characteristics, Tiebout equilibrium, and the incentive effects of competition among jurisdictions. *American Economic Review* 96 (4): 1333–1350.

———. 2017. Measuring the impact of teachers: comment. *American Economic Review* 107 (6): 1656–1684.

Rudolph, Frederick. 1962. *The American College and University: A History.* Athens: The University of Georgia Press, 1990.

———. 1977. *Curriculum: A History of the American Undergraduate Course of Study Since 1636.* San Francisco: Josey-Bass Publishers.

Rudy, Willis. 1984. *The Universities of Europe, 1100–1914: A History.* London: Associated University Presses.

Rüegg, Walter. 1992. Epilogue: The Rise of Humanism. *A History of the University in Europe: Volume I, Universities in the Middle Ages.* Edited by Hilde De Ridder-Symoens. Cambridge: Cambridge University Press, 2003.

Ruggles, Samuel B. 1854. *The Duty of Columbia College to the Community, and its Right to Exclude Unitarians from its Professorships of Physical Science.* New York: John F. Trow.

Rummel, Erika. 1999. *Jiménez de Cisneros: On the Threshold of Spain's Golden Age.* Tempe: Arizona Center for Medieval and Renaissance Studies.

Saavedra, Juan E. 2009. The learning and early labor market effects of college quality: A regression discontinuity analysis. Unpublished paper. Harvard University.

Saez, Emmanuel. 2001. Using elasticities to derive optimal tax rates. *Review of Economic Studies* 68: 205–229.

Samuels, Warren J. 1991. The firing of E. A. Ross from Stanford University: injustice compounded by deception? *The Journal of Economic Education* 22 (2): 183–190.

Sandstrom, F. Mikael and Fredrik Bergstrom. 2005. School vouchers in practice: competition won't hurt you. *Journal of Public Economics* 89: 351–380.

Sappington, David E. M. 1995. Revisiting the line-of-business restrictions. *Managerial and Decision Economics* 16 (4): 291–300.

Scheuer, Florian and Iván Werning. 2016. The taxation of superstars. *The Quarterly Journal of Economics* 132 (1): 211–270.

Schmidt, William H., Richard T. Houang, Leland S. Cogan, and Michelle L. Solorio. 2019. *Schooling Across the Globe: What We Have Learned from 60 Years of Mathematics and Science International Assessments.* Cambridge: Cambridge University Press.

Schmutte, Ian M. 2015. Job referral networks and the determination of earnings in local labor markets. *Journal of Labor Economics* 33 (1): 1–32.

Schrecker, Ellen W. 1986. *No Ivory Tower: McCarthyism and the Universities.* New York and Oxford: Oxford University Press.

Scott, Joan Wallach. 2018. The tension between the university and the state. In *Academic Freedom: The Global Challenge.* Edited by Michael Ignatieff and Stefan Roch. Budapest: Central European University Press.

Shaw, Wilfred B., ed. 1942. *The University of Michigan: An Encyclopedic Survey.* Ann Arbor: The University of Michigan Press.

Shils, Edward. 1978. The order of learning in the United States: the ascendancy of the universities. *Minerva* 16 (2): 159–195.

Sinclair, Bruce. 2012. Mergers and acquisitions, in *Becoming MIT: Moments of Decision.* David Kaiser, Ed. Cambridge and London: MIT Press.

Siow, Aloysius. 1998. Tenure and other unusual personnel practices in academia. *Journal of Law, Economics, and Organization* 14 (1): 152–173.

Sloan, Douglas. 1971. *The Scottish Enlightenment and the American College Ideal.* New York: Teachers College Press.

Slosson, Edwin E. 1910. *Great American Universities.* New York: The MacMillan Company.

Smith, Merritt Roe. 2012. God speed the institute: the foundational years. In *Becoming MIT: Moments of Decision.* Edited by David Kaiser. MIT Press.

Smith, Thomas E. V. 1889. *The City of New York in the Year of Washington's Inauguration, 1789.* New York: Anson D. F. Randolph & Co.

Snow, Louis Franklin. 1907. The college curriculum in the United States. New York: PhD dissertation, Teachers College, Columbia University.

Solow, Robert M. 1956. A contribution to the theory of economic growth. *The Quarterly Journal of Economics* 70 (1): 65–94.

Sovern, Michael I. 2014. *An Improbable Life: My Sixty Years at Columbia and Other Adventures.* New York: Columbia University.

Spence, A. M. 1976. Product selection, fixed costs, and monopolistic competition. *The Review of Economic Studies* 43 (2): 217–236.

Spence, Michael. 1973. Job market signaling. *The Quarterly Journal of Economics* 87 (3): 355–374.

Squicciarini, Mara P. and Nico Voigtlander. 2015. Human capital and industrialization: evidence from the age of enlightenment. *The Quarterly Journal of Economics* 130 (4): 1825–1883.

Starr, Paul. 1982. *The Social Transformation of American Medicine.* New York: Basic Books.

Stigler, George J. and Robert A. Sherwin. 1985. The extent of the market. *The Journal of Law & Economics* 28 (3): 555–585.

Storr, Richard J. 1953. *The Beginnings of Graduate Education in America.* Chicago: The University of Chicago Press.

Straumsheim, Carl. 2016. Critics see mismatch between Coursera's mission, business model. Unpublished paper. Inside Higher Ed.

Sullivan, Andrew. February 9, 2018. We All Live on Campus Now. New York Magazine.

Synnott, Marcia Graham. 1979. *The Half-Opened Door: Discrimination and Admissions at Harvard, Yale, and Princeton, 1900–1970.* New Brunswick, NJ: Transaction Publishers, 2010.

Syverson, Chad. 2011. What determines productivity? *Journal of Economic Literature* 49 (2): 326–365.

Taylor, Kate (November 10, 2017). Upper West Side schools zones changed, but not all parents went along. New York Times.

Tewksbury, Donald G. 1932. *The Founding of American Colleges and Universities Before the Civil War: With Particular Reference to the Religious Influences Bearing Upon the College Movement.* Mansfield Centre, CT: Martino Publishing, 2011.

Thelin, John R. 2004. *A History of American Higher Education.* Baltimore, MD: The Johns Hopkins University Press, 2011.

Thompson, D. G. Brinton. 1946. *Ruggles of New York: A Life of Samuel B. Ruggles.* New York: Columbia University Press.

Tiebout, Charles. 1956. A pure theory of local expenditures. *Journal of Political Economy* 64 (5): 416–424.

Toivanen, Otto and Lotta Vaananen. 2016. Education and invention. *Review of Economics and Statistics* 98 (2): 382–396.

Turner, Lesley. 2017. The incidence of student financial aid: evidence from the Pell grant program. Unpublished paper. University of Maryland.

Ubell, Robert. 2017. Three steps for making MOOCs money makers. Unpublished paper. Inside Higher Education.

Urquiola, Miguel. 2005. Does school choice lead to sorting? Evidence from Tiebout variation. *American Economic Review* 95 (4): 1310–1326.

———. 2016. Competition among schools: traditional public and private schools. *Handbook of the Economics of Education.* Edited by Eric Hanushek, Stephen Machin, and Ludger Woessmann. Amsterdam: Elsevier.

Urquiola, Miguel and Eric Verhoogen. 2009. Class-size caps, sorting, and the regression discontinuity design. *American Economic Review* 99 (1): 179–215.

Valenzuela, Juan Pablo, Cristián Bellei, and Danae De Los Rios. 2013. Socioeconomic school segregation in a market-oriented educational system: the case of Chile. *Journal of Education Policy* 29 (2): 1–24.

Valero, Ana and John Van Reenen. 2016. The economic impact of universities: evidence from across the globe. National Bureau of Economic Research Working Paper No. 22501.

Van Reenen, John. 1996. The creation and capture of rents: wages and innovation in a panel of U.K. companies. *The Quarterly Journal of Economics* 111 (1): 195–226.

Vandermeersch, Peter A. 1996. Teachers, in *A History of the University in Europe: Volume II, Universities in Early Modern Europe*. Edited by Hilde De Ridder-Symoens. Cambridge: Cambridge University Press, 2003.

Verger, Jacques. 1973. *Les Universités au Moyen Age*. Paris: Presses Universitaires de France.

———. 1986. *Histoire des Universités en France*. Toulouse: Bibliotèque Historique Privat.

Veysey, Laurence R. 1965. *The Emergence of the American University*. Chicago: The University of Chicago Press.

Von Wachter, Till and Stefan Bender. 2006. In the right place at the wrong time: The role of firms and luck in young workers' careers. *American Economic Review* 96 (5): 1679–1705.

Wahls, Wayne P. 2018. High cost of bias: diminishing marginal returns on NIH grant funding to institutions. Unpublished paper. bioRxiv.

Waldinger, Fabian. 2010. Quality matters: the expulsion of professors and the consequences for PhD student outcomes in Nazi Germany. *Journal of Political Economy* 118 (4): 787–831.

———. 2012. Peer effects in science: evidence from the dismissal of scientists in Nazi Germany. *Review of Economic Studies* 79 (2): 838–861.

———. 2016. Bombs, brains, and science: the role of human and physical capital for the creation of scientific knowledge. *The Review of Economics and Statistics* 98 (5): 811–831.

Waldman, Michael. 1990. Up-or-out contracts: a signaling perspective. *Journal of Labor Economics* 8 (2): 230–250.

Walters, Christopher R. 2018. The demand for effective charter schools. *Journal of Political Economy* 126 (6): 2179–2223.

Walton, Richard J. 1986. *Swarthmore College: An Informal History*. Swarthmore, PA: Swarthmore College.

Warch, Richard. 1973. *School of the Prophets: Yale College, 1701–1740*. New Haven, CT: Yale University Press.

Wayland, Francis. 1850. Report to the Corporation of Brown University on Changes in the System of Collegiate Education. Providence, RI: George H. Whitney.

Weber, Max. 1930. *The Protestant Ethic and the Spirit of Capitalism*. London: Unwin Hyman.

Weinstein, Russell. 2017a. Employer screening costs, recruiting strategies, and labor market outcomes: an equilibrium analysis of on-campus recruiting. IZA Institute of Labor Economics Working Paper No. 10912.

———. 2017b. Geography and Employer Recruiting. Unpublished paper. IZA Institute of Labor Economics Discussion Paper No. 11224.

Weissmann, Jordan. 2015 (September 7). Is it time to tax Harvard's endowment? Slate Magazine.

Weisz, George. 1983. *The Emergence of Modern Universities in France, 1863–1914*. Princeton, NJ: Princeton University Press.

Werner, Anja. 2013. *The Transatlantic World of Higher Education: Americans at German Universities, 1776–1914*. New York: Berghahn Books.

Wertenbaker, Thomas Jefferson (1946). *Princeton: 1746–1896*. Princeton, NJ: Princeton University Press, 1996.

Whitehead, John S. 1986. How to think about the Dartmouth College case. *History of Education Quarterly* 26 (3): 333–349.

Williams, Adam M., Derek R. Slagle, and Darrin Wilson. 2014. Ranking universities for scholarship in public administration research. *Journal of Public Affairs Education* 20 (3): 393–412.

Wilson, Robin 2010. Tenure, RIP: what the vanishing status means for the future of education. *Chronicle of Higher Education*.

Woessmann, Ludger. 2016. The importance of school systems: evidence from international differences in student achievement. *Journal of Economic Perspectives* 30 (3): 3–32.

Yeomans, Henry Aaron. 1948. *Abbott Lawrence Lowell: 1856–1943*. Cambridge, MA: Harvard University Press.

Young, Jeffrey R. (May 10, 2017). Three Years In, Minerva's Founder On For-Profits, Selectivity, and His Critics. EdSurge.

Zimmerman, Seth. 2016. Making the one percent: The role of elite universities and elite peers. National Bureau of Economic Research Working Paper No. 22900.

Zink Clifford, W. 2017. *The Princeton Eating Clubs*. Princeton, NJ: Princeton Prospect Foundation.

Zuckerman, Harriet. 1977. *Scientific Elite: Nobel Laureates in the United States*. New York: The Free Press.

Acknowledgments

I AM GREATLY INDEBTED to colleagues who provided comments on a draft of this book: John Coatsworth, Jonathan Cole, David Figlio, Roger Geiger, Claudia Goldin, Patricia Albjerg Graham, W. Bentley MacLeod, Ofer Malamud, Robert McCaughey, Michael McPherson, María Victoria Murillo, Suzanne Nichols, Joseph Salvatore, and Aaron Wasserman. Some of these individuals are long-time friends I could ask a favor of; several I had never met and they were nevertheless extremely generous with their time. All remaining errors of omission and commission are mine.

I also greatly benefited from conversations with numerous colleagues: Robert Ainsworth, John Alcorn, Manuela Angelucci, Peter Bergman, Nicola Bianchi, Ernesto Dal Bó, Jeremiah Dittmar, Alexander Eble, Fernanda Estevan, Pamela Giustinelli, Jacob Hacker, Kate Ho, Caroline Hoxby, Chang-Tai Hsieh, Simon Jäger, Ravi Kanbur, Ju-Ho Lee, Alessia Lefébure, Henry Litwhiler, Patrick McEwan, Robert McMillan, Robert Metcalfe, Andreea Mitrut, Enrico Moretti, Andrea Moro, Cristian Pop-Eleches, Andrea Prat, Patrick Puhani, Evan Riehl, Jonah Rockoff, Sebastian Siegloch, Mara Squicciarini, Stefanie Stantcheva, Ulrich Trautwein, Pierre Verschueren, Fabian Waldinger, and Simon Wiederhold.

I also thank Ian Malcolm, my editor at Harvard University Press. I was lucky to meet Ian just as I had begun thinking of this project, and he was unfailingly supportive once I sent him a draft a couple of years later. He also introduced me to Madeleine Adams, who provided useful editorial suggestions.

For research assistance, I thank several excellent (then) undergraduate research assistants: Kaatje Greenberg, Lennart Hardenberg, Sanat Kapur, Brian Lu, Vu-Anh Phung, and especially Henry Litwhiler, who helped to bring many elements of the data together.

Last but not least I thank my parents, my siblings, and Claudia, Elena, and Joe. This book is dedicated to them.

Index

Abdulkadiroglu, Atila, 136
ability: admissions exams and, 109–112;
   homogeneity in, 100; research quality
   and, 126; school's wealth and, 119;
   socioeconomic background and, 110;
   sorting and, 85, 86–87, 108–109 (*see
   also* selectivity)
academic freedom, 138–140
academic outcomes: diversity and, 96;
   reputation and, 108
academic units: at Columbia, 72;
   segregation into, 57–58. *See also* fields;
   specialized instruction
Acemoglu, Daron, 206
ad fontes, 166
Adams, Charles, 49, 105, 138. *See also*
   Cornell University
admission by certificate, 83
admission by examination, 83
admissions: corruption and, 111; legacy
   students and, 108; loss of control over,
   95–96; open, 83, 84. *See also*
   selectivity; sorting
admissions exams, 97, 109–112
Agassiz, Louis, 55–56
agency, 19
alumni: advice from, 113; donations by, 111,
   112–115, 116, 199; of early universities,
   155–156; power of, 113, 155–156
American Association of University
   Professors (AAUP), 139

American universities: evolution of
   research performance, 14; gradual
   improvement of, 10, 12; initial
   weakness of, 18, 19; mentions of, 12;
   recruitment of talent, 16; rise to
   dominance, 8. *See also* colleges,
   antebellum; *individual colleges*
Anabaptists, 169
ancient texts, 166–167
Angell, James, 63, 64, 78, 98. *See also*
   Michigan, University of
Anglican church, 169, 190–192. *See also*
   Columbia University; religion
antebellum colleges. *See* colleges,
   antebellum
antisemitism, 95, 97, 100–102. *See also*
   Jewish students
applications, college, 202
Aquinas, Thomas, 162
Archdeacon, Thomas J., 185
Asimov, Isaac, 101
athletics, 105–106, 113–114, 199
autonomy. *See* self-rule / autonomy
Avery, Christopher N., 133
Axtell, James, 47, 106
Aydelotte, Frank, 107

*b*accalorius, 26
Bachelor of Arts, 57
Bachelor of Literature, 57
Bachelor of Science, 57

Civil War, colleges before. *See* colleges, antebellum

civitas christiana (holy city), 168. *See also* city upon a hill

Clark, Burton R., 197

Clark University, 78

class: role in sorting, 32. *See also* socioeconomic background

Clement VII (pope), 159

clergy, 165–166; as professors, 22; training of, 169–170, 187, 188

Clotfelter, Charles T., 114, 116

clubs, 88–96; alumni loyalty and, 113–114; fraternities, 93–94; harms caused by, 94–95; at Harvard University, 89–92; loss of control over admissions / student experience and, 95–96; at Princeton, 92, 104; undesirable student conduct and, 96; at Yale, 93

coeducational institutions, 62, 73–74, 83

Cole, Jonathan R., 4, 10, 124

College Entrance Examination Board (CEEB), 109

College of New Jersey, 189. *See also* Princeton University

colleges: in colonies (*see* colleges, antebellum; colleges, colonial); desire to eliminate, 99; disappearance of in Europe, 172–173; emergence of, 162–164; in England, 172; innovations in governance, 164; strengthening, 100; support of research, 199; teaching reform and, 107; value of, 98–99

colleges, antebellum, 21–48; academic freedom in, 138; age of students, 42, 43; arbitrary dismissal of faculty, 138; assessment of, 47–48; backsliding of collegiate system and, 39; compared to

European colleges, 43–44; control of student conduct, 47; creation of, 33; curriculum in, 25–26, 28, 30, 44–47; demand for educational expansion and, 39–44; denominational college creation and, 39–40; exit of, 37; failures in teaching reforms, 50–59; growth of, 24; homogeneity of students in (*see* sorting); labeling ambiguity, 42–44; number of students in, 37; preparedness of students in, 41–42; public aid for, 37; purposes of, 47–48; religion and, 30; research produced by, 21, 28, 48; resource constraints, 37; science in, 29–30; selectivity of, 41; sorting by, 21, 32–37, 85–87 (*see also* sorting); teaching in, 21, 26–28 (*see also* teaching in antebellum colleges); traditionalist view of, 48; transformation of, 50 (*see also* teaching reform)

colleges, colonial: abandonment of territorial-confessional model, 188–193; free market and, 174; limitations on entry, 182–183; Middle Atlantic, 183–194; religion and, 175–176, 186–193. *See also* Brown University; Columbia University; Dartmouth College; Harvard University; Pennsylvania, University of; Rutgers University; William and Mary, College of; Yale University

Colombia, education in, 136

colonial colleges. *See* colleges, colonial

colonies, American, 168; religious homogeneity in, 183–186. *See also* colleges, antebellum; colleges, colonial

Columbia University, 4, 98; academic units at, 72; creation of, 190–192; endowment, 71, 72; Hosack property,

schools and, 84. *See also* identity-related concerns

dormitories, 88–89, 92, 104–105; at Harvard, 89, 90; house system, 105; selectivity and, 100. *See also* clubs

Dunster, Henry, 25, 177–178, 179

Dutch Reformed, 192. *See also* religion; sorting: denominational

Dwight, Timothy, 23, 43–44, 112. *See also* Yale University

eating clubs, 92, 104

Eaton, Nathaniel, 177

economic growth, 150

economics: rankings by, 14, 230–233. *See also* fields; specialized instruction

education: average years of, 3, 4; demand for, 49 (*see also* training); expanded access to, 39–44; free market approach to, 16–20 (*see also* free market); as investment good, 17, 133; rewards to, 150. *See also* high schools; K-12 education; schools; secondary education

Eire, Carlos M. N., 156, 165, 166, 168, 170

Eisenhower, Dwight, 80

electives, 57, 62, 68–69, 73, 106

Eliot, Charles, 23, 28, 41, 42, 56, 58, 63–64, 66, 67–71, 74–75, 77, 78, 82, 83, 84, 89, 94, 95, 106, 109, 205. *See also* Harvard University

Ely, Richard, 138–139

employees, graduate students as, 161

endowments, 38, 114, 162; Columbia's, 71, 72; of English colleges, 172. *See also* resources

England. *See* Cambridge University; Europe; Oxford University; U.K.

Enlightenment, 28–30

enrollment, growth in, 82–85

enrollment caps, 107–108. *See also* selectivity

entry, free. *See* free entry

entry, massive. *See* massive entry

Episcopal Church, 85. *See also* Anglican church; religion

Epple, Dennis, 115

Erasmus of Rotterdam, 167

Europe, 147–173; appearance of universities in, 149–164; centralized spirit of education in, 40; decline of free university market in, 164–173; early schools in, 150–153; educational expansion in, 40; emergence of colleges and, 162–164; faculty as public servants in, 147; federal research funding in, 148; free market in, 20, 148, 149–173; historical research conditions in, 4; Protestant Reformation, 27, 148, 164–165, 167–168; secondary schools in, 28, 172–173; tracking in, 40. *See also* France; Germany; states; U.K.

European universities: American enrollments in, 12; control of, 147, 148, 170–173, 178, 196–197; in 1800s, 28–29; Enlightenment and, 28–29; free entry and, 158–160; influence of, 26–27; massive entry and, 159–160; scope in, 147; self-rule and, 177; states and, 144, 147; transformation of teaching in, 30. *See also* Cambridge University; France; German universities; Oxford University; Paris, University of; universities, early

Every Student Succeeds, 41

expertise, 23–24, 66, 127. *See also* specialized instruction

Eyring, Henry J., 201

faculty: American Association of University Professors (AAUP), 139; antebellum, 23, 24 (*see also* teaching in antebellum colleges); arbitrary dismissal of, 138–140; control by, 178, 181; diversity of, 79; expertise of, 66; hiring of junior professors, 79; hiring of school's students, 79; at Johns Hopkins, 66; medieval, 161; pay of, 80; poaching of, 78; professionalization of, 79; as public servants, 147; quality of, school reputation and, 108; renewable term contracts, 139–140; requirements for, 76; self-rule and, 177; sorting of into universities according to research talent, 80–81; specialization of, 19, 55–56, 75, 161; status / power of, 80; supply and demand, 76; teaching reform and, 75–81; teaching requirements, 80; working conditions, 80. *See also* masters; minds; scholars, medieval; teaching; tenure

Field, Walter Taylor, 26

fields: development of, 75; rankings by, 14, 224–244. *See also* chemistry; economics; medicine; physics; specialized instruction

finishing clubs, 90–92

Finke, Roger, 183

first mover advantage, 134–135

food: dining halls, 88; eating clubs, 92, 104; emergence of colleges and, 162–164; in medieval universities, 152–153

France, 147; colleges in, 163; equality of universities in, 148; *grandes écoles*, 147; institutional model for, 149; *lycées*, 28; research output in, 173; state control of universities in, 171. *See also* Europe; Paris, University of

Franklin, Benjamin, 186, 193

fraternities, 93–94, 96

free entry, 17, 158–160, 198; in antebellum period, 33; colonial colleges and, 174; Cornell and, 62; denominational sorting and, 35–36; end of in Europe, 164; limitations on, 182–183; principles behind, 193; proximity and, 35; teaching reform and, 53, 67. *See also* free market

free exit, 37

free market, 6, 16–20, 117, 144, 198; customers and, 18; decline of, 164–173; development of, 20; early American colleges and, 174; in Europe, 20, 148, 149–173; free scope and, 160–164; inequality and, 118–119; invention of, 148; K-12 education and, 20; performance and, 136; religion and, 174; research performance / quality and, 143; self-rule and, 154–158; teaching reform and, 81. *See also* free entry; free scope; self-rule / autonomy; sorting

free scope, 17, 160–164, 198. *See also* free market

Frelinghuysen, Theodore, 192

Friedman, Milton, 136

funding, 119; concentration of, 126; focus on research and, 127–137; foundation support, 123; inequality and, 117, 205. *See also* money; resources; spending

funding, federal, 19; concerns about, 207; debate about, 119–123; in Europe, 148; inequality and, 118–127; MIT and,

124; project selection, 120; Stanford University and, 125; universities' ranks in, 125–126

Gallatin, Albert, 55
García Marquez, Gabriel, 113
Geiger, Roger L., 12, 24, 44, 78, 79, 119
Georgetown University, 43
German universities, 207; Americans at, 12; control of, 196; decline of in mentions, 12; equality of, 148; institutional model for, 149; research at, 131. *See also* European universities; universities, early
Germany, 147; Berlin, University of, 60; disappearance of colleges in, 172–173; Göttingen, 66; *gymnasia*, 28, 44; historical research conditions in, 4; number of mentions, 10; religion in, 167–168; research output in, 173; seminar in, 66; state control of universities in, 171. *See also* Europe
Gibbs, Wolcott, 53, 55
Giessen, University of, 7
Gilman, Andrew, 63–67, 70–71, 128, 129, 138. *See also* Johns Hopkins University
Gilman, Daniel, 59. *See also* Johns Hopkins University
Goastellec, Gaele, 148
Gold Coast, 89, 90, 97
Goldin, Claudia, 39, 40, 49, 116
Göttingen, 51, 54, 66
governance. *See* control; presidents; self-rule / autonomy
grace, 187
graduate instruction: adding, 55–56; at Columbia, 73; Cornell and, 63–64; demand for, 64; at Harvard, 69, 70–71; relation with undergraduate

programs, 114–115; resistance to, 73; selectivity and, 103; teaching reform and, 59. *See also* professional schools; specialized instruction; teaching reform
Graduate Record Examination (GRE), 109
graduate students, as employees, 161
Graham, Hugh Davis, 10
Graham, Patricia Albjerg, 43, 94
grandes écoles, 147. *See also* France
Gray, Asa, 30
Great Schism, 159–160
Greek language, 45
Green, Ashbel, 22
Gregory VII (pope), 150
Gregory IX (pope), 158
Gregory XI (pope), 159
Grosseteste, Robert, 162
Gruber, Jonathan, 10, 207
Guibert de Nogent, 150
guilds, 152, 154, 161
Gumbel, Peter, 147
gymnasiums, 28, 44

Hamilton, Alexander, 42, 86
Harkness, Edward, 104–105
Harper, William, 78, 80, 98
Harper's Weekly, 62
Harriman, Averell, 93
Harvard, John, 177
Harvard University: admissions exams and, 109–110; admissions to, race and, 32; antebellum curriculum, 25; Board of Overseers, 178, 179; clubs, 89–92; college at, 99, 100; control of, 177–179; Corporation, 178–179; creation of, 176–179; dormitories, 89, 90, 97, 104–105; Dunster, 25, 177–178, 179;

innovation, incentives for, 206
Institute of 1770, 91
investment good, education as, 133
Ivy League, 62

James, Henry, 27
Jefferson, Thomas, 36, 68, 71
Jencks, Christopher, 36, 42, 79, 85, 114–115
Jewish immigrants, 185
Jewish students, 97, 100–101, 107, 108.
     See also antisemitism
John, Wheelock, 194
Johns Hopkins Press, 65–66
Johns Hopkins University, 59, 128;
     free entry and, 67; reform and, 60,
     63–66; teaching reform at, 70–71;
     undergraduate college, 66–67. *See also*
     Gilman, Daniel
Johnson, Samuel, 191
Johnson, Simon, 10, 207
Jordan, David, 98, 139
journals, 76–77. *See also* publication;
     research

K-12 education: free market approach
     and, 20; performance in, 136; school
     choice in, 136–137; sorting in, 129–130,
     137. *See also* education; high schools;
     schools; secondary education
Karabel, Jerome, 79, 91, 93, 95–96, 102
Katz, Lawrence F., 39, 40, 49, 116
Keller, Morton, 69
Keller, Phyllis, 69
Kelley, Brooks Mather, 24, 182, 187
Kerr, Clark, 110, 132
Kilgore, Harley, 120
Kingsley, James, 45
Kirkland, John, 52. *See also* Harvard
     University

Knox, John, 169
Koch, James, 90
Krugman, Paul, 206

Lafayette College, 109
land grants, 61
Latin, 45–46
Lawrence, Ernest, 79
Lawrence Scientific School, 58, 69
lecture (*lectio*), 26, 69
legacy students, 108. *See also* alumni
Lemann, Nicholas, 85, 110
Leslie, W. Bruce, 94
Lindsley, Phillip, 35. *See also* Princeton
     University
Livingston, William, 191–192
lodging. *See* clubs; dormitories; housing
Louis IX (king of France), 158
Louis XII (king of France), 171
Louis XIV (king of France), 171
Louisiana, 136
Low, Seth, 74
Lowell, Abbott, 97, 100, 101, 102, 103,
     104, 105, 107, 115. *See also* Harvard
     University
Lowell, Lawrence, 99
Luther, Martin, 165, 167–168, 170. *See also*
     Protestant Reformation

MacLeod, W. Bentley, 87, 88, 115, 133
magister scholarum, 150
Magisterial Reformation, 174
magisters, 168
managerial talent, productivity and,
     120, 127
Manhattan Project, 119
Mantz, Felix, 169
market forces: performance and, 135–137.
     See also free market

Obama administration, 41
Oberdorfer, Don, 113, 190
Ocasio-Cortez, Alexandria, 205
Office of Scientific Research and
Development (OSRD), 119, 120
online instruction, 201. *See also*
MOOCs
open enrollment policies, 83, 84
OSRD (Office of Scientific Research
and Development), 119, 120
Oxford University, 149; autonomy of,
158; colleges in, 163; curriculum and,
106; migration from, 155, 157; violence
in, 153. *See also* European universities;
U.K.

Packard, David, 125
Palmer, Alice Freeman, 78
parallel programs, 57, 58, 59
Paris: colleges in, 163. *See also* Europe;
France
Paris, University of: autonomy of, 157–
158; excommunication of masters at,
157–158; influence of, 149; migrations
from, 155; state control of, 171; vio-
lence in, 153. *See also* European
universities; France
Parrington, Vernon, 105
paternalism, 47
Patton, Cornelius Howard, 26
Paulsen, Friedrich, 171, 207
Peasants' War, 169
peer effects, 115
peer groups, 31. *See also* sorting
peer review, 76
Penn, William, 185
Pennsylvania, University of, 193–194.
See also colleges, colonial
Phi Beta Kappa, 90

Philadelphia, 185–186
Philadelphia Synod, 189
Philip II (king of France), 157
Phillip the Fair (king of France), 155
physics, rankings by, 14, 240–244
Picketty, Thomas, 205
Pierce, Benjamin, 128
political support of research, 199
popes, 156; early universities and, 156;
entry and, 159–160; Great Schism,
159–160. *See also* Catholic Church;
church; religion
population, research performance and,
10, 219
Porcellian, 90, 91
Porter, Noah, 27, 63, 64, 99, 113. *See also*
Yale University
preceptors, 106
Presbyterians, 35, 186–189. *See also*
Calvinism
presidents, 22, 177–178, 181, 187
prestige, 148
Price, Tom, 205–206
Princeton University: antisemitism at,
95; black applicants to, 84; clubs at,
92, 104; college at, 99; control of,
189–190; creation of, 188–190; eating
clubs, 92, 104; religion and, 35,
189–190; resources per student,
38–39; selectivity and, 103. *See also*
Bowen, William; Lindsley, Phillip;
McCosh, James; Wilson, Woodrow;
Witherspoon, John
printing, movable-type, 167
productivity, 117–143; improvements in,
209–210; managerial talent and, 120,
127; matching minds and money,
126–127; sorting's interaction with
tenure and, 137; tenure's effects on,

student economic background and, 162. *See also* European universities

university, designation of, 74

urban schools: diversity and, 84. *See also* cities; Columbia University

Urban VI (pope), 159

urbanization, 150, 167

Urquiola, Miguel, 87, 88, 115, 133, 137

Valla, Lorenzo, 166

value added, researcher, 135

Verdier, Thierry, 206

Verger, Jacques, 161, 173

Veysey, Laurence R., 12, 68, 84, 94, 104, 114

violence, in early universities, 153

Virginia: religion and, 176. *See also* colleges, colonial; William and Mary, College of

Virginia, University of, 36, 68

vouchers, 136–137

Walker, Amasa, 23

Walsh, Raymond, 140

Warch, Richard, 182

Warfield, Ethelbert, 109

Wayland, Francis, 56–58

wealth. *See* class; endowments; funding; socioeconomic background; spending

Webster, Daniel, 195

Weinstein, Russell, 133

Wentworth, John, 194

Western Reserve College, 33

Westphalia, Peace of, 186

Wheeler, Benjamin, 79. *See also* Berkeley, University of California

Wheelock, Eleazar, 183, 194

Wheelock, John, 37

White, Andrew, 60, 63, 65, 67, 70. *See also* Cornell University

Whitefield, George, 186, 187, 189, 193

Whitehead, John S., 195

William and Mary, College of, 36, 42, 90, 180–181; control of, 180–181; religion and, 176, 180. *See also* colleges, antebellum; colleges, colonial; Virginia

Wilson, Woodrow, 84, 95, 96, 99, 104. *See also* Princeton University

Winthrop, John, 168

Wisconsin, 138

Witherspoon, John, 29, 86. *See also* Princeton University

women: admission of, 73–74, 103 (*see also* coeducational institutions); exclusion of, 83

Woolsey, Theodore, 56. *See also* Yale University

World War II, 10, 12

Yale Law School, 87

Yale Report of 1828, 45–47

Yale University: alumni donations to, 112; clubs at, 93, 95–96; college at, 99; control of, 187; creation of, 181–183; dormitories at, 104–105; enrollment caps at, 107; graduate instruction at, 56; religion and, 35, 176, 181–182, 187; selectivity of, 102; Sheffield Scientific School, 58, 65; training for ministry and, 189. *See also* colleges, antebellum; colleges, colonial; Day, Jeremiah; Dwight, Timothy; Porter, Noah; Sproul, Robert; Woolsey, Theodore

Zink, Clifford W., 95

Zurich, University of, 7

Zwingli, Ulrich, 168